A SCANDALOUS PROPHET

A SCANDALOUS PROPHET

The Way of Mission after Newbigin

Edited by

Thomas F. Foust,
George R. Hunsberger,
J. Andrew Kirk,
and Werner Ustorf

WILLIAM B. EERDMANS PUBLISHING COMPANY
GRAND RAPIDS, MICHIGAN / CAMBRIDGE, U.K.

© 2002 Wm. B. Eerdmans Publishing Co.
All rights reserved

Wm. B. Eerdmans Publishing Co.
255 Jefferson Ave. S.E., Grand Rapids, Michigan 49503 /
P.O. Box 163, Cambridge CB3 9PU U.K.

Printed in the United States of America

07 06 05 04 03 02   7 6 5 4 3 2 1

ISBN 0-8028-4956-3

www.eerdmans.com

Contents

v

CONTENTS

Contents

CONTENTS

Introduction

"After Newbigin" was the title of the international conference held in Birmingham on 2-3 November 1998 and sponsored by the School of Mission and World Christianity, on behalf of the Selly Oak Colleges, and by the British and Foreign Bible Society. As its subtitle indicated, this conference was a missiological inquiry in honor of Lesslie Newbigin. We thought the best way the world of learning had to honor one of its productive and controversial thinkers was to explore his ideas critically, and take some of them further. These ideas are often surprising in their range and lateral associations, frequently brusque in their ruggedness, and occasionally disturbing. Lesslie Newbigin was certainly not a one-dimensional thinker.

When preparing the conference and, now, this volume, we have done our best to avoid the domestication of Newbigin by preventing his memory from being "snatched" by what might be called "Newbiginologists" of one sort or another. We cannot judge to what extent we have achieved this goal. However, we have tried to offer a variety of interpretations and perspectives in worldviews, cultural assumptions, religious and denominational affiliations, geographical backgrounds, and gender. Newbigin had the rare ability to attract people of quite diverse missiological convictions to take his thought seriously and enter into debate with it.

The conference, with its more than thirty prepared contributions, clearly had a dialogical and participatory structure, and Jan van Butselaar and Dan Hardy, the two "rapporteurs," gave final and critical assessments of the overall process — which function in this volume in lieu of a conclusion. The interaction and discussion, at the conference and after (Heather Ward's letter, included in section 2, represents a plethora of follow-up reactions), are less obvious in the book, as limited space permits only a selection of the materials.

The initial invitation to the contributing scholars outlined only that the format within each session would follow this procedure: an initial paper by one participant, a response paper by a second participant, a rejoinder by the first participant, and then a discussion open to all those attending. Thus, all those who prepared papers for the colloquium are to be commended, for they all agreed to take part in the event without first knowing their specific assignments. It was only after confirmation of the list of participants that papers were assigned. The acceptance of the invitation by such an esteemed group of scholars under such terms demonstrates the wide respect for Newbigin within the academic community.

The ideal for each session was to provide the second participant with the first participant's paper prior to the conference so that, if desired, a direct response could be given to the first essay. Furthermore, so far as possible, the first participant was provided a copy of the second participant's paper in advance of the colloquium so that a rejoinder could be prepared. Following the rejoinder the audience was invited by the moderator to participate in a discussion of the topic at hand. And with over one hundred people in attendance at the event, there were many invaluable discussions.

During each session of the two-day conference, two discussions took place concurrently in venues near to each other. Additionally, there were four "workshops," one within each of the sections described below, each in a time slot all its own so that four young scholars might present new ideas related to Newbigin to all attending the conference. It was hoped that by bringing all the attendees together in these workshops an environment for discussion, interaction, and "group thinking" would be created. (The Appendix provides a copy of the program of the colloquium and how one may obtain a tape recording of any or all of the participants' contributions.)

In any such venture as the colloquium, cancellations due to illness, papers not received in time, and other unexpected circumstances were inevitable. Thus, in a few instances, some very brave and charitable people took on assignments on very short notice. Consequently some of the sessions consisted of a pair of presentations that did not have the possibility of interacting with each other and instead widened the scope of reference.

In order to offer the reader some sense of the "feel" of the conference, we have preserved in the main headings of the book those that were used to organize our missiological inquiry into Newbigin's contribution to the ecumenical and missionary movement. They are: (1) "The Universal Church and the Ecumenical Movement"; (2) "Trinitarian Missiology"; (3) "Enlightenment, Postmodernity, and Mission"; and (4) "Globalization and the Gospel." Each section contains roughly the same number of presentations. The headings were selected to coincide broadly with areas in which Newbigin was involved in his life and theology. We have taken the liberty of including papers written by two of the primary organizers of the colloquium (J. Andrew Kirk and Werner Ustorf) that were not actually given at the conference but are directly related to its essential themes.

Four papers were selected from the colloquium to appear in the first section of this book, "The Universal Church and the Ecumenical Movement," a theme which captures some of the primary concerns of Newbigin's life and work. Two of the essays in this subdivision, those by Duncan Forrester and Michael Goheen, provide keen analyses of distinct aspects of Newbigin's theology. Forrester's insight into the public figure of Newbigin highlights how considerable his contribution was to the public theology of the church. However, Newbigin's theology seldom addressed itself directly to those outside the church, thus limiting its contribution beyond the church's sphere of influence. The workshop paper presented by Michael Goheen (who recently completed his doctoral studies on Newbigin) gave colloquium attendees an opportunity to explore the emphasis Newbigin gave, following in the tradition of J. H. Oldham, Hendrik Kraemer, and others, to the missional callings of individual believers. He shows how this emphasis might serve to authenticate an alternative community model needed by the church today. L. A. (Bert) Hoedemaker outlines the contours of the ground between the Christian faith and modernity and then identifies and evaluates Newbigin's position within the scope of his subject. And, on a different note altogether, Peter Cruchley-Jones broadly addresses issues raised by Newbigin against the backdrop of a paradigmatic exilic theme.

Deeply rooted in Newbigin's theology was the concept of the Trinity, which for him was one of the twin pillars, along with the incarnation, that formed "the starting point for a way of understanding reality as a whole" (*Foolishness to the Greeks* [Grand Rapids: Eerdmans, 1986], p. 90). This important aspect of Newbigin's theology gives shape to the second section of the book, "Trinitarian Missiology," which has five contributions. The first three essays, by Perry Schmidt-Leukel, Colin Greene, and Heather Ward, should be read in concert. During the colloquium the exchange between Schmidt-Leukel and Greene was an important and lively one. Utilizing a more precise understanding of the typology of the widely accepted "exclusivism, inclusivism, and pluralism," Schmidt-Leukel argues that "there is no such thing as the trinitarian model for understanding mission." Greene, who sharply counters Schmidt-Leukel's claim with the contention that one cannot go around Newbigin in present-day missiology, responds with a paper largely sympathetic to Newbigin's trinitarian position. As noted above, Heather Ward's letter, written after the colloquium had passed, is included in this section as an example of the kind of response the colloquium hoped to elicit in order to stimulate further investigation.

In this same second section, two papers attempt to go "after Newbigin" in different ways. Philip Kenneson contends, like Newbigin, that the Trinity adequately expresses the reality that humans are constituted as persons through their social relations. That is, in ways analogous to the divine personhood, "part of what it means for us to be a person is to 'dwell in' other people and to have them 'dwell in' us." Kenneson advocates this as one direction our attention ought to go "after Newbigin" in place of Newbigin's epistemological quest, now that the religious "playing field" is more or less level. On the other hand, Frances Young reminds us that a study of the essence of the Trinity is an attempt to understand the God who cannot be comprehended or contained. God is the one who contains but who cannot be contained.

Although Newbigin interacted more directly with modernism than postmodernism, George Hunsberger maintains in his essay that Newbigin's last great project (The Gospel and Our Culture) "stood on the ground of the emerging postmodern critique of the most fundamental confidences of the modern age." That is the note upon which the third section of the book, "Enlightenment, Postmodernity, and Mission," begins. The six essays in this section explore the interrelationships between these three themes that were so directly a part of Newbigin's postretirement missional activity. Hunsberger's essay engages those themes by focusing on ecclesiological vision, identifying three hallmarks of the church during this transitional period sometimes called postmodernity. The church must be: truly the community, a community of the true, and a community in missional relationship with the world. In response to Hunsberger's essay, Lynne Price holds that his approach, like Newbigin's, begins in the wrong place. Rather, Price outlines a different methodology for the church of today and, using Leslie Weatherhead as a model, calls it "faithful uncertainty."

The third and fourth papers within the third section are those by editor-organizers Andrew Kirk and Werner Ustorf. In "Mission in the West: On the Calling of the Church in a Postmodern Age," Kirk offers a précis on a wide-ranging set of issues. Ustorf, in his essay "The Emerging Christ of Post-Christian Europe," focuses his critical eye on the present-day christological problem. The final contributors to this section are Andrew Walls and Thomas Foust. Walls's analysis of the current worldwide missiological climate contains a healthy reminder that Christianity began the twentieth century as primarily a Western religion, but that by the end of the century the majority of all Christians lived in Africa, Asia, Latin America, or the Pacific. "That is, Christianity enters the twenty-first century as a mainly non-Western religion." While this prophetically pinpoints that the identity of the church will be significantly shaped more and more by the southern continents, it is also a sharp reminder that the West is indeed the new mission field. On a different note altogether, Foust, who gave the workshop paper for this section, questions whether or not within Newbigin's epistemology there is an "internal dialogue." He asserts that to understand Newbigin's philosophy and theology, one must always bear this "dual discourse" in mind.

Kalarikkal Aleaz, Mahmut Aydin, Charles Taber, Robert M. C. Jeffery, David Kettle, and Jenny Taylor are those whose essays are included in the fourth section, "Globalization and the Gospel." In contrast to Newbigin, Aleaz asserts that a pluralist understanding of the gospel is the opportunity to counter the globalization process, a globalization of poverty acquiescing to a free-market economy. Writing in response to Aleaz, Mahmut Aydin sees pluralism more problematic for Christians than for Muslims. He suggests that the way forward for Christians is to relativize the Christ event by understanding Jesus to be "the unique and normative revelation of God for those who follow his way, not for those who follow other ways." And in a globalized world, instead of claiming a priori the superiority of one's religious tradition, the validity of one's religious claim lies in the degree to which it brings liberation to the poor and how much it contributes to the development of the common good. Both Christians and Muslims, Aydin proposes, should seek mutual transformation toward what he calls the Transcendent Reality and not try to convert the other to their own faith. Following the Aleaz-Aydin exchange is the one between Charles Taber and Robert Jeffery. In his essay Taber perceives three ways of understanding and dealing with globalization: the modern way, the postmodern way, and what he terms the "gospel" way. Following along lines similar to Newbigin, Taber recommends this third way, suggesting that "the gospel of the kingdom of God is the only valid universal meta-narrative." Correctly understood, it alone is the perspective that is neither homogenizing nor totalitarian. Jeffery challenges the validity of Taber's singular "gospel perspective" on the grounds of cultural relativism. This leads Jeffery to conclude "that there is not one solution to our reaction to globalization" and that the uniqueness of Christ is understood in different ways through the many expressions of Christianity.

The penultimate paper in this section is by David Kettle, who provides an overview of authority by tracing its forms from what he calls "traditional societies" to present Western societies. In the end, he suggests a type of Christian "inner direction," under the authority and grace of God in Christ, as a way of renewal for Christians in today's global situation. The last essay is

INTRODUCTION

Jenny Taylor's workshop paper which offers her appraisal of Newbigin's perspective on Islam, a task for which she is uniquely suited, having coauthored with Newbigin and Lamin Sanneh the book *Faith and Power: Christianity and Islam in "Secular" Britain* (London: SPCK, 1998).

At the end of each of the two days of the colloquium, a rapporteur summed up the day's events and discussions. Daniel Hardy and Jan van Butselaar, the two rapporteurs, provided keen insights in their observations. We thought it fitting to include their remarks as section 5 of this work to give the reader a more summary sense of the colloquium. These, together with the critical assessment of Michael Taylor, serve as concluding remarks for this volume.

Finally, at the end of the book we include a comprehensive and briefly annotated bibliography of Newbigin's writings, including not only his published works but also a number of significant unpublished written items and a selection of audio and visual recordings of addresses he made in various circumstances. Alongside his own works, the bibliography includes an extensive list of published reviews of his books and a bibliography of the most substantive material interacting with his writings and thought. The bibliography has been compiled by Tom Foust and George Hunsberger with the anticipation that it provides the foundation for continuing efforts to expand and keep current a full bibliographical resource for research into Newbigin's contributions, making that available in every appropriate print and digital way. See also the United Kingdom and North American websites listed on p. 324.

Last but not least, we ought to mention one memorable and unusual occurrence that took place on 2 November 1998, in the main auditorium of the conference: Saint Augustine "appeared" in the flesh (many thanks to actor Andrew Harrison), wearing sandals and a dark brown habit and reciting passionately and eloquently a selection from his *City of God* (book 11.2). We thought it worthwhile to include Saint Augustine's speech as a prologue to the whole volume as a worthy reminder of the tradition in which we follow. We cannot be sure whether Lesslie Newbigin would have appreciated this reminder of the historical continuity in which is set his own quest for a faithful relationship between Christian faith and cultural particularities. But we think he would have been pleased to be placed in such company! We certainly thought it most appropriate.

Tom Foust,   George Hunsberger
Andrew Kirk,   *Holland, Michigan, USA*
Werner Ustorf
Birmingham, England

Contributors

Kalarikkal Poulose Aleaz is Professor of Religions at Bishop's College as well as at the North India Institute of Postgraduate Theological Studies, Calcutta, India. He is also associated with the South Asia Theological Research Institute, Bangalore, India, where he guides doctoral candidates. His areas of specialization are Indian philosophy and Indian Christian theology. He is the author of eleven books and numerous articles. He was the William Paton Fellow of the Federation of Selly Oak Colleges, Birmingham, in 1997.

Mahmut Aydin is Associate Professor of History of Religions and Interreligious Dialogue at Ondokuz Mayis University, the Faculty of Theology in Samsun, Turkey. He received his B.A. and M.A. from the University of Ondokuz Mayis. He completed his Ph.D. on Christian-Muslim relations at the Centre for the Study of Islam and Christian-Muslim Relations, Birmingham University, in 1998.

G. Jan van Butselaar taught African church history at the Theological College in Butare, Rwanda, and as a guest lecturer at the United Theological College in Rikatla, Mozambique. He has published several books and articles on missiology and on African church history, such as *Africains, missionnaires et colonialistes. Les origines de l'Eglise Presbytérienne du Mozambique (Mission suisse), 1880-1894*, Ph.D. thesis (Leiden: Brill, 1984). He is presently General Secretary of the Netherlands Missionary Council in Amsterdam. In that capacity he has been engaged in the study project "Missiology for Western Culture," an offshoot of the "Gospel and Western Culture" debate that was started by Lesslie Newbigin.

CONTRIBUTORS

Peter Cruchley-Jones is a minister in the United Reformed Church in the UK. He is currently in pastoral charge on a large council housing estate in Cardiff, Wales. He completed his Ph.D. in missiology at the University of Birmingham in 1999.

Duncan B. Forrester was ordained as a presbyter of the Church of South India in 1962, and taught politics at Madras Christian College for eight years. After a period as Chaplain and Lecturer in Politics and Religious Studies at the University of Sussex, he was appointed in 1978 to the Chair of Christian Ethics and Practical Theology in New College, University of Edinburgh. He is at present Dean of the Faculty of Divinity and Director of the Centre for Theology and Public Issues. His recent publications include *The True Church and Morality: Reflections on Ecclesiology and Ethics* and *Christian Justice and Public Policy.*

Thomas F. Foust assists CMF International of Indiana, USA, with their work in Great Britain and is a postgraduate student at the University of Birmingham, England, where he is also an Honorary Lecturer. In addition to coediting this volume, his other publications include the book *Adventuring for Christian Unity and Other Essays by Dean E. Walker* (1992), edited with William Richardson.

Michael Goheen is Associate Professor of Worldview Studies, Mission and World Christianity in the Religion and Theology Department of Redeemer University College, Ancaster, Ontario, Canada. He holds a Ph.D. from the University of Utrecht, Netherlands, where he completed a dissertation entitled "As the Father Has Sent Me, I Am Sending You: J. E. Lesslie Newbigin's Missionary Ecclesiology," which was published by Boekencentrum Press, Zoetermeer, Netherlands (January 2001). He is also minister of preaching at First Christian Reformed Church in Hamilton, Ontario.

The Rev. Dr. Colin Greene is Head of Theology and Public Policy for the Bible Society, and Visiting Professor of Systematic and Philosophical Theology at Seattle Pacific University, USA. He is author of *Christology and Atonement in Historical Context* and the forthcoming *Marking Out the Horizons: Christology in Cultural Perspective.* He is consultant Editor for the Scripture and Hermeneutics Seminar and contributor to the first and second volumes, *Renewing Biblical Interpretation* and *After Pentecost: Language and Biblical Interpretation.* He has also contributed to *The Lectionary Commentary: Theological Exegesis for Sunday's texts* (3 vols.; Eerdmans, 2001).

Contributors

Daniel Hardy was formerly Van Mildert Professor of Divinity, University of Durham, and Residentiary Canon of Durham Cathedral. He later served as Director of the Center of Theological Inquiry at Princeton Theological Seminary before becoming consultant to the Centre for Advanced Religious and Theological Studies, Faculty of Divinity, University of Cambridge.

Libertus (Bert) A. Hoedemaker is Professor of Missions and Ecumenics at the State University of Groningen, the Netherlands. He studied at Utrecht University and at Yale Divinity School. Prior to coming to Groningen, he taught at the Theological Seminary in Jakarta, Indonesia. His English-language publications include *The Theology of H. Richard Niebuhr* (1970), *Missiology — An Ecumenical Introduction* (editor and contributor, 1994), and *Secularization and Mission* (1998).

George R. Hunsberger is Professor of Missiology at Western Theological Seminary of Holland, Michigan, USA, and coordinator of the Gospel and Our Culture Network in North America. He is a minister of the Presbyterian Church (USA) and received a Ph.D. in ecumenics, missiology, and the history of religions from Princeton Theological Seminary. He has been a pastor, a teacher, a campus minister, and a mission administrator in the USA, Kenya, and Uganda. He is the author of *Bearing the Witness of the Spirit: Lesslie Newbigin's Theology of Cultural Plurality* and coauthor of *Missional Church: A Vision for the Sending of the Church in North America*. He edits the *Gospel and Our Culture Newsletter*.

Robert M. C. Jeffery is Sub Dean and Canon of Christ Church, Oxford. After two curacies, he served for five years with Canon David Paton in the Missionary and Ecumenical Council of the Church Assembly of the Church of England. He was then Secretary of the Division of Mission and Unity at the British Council of Churches. After serving as a vicar in Oxford, he was then diocesan missioner and subsequently an archdeacon in the Lichfield Diocese. Before returning to Oxford, he was the dean of Worcester Cathedral for nine years. He was recently awarded the honorary D.D. at the University of Birmingham. He has written regularly on matters of mission, ecumenism, and spirituality.

Philip D. Kenneson is Associate Professor of Theology and Philosophy at Milligan College in Tennessee. He is the author of *Selling Out the Church: The Dangers of Church Marketing; Beyond Sectarianism;* and *Life on the Vine: Cul-*

tivating the Fruit of the Spirit in Christian Community. He is currently at work on a book on ecclesiology to be published by Blackwell.

David Kettle is an Anglican priest living in Cambridge. He is Co-ordinator of the Gospel and Our Culture Network, and assists in the parishes of Bottisham, Lode, and Quy. From 1991 to 1997 he was Anglican chaplain at Massey University, New Zealand, in which country he has had many articles published on gospel and culture themes.

J. Andrew Kirk is Director of the Centre for Missiology and World Christianity in the Department of Theology of the University of Birmingham. He has published thirteen books on mission-related subjects and worked for twelve years in Latin America.

Lynne Price is a freelance theologian based in Birmingham, England. Her latest book, *Theology Out of Place: Walter J. Hollenweger,* will be published by Sheffield Academic Press in July 2002. She is the author of *Faithful Uncertainty: Leslie D. Weatherhead's Methodology of Creative Evangelism* (Peter Lang, 1996) and a coeditor of *Mission Matters* (Peter Lang, 1997).

Perry Schmidt-Leukel is Professor of Systematic Theology and Religious Studies and Chair of World Religions for Peace, University of Glasgow, Faculty of Divinity. He was formerly Wissenschaftlicher Oberassistent at the Roman Catholic Theological Faculty of Munich University, Germany. He is the author of numerous works in the fields of systematic theology, theology of religions, and Christian-Buddhist dialogue.

Charles R. Taber is Professor of World Mission Emeritus at Emmanuel School of Religion in Johnson City, Tennessee. His Ph.D. is from the Hartford Seminary Foundation. He has served as a missionary in the Central African Republic and as a translations consultant of the United Bible Societies (West Africa). He was editor of *Practical Anthropology* (1968-72) and *Gospel in Context* (1978-79).

Jenny Taylor is variously a journalist, writer, and commissioning editor, and is reading for a doctorate in secularization and public policy at the School of Oriental and African Studies at London University. She was the first Race Relations Correspondent in the Westminster Press Group in the early 1980s, and for the four years leading up to its Gospel as Public Truth Conference in 1992 she was a member of the Gospel and Our Culture's management group and its publicist. She has edited the house magazine of the international charity Interserve, founded to work among women in purdah in India, and now works freelance from her home in north London.

Michael H. Taylor is President of Selly Oak Colleges in Birmingham and Professor of Social Theology in the University of Birmingham. He has served as minister of several Baptist churches and as principal of the Northern Baptist College in Manchester. He was Director of Christian Aid from 1985 to 1997. He is the author of articles on worship, theology, ethics, and development and several books, including *Good for the Poor: Christian Ethics and World Development* and *Not Angels but Agencies: The Ecumenical Response to Poverty.*

Werner Ustorf has taught at the universities of Hamburg and Heidelberg and at Tamil Nadu Theological Seminary. Since 1990 he has been Chair of Mission at the University of Birmingham. He has published on questions of mission history, Christianity in Africa, and currently on the relationship between mission and Nazism and on the rise of neopaganism in Europe.

Andrew F. Walls is a former missionary to Sierra Leone and Professor Emeritus at the Centre for the Study of Christianity in the Non-Western World at the University of Edinburgh. A collection of his thoughts is to be found in his *The Missionary Movement in Christian History: Studies in the Transmission of Faith* (1996).

Heather Ward teaches moral and human development for the Merrivale Institute in Birmingham. She holds an M.Ed. degree in religious education and a doctorate in nineteenth-century literature and theology. Her publications include *The Gift of Self* and *Streams in Dry Land.*

Frances Young since 1986 has held the Edward Cadbury Chair of Theology at the University of Birmingham, where she has taught since the early 1970s. She is currently one of the Pro-Vice Chancellors of the University of Birmingham. Her principal interests lie in the areas of New Testament studies and early Christianity; its culture, doctrine, and biblical exegesis in particular. She was ordained a Methodist minister in 1984.

Acknowledgments

The success of the international conference convened in the Selly Oak Colleges at the beginning of November 1998, and from which this book has arisen, is due to the interlocking contributions of many people. Without their support and tireless efforts, many aspects of the project would have been much less effective.

At the head of the list comes Tom Foust, who undertook the bulk of the organization of the conference and all the initial work on the book. His skills in working against a very tight time schedule and his unfailing courtesy and cheerfulness are wonderful gifts which greatly enhanced the smooth running of the conference. He was ably supported by Beverley Stubbs, administrator of the School of Mission and World Christianity, who did a lot of the correspondence and other administrative tasks in a most efficient way.

The idea of having a conference to honor the contribution of Lesslie Newbigin to the worldwide mission of the church was enthusiastically supported by Lesslie's son John and daughter Dr. Margaret Beetham. We thank them for their help and encouragement. Michael Taylor, the President of the Selly Oak Colleges, was also a great source of stimulus, playing an important part in ensuring that the momentum for the conference did not lag. He played a key role at various points during the proceedings.

The conference would not have been possible without the considerable generosity of the British and Foreign Bible Society (BFBS), who made available a large donation which underwrote the expenses, particularly those of bringing distinguished speakers from other parts of the globe. Thanks are particularly due to Rev. Dr. Martin Robinson, one of the directors, and to Rev. Dr. Colin Greene, for enabling the participation of the BFBS.

ACKNOWLEDGMENTS

Several people took part, either as convenors for one of the days, or in chairing one of the sessions or presenting a paper (not included in this volume). They too contributed substantially to the achievements of the meeting. In this respect our thanks go to Michael Amaladoss, Allan Anderson, H. Dan Beeby, Jabal Buaben, Emilio Castro, Eleanor Jackson, Aasulv Lande, Emmanuel Lartey, Dennis Lindsay, Hugh Montefiore, Murray Rae, Philip Seddon, Israel Selvanayagam, and Denys Turner. Andrew Harrison, an actor, represented Augustine for a few astonishing and stimulating minutes with great verve.

We would like to thank Reelife Recordings (of Laverick Hall, Halton, Lancashire, LA2 6PH, Tel. 01524 811282) for recording all the sessions and making available tapes of what transpired. They may be contacted to purchase the tapes of any or all of the sessions. We would also like to thank Mike Bishton for the excellent and very modestly priced food that he supplied — his work was particularly complicated because of the difficulty of ascertaining accurate numbers (a caterer's nightmare) — and Timothy Aho, Walter Donaldson, Debbie Foust, Georgina Lord, Triin Rait, Ally Rose, Rachel Atkinson, Charles and Barbara Cook, and Mark Newman for being extra pairs of hands to Tom Foust.

We are extremely grateful to Bill Eerdmans for being so willing to publish, and for all the help the staff have been in getting the manuscript in order. Dr. Rachel Rakotonirina has also played a major part in working through the various presentations to bring them into a standard form. This is exacting and often rather tedious work, and we are most grateful to her for the excellent job she has done.

Finally, thanks are due to Werner Ustorf and Philip Seddon for overseeing the whole process. The idea arose within the School of Mission and World Christianity with which Lesslie had had such a fruitful relationship over many years, and was strongly supported by the Selly Oak Colleges. To all of you, we are deeply appreciative. May our homage to Lesslie contribute in some small measure to his overriding passion to communicate appropriately and effectively the gospel of the risen Jesus Christ, Lord of the universe, to all peoples and to their cultures.

J. Andrew Kirk

AFTER NEWBIGIN

A Missiological Inquiry in Honor of Lesslie Newbigin

• •

SAINT AUGUSTINE'S SPEECH

Speaking from *City of God,* book 11, no. 2

• •

2-3 November 1998

Andrew Harrison, Actor

"Of the knowledge of God, to which no man can attain save through the Mediator between God and men, the man Christ Jesus."

It is a great and very rare thing for a man, after he has contemplated the whole creation, corporeal and incorporeal, and has discerned its mutability, to pass beyond it, and, by the continued soaring of his mind, to attain to the unchangeable substance of God, and, in that height of contemplation, to learn from God Himself that none but He has made all that is not of the divine essence. For God speaks with a man not by means of some audible creature dinning in his ears, so that the atmospheric vibrations connect Him that makes with him that hears the sound, nor even by means of a spiritual being with the semblance of a body, such as we see in dreams or similar states; for even in this case He speaks as if to the ears of the body, because it is by means of the semblance of a body He speaks, and with the appearance of a real interval of space — for visions are exact representations of bodily objects. Not by these, then, does God speak, but by the truth itself, if any one is prepared to hear with the mind rather than with the body. For He speaks to that part of man which is better than all else that is in him, and than which God Himself alone is better. For since man is most properly understood (or, if that cannot be, then, at least, *believed*) to be made in God's image, no doubt it is that part of him by which he rises above those lower parts he has in common with the beasts, which brings him nearer to the Supreme. But since the mind, itself, though naturally capable of reason and intelligence, is disabled by besotting and inveterate vices not merely from delighting and abiding in, but even from tolerating His unchangeable light, until it has been gradually healed, and renewed and made capable of such felicity, it had, in the first place, to be impregnated with faith, and so purified. And that in this faith it might advance the more confidently towards the truth, the truth itself, God, God's Son, assuming humanity without destroying His divinity, established and founded this faith, that there might be a way for man to man's God through a God-man.

SECTION 1

THE UNIVERSAL CHURCH AND THE
ECUMENICAL MOVEMENT

Lesslie Newbigin as Public Theologian

Duncan B. Forrester

The Roots of Ecumenical Public Theology

Lesslie Newbigin was deeply shaped by the ecumenical biblical theology which emerged out of the German Church Struggle and the embryonic ecumenical movement in the 1930s, and which became a dominant orthodoxy in the early postwar period among Protestants. Newbigin became a major practical exponent of this theology, which he never deserted in the theologically swinging sixties or the more skeptical and secular seventies, eighties, and nineties.

This theology was perhaps most clearly represented by Karl Barth and the Theological Declaration of Barmen of 1934, of which Barth was the chief author. Newbigin himself for many years found the thought of Emil Brunner more congenial than that of Barth, but later in life seems to have moved in a more Barthian direction, making particular use of the kind of confessional approach represented by Barmen. The new dialectical theology arose out of the deep disillusion with liberal optimism engendered by the First World War, the Bolshevik Revolution in Russia, and the rise of Hitler in Germany. Against the *Führerprinzip* it set the Lordship of Christ.

The German Church Struggle and the Second World War appeared far more clearly than the First World War to involve a fundamental conflict of good and evil, of competing faiths, conflicting ideologies, and contrasting loyalties. It was also understood as a conflict between the true church and the idolatry of the *Volk*. The victory of 1945 seemed to many to be a kind of vindication of this particular theology and of the Christian church over a demonic movement which had been of apocalyptic proportions. It is not surprising that after 1945 the theology that had provided a rationale for resistance to Hitler went through a period of great confidence, and the churches in many places prospered and attracted the brightest and the best of the younger generation.

This was theology which was confessional. It taught that the heart of the matter was the confession in words and action of the truth that is to be found in Jesus Christ; and such confession inevitably brought the believer into conflict with alternative ideologies and claims to loyalty which were totalitarian or idolatrous. It was an ecclesial theology in the sense that it saw Christian faith as inseparable from the church; only in the church could faith be lived and believers nurtured; and more: the church represented an alternative community and way of being. It was significant that Karl Barth changed the title of his massive project in the early 1930s from *Christian Dogmatics* to *Church Dogmatics* — without the church there is no Christian theology, and the theologian's primary responsibility is to help the church to be the church and to monitor and encourage its proclamation. This theology, then, claimed to be public truth, capable of engaging successfully in the public arena in battles against the brutal ideologies and political systems which degraded humankind by their falsity. It assumed that any serious theology would be significant in the public arena. It did not follow the 1960s slogan of "letting the world set the agenda"; indeed, it did the opposite. Theology itself should control its business, but its agenda was decidedly not confined to a religious ghetto or the in-house converse of a timid sect of "cognitive deviants"; it was public truth. Barth's theology, to take the most obvious example, was public theology because it was serious theology which actually transformed the terms of debate. As committed and probing theology, it was also publicly relevant and constructive.

This was a public theology in as far as it claimed to be true in a way which was inspectable in the academy; but it was also an ecclesial theology which constantly emphasized its grounding in the life and witness and proclamation of the church. It recognized a strong version of biblical authority: Christian theology must speak to the world of today and its problems from within "the strange world of the Bible." There was an implicit emphasis on the unity of the biblical witness, exemplified, for instance, in the series of little books published in preparation for the Evanston Assembly of the WCC as Ecumenical Biblical Studies, with titles such as *The Biblical Doctrine of Man in Society, The Biblical Doctrine of Work,* and *The Biblical Doctrine of Justice and Law.* The definite article is significant: the Bible is assumed to teach one thing on every major subject, and the movement from Scripture to doctrine was sometimes treated in rather too simple a way. But a galaxy of theologians and church leaders such as D. T. Niles from Sri Lanka and M. M. Thomas from India espoused this theology, delighted in the Bible, and brought Christian faith vividly to light in the imagery of Scripture.

Newbigin as Public Theologian

From early on, Newbigin stood squarely in the theological school I have outlined above. During his years in India and in Geneva; his days as a district missionary, and later a bishop; as a leader in the negotiation of the South India scheme for unity; and as a global ecumenical leader, his major coordinating themes were mission and unity. But he was, as an alien, somewhat reticent at that time on political and economic matters. When he returned to Britain on his retirement, he threw himself into theological debate and quickly showed himself still to be a doughty warrior as he crossed swords with those who taught that the incarnation was no more than a myth, or suggested that all religions boil down to the same thing, or capitulated to the onslaughts of Thatcherism on the welfare state.

Mission, unity, and ecclesiology were still major themes, but Newbigin felt able, as he had not been in India, to engage as a theologian in political controversy. He found Britain, and indeed the West in general, in urgent need of a "genuinely missionary encounter" between the gospel and post-Enlightenment culture. The heavenly city of the Enlightenment philosophers, he claimed, has failed, and indeed has become demonic, for "the project of bringing heaven down to earth always results in bringing hell up from below."[1] No longer is it possible, let alone desirable, to attempt to restore Christendom or return to a pre-Constantinian and pre-Enlightenment innocence. He could affirm, in terms that could almost come from Stanley Hauerwas, that "The most important contribution which the church can make to a new social order is to be itself a new social order."[2] But it must also seek to unmask and confront the false economic, social, and political ideologies of the age as well as the simplistic pragmatism so characteristic of the Anglo-Saxon mindset. In an age when the West was in an advanced stage of syncretism, theology and the church had to resist relegation to the private and domestic domain, and steadfastly confess the Lordship of Christ over the whole of life. With

1. Lesslie Newbigin, *Foolishness to the Greeks: The Gospel and Western Culture* (London: SPCK; Grand Rapids: Eerdmans; and Geneva: WCC, 1986), p. 117.

2. Lesslie Newbigin, *Truth to Tell: The Gospel as Public Truth* (Grand Rapids: Eerdmans; Geneva: WCC Publications; and London: SPCK, 1991), p. 85.

Calvin and Luther and indeed the whole premodern tradition, he affirmed that it would be blasphemy to suggest that economic and political behavior lay outside the jurisdiction of theology. The task, as he saw it, was essentially public confession which simultaneously denounced falsehood and oppression and announced the good news of the gospel.

In the depths of Mrs. Thatcher's reign he tried, without success, to instigate a Barmen-style anti-Thatcherite theological declaration. "No society can cohere and no government can continue to govern indefinitely," he wrote, "when the exploitation of the weak by the strong passes a certain point and the political order has lost its moral credibility. The contemporary attempts of the governments of Prime Minister Thatcher in Britain and of President Reagan in the United States can only destroy our societies."[3] Newbigin himself went on record again and again as a prophetic figure who was not afraid to speak his mind on public affairs. When he visited South Africa under apartheid, he told the minister of justice to his face that he was under judgment by God for the injustices and atrocities perpetrated in his name.

Rights, Needs, and Wants

Newbigin both engaged in debates about theory and also addressed a few fairly specific political questions. Christianity, for him, represented in both theory and practice a third way, distinct from the orientations of right and left, which both shared Enlightenment assumptions. Both speak in terms of individual rights: the Right asserts each individual's right to define and pursue a specific good without interference on the grounds of a higher common good; the Left asserts that every person has the right to have basic needs met by the community. Each of us, according to the Enlightenment worldview, has the right not only to pursue happiness and fulfill our needs, but to decide what is our good, and what our needs are, for ourselves.

This modern worldview provides no way of establishing as "public truth" some understanding of human beings and the goal of human life which would allow us to affirm an objective ordering of human needs or the good for human beings. In short, "if there is no publicly accepted truth about the ends for which human beings exist, but only a multitude of private opinions on the matter; then it follows, first that there is no way of adjudicating between needs and wants, and second that there is no way of logically

3. Newbigin, *Foolishness to the Greeks*, pp. 121-22.

grounding rights either in needs or in wants."[4] Both the socialist and the capitalist accounts of human nature, Newbigin concludes, are false and lead to seriously flawed policies which are, at the end of the day, destructive of true community and human flourishing.

The Welfare State Debate

The advent of the British welfare state had been greeted with tremendous enthusiasm, and it has continued to enjoy massive popular support despite criticisms and acknowledged problems, not least from the Christian churches which have tended to regard it as essentially Christian in its concern for the welfare of all.[5]

Many of the problems that the welfare state ran into in the 1960s and 1970s had to do with inflated expectations and the insatiability of some basic human needs. Some people accused the welfare state of trying to play God, by attempting to make the human condition unproblematic; others saw it as taking over in secular guise central functions of the Christian church. The demand for health care in particular seemed to have no limits, as life span lengthened and increasingly expensive and sophisticated forms of treatment were developed. Many people began to wonder whether the economy could stand the escalating costs of the welfare state. Furthermore, there were on the one hand increasing worries that existing patterns of welfare provision led to an enervating dependency on a "nanny state" and the erosion of economically vital incentives, and on the other hand it was demonstrated by a variety of researchers that the middle classes benefited disproportionately from health care, education, and housing in particular. A welfare state based on communitarian and egalitarian ideals was clearly not working as it should.

Criticisms of the welfare state came from both right and left. The extreme Left had all along seen the welfare state as a palliative which obstructed the possibility of radical change by obscuring the harmful effects of a market economy. The Right increasingly saw market provision of welfare which allowed more choice to the client as the desirable way forward, and sought to replace universal provision with the provision of a "safety net" of "targeted benefits" for the weakest and poorest. The moderate Left continued to see the welfare state as a tool of social engineering rather than a safety net, but sought more cost-effective, decentralized, and participative ways of providing welfare.

4. Lesslie Newbigin, "The Welfare State: A Christian Perspective," *Theology* 88 (May 1985): 179.

5. See my *Christianity and the Future of Welfare* (London: Epworth, 1985).

A Christian view must be in tension with both right and left, Newbigin suggests, and it will provide a critique of the past and some clues as to the way forward, precisely because it is "public truth." In a superb passage Newbigin sums up his argument: what theology has to offer is true — the Christian view of the nature and destiny of human beings, which

> is that for which the church exists as sign and witness. It is entrusted to the church, not as one among a variety of options for the private cultivation of the religious life, but as the publicly revealed truth for which Jesus Christ bore witness before Pontius Pilate, the rock of reality against which all other claims to truth have to be tested. It is that human beings are created in love and for love, created for fellowship with one another in a mutual love which is the free gift of God whose inner life is the perfect mutuality of love — Father, Son and Spirit; that happiness consists in participation in this love which is the being of God; and that participation in it is made possible and is offered as a gift to sinful men and women by the justifying work of Christ and the sanctifying work of the Holy Spirit. In the light of this given reality, all projects for the pursuit of happiness as the separate right of each individual human being are exposed as folly, and all definitions whether of want or of need are to be tested in the light of this, the one thing needful — which is to be, along with one's brothers and sisters, on the way which does actually lead to the end for which all things were created and in which all human beings can find their blessedness.[6]

This is heady, helpful rhetoric, more theologically sophisticated than Frank Field's similar assertion that the ills of the welfare state can be traced back to a false and naively optimistic view of human nature. Field also advocates a return to the kind of balanced Christian understanding of human nature which was represented by R. H. Tawney. But Field takes the step that Newbigin seems reluctant or incapable of taking. He asks in quite specific terms what a welfare state that rested on a Christian view of human nature would look like. Field's thought is concrete; Newbigin is reluctant, perhaps on grounds of competence, to enter into specifics. Newbigin is strong and challenging on generalities and principles, but has little to say about application. But, as R. H. Tawney said, "to state a principle without its application is irresponsible and unintelligible."[7] We look in vain to Newbigin for any serious engagement with questions of application, save in the life of the church.

6. Newbigin, "The Welfare State," p. 179.
7. R. H. Tawney, *The Attack and Other Papers* (London, 1953), p. 178.

Christian Justice

Newbigin is sensitively aware of the problem of justice in a morally fragmented society, which I explore in chapter 2 of my *Christian Justice and Public Policy*.[8] He is convinced that there is "no possibility of achieving an agreed definition of justice within the conceptual framework of secular 'Liberalism.' It is bankrupt."[9] The huge problems for society that arise from this confusion and uncertainty are not Newbigin's primary concern. He is more interested in presenting and commending a Christian account of justice which is relevant to the healing of society's problems and capable of coping with deeply entrenched injustice. Like the rest of us, he hears today "a long cry of anguish and distress. And who can be deaf to this cry?"[10] But for him the task is not to amplify or relay that cry, but rather to unmask the illusions and confusions about justice which are so hurtfully dominant in our society, and then to "set forth the quite different conceptual framework which is offered by the Bible and the Christian tradition." This is the "proper work" of the church.

Justice is the other face of love, and both terms are given distinctive content in the Christian tradition. The true context of justice is the holy, generous, justifying love of God. Other ways of understanding justice lead to disaster. Let Newbigin speak for himself:

> Justice means giving to each what is due, but it is of the essence of the fallenness of human nature that I overestimate what is due to me and underestimate what is due to others. Thus we fight one another for justice with all the fervour of a moral crusade, and it eludes us while we tear the fabric of society to shreds. But what is really due to each person is to be loved and honoured as made in God's image and for God's love, then the struggle for justice (which is always necessary among sinful human beings) is protected from that demonic power which always takes over when I identify justice for me with the justice of God. We struggle for more justice in a world where absolute justice cannot be, but we live by grace as debtors to the charity of God; and the stigma has been borne by another.[11]

True justice is relational. Its source is in the being of the triune God, "in the eternal giving and receiving of love which is the being of the Godhead."

---

8. D. B. Forrester, *Christian Justice and Public Policy* (Cambridge: Cambridge University Press, 1997).

9. L. Newbigin, "Whose Justice?" *Ecumenical Review* 44 (1992): 308-11, here 310.

10. Newbigin, "Whose Justice?" p. 308.

11. Newbigin, "The Welfare State," pp. 181-82.

God's justice reflects his covenant faithfulness, even to the unfaithful and ungodly — indeed, particularly in the justification of the ungodly. Thus "at the centre of the Christian understanding of justice there stands the cross, not a symbol but a historic deed in which the justice of God was manifested in his covenant faithfulness right through to the point where the just died for the unjust."[12]

This is fine theology. But because it floats free of concrete earthing, it is perhaps not hard to understand why Newbigin's thought on justice has attracted so much less attention outside the confines of the church than the speeches of David Jenkins, or reports such as *Faith in the City* or *Unemployment and the Future of Work* which speak of implementation and go into specifics. It has its limitations as public theology.

The Church as Exemplar of Public Truth

For Newbigin the role of the church is central. Involvement in the public arena is a form of confession and of mission, of which the church provides a necessary hermeneutic. "The missionary action of the church," he writes, "is the exegesis of the gospel."[13] The Ceylon minister and theologian D. T. Niles illustrates this hermeneutic process dramatically and in simple terms:

> It is a common experience in India or Ceylon, when an evangelistic team visits a village, that in the meeting that is organised the small Christian community in the village will be sitting in the middle while the Hindus and Muslims will be standing all around. And, in that situation, the evangelist is aware that whereas he is pointing to Christ, his listeners are looking at that small group sitting in front of them. The message will carry no conviction unless it is being proved in the lives of those who bear the Name that is being declared. This village situation is the world situation too, and for good or ill it is still the Christians of Western lands who are sitting in the middle.[14]

Newbigin develops the image further, emphasizing that in a village in South India, "the local community is the local community. Your neighbour who lives in the next door house is also the man you meet at work, in your lei-

12. Newbigin, "Whose Justice?" p. 310.
13. Newbigin, *Truth to Tell*, p. 35.
14. D. T. Niles, *Upon the Earth: The Mission of God and the Missionary Enterprise of the Churches* (Madras: Christian Literature Society, 1962), p. 197.

sure, on holidays and on work days. And even though Christians may be a small minority, the church stands in the village as a visible invitation to the whole community." In such villages the Christians rarely have a church building; they worship in the open or under the shade of a tree, visible to all. Here "[o]ne administers the sacraments and preaches the word to a group of believers surrounded by a wider circle of those who do not yet believe, but for whom also Christ came. One speaks to all, and the words spoken to the church are heard by those outside."[15] The message of the gospel is public truth which cannot be separated from the actual, day-to-day life of the community of faith. The life and nature of that community is a hermeneutic of the gospel.

If it is true that others understand the faith in the light of what they know and have experienced of the Christian community, the church, so also Christians may not separate their understanding of justice, rights, community, welfare, and so on from the fellowship that is called church. For the church is called to embody and manifest the justice and the love of God, and in fulfilling this task it manifests the fullness of life and the salvation that is promised in Christ. This is its mission, its calling, not for its own sake but for the life of the world and the welfare of the broader community.

Stanley Hauerwas provides, as it were, an explication of Newbigin and Niles's model:

> The task of the church [is] to pioneer those institutions and practices that the wider society has not learned as forms of justice. (At times it is also possible that the church can learn from society more just ways of forming life.) The church, therefore, must act as a *paradigmatic community* in the hope of providing some indication of what the world can be but is not. . . . *The church does not have, but rather is a social ethic.* That is, she is a social ethic inasmuch as she functions as a *criteriological institution* — that is, an institution that has learned to embody the form of truth that is charity as revealed in the person and work of Christ.[16]

In thousands of congregations throughout the world, Newbigin writes,

> it becomes possible for the church as a local fellowship to be an agency of God's justice. In its liturgy it continually relives the mystery of God's ac-

---

15. L. Newbigin, *Honest Religion for Secular Man* (Philadelphia: Westminster; London: SCM Press, 1966), p. 108.

16. Stanley Hauerwas, *Truthfulness and Tragedy* (Notre Dame: Notre Dame University Press, 1977), pp. 142-43, emphasis mine.

tion in justifying the ungodly. In its common life and the mutual care and discipline of its members it embodies (even if very imperfectly) the justice of God which both unmasks the sin and restores relation with the sinner. In its action in the society of which it is a part it will seek to be with Jesus among those who are pushed to the margins. But in all this it will point beyond itself and its own weakness and ambivalence, to the one in whom God's justice has been made manifest in the strange victory of the cross.[17]

It is concrete actions by the local Christian community which express a special balance between realism and hope, and embody in specific contexts the justice of God. "The most important contribution which the Church can make to a new social order," Newbigin writes, "is to be itself a new social order."[18]

In this strong ecclesiological emphasis, Newbigin lays down a foundation for public theology which is often rather neglected elsewhere. His public theology insists that Christians' contributions to public affairs must be theologically based and distinctive. Otherwise it is well for us to hold our tongues. And the institutional church must take seriously for its own inner life the message it addresses to the broader society, trusting that in some way the life and worship of the church, in all its weakness and confusion, may manifest the attractive truthfulness of the message proclaimed.

17. Newbigin, "Whose Justice?" p. 331.
18. Newbigin, *Truth to Tell*, p. 85.

Rival Conceptions of Global Christianity: Mission and Modernity, Then and Now

Bert Hoedemaker

Introduction

This contribution focuses on some of the presuppositions of the vision of global Christianity that were dominant in the formative years of the twentieth-century ecumenical movement (roughly: 1928-68), and it considers those in the light of present-day experiences of globalization and fragmentation which seem to call for an alternative conception of mission and ecumenism. The argument is that Lesslie Newbigin was a major exponent of the "dominant conception," and that the discussion of his recent work on gospel and (Western) culture will benefit by such a comparison.

To summarize briefly at the outset: the dominant conception is preoccupied with the problem of unity and diversity, of "one gospel and many cultures"; it is intent upon the coherence and the witnessing power of emerging global Christianity as a rival to major alternatives such as "secular civilization" and non-Christian religions; and it seeks to unify the diversity of missionary movements and spiritual traditions with the aid of the concept of *missio Dei*. By contrast, the most urgent contemporary question seems to be: What role can there be for the gospel tradition in a world plagued by pluralism and fragmentation? The survival, coherence, and reconciliation of the human race has as such become a theological problem; the identity of "global Christianity" depends on its ability to reconstruct its various traditions in the perspective of this question. Against the background of the contrast between dominant conception and present-day experience, the tensions between Western and non-Western Christianity that began to undermine the dominant conception from the late 1960s onward appear to be just a prelude, an intermediate phase, leading up to the global problem of unity and fragmentation of humankind.

The following treatment will be introduced by brief comments on the general theological concerns of the dominant conception and on the way the question of the relation between mission and church unity emerged in the context of those concerns. A closer look at the approaches to "culture" and "modernity," characteristic of the dominant conception, will follow, and a comparison with more recent approaches will be attempted. "Culture" and "modernity" appear to be the crucial issues in a discussion about contemporary global Christianity, and they might turn out to be crucial as well in a discussion about Newbigin's recent work.

General Theological Concerns in the Formative Years

After the First World War the missionary movement was confronted with problems that called for reflection and organization on a more or less centralized global level. Indigenization, the self-affirmation of other religions, secularization and economic inequality, and the autonomy of the "young" churches — all these issues challenged the self-understanding of the missionary movement and its worldview. The non-Western, non-Christian world could no longer be defined in an undifferentiated way as "pagan"; the First World War placed the world on the political agenda as a problem of peace and justice, and that could not leave Christianity unaffected. Here lies the origin of the ecumenical movement and of the "logic" of the integration of the missionary movement into a worldwide communion of churches. In this situation the missionary movement gradually came to be (re)defined as the effort to create a worldwide network of churches that would become centers of witness each in its own context. World Christianity was to become the paradigm of a world society in the perspective of the kingdom of God; without this institutionalized reference to the coming kingdom the world would be left to chaos — a chaos in which religions, ideologies, and above all "secular civilization" would try in vain to create some order.

In due time these theological concerns found their label in the concept of *missio Dei*. This concept expresses a trinitarian view of the God-world relation: the divine plan of salvation is realized in the gathering of the people of God (church) and the establishing of signs of the coming kingdom (mission). Mission, in other words, is seen as part of an encompassing, overarching action of God in which "world" and "kingdom" are held together. In this sense the concept of *missio Dei* signals a critical review and a firm theological

14

grounding of the history of the missionary movement; and it is a typical expression of the "ideology" of the construction of a strong ecumenical movement, which Raiser calls "christocentric universalism."

The integration of the International Missionary Council (IMC) and the World Council of Churches, which was in Newbigin's portfolio when he was general secretary of the IMC, was a logical outcome of the theological concerns sketched above. At the time, Newbigin's main concern was to retain a strong emphasis on mission in a setting in which interchurch development aid seemed to receive the highest priority.[1] In hindsight, however, it appears that the integration implied a more fundamental question. In what sense could and should churches be regarded as agents of mission, and what did it mean to call churches to missionary responsibility? Should the ecumenical movement be characterized by churches carrying out a "missionary responsibility" together, or was it to be defined as ongoing missionary mobility in which "churches" would be something like temporary halting places? The question is by no means artificial, as the discussions at the Willingen conference make clear.[2] Implicitly, the World Council opted for the first alternative, but the question was never dealt with in a satisfactory way. In the shadow of the *missio Dei* concept, it virtually disappeared. As a result, ecumenical theology remains weak on this point, caught between the evangelical emphasis on "mission" and the Roman Catholic emphasis on "church." Because of this weakness, the dominant conception ultimately fails to clarify how "global" and "Christianity" hang together.

What the integration did accomplish was to bid farewell to the geographic concept of mission. From now on mission would be a six-continents affair; the "home base" could be anywhere; the "Western world" was to be included in the mission fields; and each local church in each place was called to mission in its own context. The six-continents approach was undoubtedly a step forward; on the other hand, it was used to support a conception of global Christianity designed as the "witnessing" counterpart to a world unified by the "secular" forces of history and technology.[3] As such, it remained captive

---

1. Newbigin's assessment of this situation can be found in scattered comments in his *Unfinished Agenda: An Autobiography* (Grand Rapids: Eerdmans; London: SPCK, 1985).

2. N. Goodall, ed., *Missions under the Cross — Addresses and Statements of Willingen 1952* (London, 1953); cf. especially the contributions of Paul L. Lehmann, "The Missionary Obligation of the Church," *Theology Today* 9 (1952): 20-38, and J. C. Hoekendijk, "The Church in Missionary Thinking," *International Review of Missions* 41 (1952): 324-36.

3. The world missionary conference at Mexico City in 1963 illustrates this point. In the section headings of the conference the word "mission" is consistently replaced by "witness," and the geographic frontier is replaced by other frontiers (other faiths, secular world, neighborhood, national and confessional boundaries). There is a consensus that the church

to some of the presuppositions of "modernity." The serious questioning of those presuppositions had not yet begun.

The Problem of Culture and Intercultural Communication

"Culture" did not become a serious issue in the debate about global Christianity until the world mission conference at Bangkok (1972/73), when it was used by Third World Christians as a tool to defend their specific identities over against the Western tradition.[4] Around the same time, new theoretical approaches to the phenomenon of culture made their entry, replacing to some extent the dominant functionalism.[5] The functionalist approach had caused a certain blindness to phenomena such as cultural change, intercultural communication, and secularization, and as such it had opened the possibility to use the polarity gospel-culture in a precritical way. Precritical means here: ignoring the hermeneutical problem of the prior intertwinement of faith formulations with religions and cultures, and underestimating the difficulties implied in the effort to define "gospel" as an independent entity over against "cultures," especially when cultures are viewed as processes of signification. Both developments — the new debate between First and Third World Christianity and the new theories of culture — began to undermine the dominant conception of global Christianity. "Cultures" could no longer be simply regarded as the expressions of the diversity of humankind, challenging the "oneness" of the gospel to a unity-in-plurality; rather, they were rediscovered as the starting points for struggles of identity, in which the "one gospel" had to become subject to plural reinterpretation.

In semiotic theory "culture" tends to be defined not as a stable system of habit, tradition, and lifestyle, but as a process of signification characterized by

---

should "take on the secular world" and its perspective of emancipation from nature as the framework for an understanding of mission. Cf. Ronald K. Orchard, *Witness in Six Continents: Records of the Meeting of the CWME of the World Council of Churches Held in Mexico City, 1963* (London, 1964).

4. "Culture shapes the voice that answers the voice of Christ": *Bangkok Assembly 1973 — Minutes and Reports of the Assembly of the CWME* (Geneva, 1973), p. 73.

5. Cf. Clifford Geertz, *The Interpretation of Cultures* (New York, 1973). The functionalist concept of culture had been a dominant tool in missions and missiological research, and that fit in well with the affinity of the missionary movement as well as of missiology to relatively closed, "primitive," tribal cultures. See Robert J. Schreiter, *Constructing Local Theologies* (London, 1985); Charles R. Taber, *The World Is Too Much with Us: "Culture" in Modern Protestant Missions* (Macon, Ga., 1991).

change and negotiation. Culture is "a dynamic process of radiation, adoption and confrontation, reception, modification, rejection, reconstruction and invention," and the same might be said of intercultural communication, as there seems to be "no master narrative that can reconcile the tragic and comic plots of global cultural history."[6] In these definitions the concept of culture is applicable only to larger units (Scottish, Southern, African culture, and so on) if it is agreed that "culture" in those cases refers to a provisional relative fixation of certain configurations of meaning, and particularly certain configurations of power.

In ecumenical-missionary discussions the words "context" and "contextualization" began to take on polemical traits along the same lines; no longer did they carry the simple meaning of social conditioning, but rather they began to refer to a junction of religious, social, and economic histories as the breeding ground for a conscious faithful choice of position by Christians, in which traditional "self-evident" ways of thinking were criticized in a fundamental way.[7] The ecumenical experience with contextuality, and from there with culture and intercultural communication as an arena of conflict, in fact signals the end of the precritical use of the polarity gospel-culture. In its concentration on the need to connect the one gospel to the many cultures, ecumenical-missionary thinking had been inclined to lose sight of the need to (re)identify the message in relation to the problematic nature of cultural plurality as such. Cultural plurality had been seen and used as an instrument in the service of evangelization, rather than as the problem itself.

There is another aspect to this to which attention should be drawn. The concept of culture belongs to the inheritance of the Enlightenment; the effort to create some order in the non-Western world by the use of the plural concept "cultures" is itself part of the project of modernity, and as such part of the problem of the asymmetrical relation between the expanding Western world and the rest of humankind. The use of the polarity gospel-culture — long popular in the missionary movement — ignores and in a sense denies this problem by treating "cultures" as basically equal units. That in itself is an abstraction from a complex process of interaction. Matters only become worse when, in the confines of this approach, an entity called "Western culture" is

6. James Clifford, *The Predicament of Culture* (Cambridge, 1988), p. 15. According to Clifford, the cultural process is motivated by the need to "make a real difference" (p. 275).

7. Examples in G. H. Anderson and T. F. Stransky, eds., *Mission Trends No. 3 — Third World Theologies* (New York: Paulist; Grand Rapids, 1976); also S. B. Bevans, *Models of Contextual Theology* (Maryknoll, N.Y., 1992); V. Küster, *Theologie im Kontext, zugleich ein Versuch über die Minjung-Theologie* (Nettetal, 1995); L. A. Hoedemaker, ed., *Theologiseren in Context* (Kampen, 1997).

isolated with its own specific problem of "modernity." This overlooks the fact that "modernity" has been part of global intercultural communication even before "cultures" were defined as partners in this communication, and that we are dealing with a long history of fundamentally problematic and asymmetrical relations. What we are inclined to call "Western culture" is not a "culture" in the traditionally missionary sense; rather, it is the cradle and the reflection of a complicated global process in which so-called cultural identities are permanently created, projected, disputed, recaptured, "cobbled together."[8] In this process the project of modernity is at work, but it also meets its limits in the widespread "local" resistance against it. Perhaps one should say that it is modernity itself that has produced and keeps producing the "clashing of cultures" and the emergence of "new histories."[9] It hardly needs to be added that these insights call for a new conception of global Christianity.

Illustrative of Newbigin's views at this point is a passage in *The Open Secret: Sketches for a Missionary Theology*,[10] in which he calls "western culture" one of the tribal cultures of humankind, which ought not export its particular worldview to other cultures. That approach reflects a precritical view of intercultural communication; it does not take into account that speaking of "cultures" already presupposes the asymmetrical Western expansion, and it mistakenly suggests that one can conceive of a global missionary movement which is untouched by this problem.

The Problem of Modernity and Secularization

The struggle of the ecumenical movement in its formative years with what was then called "secular civilization" or "the secular world" constitutes a fascinating story. It begins at the world missionary conference at Jerusalem (1928), where Rufus Jones presented an influential paper entitled "Secular Civilization and the Christian Task,"[11] which already foreshadows the domi-

8. Robert J. Schreiter, *The New Catholicity: Theology between the Global and the Local* (Maryknoll, N.Y., 1997), p. 59.

9. Cf. on this: Mike Featherstone, *Undoing Culture: Globalization, Postmodernism, and Identity* (London, 1995).

10. Lesslie Newbigin, *The Open Secret: Sketches for a Missionary Theology* (London: SPCK; Grand Rapids: Eerdmans, 1978), p. 171. In the revised edition this passage was not changed.

11. Rufus M. Jones, "Secular Civilization and the Christian Task," in *The Christian Life and Message in Relation to Non-Christian Systems*, Report of the Jerusalem Meeting, vol. 1 (London, 1928), pp. 284-338.

nant conception of global Christianity as a paradigmatic alternative to global secularism; and it (provisionally) ends with the world missionary conference at Mexico City (1963) and the report of the "missionary structure of the congregation" project (1967), which both defined the secular world as the place of God's action and as a necessary point of reference for the church and its mission.[12] It is clear that the dominant conception of global Christianity was formed in the time the "secular" creation of a certain global unity — first negatively, through two world wars, then more positively, through a concerted effort at worldwide development — made considerable advances and did not fail to impress the architects of the ecumenical movement. During the 1960s ecumenical thinkers such as M. M. Thomas and C. C. West developed views that placed global Christianity in the context of a broader framework of God's "worldly" action in the whole of human history and in a sense relativized the significance of the church.[13]

To a certain extent, Newbigin accepted these emphases at the time of the integration of the missionary and ecumenical movements; but they also presented a severe challenge to him, as they seemed to undermine the *raison d'être* of the (traditional) missionary movement.[14] As stated above, Newbigin's main concern during those years was to retain a strong emphasis on mission in a setting in which interchurch (development) aid seemed to receive the highest priority. "Mission" seemed to be passé in Geneva. Matters became worse, in his view, at the notorious ecumenical student conference at Strasbourg (1960), where all more traditional references to church and mission were declared obsolete, and also by the publication of John Robinson's *Honest to God* (1963), which made short work of any belief in a God "out there." Newbigin felt that a legitimate emphasis on the significance of "secular history" could not and should not lead to the erosion of all references to the transcendent God. He saw this as a typically Western problem; the Asian

---

12. Newbigin reports: "If the Tambaram meeting had placed the Christian mission firmly in a churchly context, and if Willingen had struggled unsuccessfully to break out of this, Mexico must be regarded as especially significant for the fact that it conceived the missionary task in the context of what God is doing in the secular events of our time." In Harold E. Fey, ed., *The Ecumenical Advance: A History of the Ecumenical Movement*, vol. 2 (London, 1970), p. 194. The names Tambaram and Willingen respectively refer to the third and fifth world missionary conferences (1938 and 1952).

13. M. M. Thomas, *Towards a Theology of Contemporary Ecumenism* (Madras, 1978); C. C. West, "Community, Christian and Secular," in *Man in Community: Christian Concern for the Human in Changing Society*, ed. Egbert de Vries (New York and London, 1966), pp. 330-58.

14. Newbigin, *Unfinished Agenda*, p. 198: "we are in the decade of the secular."

M. M. Thomas, in his opinion, approached the issue of secularization in a much more balanced way.

The whole quandary about the situatedness of global Christianity in the secular world led Newbigin to the firm conviction that the Christian tradition would only be able to retain its identity if it would continue to take seriously its basic point of departure, that the revelation of God in Christ was the only clue to the understanding of the whole of (secular) history. In a sense he picked up the emphases of the early world missionary conferences: Jerusalem (1928) on the need for a Christian-religious alternative to a global secular civilization, and Tambaram (1938) on the need to develop a specifically Christian witness over against the pagan ideologies of the time. But under the pressure of the later discussions on secularization, he practically reduced those emphases to a fundamental, and therefore also in a certain sense formal, distinction between Christian and secular worldviews. For him the transcendent reference point became the cornerstone of the conception of global Christianity. His conviction, that this was the basic contribution of the missionary movement to the ecumenical movement, was elaborated in his most significant theological books: *Honest Religion for Secular Man* (1966) and *The Open Secret* (1978).

In hindsight it is obvious that this whole discussion remained within the confines of modernity. It belongs to the context of negotiation and polemical debate between Christian and secular worldviews — a debate which reveals the basic affinity between those worldviews, as they were then conceived, and also makes clear how much the ecumenical movement in its heyday was allied to the "project" of modern Western culture. Even the critical position of Rufus Jones in 1928 did not dispute the necessity of a rational, Western-based worldview. Rufus Jones only wanted to connect it to God and to the tradition of Christian belief.

Newbigin was faithful to this consensus. In his (implied) concept of culture he remained indebted to functionalism and thus could not see the crucial significance of the struggle of contextual theology and the importance of intercultural hermeneutics for the understanding of the gospel. The proclamation of the gospel remained a universal project for him. In the same way, in his approach to modernity Newbigin remained trapped in the presuppositions of the project of modernity itself, and thus could not see that an adequate handling of the problem of the alliance of Christian faith and "modern culture" required a prior awareness of the problems created by this alliance in a global setting. In order to move "beyond Newbigin" on these issues, at least the following two considerations will have to be brought into the discussion and worked out in more detail.

First: Christianity and modernity have been traveling companions in history ever since the fifteenth and sixteenth centuries. In the worldwide western expansion, "religious forms of modernity" and "modern forms of religion" have gone hand in hand in mutual stimulation, even mutual definition.[15] It seems justified to regard Western Christianity and modernity as growing up together in kinship and rivalry, rather than as successive and fundamentally incompatible designs. Christian faith, conceived as a permanent process of reconstruction of tradition, cannot place itself outside this ongoing kinship and rivalry, even when it is critical of its own history and its own previous alliances. In other words: it cannot define itself as a meta-project, over against the meta-project of modernity. To describe the "Christianity and modernity" problem in terms of a confrontation between two worldviews or two rationalities, as Newbigin does, ignores the historical reality of the kinship and rivalry. What is more, it remains within the confines of modernity and models Christian faith with the aid of "modern" presuppositions.

Second: all this is not to deny that Christianization and modernization — even in their kinship and rivalry — can be distinguished as two historical projects, as schemes to "organize" the cultural and religious plurality of the (Western) world, as "grand narratives," each intent on becoming the major defining factor in Western culture. The various efforts to define the present state of Western culture as "postmodern" all testify to the fact that both projects have remained incomplete: they have met and still meet their limits in the stubborn reality of (worldwide) cultural and religious plurality. The project of Christianization has undergone major redefinition and transformation in the missionary movement and in the development of a plural world Christianity. The project of modernization has created some semblance of "completed modernity" in the processes of globalization, but the aims and presuppositions of these processes are challenged by various forms of cultural and religious self-assertion. In view of all this, it might be more adequate not to define the "Christianity and modernity" problem as a specifically Western hang-up, but to place it in the framework of the worldwide tension between the power of a narrow functional rationality on the one hand and the potency of human religious traditions on the other: traditions that keep insisting on raising "transcending" questions about humankind, its unity, and its reconciliation.[16] In

---

15. See for this point: T. Asad, *Genealogies of Religion; Discipline and Reasons of Power in Christianity and Islam* (Baltimore, 1993); P. van der Veer, ed., *Conversion to Modernities: The Globalization of Christianity* (1996).

16. See Bert Hoedemaker, *Secularization and Mission: A Theological Essay* (Harrisburg, Pa., 1998).

that perspective, Christian faith as the reconstruction of the Christian tradition takes its clue from the essential incompleteness of both Christianization and modernization.

Concluding Remarks

In order to save and refocus Newbigin's important appeal to the modern Christian conscience to consider the necessity of a new missionary approach to contemporary Western culture, it might be necessary to free it from the restrictions of what this paper has called the "dominant conception" of global Christianity. Within those restrictions the appeal remains captive to the presuppositions of modernity itself and cannot, therefore, grasp the problem in its full scope. It concentrates on foreground issues, such as the tension between public and private, objective and subjective knowledge, universal history and decisive events, and so on; and it is inclined to do so in a rationalistic, not to say dogmatic, way. I suggested above that Newbigin ultimately takes refuge in a formal distinction between Christian and secular worldviews.[17] This is characteristic of the way the dominant conception placed world and kingdom, world and witness, secularity and Christianity next to and over against each other.

If we attempt to develop the concepts of "culture" and "modernity" with the aid of recent theory, and to reformulate the "Christianity and modernity" problem as one of globalization and fragmentation, we will need an eschatology that focuses on the unity and reconciliation of humankind — an eschatology that reaches beyond forms of unity that create new dichotomies and give rise to more radical "transcending" questions, and also beyond the fragmentation that seems to legitimize ongoing conflict. The twin projects of Christianization and modernization had — and still have — precisely that eschatological potential in them, but this potential has tended to give way to totalitarian tendencies also present in the projects. Eschatology needs to return as criticism of these tendencies, and as an instrument to recover the perspective of a true unity of humankind.

---

17. This can be illustrated by the formal way he presents his basic theological choices in *The Open Secret.* Jesus' *exousia* and the believer's commitment (in chap. 2, "The Question of Authority") are not elaborated in terms of choice for content but in terms of allegiance to principles. The same is true for the crucial chapter on election (7).

Entering Exile: Can There Be a Missiology for "Not My People"?

Peter Cruchley-Jones

This paper seeks to address some of the broad issues raised by Newbigin and the Gospel and Culture movement through the biblical paradigm of exile. This paper emerges from a Ph.D. thesis, but more importantly from a people and a place. The application of the exile paradigm has come out of the theological reflections of people in the congregations and community I serve in South Wales. I am a United Reformed Church minister serving three congregations in Ely, a large council housing estate in Cardiff. Ely is a community beset by poverty, with high unemployment, youth disaffection, and poor health. It is also a proud and resistant community which seeks to tackle together its problems.

The three churches I serve are small but talented, and our existence is precarious if determined. In a community of thirty thousand we number a little over one hundred. Church people have a memory of stronger days with full churches and respect shown. But there is a deep sense in some of disparagement about the world today. We feel ignored and isolated and far from the center of things, and we exert a lot of energy trying to get back there. As we reflected on these thoughts and experiences, we began to turn to the exile stories as a starting point for our analysis. It has unexpected and disturbing implications. There is a longer discussion of these themes in my book Singing the Lord's Song in a Strange Land *(Frankfurt: Peter Lang, 2000).*

PETER CRUCHLEY-JONES

"The World Is a Terrible Place. It Was Much Better during the War."[1]

It seems to me that this sense of the church's disorientation in society underlies much of Newbigin and the general theme of exploring the nature of the relationship between gospel and cultures in contemporary society. Both those who would argue for a rejection of plurality and those who would argue for an embrace of it do so to reorient the church for its contemporary society and for it to grasp more fully the ideal of being God's people in contemporary society. And underlying this is an intriguing question: Is God silent in our culture (especially if he seems to say so little of value in the church)?

Various approaches could be made to these questions. My approach is to come via the theological medium of the exile experience of Israel and of Ely. I believe the fruitfulness of exile as a paradigm is that it enables a critique not just of culture but also of church. Thus it is not sufficient to judge if "gospel" can accommodate a certain culture.[2] It is also necessary to ascertain if "gospel" can accommodate church. It is to allow an important recognition, which is that church defines "gospel" in the relationship "gospel and culture" just as it defines culture. Thus church, with such an integral and dominating role in this relationship, needs to be included within the critique and analysis.

Exile as the Loss of the Public Center

I would suggest there is no more fundamental experience of disorientation for God's people than the exile experience.[3] It is worth listening to one of the biblical voices of exile in its entirety to realize how scalded Israel was by exile.

> By the rivers of Babylon —
> there we sat down and there we wept
> when we remembered Zion.

---

1. I have explored this with several women's groups in churches and had the same general response about wartime. The men who were there are not quite so sure! But an astonishing 20 percent of the sisterhood in one of my churches thought the world was worse now than it was two hundred years ago!

2. As Newbigin seeks to do. See Lesslie Newbigin, *The Gospel in a Pluralist Society* (London: SPCK; Grand Rapids: Eerdmans; and Geneva: WCC Publications, 1989), p. 222.

3. This is borne out both in biblical historical studies like those of Peter Ackroyd (see *Exile and Restoration* [London: SCM Press, 1968]) and in the more recent biblical theological studies of Walter Brueggemann (see, for example, *Hopeful Imagination* [Philadelphia: Fortress, 1986]).

On the willows there
    we hung up our harps.
For there our captors
    asked us for songs,
and our tormentors asked for mirth, saying,
    "Sing us one of the songs of Zion!"
How could we sing the Lord's song
    in a foreign land?
If I forget you, O Jerusalem,
    let my right hand wither!
Let my tongue cling to the roof of my mouth,
    if I do not remember you,
if I do not set Jerusalem
    above my highest joy.
Remember, O Lord, against the Edomites
    the day of Jerusalem's fall,
how they said, "Tear it down! Tear it down!
    Down to its foundations!"
O daughter Babylon, you devastator!
    Happy shall they be who pay you back
    what you have done to us!
Happy shall they be who take your little ones
    and dash them against the rock!   (Ps. 137 NRSV)

The exile stories of the Old Testament witness the loss of place and privilege for the people of God. This loss occurs politically in the loss of nationhood and theologically in the loss of election. The temple is destroyed, the king is variously exiled or blinded and exiled, the land is defiled, and the covenant is seemingly forgotten by a silent (?) God.[4]

Exile brings the world of Zion crashing to the ground, and with it, in Newbigin's borrowed phrase, its plausibility structure.[5] The degradation of Zion by Babylon, Assyria, and Egypt portrays a scene of cultural encounter in which the seemingly pure covenantal tradition of Zion is diluted, adulterated, and ultimately overpowered by the unclean and alien cultures of the Canaanites, the Assyrians, and the Babylonians.

The cost of all this idolatry is marginalization from the land for the wealthy and marginalization *in* the land for the poor. The cost is also the loss of Zion, that most potent of images of the public center and public truth. Is-

---

4. Ezek. 8:12.
5. See Newbigin, *The Gospel in a Pluralist Society*, pp. 27-38.

rael's response to exile, if we take Psalm 137 as an example, is largely to lament the loss, endure the loss, and hope for restoration and revenge.

This has a resonance in this gospel and culture debate. Ezekiel bemoans those of God's people who worship wood and stone,[6] just as Newbigin bemoans those who give in to the ideology of pluralism.[7] Exile could be the result of God's people being open to plurality rather than remaining pure, or it could be the result of remaining "pure" and not being open to plurality.

One should recognize that the exile inhabits a contested place within its various biblical narratives. The official version of exile according to the priestly organized histories of Kings suggests that exile comes as an inevitable consequence of idolatry, of theological insubordination.[8] God's people started fraternizing with the Canaanites, and before long began to worship the queen of heaven.[9] They gave ground on the public center and public truth that the covenant alone deserved and warranted. The geopolitical expansion of Assyria, Egypt, and Babylon, though they were eager for land and power, is put in a theo-political framework of the repercussions of Israel's lusting adultery and disobedience against Yahweh.

We might like to think that the lesson of exile for Israel is to learn to keep a pure covenant, and restoration is dreamt of and acted upon in terms of the restoration of the old certainties, particularly the temple. Certainly the priestly inspired restoration suggests this in Ezra and the emphases of the priestly redacted postexilic biblical material.[10] If this is all there is to it, then the Newbigin argument about fostering methods of being church which regain the public center for the official gospel is compelling.

But the exile story is not as univocal as that. Alongside idolatry should be placed covenantal complacency. Jeremiah's temple sermon (Jer. 7:1-15) makes very clear that Zion is no refuge: "Do not trust in these deceptive words: 'This is the temple of the LORD, the temple of the LORD, the temple of the LORD'" (Jer. 7:4 NRSV). Defining the people of God as those who preserve and police the internal institutions of Zion or the gospel is not enough.

---

6. Ezek. 20:32: "What is in your mind shall never happen — the thought, 'Let us be like the nations, like the tribes of the countries, and worship wood and stone'" (NRSV).

7. See Newbigin's discussion of contextualization as domestication in Newbigin, pp. 141-54.

8. This can be illustrated with the Deuteronomic attitudes to (idolatrous) kings like Saul (1 Sam. 28:7ff.), in the northern kingdom Jeroboam (1 Kings 13:33-34) and Ahab (and, of course, Jezebel) (1 Kings 21:17-26), and in the southern kingdom Manasseh (2 Kings 21:1-16).

9. Jer. 7:18.

10. E.g., the Deuteronomic covenantal equation of disobedience met by punishment, obedience by blessing.

Jeremiah points to a feature that is still visible for us in Ely, and this is the ascription of ontological primacy to liturgy. Righteousness and covenantal obedience had been reduced to the practice of the temple cult. The opening chapter of Isaiah, for example, seeks to tear down this ideology of the sufficiency of the temple and its liturgy.[11] This emphasis on the ontological primacy of liturgy and worship establishes a self-perpetuating, self-fulfilling ideology of God's people that supplants praxis with doxology. I would suggest this is visible in the church.

Newbigin himself expresses this ecclesio-centric view when he discusses the church and the Christian's response to the sociopolitical realities and choices of our time: "What we do in the liturgy and life of the church has an ontological primacy and an evolving reality far beyond these choices we make."[12] Speaking as one from Ely who faces with others some of the most crushing sociopolitical forces in Western society, I say this would be a really neat trick. It may be comforting, but it is ultimately deceitful.

Exile exposes and also stems from Zion and the church's ecclesio-centrism. It stems from the natural and genuine but misguided assumption by God's people that they and their internal mechanisms and ideologies have a privileged and prior place in the affection and action of God.[13] In general it means making the church the locus for God.[14] Inevitably, if the church has such a privileged position, pluralism is to be rejected.

Exile as the Loss of the Theological Center

The loss of the public center through the crushing of Zion's physical and theological institutions and dominance sent out shock waves. The majority response is anger, dismay, and lamentation. The loss of a public center provoked the dreadful prospect that Zion is not at the theological center either. Exile suggests that God is not acting against Babylon, God is acting against Zion. God is not rejecting Assyria, God is rejecting Israel.

The paradigm of exile does not assume that the prevailing exiling cul-

---

11. Isa. 1:10-17.

12. Newbigin, *The Gospel in a Pluralist Society*, p. 139.

13. This can mean for some that election is understood as privilege, and I know Newbigin argues against this. It means for others that it is appropriate to maintain the structures and edifices of church, local and denominational, against all comers.

14. This is something Newbigin effectively advocates in his chapter on the church as the locus for mission and God's action in the world; see Newbigin, *The Gospel in a Pluralist Society*, pp. 116-27.

ture is automatically antithetical. Exiles might like to say that this is so, but there is danger that this is just a product of lamentation over lost power. If we are to understand exile theologically, the issue is not that the host culture is antithetical to God's people, but that God's people are antithetical to God.

In this way one can understand exile as an act of God not against Babylon but against Israel, not against secular plural Western culture but against secular Western monocultural Christianity. Not against Enlightenment but against ecclesio-centrism. "When she had weaned Not pitied, she conceived and bore a son. And the LORD said, 'Call his name Not my people, for you are not my people and I am not your God'" (Hos. 1:8-9 RSV).

This decommissioning of God's people is an appalling prophecy and a terrifying prospect. This is where the exile paradigm begins to hurt. If exile is to be taken seriously as a paradigm, then it needs to be seen as more than a minority in an alien environment.[15]

The issues are not just questions of rejection, engagement, or assimilation to our hostile alien cultural environment. They are also about questions of rejection, engagement, or assimilation to God and God to us. It concerns us with the breaking down of our images of God and (God) breaking down our images of ourselves.

But exile further shocks because the locus for God is not Zion; the locus for God in exile is the East. When God withdraws from Zion in Ezekiel, it is through the east gate, and away into the east he departs.[16] It seems that the East, as for us in the UK, held a sense of promise and threat for Israel. It was an east wind that drove back the Red Sea,[17] but it was also from the east that invasion came from foreign nations.[18]

While I do not want to overplay the significance of this verse, the loss of the theological center through exile provokes a new decentered perspective in Amos.

Are you not like the Ethiopians to me,
   O people of Israel? says the LORD.
Did I not bring Israel up from the land of Egypt,
   and the Philistines from Caphtor and the Arameans from Kir?[19]

---

15. Though I would argue that this is something important to accept.
16. Ezek. 10:1–11:25.
17. Exod. 14:21.
18. See Ezek. 25:4, for example.
19. Amos 9:7 NRSV. I am grateful to a friend and colleague, Rev. Mark Gray, for this insight.

Amos is here suggesting that the exodus story is not a publicly defining integrating moment in the life of Israel alone. The action of God *(locus and mission)* is hardly restricted to Zion alone if such prophetic words as these are to stand. If Amos points to Yahweh provoking alternative exodus stories in the lives of other nations, should the outworking of the gospel be constrained to the confines of the church?

Exile reminds us that there is no preeminence for God's people before God, and if this is so, there is no preeminence for God's people and what they own in the public center either. So is restoration all that is to be learned about from exile? Is the point of exile restoration? Is the point of Western Christianity in its presently threatened existence to return to the public center, and as quickly and with as much integrity as possible?

While I think restoration is one of the chief preoccupations of exile, I think it is also appropriate to see the exile and exilic culture as part of the *missio Dei*. Exile is not of itself a mistake best soon rectified. It is a place of potentially epiphanous and ontophanous significance. In exile we have an opportunity to reorient ourselves to God (epiphany) and to our purposes as Not My People (ontophany).[20]

Our epiphanous, if decentered, theological location in Ely can be expressed in two incidents in my personal experience of ministry in Ely.

I met John's mum and dad two days after he died in the ambulance, having sniffed lighter fuel in the car park of our local leisure center. He was seventeen. I called without introduction; they were not church people. John's mum had been to Sunday school as a girl, so she knew God was punishing her and John. Sunday school had taught her this, and she was afraid he was in hell, because when his friends came for her and she went to him she found him so cold and lifeless. And what made her full of agony was not just that her son had died, but that God had done it, and that he was so bloody silent.

I tell this story not to make any comment on the outworkings of a time when the gospel was at the public center in the Sunday school movement,

---

20. In Ely we have attempted to explore the epiphany and ontophany of exile. Just as exile has helped us confront ourselves as Not My People, exile has also helped us identify the exile of "(I am not your) God." So we have attempted to articulate our sense of the presence of God as one which is to be encountered as a living presence, a dying presence, and a rising presence in human experience. This is expressed in a little more detail in my essay in Lynne Price, Juan Sepulveda, and Graeme Smith, eds., *Mission Matters,* Studies in the Intercultural History of Christianity, vol. 103 (Frankfurt: Peter Lang, 1997), pp. 109-20.

though conceivably it could be that. I tell it because it speaks so powerfully and tragically of the silence of God within the theological frameworks in which God is constrained. It seems to me that as we begin to address the issues of gospel and our contemporary culture, space is needed for the ambiguity of a God who is silent and silenced not just within culture, but within church.

> I came home from taking a church group on retreat to find a large group of young people huddled by a bus shelter in pouring rain, all with candles and flowers. I drove past about half an hour later, having found out that the night before a fifteen-year-old girl had been run over there and killed by someone driving recklessly in a stolen car. I stopped and joined them; there were about thirty young people, none older than sixteen. There were no adults apart from me. They all had candles and had laid flowers and had written tributes to Sian all over the bus shelter. I listened to a few of them and looked at the flowers. I even told them what I was (a vicar). They told me some of them had prayed, but mostly they were just being there where it happened. One of my churches is about two hundred to three hundred meters down the road from that bus stop. I considered opening it for them. But they needed to be at this spot. They didn't need the church, and though they were glad I'd come and joined them, they didn't really need me. So I left after about half an hour. They were there for three nights running, often in the rain. But they kept vigil and they sought light for the dark.

I tell this story not to illustrate a theological response in a time and setting when the gospel is not at the public center, though conceivably it could be that. I tell it because it illustrates for me two further issues for gospel and culture discussions. First, the irrelevance of the church as a meaningful place for people's theology but that people still act and think theologically. Secondly, it illustrates the deep-seated need for the church to commandeer and baptize the theological responses of others. I felt I should offer them the church building because the weather was so dreadful, but really I wondered whether I wanted them to see the church as the proper place for this and that I was the proper person for it. Instead I chose — what was inevitable anyway — to let them be in control and allow myself to be on the margins of it.

The epiphanies of exile point to a pluralizing, even syncretizing God, a God who breaks out of the safe confines God's people have grown accustomed to preserve and police. Exile points to God pluralizing Babylon and Zion with each other. Zion finds that God no longer views them as the public center. Zion finds its election is more within itself than above the nations. Its exodus paradigm is shared with others, and is relativized and intensified as a paradigm in which to discover not the superiority of Zion but the liberating power of Yahweh.

Exile points to a collapsing and syncretizing of the theologies of Zion. This is not simply a matter, for example, of the blending of sources and traditions in Old Testament thinking, as with the influence of the Babylonian myth, the Enuma Elish, on the Genesis tradition of creation, or in other aspects of the Wisdom tradition. To speak of God's syncretizing is to recognize God's subversiveness of our official theological systems, and particularly the values and hegemonies they represent. In exile the theological and ecclesiological systems of curse and blessing, of alienation and presence, of power and weakness no longer cohere as they should. Zion is to be understood as a place of blessing and curse, a place of presence and alienation. Babylon is also a place of blessing as well as curse, a place of presence as well as alienation. It is not that Zion is replaced by Babylon, but instead that Zion is to be understood alongside Babylon. In the theological response of her friends, the bus stop where Sian was killed is a place of curse and alienation, but also of blessing and presence.

Even though the priestly-monarchical alliance reexerts control after restoration, it does so recognizing that the actions of the king, and the overreliance on the ontological primacy of liturgy, are key triggers to the crisis of exile. Patterns of power are challenged as Yahweh calls both the priest Ezekiel and the goat herder Amos, not to mention the mighty Persian emperor Cyrus. Once again it is not that the theological power of the king is replaced (revolution), but that it is pluralized. Speaking as an officer of ecclesiology (if not as august an officer as Newbigin or others), one should be wary of the words of those who in exile lose not just public center but also public recognition. As one of my congregation put it, "Don't forget. We'll be here when you've gone." In the context of decline, and especially of indicating the blame for decline, one should be wary of mission as a masked, if good-intentioned, will to power.

Thus, if there is a missiology in exile, it hinges on accepting being made "Not My People." This is to accept just how much it is the *missio Dei*, not the *missio ecclesiae*. This is to accept just how provisional we are. It is not just "all flesh" which is like grass. We should not mistake the promise of God to be with us, even to the end of the age, to suggest with the old rhetoric of religious war that God is on our side. The more one reflects on the identification in history of one people as God's people, the more startling is the story of their exile — not least as it is enshrined in their own theological story. There can be little more relativizing for and of us than the exile story. It would be good to add to the injunction to remember when you were slaves in Egypt, the injunction to also remember when you were exiles.[21]

Not Exodus, Not Return: The Vocation of Exile
for People of a Subversive God

Accepting exile is not meant to be cheap grace, or a theological form of psychobabble therapy by which one is forgiven but then continues in the same old narcissistic way. Exile offers at least three methods to take the strain and opportunity of being a distinctive minority in an alien environment.

Assimilation is one of these methods, becoming Babylonian as it were, or worshiping gods of wood and stone. The foreclosure of such a route for a minority that wishes to remain distinctive is obvious, if it were not for the fact that it is happening all the time. The second route is to maintain ritually and imaginatively the world that was lost and work and pray for its restoration-replication. This is common to many exiles. Contemporary writers on exile recommend it as long as it is the world/way-of-living of God's kingdom which is imagined.[22] I have sympathy with this view. However, I am concerned that this approach is not sufficiently alert to the power of the ideologies of restoration, and that it is an approach ultimately suborned by the need to get out of exile and reassert preeminence.

Exile can be affirmed. Exile is part of the new thing God does, and it, not restoration, is our vocation.[23] Jeremiah shocks his people with this affirmation of exile with a vision of two baskets of figs, the bad figs representing those left behind, and the good figs those taken into exile (Jer. 24:1-9). Exile is still to be understood as God acting in history, as moving toward the accomplishment of the *missio Dei*. Exile threatens to crush the people of God, but it also threatens to break us open. Keeping pure as a holy remnant is a way to cope with exile, but it requires not just a barrier to culture, but within this way of reading exile it requires a barrier against God. If God goes east, into exile, the remnant mentality is to stay within the walls of the sanctuary. But Ezekiel makes a harrow-

---

21. Perhaps this is implied in the opening verses of 1 Pet. 1.

22. See especially the works of Walter Brueggemann: *Hopeful Imagination* and *Prophetic Imagination* (Philadelphia: Fortress, 1978).

23. As Daniel L. Smith comments, "Exodus is the road to nationalism and power" (*Religion of the Landless* [Bloomington, Ind.: Meyer Stone, 1989], p. 205). It is inappropriate for us to approach exodus with an imperial history and think that it can be used to spur us to a renewed prophetic church. Instead, it is in danger of inflaming old desires for dominance.

ing image for this mentality for the sanctuary as no longer protective when he likens besieged Jerusalem to a corroded, boiling pot.[24]

The paradigm of exile offers us a self-challenging critique.[25] But it also critiques Babylon. Nebuchadnezzar still has feet of clay. The epiphanous and ontophanous potential of exile, of Babylon, and the promise of pluralism are still to be understood as provisional and insufficient, just as are the promises of restoration, Zion, and the gospel.

If the paradigm of exile is to hold out a way of reorienting ourselves theologically, it needs to be kept within the confines of exile, with the emphasis on living in exile, not waiting for return. This means that we remain focused. It is not a matter of rejecting the outside world or of bemoaning it. Nor is it a matter of seeking techniques to reform and restore church-gospel. By remaining focused on living in exile we remain alert to the critique of Zion and Babylon, of church-gospel and culture. If exile is to enable "Not the Body of Christ" to live with this contemporary experience of being the church and rediscover how to become the "Body of Christ" afresh, it needs to be on the basis of rejecting restoration and resettlement and rejecting assimilation. This is perhaps best expressed as:

Making Ourselves Not at Home: Being outside the Gate

So Jesus also suffered outside the gate in order to sanctify the people through his own blood. (Heb. 13:12 RSV)

The practice of British Christianity has largely been at the center of society, seeking the recognition of the establishment. It is comfortable in mainstream suburban life, even as it slowly decays in such places. The crisis of exile stems in part from the increasing marginalization of our role as churches, even in the suburbs. We are not comfortable at the margins; we are not comfortable outside the gate. But it is possible that this is an important place to be the church.

Hebrews suggests that Christ's death outside the gate established a new place of salvation, one in contrast to the center ground taken by the temple. Jesus' death on Golgotha moves this place of sacrifice, sanctification, and sal-

---

24. Ezek. 24:1-14.

25. Not that exile prevents the recrudescence of the desire to be back in control, Smith warns, but "the temptation is to artificially end exile before God ends our exile. The temptation is to engage in the idolatry of Hananiah's false promise and to 're-enter history' with a share of worldly power" (Smith, p. 207).

vation outside the gate among the outcast and disenfranchised,[26] from the center to the periphery.

The liberation theologian Orlando Costas critiques the Western church for seeking to get back into the enclosure through the fostering and enforcing of a revised Christendom ideal. Costas feels that even if Christendom has disappeared politically, it continues mentally in the attitudes and aspirations of the church.[27] Thus, through the paradigm of Christendom, the church has created for itself a position to preserve or, in our case, regain. Even as that position has decayed, its mentality has lived on through a tendency to elicit suspicion of all those outside the gate, beyond the agreed confines of tradition and membership, and so build up boundaries rather than cross them.

But we might want to argue that mission is not about others crossing our boundaries but about us crossing our boundaries, our going outside the gate. Equally the *missio Dei* is about God's own crossing of boundaries of going outside the gate.[28] But we have to be alert to the danger of reformulating the binary oppositions of Christendom. We in Ely are trying to discover that we are not at home in our setting because we are called to be creatures of God's kingdom. But seeing ourselves as culturally alien from our community can still lead us to feel superior and once again preeminent. We require a more sophisticated and subtle view of our culture than is sometimes allowed.[29]

A missiology in exile is not for me about "feeling at home" or about returning home. But it is about realizing we are not at home in exile, and because it is a missiology and not an ecclesiology, it is about recognizing that we do need to be alive and at work in exile. It is to engage with the subverting experience of exile and the subverting cultures of exile and the subverting God of exile, even though it seems to undermine all that people want to stand for and keep pure.

It is clear that being the church in exile in Ely has provoked many ques-

---

26. Orlando E. Costas, *Christ outside the Gate: Mission beyond Christendom* (New York: Orbis, 1982), pp. 188-89.

27. Costas, pp. 190ff. I think one could argue that the move in British ecclesiologies toward church as community center can be an example of a rehabilitated ideal of Christendom. It is not the ideal of service that suggests this, but the desire to be at the center.

28. Costas talks about it in traveling and exilic terms defining the church as *paroikia*, a temporary abode, "a tent in the wilderness, not a fortress or an insulated castle." But Costas places the focus of the church on identification with the crucified Christ and his permanent commitment to the outcast, not on identification with modernity (pp. 192-93).

29. See, for example, Werner Ustorf's critique of Newbigin's gospel-and-our-culture approach in *Christianized Africa — De-Christianized Europe* (Korea: Tyrannus, 1992), pp. 149-63.

tions about how we do things, about the nature and style of worship and the nature and style of outreach into the community. But these questions may still be answered through an "acquisitive ecclesiology." We may develop structures and styles that encourage people to become part of a church, rather than part of the people of God. It is the questions about who we are and what we are for that exile provokes most. These are the questions to attend to most. Exile challenges us to see that being God's people is not a once and for all thing, conferred by covenant, king, and temple or by baptism and Eucharist. Exile challenges us to see being God's people as a dialectical process of "living and becoming." In other words, it has to be lived out over and over again in a multiplicity of ways in our multiplicity of contexts.

Living and Becoming

Exile offers us this dialectic of "living and becoming" through a valuable if disturbing self-critique of "My People"–"Not My People," "Body of Christ"– "Not the Body of Christ." It gives a critique that is rooted ethically and missiologically. This is essential because being God's people requires a constant living out of what it means to be God's people. It requires a constant becoming in relation to the contexts God's people live in, and a constant becoming in response to the failings of God's people. In this way it recognizes that being God's people derives from how we act or do not act.[30] It is suspicious, alerting, and challenging; it offers the question: Is this the action of the body of Christ or of Not the body of Christ? It leads us to be skeptical of our own pronouncements, our own ecclesiological rhetoric dressed as theology. It questions the agendas upon which we act: Are they appropriate to the people of God or to the institution of the people of God? It admits the possibility that we might not just be misguided, we might be wrong,[31] that we are Not the body of Christ if we act like this.

This sounds like the triumph of law over grace, or worse, kicking someone when he or she is down. But I want to argue that this is not the case. First and foremost the grace of God is what enables us to mature as God's people, to grow as God's people, to take our responsibilities seriously as God's people. This means the taking of responsibility for our actions and the impact of our actions on others, on God, on ourselves. God's grace does this by challenging

---

30. One might want to make a universalist claim that all people are God's children, but that maturity into God's people requires more than a gracious birthright.

31. Here the usage of the inclusive "we" is an articulation of our reflections in Ely.

us, inviting us, and allowing us to change. God's grace is not meant to be the safeguarding of our cosmological preeminence as God's people.

Jeremiah emphasizes this subversiveness of God through exile. God makes it clear to Jeremiah: "Do not pray for this people [Israel], or lift up a cry or prayer on their behalf, for I will not listen when they call to me in the time of their trouble"[32] so that God subverts Israel's piety. But then in Jeremiah's letter to the exiles, he advises them to pray for the cities in which they are set,[33] and through this God subverts afresh the exiles and their leaders and their sense of lamentation.[34] God then subverts the desolation of exile which had been taught the exiles by their theology of the land and temple rather than by the action of God. "Seek me and you will find me,"[35] says God to those who thought they could not sing the Lord's song in this foreign land (or should that be foreign plausibility structure?).

Indeed, this letter makes clear the vocation in and for exile to which God has called his people. It makes clear that God is in exile and the *missio Dei* is at work in exile, which includes the culture in which God's people feel exiled and which seems so antithetical to God's people — gospel. It also suggests that God is not necessarily at work in his so-called proper locus, the church. Discerning this in practice could begin a missiology for "Not My People" without it requiring restoration, a critical pluralism that is expectant of God's presence and absence in church-gospel and culture.

32. Jer. 11:14 NRSV; see also Jer. 14:11-12.
33. Jer. 29:7.
34. See Jer. 29:24ff.
35. See Jer. 29:13.

The Missional Calling of Believers in the World: Lesslie Newbigin's Contribution

Michael Goheen

In one of his last articles David Bosch distinguishes five different traditions of the relationship of the church to civil authorities: Constantinian, pietist, reformist, liberationist, and Anabaptist.[1] He dismisses the first two — Constantinian and pietist — as otherworldly. He sees the other three as "world-formative" and "much closer to each other than may appear at first glance."[2] I believe we can broaden the scope of these categories to assess the relationship of the gospel to all of culture and not simply the civil authorities. If we do so, it is the Anabaptist tradition — which Bosch also calls in other places the alternative community and countercultural model — that has been gaining tremendous ground in the North American context especially among those who, following Newbigin, are calling for a missionary encounter with Western culture.[3] It is my contention that while this is a helpful and necessary corrective, valuable elements of the reformist tradition that were essential to Newbigin's understanding of mission in the public square are being neglected. Specifically, the calling of believers in the world has received little attention. In this paper I propose to do three things. First, I will briefly sketch the Anabaptist tradition as it is taking form in the North American context. Second, in the major part of the paper I will elaborate on this aspect of

1. D. J. Bosch, "God's Reign and the Rulers of This World: Missiological Reflections on Church-State Relationships," in *The Good News of the Kingdom: Mission Theology for the Third Millennium*, ed. Charles Van Engen, Dean Gilliland, and Paul Pierson (Maryknoll, N.Y.: Orbis, 1993), pp. 89-95.
2. Bosch, "God's Reign," p. 94.
3. D. J. Bosch, "How My Mind Has Changed: Mission and the Alternative Community," *Journal for Southern Africa*, no. 41 (December 1982): 6-10.

Newbigin's understanding of the calling of believers in the world, a theme neglected by the growing alternative community emphasis. Finally, I will close with a brief evaluative comment.

The Alternative Community Model in North America

Douglas John Hall begins his little book *The End of Christendom and the Future of Christianity* by dividing church history into three primary eras: the early church, Christendom beginning with Constantine, and the present.[4] There have been two major shifts that account for this division. The first occurred under the Roman emperors Constantine and Theodosius when the church was officially established. The church moved from a marginal position to a dominant institution in society; from being socially, politically, intellectually inferior to a position of power and superiority; from being economically weak and poor to a position of immense wealth; from being an oppressed minority to being an oppressive majority; from being an illegal religion to becoming the only religion of the state; from being resident aliens to a territorial understanding of the faith whereby the Roman Empire is considered Christian. This official establishment characterized the position of the church throughout the remainder of the Roman Empire and then in Europe. This pattern continued in North America, even though the church was only temporarily established in some places. A functional Christendom prevailed in which the church's power is experienced in terms of a cultural establishment.[5]

The second major shift is the disestablishment of the church today that is taking place all across the Western world. The church has lost the official power it has known for so many years and is again being pushed to the margins of society. This disestablishment is considered a positive development, because now the church can recover its identity as shaped by the scriptural story rather than the cultural story.

During the early years of its life, the church understood her identity as resident aliens. There was a redemptive tension between the church and her culture. The church understood itself to be an alternative community that was nourished by an alternative story. This contrast community was not one that ignored the public life of society by being reshaped into a private institu-

---

4. D. J. Hall, *The End of Christendom and the Future of Christianity* (Valley Forge, Pa.: Trinity Press International, 1997).

5. D. Guder, ed., *Missional Church: A Vision for the Sending of the Church in North America* (Grand Rapids: Eerdmans, 1998), pp. 47-60.

tion that provided an otherworldly and spiritual salvation for its members. Rather it was publicly subversive by a life of radical discipleship that existed as a kind of antibody in society. However, with the Constantinian shift the story that governed the church's life and the story that governed cultural development were merged. The redemptive tension was lost as the church became part of the constellation of powers within the empire. Her identity was shaped by her place in culture rather than by the story of the kingdom of God. The end result was cultural captivity. This domestication continued in the modern period as the church took her place in culture as chaplain of society, influencing the moral and private religious beliefs of the citizens.

When one sees how the church has been absorbed into culture and deeply compromised by Christendom, it is easy to see the compelling power of the alternative community model. The renewed stress on alternative emphasizes that the church is a community that is shaped by a different story than the dominant cultural story. The word "community" stresses that the mission of the church is a communal affair; the church is to embody a social order that faithfully points to the coming kingdom.

I find the logic of this compelling. I also believe that most of what has been said could be found in the writings of Newbigin. Indeed, there are two events which would suggest that Lesslie Newbigin would feel quite comfortable with this emphasis. The first was a workshop given by Stephen Bevans at a Gospel and Our Culture Network meeting. After he had written his little book *Models of Contextual Theology,* in which he outlines five models of contextualization, he outlines a sixth model.[6] He named this model the "countercultural model," and included Newbigin along with Hauerwas and Willimon as exponents. Bevans would include Newbigin in this growing shift to an alternative community model.

The second event was a colloquium held in Leeds, England, during the summer of 1996. It was a dialogue between a number of scholars in the Dutch neo-Calvinist tradition and Lesslie Newbigin on the topic of mission in the public life of Western culture. In a paper given by the Dutch philosopher Sander Griffioen entitled "Newbigin's Philosophy of Culture," he makes a distinction between the negative Christian responsibility of critiquing sinful idolatry in culture and positive involvement as a steward participating in the cultural development of society. Griffioen believes that in Newbigin's discussion of contextualization, "he pays virtually no attention to the gospel as an agent of inner reformation or cultural renewal. All the emphasis is on the

---

6. Stephen Bevans, "Doing Theology in North America: A Counter-Cultural Model?" (paper given at Gospel and Our Culture Network conference, Chicago, 1993).

critical and judging function of the Word."[7] Griffioen too believes that Newbigin's stress is on the countercultural.

These two illustrations show that Newbigin has strongly stressed the importance of the church as an alternative community living in a different story over against the idolatry of the prevailing culture. However, there is a stress in Newbigin's work that has been neglected, even eclipsed, in the writings of many in North America who advocate this countercultural model. Newbigin has maintained throughout his life that the task of believers in their various callings in culture is the primary place where a missionary encounter takes place. While this emphasis is not denied in the emerging alternative community emphasis, it is smothered by neglect and a studied indifference. The stress on alternative and on community does not seem to have a place for this "declericalized or lay theology," as Newbigin calls it. The recent stress of the alternative community model is to eschew power and simply impact the public life of culture through a corporate life. Perhaps this contrast can be seen most sharply by noting that at the same time Newbigin was calling for the pursuit of a Christian society, Douglas John Hall stated that "it is wicked to seek a Christian society"! The tone in Newbigin's missiology and ecclesiology is quite different. Until the end of his life the calling of individual believers in the world remained a pillar in his understanding of the church's missionary encounter with culture and more specifically the public square.

In the remainder of the paper I will sketch Newbigin's position on the mission of individual believers in their callings and argue that it is only with this stress that the alternative community model can be authentic.

Newbigin's Understanding of the Mission of Individual Believers in the World

Newbigin's stress on the callings of individual believers in the world is neither recent nor original. It is not recent; this has been a primary emphasis of Newbigin missionary thought and practice throughout his entire life. It is not original; he has developed his position in the context of the ecumenical tradition's growing emphasis on the laity. J. H. Oldham and the Oxford World Conference on Church, Community, and State in 1937; the establishment of lay academies throughout Europe after 1945; the founding of the Ecumenical Institute at Bossey in 1946, led by Suzanne de Dietrich and Hendrik Kraemer;

---

7. S. Griffioen, "Newbigin's Philosophy of Culture" (paper presented at a colloquium on the gospel and the public life of Western culture, Leeds, England, 1996), pp. 12f.

the establishment of the Department on the Laity in the WCC in 1955, led by Secretary Hans-Ruedi Weber; and books by Kraemer (1958) and Yves Congar (1957) on the laity and the church are highlights in this growing concern for the laity that shaped Newbigin.[8]

The remainder of this section will be devoted to explicating Newbigin's understanding of the calling of believers in the world.

Eschatological, Soteriological, and Christological Foundations

There are at least three fundamental theological convictions that undergird Newbigin's commitment to the mission of the believer in his or her societal callings. The first is his understanding of the church in an eschatological context. The church has been traditionally understood from the aspect of a gathered community that engages in cultic or "religious" rituals, while the fact that the majority of its life and work takes place outside the bounds of this institutional and gathered expression has been largely neglected. Newbigin's understanding of the church goes a long way to healing this split.

Newbigin's understanding of the church is always in an eschatological context. The gospel is a gospel of the kingdom, and the kingdom involves God's rule over all of creational life. The most common way he describes the church is with the terms "sign," "instrument" (or "agent"), and "first fruit" (sometimes "deposit" or "foretaste") of the kingdom. As he comments: "Each of these three words is important. They are to be a *sign*, pointing men to something that is beyond their present horizon but can give guidance and hope now; an *instrument* (not the only one) that God can use for his work of healing, liberating, and blessing; and a *firstfruit* — a place where men and women can have a real taste now of the joy and freedom God intends for us all."[9]

The formal definition he often gives of the church points to the same thing even more clearly. "The church is the provisional incorporation of mankind into Jesus Christ."[10]

---

8. Y. Congar, *Lay People in the Church* (Westminster, Md.: Newman, 1957); H. Kraemer, *A Theology of the Laity* (London: Lutterworth, 1958).

9. L. Newbigin, *A Word in Season: Perspectives on Christian World Mission*, ed. Eleanor Jackson (Edinburgh: Saint Andrew Press; Grand Rapids: Eerdmans, 1994), p. 33.

10. L. Newbigin, "The Form and Structure of the Visible Unity of the Church," in *So Sende Ich Euch: Festschrift für Dr. Martin Pörksen zum 70. Geburtstag*, ed. Otto Wack et al. (Korntal bei Stuttgart: Evang. Missionsverlag, 1973), p. 111. Originally published in two parts: "The Form and Structure of the Visible Unity of the Church," *National Christian Council Review* 92 (1972): 444-51; 93 (1973): 4-18; cf. Newbigin, *A Word in Season*, p. 53.

Both descriptions point to the fact that Newbigin does not understand the church simply as a religious community gathered to engage in certain religious rituals. Rather the church is the new humankind that already shares in the life of the kingdom of God, and that life spans the whole of human affairs.

New Testament scholar Herman Ridderbos has noted that the word *ekklesia* is used in three different ways in the New Testament. The first is of the new people of God in the totality of their lives as the reconstitution of humankind in Jesus Christ. As such her life comes to expression in the totality of her existence and not only as she gathers for worship. The second use is of local identifiable congregations. These congregations are organized as communities, and each is recognizable as a human community in a certain place. The third use of the word *ekklesia* points to a community gathered for certain "religious" activities — worship, prayer, sacraments, and so forth.[11] It is the first of these definitions that the Evanston Assembly of the WCC (1954) used in an attempt to redefine the church in terms of a new humankind over against long-established patterns of ecclesial definition. "[T]he laity are not mere fragments of the church who are scattered about in the world and who come together again for worship, instruction, and specifically Christian fellowship on Sundays. They are the church's representatives, no matter where they are."

It is this fundamental ecclesiological conviction that shapes Newbigin's commitment to the importance of the witness of believers in the totality of their lives as an important dimension of the missionary church. It may be asked, however, whether or not Newbigin was always consistent with this insight. Sometimes Newbigin follows the more traditional and common understanding and limits his use of the word "church" to the gathered local institutional expression and falls into the trap of seeing the laity as a fragment of the church scattered about in the world. An example pertinent to our present topic is when he speaks of the activities of believers in their individual callings as "in the line of God's will as revealed in Christ but which fall outside of the boundaries of that body explicitly committed to Christ by faith and baptism."[12]

While Newbigin may not have been consistent with this theological insight concerning the church, it is clear that his primary understanding of the *ekklesia* is shaped by the broad scope of the coming kingdom. The believers at work in their various callings are the church at work.

---

11. Herman Ridderbos, *Paul: An Outline of His Theology* (Grand Rapids: Eerdmans, 1975), pp. 328-30.

12. L. Newbigin, "The Spiritual Foundations of Our Work," in *The Christian College and National Development* (Madras: Christian Literature Society, 1967), p. 6.

The second theological conviction foundational for Newbigin's "lay theology" is his understanding of the salvation of which the new humankind now has a foretaste. Salvation is comprehensive in scope and restorative in nature. Salvation is comprehensive in scope; it is not simply the salvation of a few individual souls but the restoration of the whole life of humankind in the context of a renewed creation. "God's promise is of a wholly renewed creation, not just reborn individuals. It is a promise not only of new men, but of new heavens and a new earth."[13] Salvation is restorative in nature; it is not the salvation of souls out of this creation but the restoration of this creation including the whole life of humankind. "The end of the story is not escape into another world. It is the triumph of God in this world . . . not the immortality of souls liberated from this world but the resurrection of the body and the re-creation of all things."[14]

This renewal is not only future but is already present as foretaste, first fruits, or deposit. If this salvation covers the whole spectrum of human life, then the witness of the people of God as previews of the kingdom is equally comprehensive. The majority of the church's witness will take place in the workplace, the marketplace, the neighborhood, the public square.

The deepest grounding for Newbigin's convictions regarding the calling of the laity is in Jesus Christ. A glimpse of the christological foundation can be seen in the sermon he delivered when he was installed as bishop of Madras. He reminded the Christians that "Christ is not just the Lord of Christians; he is Lord of all, absolutely and without qualification." Therefore, "the entire membership of the Church in their secular occupations are called to be signs of his lordship in every area of life."[15]

It is these three foundational theological assumptions that shape Newbigin's commitment to the importance of the callings of individual believers in any missional church. The church is the new humankind that shares in foretaste a salvation that is the restoration of its entire life in Jesus Christ. Witness to this eschatological salvation will find expression in the totality of life.

13. L. Newbigin, *Behold I Make All Things New* (Madras: Christian Literature Society, 1968), p. 22. Talks given at a youth conference in Kerala, May 1968; cf. L. Newbigin, *Journey into Joy* (Grand Rapids: Eerdmans, 1973), p. 93.

14. L. Newbigin, "The Bible Study Lectures," in *Digest of the Proceedings of the Ninth Meeting of the Consultation on Church Union* (COCU), ed. Paul A. Crow (Princeton: Consultation on Church Union, 1970), p. 220. Lectures given in St. Louis, 9-13 March 1970; cf. Newbigin, *Behold I Make*, p. 22.

15. L. Newbigin, *Unfinished Agenda: An Updated Autobiography* (Edinburgh: Saint Andrew Press; London: SPCK; and Geneva: WCC Publications, 1993), p. 203.

Focal Point of Mission

In Newbigin we can distinguish three different forms of mission by the church. First, the community of the church bears witness to Christ by modeling in its own corporate life as an alternative community the life of the kingdom. In 1991 Newbigin even said that "the most important contribution which the Church can make to a new social order is to be itself a new social order."[16] The second is corporate witness in which the local congregation together reaches out in service and evangelism to its community and to the ends of the earth. The third is the witness of the various members in their daily lives at home and work, in their neighborhoods, and so forth. He expresses the conviction that it is in this third form of mission where we find that "the primary witness to the sovereignty of Christ must be given"[17] because the "enormous preponderance of the Church's witness is the witness of the thousands of its members who work in field, home, office, mill or law court."[18]

This concern for the calling of individual believers in the public square is a long-standing one for Newbigin. When he was a student at Cambridge, his disappointment with the Student Christian Movement's practice of simply emphasizing the ordained ministry as the primary place of Christian service led him to form a "Christians in Business" society. This group was to provide a forum for Christians who were entering business to struggle with what it meant to be faithful to the gospel in that sector of life.[19] As a newly appointed bishop, he expressed the conviction that if the church in Asia was to become a missionary church, they must attend to "the task of training Christian laymen to be effective Christians within their own special vocations." He continues: "We have to help the church member be a Christian *in his job.*"[20] A

16. L. Newbigin, *Truth to Tell: The Gospel as Public Truth* (Grand Rapids: Eerdmans; Geneva: WCC Publications; and London: SPCK, 1991), p. 85.

17. L. Newbigin, "The Work of the Holy Spirit in the Life of the Asian Churches," in *A Decisive Hour for the Christian World Mission,* John R. Mott Memorial Lectures, 1959 (London: SCM Press, 1960), p. 28.

18. L. Newbigin, "Our Task Today" (a charge given to the fourth meeting of the diocesan council, Tirumangalam, 18-20 December 1951), p. 6.

19. Newbigin, *Unfinished Agenda,* p. 17.

20. L. Newbigin, "The Evangelization of Eastern Asia," in *The Christian Prospect in Eastern Asia: Papers and Minutes of the Eastern Asia Christian Conference, Bangkok, December 3-11, 1949* (New York: Friendship, 1950), pp. 77-87. The paper was read at a conference entitled "The Task of the Church in Changing East Asia," held at Bangkok, December 1949, and republished in *International Review of Missions* 39 (1950): 137-45, here 144, emphasis Newbigin's.

year later in his address to the diocese, he outlined the four most pressing needs facing the church in India. Since the most important witness of the gospel will be done by believers in their various callings in the world — "the Church's front-line troops in her engagement with the world"[21] — much more time must be given to equipping these people. As a veteran missionary, he expressed the concern that the mission of the church in society had been reduced to the maintenance of educational, healing, and service institutions that led to the "deep-seated and persistent failure of the churches to recognize that the primary witness to the sovereignty of Christ must be given, and can only be given, in the ordinary secular work of lay men and women in business, in politics, in professional work, as farmers, factory workers and so on."[22] In response to the urging of Hendrik Kraemer, Newbigin established a study center in Madurai whose task was *inter alia* to equip the church's lay membership for its "secular witness."[23]

His time in Geneva coincided with a growing interest in the calling of believers in the world fueled by the breakdown of the *corpus Christianum* and growing secularism. In 1954 the department of the laity had been established in the WCC. At the New Delhi assembly of the WCC in 1961, the laity had become a central issue. This led to a deepening conviction on his part of the centrality of the witness of believers in the world. When he returned to India as bishop of Madras, these deepening convictions begin to emerge and find expression. He describes his earlier understanding of mission as being "too narrowly ecclesiastical." At his installation service he preached Christ as Lord of all of life, insisting that "the entire membership of the Church in their secular occupations are called to be signs of this lordship in every area of public life."[24] As bishop he understood his task to equip believers for this task, and indeed, this continued to be a major preoccupation during this time. He urged structural reforms that would equip all believers for their calling.

His return to the West did not dampen this concern. In fact, a major pillar in his call for a missionary engagement with the public square of Western culture was the calling of individual believers.[25] Newbigin continues to refer

---

21. Newbigin, "Our Task Today," p. 6.

22. Newbigin, "Holy Spirit," pp. 27f.

23. Newbigin, *Unfinished Agenda,* pp. 118f.

24. Newbigin, *Unfinished Agenda,* p. 203.

25. L. Newbigin, *The Other Side of 1984: Questions for the Churches,* Risk Book Series, no. 18 (Geneva: WCC, 1983), pp. 41f.; *Foolishness to the Greeks: The Gospel and Western Culture* (London: SPCK; Grand Rapids: Eerdmans; and Geneva: WCC, 1986), pp. 141-44; *The Gospel in a Pluralist Society* (London: SPCK; Grand Rapids: Eerdmans; and Geneva: WCC Publications, 1989), pp. 229-31; *A Word in Season,* pp. 156, 174.

to this dimension of the church's mission as primary.[26] And so he writes: "There is urgent need for the Church to give higher priority to the formation of groups of Christian men and women in particular sectors of public life. These would include education, industry, commerce, politics, drama, the arts, the natural and social sciences, and historical studies. The groups would explore ways in which a Christian perspective can be developed in these areas, and ways in which this perspective can challenge and redirect contemporary practice."[27]

In his third lecture at Western Seminary, published in *Truth to Tell*, he outlines three concrete points to enable the church to "speak the truth to Caesar." It is the third that many in North America have emphasized; it calls for the church to impact the public life of Western culture by itself being an embodiment of the new order of the kingdom. However, the other two points have to do with the calling of individual believers in culture. First, "it must be the responsibility of the Church to equip its members for active and informed participation in public life in such a way that the Christian faith shapes that participation."[28] "Second, if such training were widely available we could look for a time when many of those holding responsible positions of leadership in public life were committed Christians equipped to raise the questions and make innovations in these areas which the gospel requires."[29]

Question of Power

Newbigin recognizes that when we speak of power to shape the public life of a nation, this clearly raises the specter of theocracy and Christendom. He addresses this issue several times. His answer is as follows.

First, Newbigin does not believe that a purely privatized Christianity or a Christendom-style theocracy are the only options available.[30] Newbigin acknowledges the contribution made by the synthesis of church and state that has shaped the life of Europe for over a thousand years. However, he does not wish to return to that synthesis.[31] He emphatically states: "What we are looking for is not a new 'Christendom,' but a society in which those whose thought and practice set the tone and direction of the different sectors of

26. Newbigin, *A Word in Season*, p. 154.
27. Newbigin, *A Word in Season*, p. 174.
28. Newbigin, *Truth to Tell*, p. 81.
29. Newbigin, *Truth to Tell*, p. 84.
30. Newbigin, *A Word in Season*, p. 168.
31. Newbigin, *Foolishness to the Greeks*, p. 124.

public life include a large number of Christian men and women who have thought through the implications of the Christian faith for those areas of the life of society."[32] On the other hand, he also wants to reject what he calls "the predominant note in contemporary answers" that takes a position over against society, emphasizes protest, and renounces all power.[33] He advances a model he calls "committed pluralism." A committed pluralism follows the model Michael Polanyi called "the republic of science." Scientists are free to differ from one another and argue. However, they are personally and responsibly committed to seeking the truth and publicly stating their findings. This model is meant to protect freedom, yet a freedom which, while acknowledging differences, is willing to seek the truth.[34] If the church allows her faith to be privatized, then the societal implication of the gospel will be seen as mere house rules for the church rather than the law of the Creator that carries jurisdiction over the entire human family.[35]

Second, Newbigin leans on the Dutch tradition of Abraham Kuyper and Herman Dooyeweerd[36] to argue that the problem with Christendom is not that Christians exercised power but that the institutionalized church exercised power. Over against this ecclesiastical totalitarianism Newbigin advocates the neo-Calvinist notion of sphere sovereignty, the doctrine that God has given in the creation order a measure of autonomy to each of the various areas of human life such as art, science, politics, and so on. The institutionalized church has no direct authority over these spheres; rather it is shaped by God's law order discerned and implemented by those within that sphere. This

32. Newbigin, *A Word in Season*, p. 173.
33. Newbigin, *Pluralist Society*, p. 125.
34. Newbigin, *Truth to Tell*, pp. 56f.
35. Newbigin, *Truth to Tell*, p. 70.
36. Newbigin believed that the Kuyperian tradition as it has developed in the Netherlands was a rich resource for mission in the public square that had been untapped (Newbigin, "Can a Modern Society Be Christian?" in *Christian Witness in Society: A Tribute to M. M. Thomas*, ed. K. C. Abraham [Bangalore: Board of Theological Education, Senate of Serampore College, 1998]; this was a lecture given at King's College, London, November 1995]). He commented following a colloquium with leading scholars in that tradition in Leeds during the summer of 1996 that while "the Gospel and Our Culture Network has hardly begun to answer the questions [of obedience in various spheres of public life]," the "Reformational, Kuyperian tradition has obviously been at work long ago spelling out concretely in the various spheres of society what it means to say 'Jesus is Lord.'" Unfortunately, he said, "this Kuyperian tradition is almost unknown in Britain," but he expressed the fervent wish that it "would become a powerful voice in the life of British Christianity" (Newbigin tapes from colloquium held at the West Yorkshire School of Christian Studies in Leeds, UK, entitled *The Gospel and the Public Life of Western Culture*, 1996).

avoids the post-Enlightenment notion of total autonomy of these spheres and the medieval understanding that each sphere is under the power of the church. So while the church as an organized body has no right to exercise power over these spheres, Christians with insight into these areas may exercise power.[37]

Third, it follows from this that it is incumbent on Christians to gain access to power if it is available, to shape the public life of the nation with the gospel.[38] In a discussion of education he says: "How is this world of assumptions formed? Obviously through all the means of education and communication existing in society. Who controls these means? The question of power is inescapable. Whatever their pretensions, schools teach children to believe something and not something else. There is no 'secular' neutrality. Christians cannot evade the responsibility which a democratic society gives to every citizen to seek access to the levers of power."[39]

Fourth, this power is not to be a coercive power in which the political power of the state and its institutions is at the service of the church.[40] Rather, power must be exercised in the way of the cross that eschews the identification of the gospel with political power and opens the way for freedom. While Newbigin wants to steer clear of a refusal to exercise political power for the sake of the justice of the kingdom, he also wants to reject a triumphalist church. Illustrations abound in history where the victim of oppression dethrones the oppressor and takes his seat on the throne and employs the same instruments of oppression.[41] The way of the cross is a way that pursues justice and right with a firm resolve while leaving wide room for freedom to dissent. Even though an Enlightenment view of freedom is not scriptural, something was gained at that time that cannot be lost. In keeping with this era of redemptive history and the nature of the gospel, freedom must be safeguarded and there must be no coercion for its acceptance.[42] However, this coercive political power is to be distinguished from the power that a Christian exercises as citizen to shape the public life in keeping with the gospel.[43]

We come here to a dilemma that, as far as I know, Newbigin never resolved. If a Christian exercises political authority, where does s/he allow room

37. Newbigin, *Foolishness to the Greeks*, pp. 143f.
38. Newbigin, *A Word in Season*, p. 171.
39. Newbigin, *Pluralist Society*, p. 224; cf. *A Word in Season*, p. 171.
40. Newbigin, *A Word in Season*, p. 170.
41. Newbigin, *Pluralist Society*, pp. 136f.
42. Newbigin, *A Word in Season*, p. 167.
43. Newbigin, *A Word in Season*, p. 171.

for freedom and dissent and where is there a required submission to the law that has been fashioned in light of the gospel?

Fifth, the victory of God's kingdom is not an intrahistorical victory.[44] The victory will come at the end when Christ returns. The use of power is not to usher in the kingdom of God but is a faithful witness to, an acted prayer for, the coming of that kingdom. The church may function as salt in society, but the fullness of God's kingdom is at the end.

Challenge Leads to Suffering

When the Christian is faithful in living the story of the gospel in his or her calling, suffering will be the result. How integral suffering is to the witness of the church can be seen in the following statement: "The closeness of our missionary thinking to the New Testament may perhaps be in part judged by the place which we accord to suffering in our understanding of the calling of the Church."[45] Why is suffering the normal badge of faithful witness?

> No human societies cohere except on the basis of some kind of common beliefs and customs. No society can permit these beliefs and practices to be threatened beyond a certain point without reacting in self-defense. The idea that we ought to be able to expect some kind of neutral secular political order, which presupposes no religious or ideological beliefs, and which holds the ring impartially for a plurality of religions to compete with one another, has no adequate foundation. The New Testament makes it plain that Christ's followers must expect suffering as the normal badge of their discipleship, and also as one of the characteristic forms of their witness.[46]

This encounter with anti-Christian ideological or religious beliefs is especially acute in the public square where the believer works. In a series of Bible studies given in Australia on 1 Peter in 1960, Newbigin contrasts the world of business driven by the profit motive with the gospel. He poses a number of questions to illustrate this antithesis in the realm of business. Does a Christian employee in a store persuade his customers to buy worthless products on orders from his employer, or does he challenge the firm and risk his livelihood?

44. Newbigin, *A Word in Season*, p. 204.
45. Newbigin, *Trinitarian Faith and Today's Mission* (Richmond: John Knox, 1964), p. 42.
46. Newbigin, *Trinitarian Faith*, p. 42; cf. *A Word in Season*, pp. 148-50.

Does a businessman challenge the whole standard of business ethics if it is wrong and risk status and livelihood? How does a businessman relate the Sermon on the Mount to the fiercely competitive market? All these examples differ, but the point is the same: obedience to the Lord of economics and business will be costly. He comments: "[I]f we take seriously our duty as servants of God within the institutions of human society, we shall find plenty of opportunity to learn what it means to suffer for righteousness' sake, and we shall learn that to suffer for righteousness' sake is really a blessed thing."[47]

Need for Communal Aspect

Newbigin's emphasis on the work of the church as it is dispersed does not diminish the importance of the church as it is gathered as a community. The witness of believers in their callings in the world requires a faithful fellowship of believers. One can feel the passion of his concern in the following questions he poses to his fellow church leaders early in his first bishopric. "Are we taking seriously our duty to support them in their warfare? Do we seriously regard them as the front-line troops? . . . What about the scores of Christians working in offices and shops in that part of the city? Have we ever done anything seriously to strengthen their Christian witness, to help them in facing the very difficult ethical problems which they have to meet every day, to give them the assurance that the whole fellowship is behind them in their daily spiritual warfare?"[48]

In his writings on the calling of individual believers, we find at least four different ways that the local instituted church equips, supports, and nourishes the church in its task in the world.

The first is as a fellowship that nourishes the life of Christ through the Word and sacraments. No understanding of Newbigin's ecclesiology is adequate if it does not recognize the stress he puts on the Word, sacraments, and prayer. In an address given to the Diocesan Council, he speaks of the "the only source of the church's life — the gospel." If the church is to fulfill her missionary calling, she must experience the saving presence and power of God himself. The Word and sacraments of the gospel are the means by which this power is mediated to the church. He asks: "Are we placing these in the very

---

47. L. Newbigin, "Bible Studies: Four Talks on 1 Peter by Bishop Newbigin," in *We Were Brought Together*, ed. David M. Taylor (Sydney: Australian Council for the WCC, 1960), p. 112.

48. Newbigin, "Our Task Today," p. 6.

centre of our church life? . . . Do we understand, do our congregations understand, that when the Word is truly preached and the sacraments duly administered, Christ Himself is present in the midst with all His saving power?"[49] There is much stress on Word and sacraments in Newbigin's writing, but the reason this quote, from a speech given in 1951, is taken is that the flow of his whole speech moves from the Word and sacraments to the life of laymen in the world. He sketches the situation of the church and outlines four main tasks that lie ahead if the church is to be a living, missionary church. The first task is to recover the presence and power of God in Word and sacrament. The second is to recover the congregation as the fundamental unit of the Christian church. He spends a large portion of this discussion on — indeed, entitles it — the "church meeting" as a structural feature that would equip members for their calling in the world (see below). The third most pressing need of the time is that God's saving power, known and experienced in the life of a redeemed community, issue in a faithful witness of the thousands of its members who work in field, home, office, mill, or law court.[50]

Along with the Word and sacraments — and perhaps even more importantly! — Newbigin puts a high stress on prayer. I do not think that either Newbigin's life or his ecclesiology can be properly understood apart from the high priority he puts on prayer. Prayer is the primary means by which one is joined to Christ, and the sap of the life of Christ flows to believers,[51] equipping them for their task in the world.

The second way the local instituted church equips, supports, and nourishes the church in its task in the world is as a fellowship that supports. In his discussion of the person engaged in business who joins the battle with powers that oppose the gospel, he comments:

> There are existential decisions which must be taken from time to time in the midst of the battle by those who are actually engaged in the battle and who will pay the price of the decision. But they are not decisions which ought to be taken in solitude. We ought not to ask each Christian in solitude to bear the burden of the real front line warfare . . . the Church must find ways of expressing its solidarity with those who stand in these frontier situations, who have to make decisions that may cost not only their own livelihood but also that of their families.[52]

49. Newbigin, "Our Task Today," p. 4.
50. Newbigin, "Our Task Today," pp. 5f.
51. L. Newbigin, *The Good Shepherd: Meditations on Christian Ministry in Today's World* (Grand Rapids: Eerdmans, 1977), pp. 140ff.
52. Newbigin, "Bible Studies," p. 111.

He never spells out explicitly what forms of support this might take, but the context of the discussion suggests that this would include at least encouragement, prayer, financial support, and insight.

The third way the local church contributes to the larger church in its task in the world is as a structure that equips. In a lecture at the founding assembly of the East Asia Christian Conference, Newbigin argues that if the church is to embody her missionary calling, at least three bold structural experiments are urgent: in forms of ministry, in equipping lay members for their different "secular" callings, and in forms of congregational life.[53] Bold experiments were necessary because present congregational structures that dominated the Western church were shaped in a time when Christianity had ceased to be a missionary religion.[54]

At this early point in his ministry, he points to three structural features that would support believers in their individual callings. The first is what he calls a church meeting, "a gathering of God's anointed people, in the power of the Holy Spirit, to find out together what witness and service He wants of them from week to week, as individuals and a body."[55] In each congregation once a month the communicant members should meet after Holy Communion *inter alia* to share experiences of God's grace in their daily lives, bring forward problems that various members face as they witness in the course of their daily callings, and discuss areas in which the whole fellowship may give special witness.[56] The second was a study center that would carry out study, research, and training on social and political issues in light of the gospel. This missiological analysis of Indian culture would provide resources that would equip Christians in their callings in public life.[57] Third, other initiatives were launched in the way of conferences and meetings that enabled "laymen" in different professions to consider together what God was calling them to do at the national and local level.

In his later bishopric in Madras, when the callings of the laity were the center of attention and when Newbigin himself gave much more attention to the social calling of the church, these structural features that would support believers in their individual callings increased. Newbigin believes at least two things have prevented the local congregation from equipping individual believers for their tasks in the world. The first is size; local churches have become

---

53. Newbigin, "Holy Spirit," pp. 30-33.
54. L. Newbigin, *Honest Religion for Secular Man* (Philadelphia: Westminster; London: SCM Press, 1966), p. 102.
55. Newbigin, "Our Task Today," p. 5.
56. Newbigin, "Our Task Today," p. 5.
57. Newbigin, *Unfinished Agenda,* p. 119.

too big. The second is character; a highly differentiated society requires more than a parish church. Newbigin suggests different structures to equip believers: training leadership for industrial workers; small-group ecumenical Bible studies formed on the basis of specialized expertise; "frontier studies," discussion and study groups of people in particular callings such as those of lawyer, doctor, businessperson, government servant, teacher, professional administrator; small groups formed around a concern for action in some particular sector of public life; a Community Service Center that coordinated and organized the task of training men and women for witness in their daily work.[58]

This concern continues during the later years of Newbigin's life when he calls for a missionary encounter with Western culture. He continues to urge the church to search for structures that will equip the believer for his or her calling in the world. "There is a need for 'frontier groups,' groups of Christians working in the same sectors of public life, meeting to thrash out the controversial issues of their business or profession in the light of their faith."[59]

The fourth way the local instituted church equips, supports, and nourishes the church in its task in the world is as a leadership that enables.[60] A leadership that equips believers in their tasks in the world is a constant theme in Newbigin's writings. In his sermons to pastors as bishop of Madras published in *The Good Shepherd: Meditations on Christian Ministry in Today's World,* Newbigin exhorts pastors to give high priority to training people in their congregations for their callings in the world. Only half the pastor's work is to gather the people together for worship. "The other half is to send them back to their daily tasks equipped to be the salt of the earth and the light of the world. If we forget this second part, the other can be positively dangerous."[61] And, he exhorts the pastors, "we ought not to be content until we can honestly say that we are helping every member of the Church to fulfill his ministry in the secular world."[62]

> At the most sophisticated level we have to think of our task in a city like Madras to train our lay members who are playing key roles in life of government, business, and the professions to become ministers of Christ in these secular situations. All of this is involved in our calling and ordination. It is for this purpose that we have set up such institutions as the Community Service Centre, in order that there may be opportunities for

---

58. Newbigin, *The Good Shepherd,* pp. 76f., 80-81.
59. Newbigin, *Pluralist Society,* pp. 230f.
60. Newbigin, *Pluralist Society,* p. 231.
61. Newbigin, *The Good Shepherd,* p. 80.
62. Newbigin, *The Good Shepherd,* p. 77.

Christians in various secular callings to learn how they can become effective ministers of Christ in their daily work.[63]

Brief Concluding Comment

One of the enduring tensions of the missionary church is how to be in the world yet not of it. The new stress of the alternative community model drawing on the rich Anabaptist tradition of not being of the world is an important corrective for the Western church who lives in a state of cultural captivity or "an advanced case of syncretism," as Newbigin has said[64] — thanks in large part to her Constantinian tradition. The further emphasis of the communal dimension is also important. However, this stress on the church as alternative community has led to a neglect of the fact that the primary place where a missionary encounter takes place is in the world, in the Monday to Saturday lives of believers. The result is that little has been done to challenge the local congregation in the way of structures and leadership to equip believers for their callings. Indeed, a stress on the calling of believers would not diminish the importance of the institutional church but would highlight the need for structures that equip the various members for mission.

Recently the Roman Catholic theologian William McConville has pointed to a danger in the growing tendency to take the image of alternative community as the primary model of the church. In his appreciative review of *Missional Church*, he warns that an alternative community can very easily become a parallel community — a separated community dissociated from any responsibility for cultural formation. I would add to this warning, that since the church cannot create a parallel community but must live in the world, talk of an alternative community could produce rhetoric that would inspire a commitment to being different (which in itself would be a good thing) but would not equip believers to live in an alternate story in the majority of their lives. What is needed is a missional ecclesiology that takes as one of its images "alternative community" but applies this to the church as the new humankind. In other words, alternative community must be an image not only for the church gathered as community but also for the church dispersed in the world. It is this kind of ecclesiology that will lead to a ministerial leadership and ecclesial structures that will equip believers for their callings. In this, I believe, Lesslie Newbigin has left us with a challenge and some direction.

63. Newbigin, *The Good Shepherd,* p. 76.
64. Newbigin, *A Word in Season,* p. 67.

SECTION 2

TRINITARIAN MISSIOLOGY

Mission and Trinitarian Theology

Perry Schmidt-Leukel

In the writings of Lesslie Newbigin we encounter the programmatic statement: "The mission of the church is to be understood, can only be rightly understood, in terms of the trinitarian model."[1] I presume that the aim of this section of the conference is to reflect on the missiological program indicated by that statement. But I'm afraid that my contribution is in a misgiving that there is no such thing as the trinitarian model for understanding mission. This is for two reasons. First, the most distinctive features of different missiological concepts do not depend on a trinitarian or nontrinitarian model but on the theology of religions for which their proponents opt. Second, trinitarian theology in general is not confined to any one of those options. You can adopt either an exclusivist or inclusivist or pluralist stand and still use a trinitarian model. However, there are important and characteristic differences in how the Trinity is understood, and these differences are clearly relevant to the choice among those three options.

I will start with a proposal about how the widespread typology of exclusivism, inclusivism, and pluralism can be made more precise. Then I will indicate how each of these three options is related to a different understanding of mission, showing that in this regard the main difference is between exclusivism and inclusivism on the one hand and pluralism on the other. I will then point out three important alternatives in interpreting trinitarian doctrines, thereby showing that there is a wide spectrum of understandings of the Trinity. Given this broad range of possible interpretations, it is clear

---

1. L. Newbigin, *The Gospel in a Pluralist Society* (London: SPCK; Grand Rapids: Eerdmans; and Geneva: WCC Publications, 1989), p. 118.

that each of the three positions in the theology of religions can legitimately work with a trinitarian model. Finally, I will mention some noteworthy affinities between some trinitarian models and the main options concerning other religions.

Exclusivism, Inclusivism, and Pluralism

The classification of exclusivism, inclusivism, and pluralism, since its introduction in the early eighties, has nowadays become a commonly used framework. But this does not mean this typology is always used in exactly the same sense. Rather, there can be found quite important differences in how the three terms are defined. And this sometimes leads to serious but unnecessary confusions.[2] In principle any classification can be either a labeling classification, that is, looking at what positions are there and then classifying them according to their most characteristic features, or it can be a strictly logical classification, not looking at what is there, but at the logical possibilities. One important difference between these classification policies is that the second aims at logical comprehensiveness, covering all the logical possibilities, while the first just gives names to the various existing theological approaches. I guess the confusions and variations in the use of the threefold typology are mainly due to the fact that it is mostly used as a labeling classification. But the wide acceptance of the threefold typology could be due to the fact that it is very close to a logical classification.

As a logical classification the scheme can best be interpreted as classifying the possible ways in which an important attribute can be distributed among the religions.[3] This can be illustrated by the diagram on page 59. The outer circles symbolize religions or — if you prefer Cantwell Smith's term — religious traditions, while the black interior circles indicate a certain attribute which is present or absent in those religions. Regarding the key issue of a theology of religions, this attribute is something like "mediation of salvific knowledge of a transcendent reality." Then you get four — and only four — logical possibilities, among which three — and only three — can count as theological possibilities.

2. See, for example, G. D'Costa, "The Impossibility of a Pluralist View of Religions," *Religious Studies* 32 (1996): 223-32.
3. For a far more extensive treatment of this typology, see my study *Theologie der Religionen. Probleme, Optionen, Argumente* (Munich and Neuried, 1997), pp. 65-97.

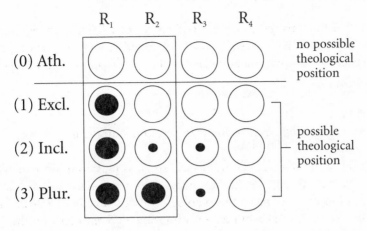

1. The atheistic or naturalistic position, saying that salvific knowledge of a transcendent reality is mediated by none of the religions because no transcendent reality exists. This is a logically possible position but cannot count as a theological option, if theology presupposes the existence of a transcendent reality. The next — and first theologically possible — position is:
2. Exclusivism, saying that salvific knowledge of a transcendent reality is mediated by only one religion — and this will naturally be that of those who hold this position.
3. Inclusivism, saying that salvific knowledge of a transcendent reality is mediated by more than one religion (not necessarily by all of them), but only one of them mediates it in a uniquely superior way. And this will also be quite naturally one's own religion.
4. Pluralism, saying that salvific knowledge of a transcendent reality is mediated by more than one religion (not necessarily by all of them), and that there is none among them whose mediation of that knowledge is superior to all the rest.

By these definitions the whole range of logical possibilities is covered, this being indicated by the square frame in the diagram: none; only one; more than one, but only one superior; more than one and none superior. Any theological option concerning the mediation of salvific knowledge by religions conforms to one of these three possibilities. There is no further position left for which theological research could look. But of course, each of the so-defined positions allows for a variety of subtypes.

Let me emphasize that the definition of exclusivism in my proposal does not entail anything about the individual chance of salvation, but deals only with the salvific function of religions. Therefore there can be three subtypes of exclusivism as regards the individual's chance of salvation: radical exclusivism, which denies any chance of salvation to members of other religions; soft exclusivism, which affirms an individual chance of salvation among members of other religions but denies any constructive function of their religions in the process of salvation (for example, the theory that for non-Christians salvation is made available through a postmortem encounter with Christ); and finally an undecided exclusivism, which leaves the question of individual salvation open but affirms that the other religions are not to be regarded as ways of salvation. So all forms of exclusivism agree in denying the mediation of salvific knowledge through other religions.

When we use this interpretation of the threefold typology, it becomes clear that Lesslie Newbigin belongs to the exclusivists and — more precisely — that he took the position I have called "undecided exclusivism." In his own words: he refuses to deny (as well as to affirm) "the possibility of the salvation of the non-Christian," but he clearly "rejects" a position "which regards the non-Christian religions as vehicles of salvation."[4]

The Missiological Consequences of Exclusivism, Inclusivism, and Pluralism

Now, what are the missiological consequences of these three options within a Christian theology of religions? To my mind, the most important consequence is that according to Christian exclusivism and inclusivism, it must remain the constant aim and ideal to convert the whole world to Christianity. And the consequence of this is that non-Christian religions or, more generally, a plurality of religions cannot be regarded as of spiritual value in any final sense. Let me explain.

If you accept my definitions, then it is clear that not all exclusivists have to make the salvation of souls the foremost motivation for mission. Only a defender of radical exclusivism will feel an absolute obligation to make as many converts as possible in order to protect people from eternal damnation. On the premises of radical exclusivism, this obligation and the resulting missionary zeal are completely fitting and could be softened only by some kind of double-predestination belief.[5]

---

4. Newbigin, p. 182.

5. If for every human being salvation or damnation is eternally predestined, then the

But soft exclusivists, and to a certain degree undecided exclusivists, can and will give priority to other reasons in their arguments for mission. One is their conviction that the true salvific knowledge of God is contained and proclaimed only within Christianity. In the eyes of Newbigin this is the most important motivation for mission.[6] And in this regard exclusivism has an important feature in common with inclusivism. The argument is quite simple and compelling: if you seriously believe that the divine revelation through Jesus Christ provides either the only or the uniquely highest form of salvific knowledge, then you will naturally wish that — at least as an ideal — every human being should come to know that truth. It is a question of strict logic: if you wish for your neighbor only the best and are at the same time convinced that the revelation through Jesus Christ is the best, then you will desire that everyone should accept that revelation. And this means that, ideally, everyone should become a Christian. But the unavoidable implication of this is that the existence of any other religion, and of a religious plurality as such, cannot have any ultimate value and should ideally be overcome — which is the regulative ideal of Christian mission. Even Karl Rahner did not hesitate to affirm precisely this.[7] Thus, even on an inclusivist basis, other religions can have only a provisional but not a final value.

If you consider this missiological implication of exclusivism and inclusivism, it will immediately become obvious that a pluralist theology of religions alone is able to provide the basis for a genuine acceptance and positive estimation of other religions and of the fact of religious plurality. May I propose a kind of self-test? Please ask yourself the following question: Would I really like the whole world to become Christian and all other religions to disappear? Or would I consider that a deplorable impoverishment? If the former, your intuition is either exclusivist or inclusivist. If the latter, your intuition is pluralist. On the basis of a pluralist theology of religions, mission can therefore not mean the Christianization of the world. On pluralist premises this is not disobedience to the Lord's command, but faithfulness to what God has already done among all humanity. So mission can and does mean for the

---

salvation of the saved cannot ultimately depend on the missionary activity of the church. Theologians like W. L. Craig have opted for exclusivism, accusing the other options of depriving the missionary calling of its urgency. But if, as in the case of Craig, exclusivism is defended and explained on the basis of double predestination, missionary efforts are no less deprived of urgency! Cf. W. L. Craig, "'No Other Name': A Middle Knowledge Perspective on the Exclusivity of Salvation through Christ," *Faith and Philosophy* 6 (1989): 172-88.

6. Cf. Newbigin, p. 125.

7. Cf. K. Rahner, "Kirche, Kirchen und Religionen," in *Schriften zur Theologie* VIII (Zürich, Einsiedeln, and Cologne, 1967), pp. 355-73.

religious pluralist the mutual sharing of different religious insights and experiences. It means deep-going dialogue, practical cooperation, and mutual transformation through genuine encounter with and learning about as well as from one another.

The Trinity

But let's come back to the question of Trinity. Could it be that trinitarian theology is as closely linked with either an exclusivist or inclusivist position as these are with the ideal of Christianizing the world? And could this be the deeper meaning of Newbigin's trinitarian missiology? To the first question my answer is negative because there is too wide a spectrum of trinitarian interpretations. Let me mention only three crucial alternatives.

1. Is the trinitarian doctrine a divinely revealed truth or a conception developed by humans in order to understand revelation? Throughout the centuries, except for the very early ones, Christians believed the former. But historical research has made it much more plausible to adopt the latter view. At least for two reasons: there was no trinitarian doctrine in the beginning,[8] and later there was not one but many trinitarian doctrines.

2. Are trinitarian formulas to be understood in a more tritheistic or a more modalistic sense? Of course, the orthodox answer would be neither/nor. But is that true to the facts? Cannot every trinitarian utterance be seen as tending either to a tritheistic or a modalistic interpretation? Is there not good reason to doubt the existence of any trinitarian doctrine that is coherent but neither virtually tritheistic nor modalistic? Consider, for example, Pannenberg's opinion that the three persons of the Trinity must be understood as three conscious centers of activity.[9] Or, as another example, consider the Roman Catho-

---

8. See, for example, the judgment of the historian Reinhard M. Hübner, "daß die Trinitätslehre ursprünglich keineswegs, weder explizit noch implizit, den christlichen Glauben kennzeichnete, vielmehr als eine 'Theologie im Werden' begriffen werden muß, deren erste Anfänge kaum vor ca. 150 n. Chr. anzusetzen sind und die ihren Vertretern die Anschuldigung des Ditheismus und Tritheismus, also der ärgsten Häresie, eingebracht hat" (R. Hübner, "Heis Theos Iesous Christos. Zum christlichen Gottesglauben im 2. Jahrhundert — ein Versuch," *Münchener Theologische Zeitschrift* 47 [1996]: 326).

9. Cf. W. Pannenberg, *Systematische Theologie*, vol. 1 (Göttingen, 1988), p. 347. Even more evident are the tritheistic tendencies in the writings of Jürgen Moltmann and Gisbert Greshake. For a sharp criticism of those modern tritheists, cf. K.-H. Ohlig, *Ein Gott in drei Personen? Vom Vater Jesu zum "Mysterium" der Trinität* (Mainz and Lucerne, 1999), esp. pp. 10-15.

lic synod for Africa speaking in an official document in 1994 of the "trinitarian family"[10] — which not only sounds like a family of three Gods but even makes one wonder about the different sexes in that "family." On the other hand, as a modalistic alternative we find for instance in the work of Kenneth Cragg the Trinity explained by the analogy that Muhammad was "prophet, husband, leader, and exemplar," but "no less, one Muhammad."[11]

3. Do trinitarian formulas correctly describe the divine reality as it is in itself, or are they to be understood as somehow analogical, metaphorical, symbolic, or mythological approximations to a reality that in itself lies completely beyond human comprehension and description? Many twentieth-century theologians have opted for the former in saying — like Barth and Rahner — that the Trinity experienced in the economy of salvation is identical with the immanent Trinity. But among the church fathers and some outstanding theologians of the Christian tradition, we find not a few saying that, in the words of Dionysius the Areopagite, the essence of God is not one, not three,[12] or, in the words of Nicholas of Cusa, that God in his infinity is neither Father, nor Son, nor Spirit.[13] Following that tradition, one could say, using the modern phrase, that trinitarian formulas refer to the human experience of God in the economy of salvation, but not to the divine reality as it is in its infinite inner being.

These three alternatives might be enough to show that there is no such thing as *the* trinitarian model, but rather a wide range of possible interpretations of the trinitarian formula, and therefore many trinitarian models.

Conclusion

Concerning theology of religions, John Hick has made abundantly clear that the prior condition for a pluralist position is the distinction between the divine reality as it is in its unfathomable inner being and the different manifestations of that reality within the manifold religious experience of humankind.[14] With regard to trinitarian theology, this means that if any trinitarian doctrine is understood as the one and only truth about God, revealed by him-

10. "Botschaft der Sondersynode für Afrika," *L'Osservatore Romano. Wochenausgabe in deutscher Sprache*, no. 23, 10 June 1994, p. 8.

11. K. Cragg, *The Call of the Minaret*, 2nd ed. (Maryknoll, N.Y., and Ibadan, 1985), p. 288.

12. *De divinis nominibus* 12.3.

13. *De docta ignorantia* 1.88.

14. See, for example, J. Hick, *An Interpretation of Religion* (London, 1989), pp. 233-96.

self (or themselves) to inform us about his (or their) nature and providing a description of the three persons of that reality which accurately depicts him (or them) as he or (they) eternally is (or are), then only an exclusivist or inclusivist theology of religions is possible. For on these premises none of the non-Christian images or concepts of the divine or the absolute could be on the same level as this highest knowledge of God. But if we understand trinitarian doctrines as humanly developed attempts to express the experience of a divine revelation through the life of Jesus, and the resulting changes in the hearts of the believers; if we therefore understand the Father, Son, and Spirit not as being three different divine persons but as pointing to three different ways the divine reality could be envisaged and approached; and accordingly if we do not pretend to possess a precise description of God's eternal being, but rather a testimony to how the divine presence came to human consciousness in one section of human religious history, then we can adopt a pluralist position and still make use of a trinitarian formula. A trinitarian model of that kind can really work, to quote John Hick, as "an acknowledgement of the plurality and diversity of the divine activity in relation to mankind . . . it can open out into an acceptance of the great world faiths as responses to different moments of divine revelation."[15]

Christian mission that works with a trinitarian model like this will not only rejoice in communicating the great experience of divine revelation in Christ, but will rejoice no less in discovering the spiritual richness of the other divine epiphanies, and it will not hesitate to give them due praise.[16]

15. J. Hick, "Islam and Christian Monotheism," in *Islam in a World of Diverse Faiths,* ed. D. Cohn-Sherbok (London, 1991), p. 9. Cf. also J. Hick, *The Metaphor of God Incarnate* (London, 1993), p. 149.

16. See a response to this paper from Heather Ward following Colin J. D. Greene's article.

Trinitarian Tradition and the
Cultural Collapse of Late Modernity

Colin J. D. Greene

The Scottish theologian John Baillie once accurately and aptly described the theological achievement of Karl Barth, and in so doing recognized that Barth marked a critical watershed in the history of modern theology. "He has changed the face of Protestant theology far more radically than any other theologian during my lifetime. . . . Whatever the measure of our agreements or disagreements with him, we have all to reckon with him. I have often said that there can be no hopeful forward advance beyond his teaching, as I fervently hope there will be, if we attempt to go round it instead of through it."[1]

This colloquium is in honor of someone who has probably similarly changed the face of the modern ecumenical and missionary movement more than we can presently recognize. Lesslie Newbigin was of course much influenced in both his theology and trinitarian missiology by the massive theological achievement represented by Barth's *Church Dogmatics*, the whole of which he read on his return from India. Let me suggest therefore that, as with his mentor before him, there will be no advance beyond the missiological directions mapped out by Lesslie Newbigin if we attempt to go round him rather than through him.

The paper offered by Dr. Perry Schmidt-Leukel falls precisely into that trap. I cannot see how Lesslie Newbigin, if he were here with us today, could do anything other than disavow the premises upon which the paper is based. There is no attempt to put Newbigin's trinitarian missiology within the wider context of the development of modern theology, neither is there any real con-

---

1. J. Baillie, *The Sense of the Presence of God* (Oxford: Oxford University Press, 1962), p. 254.

cern to exegete the main tenets of Newbigin's trinitarian theology of mission from the basis of his own writings, and finally there is a near fatal failure to recognize that Newbigin's trinitarianism, if we are to go through it rather than round it, constitutes the basis upon which he critically engages with what he refers to as the cultural collapse of late modernity. By way of response, let me try a typical exercise in Irish arrogance by following the schema just suggested.

The Context of Newbigin's Missiology within Modern Theology

Lesslie Newbigin, always one to recognize the importance of tradition, especially what the Old Testament scholar Gerhard von Rad referred to as the history of the transmission of religious tradition, stands himself within such a tradition. It is the history of the recovery of trinitarian theology which is such a distinctive feature of modern twentieth-century theology. It was of course initiated by Karl Barth and has been further developed by theologians as diverse as Wolfhart Pannenberg, Jürgen Moltmann, Karl Rahner, Walter Kasper, Leonardo Boff, Robert Jenson, Eberhard Jüngel, Tom Torrance, John Zizioulas, and Miroslav Volf. As early as 1963 Newbigin recognized the importance of this renewal of trinitarian theology for the modern missionary movement. He argued that the church would not be able to maintain the centrality of Christ in its missionary concerns "except within the framework of a fully and explicitly trinitarian doctrine of God."[2] Firmly positioned as Newbigin was within the ecumenical circles of the World Council of Churches and its denominational subsidiaries, he was well able to see the emergence of a rival theology of missions which was beginning to espouse an alternative viewpoint. In that sense he would have agreed with the contention of Carl Braaten that there were basically two types of theology in modern Christianity. "The one anchors itself in the biblical witness to God's salvation-historical dealings with the world, centred in the revelation of Christ and elaborated in the doctrine of the Trinity as a tripersonal communion of reciprocal relations."[3] The other earths itself within the burgeoning field of religious studies and was much influenced by the phenomenological study of religion.

Newbigin positioned himself firmly within the former tradition; he remained convinced throughout the rest of his life that the doctrine of the Trin-

2. L. Newbigin, *Trinitarian Faith and Today's Mission* (Richmond: John Knox, 1964), p. 31.
3. C. E. Braaten, *No Other Gospel* (Philadelphia: Fortress, 1992), p. 111.

ity was the only suitable theological framework for Christology, ecclesiology, and therefore also the theology of mission. Newbigin also remained implacably opposed to the alternative type of modern theology which was emerging from the new scientific study of the religions and, certainly within the academic fraternity, was marked by a similar broad ecumenical consensus. An equally impressive array of names can be summoned as representatives of what became known within missionary circles as the new Copernican revolution, or what Paul Knitter described as the move away from ecclesio-centrism and Christocentrism to a new pluralistic, nontrinitarian theocentrism. David Tracy, Langdon Gilkey, Gordon Kaufmann, Schubert Ogden, John Cobb, Tom Driver, Sallie McFague, Wilfred Cantwell Smith, Stanley Samartha, Diana Eck, James Gustafson, Paul Knitter, John Hick, and Mark Taylor, to name but a few, all espouse a similar position. I fail to see how Dr. Schmidt-Leukel can claim that the pluralist position can successfully be housed within a trinitarian framework because, as he himself admits, it commits the same fallacy first introduced to dogmatic theology by Thomas Aquinas; namely, the fateful separation of the one God as he is in his own being and as he is in his trinitarian revelation, although the Western tradition in theology had leaned in this direction since Augustine. Against just such a position Karl Rahner directed his now famous dictum that the economic Trinity is the immanent Trinity and the immanent Trinity is the economic Trinity. To refuse such a trinitarian identification is to cut the doctrine of the Trinity loose from its biblical moorings and, like Schleiermacher, consign it to the status of an afterthought in dogmatics instead of the fertile source of a proper theology of the church, its unity and its mission. In its place emerges the now equally famous separation of the religions into a schema labeled exclusivist, inclusivist, and pluralist — an overly neat framework which Newbigin remained convinced, as did David Bosch, was fatally flawed, if not in its conceptuality, most certainly in its application to the theology of mission.

An Exegesis of Newbigin's Trinitarian Missiology

Let us now turn to a brief exegesis of Newbigin's trinitarian missiology. The best place to start is not with *The Gospel in a Pluralist Society,* but with *The Open Secret,* first published in 1978. Here Newbigin claims that the doctrine of the Trinity is the only satisfactory answer to the question raised in the New Testament itself: Who is Jesus? He utilizes the introduction of Mark's Gospel to show that Jesus is described as the one who both announces and inaugurates the kingdom of God. In this way he is acknowledged as the Son of God.

Similarly throughout the Gospels he is attested as the obedient Son of the Father who does not organize or implement his own program but fulfills the Father's mission and so glorifies the one by whom he is sent (John 1:4). He is also understood as the one who in some special way is anointed by the Spirit. In the Gospels Jesus announces the beginning of his ministry in the words of Isaiah 61, a clear reference to the liberating presence and power of the Spirit. He is the beloved Son whose vocation is to bring forth justice to the nations.

By way of summary, then, the Gospels acknowledge a Jesus who announces the advent of the kingdom; in his baptism identifies himself with a sin-burdened humanity longing for the kingdom; through his ministry manifests the signs of the kingdom, and by his death and resurrection opens up a new way for people to receive the kingdom, albeit it in provisional form. If there is one criticism of Newbigin's exegesis of the New Testament answer to the question of who is Jesus, it would be that he doesn't sufficiently underscore the importance of the resurrection as God's answer to that same question. Consequently, as Pannenberg recognizes, "Only by his resurrection from the dead did the Crucified attain to the dignity of the Kyrios (Phil. 2:9-11). Only thus was he appointed the Son of God in power (Rom. 1:4). Only in the light of the resurrection is he the pre-existent Son. Only as the risen Lord is he always the living Lord of his community."[4]

When the gospel was taken beyond the confines of Judaism out into the Greco-Roman world, that same question was answered from within another conceptual framework. The implicit and eschatologically orientated trinitarianism of the Gospels makes way for the explicit, protologically directed trinitarianism of Tertullian, Origen, Athanasius, the Cappadocian Fathers, and Augustine. It was this very same trinitarianism which broke apart the ancient dichotomies of the Neoplatonic worldview and allowed a new relationship between God and the creation to be conceived. Trinitarianism is most certainly based on a number of presuppositions which do not sit easily with the new pluralistic theology of the religions. First of all, it refuses to speculate about a god who is ultimately an unknowable monad because such a belief evacuates history of any meaning or significance and renders a view of God as an utterly remote divine being with whom we can never really converse. Secondly, it affirms that it is a trinitarian conceptual framework which most aptly describes the story which unfolds in the Bible: the God who revealed his reconciling purposes for humankind in the election of Israel, the sending of the Son, and the establishment of the Christian church. Consequently Newbigin believes there is good warranty to develop a theology of mission conceived "as the pro-

---

4. W. Pannenberg, *Systematic Theology*, vol. 2 (Edinburgh: T&T Clark, 1994), p. 283.

claiming of the kingdom of the Father, as sharing the life of the Son, and as bearing the witness of the Spirit."[5] In this way the gospel message remains an open secret. It is not a universal gnosis available to everyone, everywhere. Only to some is given the secret of the kingdom of God received through faith and repentance. "To repent is to do the U-turn of the mind which enables you to believe what is hidden from sight, the reality of the presence of the reign of God in the crucified Jesus."[6] But the task of every Christian is to test the gospel's claim to universal veracity by publishing it abroad among the nations.

In *The Gospel in a Pluralist Society*, Newbigin utilizes the same trinitarian framework to work out the parameters of what he refers to as the logic of mission. This entails that the church is not the source or the agent of mission but the locus of mission. Mission issues forth from the trinitarian history of God. The church is not an imperialistic movement which seeks to take control of history but the community that lives by "the story of the self-emptying of God in the ministry, life, death, and resurrection of Jesus."[7] It is this story which clarifies the true goal of mission, which is not, surprising is it may seem, the salvation of individuals from the world but, as demonstrated by the ministry of Paul, the establishment of believing communities throughout the world. The center of mission is consequently not the saving of, or the failure to save, individual souls from perdition but the disclosure of the true meaning of the human story in the person of Christ. If the central facts of this story cannot be verified by reference to another extraneous authority, how can the gospel be rescued from the charge of subjectivism? Only through mission, because this is the way we test the claim that the gospel reveals the clue to the meaning of universal history. The true purpose of mission is not then the growth of the church, the saving of souls, or the humanization of society, but an acted-out doxology. It is that God may be glorified on earth as in heaven.

The Cultural Collapse of Late Modernity

Let us turn now to Newbigin's contention that the alternative viewpoint, a pluralistic nontrinitarian theism, is really a profound manifestation of the cultural collapse of modernity. Newbigin aptly describes the reigning plausi-

---

5. L. Newbigin, *The Open Secret: Sketches for a Missionary Theology* (London: SPCK; Grand Rapids: Eerdmans, 1978), p. 31.

6. L. Newbigin, *The Gospel in a Pluralist Society* (London: SPCK; Grand Rapids: Eerdmans; and Geneva: WCC Publications, 1989), p. 117.

7. Newbigin, *Pluralist Society*, p. 120.

bility structure of pluralism: "But for those who have shared in the multifaith, multiculture, multirace world of today it seems preposterous to maintain that in all the infinite pluralities and relativities of human affairs there should be one absolute against which everything else is to be measured."[8]

He notes that what is referred to as exclusivism is perceived by the pluralists as really a manifestation of the old colonial imperialism which is utterly out of keeping with modern historical consciousness. Instead the pluralists point to what Jürgen Moltmann has referred to as a universal soteriological situation which is a distinctive feature of late modernity. Moltmann isolates three debilitating effects of modernity which threaten to engulf us all, namely, the continued threat of nuclear extinction, the all-pervasive nature of the ecological crisis, and the economic disparity between the Two-Thirds World and the First World.[9]

Newbigin, like Moltmann, accepts that in the midst of this perilous situation there is indeed a need to find an adequate basis for the unity of humankind. But whereas Moltmann finds it in a new eschatological Christology, the pluralists locate it in the jettisoning of all particularist Christologies altogether. The connection here is far from obvious, except in what Christopher Duraisingh refers to as the "collective human search for meaning and sacredness," which somehow must be located within the universe of faiths and not in one particular religious tradition.

Newbigin asks what are the presuppositions upon which this new quest for the unity of humankind are to be based. For Kaufmann it is simply "modern historical consciousness," which is somehow elevated to a position of epistemological immunity. For Cantwell Smith it is the equally unsubstantiated conviction that all religions are really variations on a single theme, which is the mystical religious experience of "the Transcendent." Why does Newbigin view such a priori convictions as evidence of the cultural collapse of modernity? Precisely because they represent a flight from traditions of rationality still upheld in the world of science, if not the world of religion, which are deeply committed to the search for a truth which will illuminate the human condition and render it a meaningful episode in the drama of universal history. The evidence he isolates constitutes a fourfold critique.

1. The almost universal acceptance that there can be no absolute in history remains for many pluralists a totally unsubstantiated dogma which is simply acquiescence to a form of debilitating relativism which affects those involved in the study of the religions like an intellectual virus. Here Newbigin

---

8. Newbigin, *Pluralist Society*, p. 157.
9. J. Moltmann, *The Way of Jesus Christ* (London: SCM Press, 1990), pp. 63-73.

is supported by Pannenberg, who comments: "The theology of the world religions that wants to be true to the empirical situation in the way the religious traditions confront each other must not evade or play down the conflict of truth claims. If we look to the history of religions in the past, there is always competition and struggle for superiority on the basis of different truth claims."[10]

2. The thesis that revelation cannot be located in the past but must confront every individual in the present. Is this not again simply a concession to a form of atomistic individualism which appears to reject tradition as the bearer of the meaning of history? "[O]ur spiritual experience is not an affair of our own individual subjectivity; it is sustained, nourished and tested by continual reference to the original witnesses of the revelation and by reference to the continuing experience of those who share with us the allegiance to Jesus."[11]

3. The tendency of modernity to elevate the individual as the sole arbiter of truth reflecting a consumeristic mentality where truth is simply that which fits our own individual preference. There simply are no criteria which could possibly help us discriminate the validity of one belief from that of another. Consequently a statement such as the Holocaust was a pernicious evil is simply a personal value judgment which is subject to no interpersonal criteria of verification.

4. The tendency of pluralists to prefer the language of universal moral values rather than the particular truth claims of the religions. A tendency which also demonstrates a penchant for abstract nouns which simply float free from the religious narratives and stories where they are actually earthed.

In conclusion, Newbigin perceives at the heart of all this a retreat into subjectivism brought about by the widespread acceptance of Nietzsche's hermeneutic of suspicion. If all knowledge is nothing but the naked will to power, then such a constructivist epistemology simply leaves the fearful anxious self at the heart of its own universe devoid of any broader context of meaning and significance. With a little poetic license we could say that the religious equivalent of this is the tripartite schema of exclusivism, inclusivism, and pluralism. At the center of this schema is a preposterous abstraction, namely, the fate of the individual soul. It is preposterous because by and large the New Testament remains agnostic in regard to this question, recognizing that judgment is the domain of God alone. And it is an abstrac-

---

10. W. Pannenberg, in G. D'Costa, ed., *Christian Uniqueness Reconsidered* (New York: Orbis, 1990), p. 102.

11. Newbigin, *Pluralist Society,* p. 164.

tion because it dislocates the individual from the corporate story of human history, which is also the story of the self-manifestation of the triune God. One central question this colloquium should also address is whether or not the advent of postmodernity is further evidence of this cultural collapse in the West or signals the possibility of cultural renewal, albeit only in dialogue with those who recognize the public dimensions of religious faith and belief. Something Lesslie Newbigin never tired of advocating.

The Use and Misuse of "Metaphor" in Christian Theology

Heather Ward

In the session led by Professor Schmidt-Leukel challenging Lesslie Newbigin's contention that "the trinitarian model" was essential to missiology, Professor Schmidt-Leukel took the responder, Colin Greene, to task for his assertion concerning the metaphorical nature of all language. The former contended, in the context of defending his position on the Trinity as a human construct, that, for example, the term "father" differed greatly in meaning when applied to God and to the human male. In so doing Professor Schmidt-Leukel revealed a fundamental misunderstanding of the nature of metaphor, confounding it with the connotative aspects of language. The grounds of this misunderstanding, I would argue, highlight an imbalance which pervaded the "After Newbigin" conference, that is, due attention to the concepts of likeness in Christian theology.

The approach to metaphor confused the power of metaphor with that of connotation. Metaphor works not by establishing multiple correspondences between the connotations of two terms, but by identifying the point of likeness between two otherwise disparate entities. "He hared along the road" identifies a common factor of speed, not a shared propensity also for shadow-boxing and madness in March. Similarly, "father" applied to God and to man points to the common factor of authorship, source of origin, as we find for example in Isaiah 64:8. Equally, when Abraham is called "father of many nations," it is his nature as progenitor which is identified; we are not concerned with other associations surrounding the term. Here the word is used metaphorically of Abraham, as one who is like God as the source of nations. This is also clear in Isaiah's treatment of the fatherhood of God and of Abraham in Isaiah 63:16. We are not invited by such usage to surround the name of Abraham with all the connotations of the word of God.

This is not simply a pedantic linguistic point from a student of literature. This recognition of the function of metaphor in pinpointing likeness within otherness highlights an essential aspect of the doctrine of the Trinity and of its implications for human activity and relationships. By regarding this doctrine as a human construct dependent on the inadequacy of metaphor which distorts more than it reveals, we remove the disturbing and challenging notion of likeness from our God concept and from our understanding of human life. The resultant affirmation of exclusive transcendent "otherness" in God certainly allows a neat solution to the problem of plurality. Plurality and "otherness" on earth are simply the consequence of multifarious and inadequate attempts to convey some understanding of an utterly transcendent unity. In taking this approach, however, we detach this doctrine from its essential Christian concomitants, the incarnation and its related doctrine of our creation in the image of God. In so doing we deny to Christianity the "otherness" we seek to respect in other faith traditions, conforming it to their likeness. Our approach to plurality in fact squeezes it out and reduces true diversity to simply another style.

Leaving aside the issues of revelation and the status of the trinitarian implications of the New Testament record, we can still see that Christian reflection on the Trinity has not been the result of a desire to construct a model of the Godhead but the consequence of meditation on the mystery of Christ as an incarnate savior. Those to whom we look for the development of trinitarian theology are also those intoxicated by the mystery of the incarnation, of divine otherness taking on humanity and completing our creation in the likeness of God, so that otherness and likeness henceforth coinhere.

Christian theology has, consequently, never been entirely apophatic. The scandal of the incarnation makes possible and necessary a kataphatic theology; the human word does, at some level, participate in the truth of the Word. The Eastern churches, while safeguarding apophaticism in their refusal to present doctrine as explanation, have never denied the human capacity for figuring truly, if incompletely and inadequately, the divine. Without such conviction we could not have the wealth of their hymnody and their liturgies, understood as participation in the divine reality. The human word, at the very least, points us in the right direction toward God, allowing us to say what he isn't. (For example, the love of God may utterly surpass human understanding, but the point of likeness between them indicates a truth enabling us to exclude ideas of indifference and hatred.)

In the West the balance was attested by the Fourth Lateran Council of 1214, which averred that in our language about God "the difference is always greater than the likeness." Similarly, within the Western mystical tradition, heavily influenced, like the East, by Pseudo-Dionysius the Areopagite, the balance remains. For Saint John of the Cross the totally transcendent God speaks completely in the Word, and it is the point of likeness in the soul, given by God, which enables the chasm of otherness to be bridged. Similarly, Meister Eckhart's apophaticism needs to be read in the light of his vernacular sermons, which deal more readily with Christ's likeness to us. Our Christian mind has found it necessary to maintain both poles of this opposition if it is to be true to its experience of God in Christ.

It is keeping the doctrine of the Holy Trinity in close association with that of the incarnation that enables the Christian to engage in mission in a plural world. We preach Christ not only as the revelation of the transcendent, "other" God, but also as the one who, "having become like us in all things but sin" (Heb. 4:15), is the revelation of humanity, into whom all diversity is gathered and recognized as sharing his features.

Trinitarian Missiology:
Mission as Face-to-Face Encounter

Philip D. Kenneson

Few missiologists in the West would hesitate to acknowledge their indebtedness to the work of Lesslie Newbigin. As a domestic missiologist of sorts, I have learned a great deal over the years from Newbigin's penetrating insight into the changing shape of Western cultures. Yet if part of the goal of this volume is to honor Newbigin by seeking to assess what directions missiology might take after Newbigin, then we must do more than gratefully acknowledge our indebtedness to him. We must also seek to identify those areas where more or different work needs to be done in the future.

One area where different work is needed is epistemology. By appropriating for mission studies the work of Polanyi and other critics of Enlightenment epistemologies, Newbigin emboldened missiologists who for too long labored under such false dichotomies as reason and faith, fact and value, objectivity and subjectivity, and public and private. In many ways Newbigin anticipated the ways in which postmodernity would level the epistemological playing field. Yet what should be our focus now that the playing field is increasingly level? In other words, what might be the next step now that epistemological concerns no longer necessarily count against the reception of Christian witness?

Since the lack of an epistemological argument against the Christian faith is not necessarily an argument in its favor — particularly in our postmodern context — missiologists might consider shifting their attention away from epistemology. Indeed, it may be that, for all his helpfulness on matters epistemological, Newbigin remained at times — like those he criticized — understandably yet regrettably fixated on epistemological concerns. Perhaps "after Newbigin," and partly as a result of his work, we may turn our attention to other matters.

But where might we turn? Obviously there are lots of possibilities, but in the brief space of this essay let me offer a few reflections about one such possibility that I believe holds some promise. My assigned topic is "Trinitarian Missiology," and it might be thought by some that no more unfortunate approach might be taken up, since many self-professed Christians find the doctrine of the Trinity to be if not impenetrable, then at least embarrassing, particularly in the missionary encounter. Can missiology in our day even hope to be enlivened and enriched by starting with what many consider a bit of outdated Christian esoterica?

I believe it can, but to do so we must be clear about the proper role of doctrine in the Christian life. For the purposes of this paper, I take it as given that doctrines are not primarily the objects of our beliefs, but are summary "grammars" or rules that govern the logic of Christian speech and thought.[1] Thus Christians don't so much believe in a doctrine of the Trinity (or try to get others to believe in such a doctrine) as they allow that doctrine to shape the ways they think about and talk about the God they worship and serve.

With such a perspective about the role of doctrine clearly in view, how might reflection on the doctrine of the Trinity enrich missiology "after Newbigin"? One short answer is this: I believe that reflection on the Trinity offers an invaluable resource as we seek to remain genuinely open to "the other" in face-to-face encounters. Now, there has been much said and written of late in academic circles about both "openness" and "otherness," but it's not clear to me how seriously either concept is taken by most people. It may be that reflection on the Trinity may enrich our understanding of both concepts.

One major obstacle to appropriating these notions is that most of us find ourselves in Western cultures that are dominated in moral and ethical matters by the language of "rights." This language, with its built-in assumption that the other is someone from whom I need to be protected and who needs to be protected from me, is too conceptually thin to encourage us to remain genuinely open to each other. In other words, rights language may keep me from harming you, but it will likely give me no reasons for believing that my life is impoverished apart from you. Moreover, while much postmodern discourse is saturated with discussions about "the other," too often such discourse is conducted at such a high level of abstraction that, paradoxically, the otherness of the other is easily erased or domesticated. When this does not happen, and the otherness of the other *is* taken seriously, the other is usually

---

1. Here I am following the argument of George Lindbeck and other so-called postliberals. See, for example, Lindbeck's *The Nature of Doctrine: Religion and Theology in a Postliberal Age* (Philadelphia: Westminster, 1984).

considered a threat. Is it possible, after Nietzsche, to acknowledge otherness or difference without this acknowledgment being an inevitable precursor to violence?

Here, it seems to me, reflecting on the doctrine of the Trinity might prove illuminating. Allow me to sketch several matters that seem to warrant further reflection by missiologists.

First, something of a consensus is emerging among many theologians that reflection on the Trinity offers us important insights into the nature of human personhood.[2] As Colin Gunton has recently pointed out with respect to the Trinity: "The persons [of the Trinity] do not simply enter into relations with one another, but are constituted by one another in the relations. Father, Son and Spirit are eternally what they are by virtue of what they are from and to one another."[3] Increasingly, theologians are making the same claims about human persons: that persons are irreducibly relational and social. In other words, like the persons of the Trinity, human persons are not self-constituted, but are constituted as persons through their social relations. In short, being a person is always being-in-relation.

Another aspect of this growing consensus is that human personhood is in some important sense *perichoretic* in ways that are analogous to divine personhood; that is, that part of what it means for us to be a person is to "dwell in" other people and to have them "dwell in" us. As Miroslav Volf puts it, divine persons are not simply interdependent and influence each other from the outside, but are personally interior to each other. "Every divine person is indwelled by other divine persons; all the persons interpenetrate each other. They do not cease however to be distinct. Rather, their interpenetration presupposes their distinctions; persons who have been dissolved in some third thing cannot be said to be interior to each other."[4]

---

2. This consensus includes Roman Catholic, Orthodox, and Protestant theologians. To name only a few who have recently echoed this theme: Cardinal Joseph Ratzinger, Walter Kasper, Leonardo Boff, John D. Zizioulas, Wolfhart Pannenberg, Jürgen Moltmann, Colin Gunton, Miroslav Volf, Anthony Thiselton, and David Cunningham.

3. Gunton, *The One, the Three, and the Many: God, Creation, and the Culture of Modernity* (Cambridge, 1993), p. 214.

4. Volf, "'The Trinity Is Our Social Program': The Doctrine of the Trinity and the Shape of Social Engagement," *Modern Theology* 14, no. 3 (July 1998): 409. For further elaboration of this matter see also Volf's *Exclusion and Embrace: A Theological Exploration of Identity, Otherness, and Reconciliation* (Nashville: Abingdon, 1996), and *After Our Likeness: The Church as the Image of the Trinity* (Grand Rapids: Eerdmans, 1998). As readers of Volf will recognize, my account of the relationship between divine and human personhood has been greatly shaped by Volf's insights.

As a result of this mutual indwelling, our identity is always something we partly receive as a gift from others, just as their identities are in turn received from us and others. Again, as Volf writes: "The self gives something of itself, of its own space, so to speak, in a movement in which it contracts itself in order to be expanded by the other and in which it at the same time enters the contracted other in order to increase the other's plenitude."[5] This suggests a circulation of gifts: a circular structure wherein we are always living from God and toward God, as well as living from one another and toward one another. If humans were capable of imaging this divine self-donation perfectly, the perfect cycle of self-donations would start moving simultaneously at all points. But since we live in a sinful world and are ourselves sinful, Christians have been called to image the way this divine self-donation intersects this world, which is precisely what the narrative about a crucified God is all about. This willingness to suffer on behalf of the other, this embrace of the other without expectation that the other will necessarily embrace us, is the cruciform life to which Christians have been called.[6]

For Christians the paradigmatic example of this is Jesus Christ, whose being and life is best understood through the concept of "self-donation." Moreover, the narrative Christians tell about the triune God insists that the Father's gifts to the world of the Son and Spirit are given so that all creation may be drawn into the very life of God, a life which remains open to our otherness.

Such a view of the Trinity and human personhood has potentially important implications for the missiological enterprise. First, it suggests that Christians ought to have at least as many reasons (if not more) than other people for remaining genuinely open to the other. Such openness is not simply a strategy for facilitating conversion, nor is it simply a toleration of difference that stems from and compounds a posture of indifference. Rather the notion of difference and otherness that should inform the Christian faith flows from our understanding of God's trinitarian nature, as well as from a deep sense of humility, a humility that creates the space not simply to give to the other but also to receive from the other. Thus any sense of "mission" that excludes reception seems destined to transform the other simply into an object of our missionary efforts or our indifference. Here we are reminded, as

---

5. Volf, "Doctrine of the Trinity," p. 412.

6. As John Milbank writes: "In a world dominated by evil and violence, self-offering, to God and others, inevitably involves suffering. This is why there is suffering at the heart of Christ's perfect self-offering to God." See "Postmodern Critical Augustinianism: A Short *Summa* in Forty-two Responses to Unasked Questions," in *The Postmodern God: A Theological Reader,* ed. Graham Ward (Oxford: Blackwell, 1997), p. 271.

Lesslie Newbigin insisted on a number of occasions, that missionary traffic must always run on a two-way street, that Christians must never assume that they exclusively possess salvation. Or said differently, however we imagine the *missio Dei,* we should never do so in such a way that this mission is only extended through us as Christians and not also to us by means of those "others" we encounter.[7] Unfortunately, many conventional uses of the word "mission" — to the extent that they exclude reception — seem to compound the problem.

To his credit, Newbigin does affirm the importance of mission work being grounded in a certain "mutual relatedness."[8] However, he does not to my knowledge ever ground human intersubjectivity in the doctrine of the Trinity, though he comes tantalizingly close to making such a move in a few passages of *The Open Secret.* Perhaps "after Newbigin" we may strengthen the theological underpinnings of his notion of mutual relatedness by rooting its implied anthropology in a Christian understanding of the Trinity.

A second implication of a trinitarian view of human personhood for mission follows closely on the first. The difference and mutual relatedness we witness at the center of the Godhead stands as a reminder that the difference of the other need not inevitably lead to violence or indifference. These two options seem to be the only ones offered within our current postmodern milieu. Yet reflection on the doctrine of the Trinity might offer us a different model for understanding and embodying our relation to "the other." Here we might pursue a theme articulated by John Milbank, who speaks of the Spirit as a "second difference" within the Godhead.[9] According to Milbank, God not only speaks the Word, which is the "first difference," but God also evokes a response to that Word through the Spirit, a response that is not mere repetition and so involves a "second difference." This suggests that God is capable of drawing into the very life of God our different responses and arranging them into a "harmony of differences," a notion that Milbank adapts from Augustine's musical ontology:

7. Newbigin writes: "The company of those so committed and so following [Christ] does not possess in itself the fullness of understanding or of obedience. It is a learning community" (*The Open Secret: An Introduction to the Theology of Mission,* rev. ed. [London: SPCK; Grand Rapids: Eerdmans, 1995], p. 140).

8. The phrase is from Newbigin, *Gospel in a Pluralist Society* (London: SPCK; Grand Rapids: Eerdmans; and Geneva: WCC Publications, 1989), p. 82.

9. Milbank, "Postmodern Critical Augustinianism," p. 274. See also Milbank's essay "The Second Difference," in *The Word Made Strange: Theology, Language, Culture* (Oxford: Blackwell, 1997), pp. 171-93.

Christianity is peculiar, because while it is open to difference — to a series of infinitely new additions, insights, progressions toward God, it also strives to make of all these differential additions a harmony, "in the body of Christ," and claims that if the reality of God is properly attended to, there can be such a harmony. And the idea of a consistently beautiful, continuously differential, and open series, is of course the idea of "music." . . . Christianity, therefore, is not just in the same position as all other discourses *vis-à-vis* postmodernity; it can, I want to claim, think difference, yet it perhaps uniquely tries to deny that this necessarily (rather than contingently, in a fallen world) entails conflict.[10]

It may be the case, therefore, that the body of Christ, to the extent that it reflects and embodies in its life together this harmony of differences, offers the world a model of community that it might not otherwise know: one capable of acknowledging and affirming difference without this recognition resulting in either indifference or violence.

Such openness to the other might also entail a third implication for the missiological enterprise: it might encourage us, if not require us, to reconsider the ways we in the West conceptualize "truth." Newbigin went a long way toward helping us understand that in an age that assumed that the dichotomy between objectivity and subjectivity was coherent, Christian claims would usually be heard as subjective preferences. But I am not sure that Newbigin helps us carve out a coherent strategy about what to do next. Rather than continuing to do the best we can within the present dichotomy — which is to assert that the truth of the gospel must be presented as public truth for all, a truth we assert with universal intent — we might be better off rejecting the dichotomy at the very beginning. We might, for example, given what was said above, begin with the assumption that truth is always "intersubjective," and hence (if we must use spatial metaphors) not so much "out there" or "in here" as "between" persons. Moreover, such a view of truth might be better served by adopting different metaphors for speaking about truth, such as truth as a "way" or "path" to be walked with other people rather than an object to be grasped and handed on to others.[11]

Such a view of truth would have several potential benefits. First, it

10. Milbank, "Postmodern Critical Augustinianism," p. 268. See also David Cunningham's chapter on polyphony in *These Three Are One: The Practice of Trinitarian Theology* (Oxford: Blackwell, 1998), pp. 127-64.

11. I have explored these matters in greater detail in my essay "Can the Christian Faith Survive If Belief in Objective Truth Is Abandoned?" *Stone-Campbell Journal* 2, no. 1 (spring 1999): 43-56.

would resonate better with the above reflections on the Trinity, as well as much of Christian Scripture. Second, it would offer a model of truth in which "knowing" and "doing" the truth were inseparable, a position to which Newbigin himself subscribed but which his continued appeal to the conventional metaphors made difficult to conceptualize. And third, such a view of truth would also likely resonate better with many persons from non-Western orientations, since for many of them the notion of the truth as a way or path is a very familiar one.

A final implication of trinitarian personhood for the missiological enterprise returns us to the issue of epistemology. It seems possible that a trinitarian view of personhood might resonate with the intriguing suggestion of those such as Emmanuel Levinas who have insisted that ethics, not epistemology, should be first philosophy.[12] For Levinas there is something about the "face of the other" that transcends and precedes all epistemological reflection. In the face of the other we meet someone who makes an irreducible claim to our attention, someone who can challenge our often facile ways of seeing and being in the world, someone who can offer us a gift we didn't know we needed. Although Christians might choose to state this point somewhat differently than Levinas has, the notion that we might be responsible for our neighbors in concrete ways before we "know" them or make judgments about them echoes throughout the Christian tradition, even if Christians have not always embodied it faithfully. Moreover, a tradition that insists that God has encountered us "face-to-face" in the person of Jesus Christ, and in doing so has called us to follow before we fully know (or perhaps even as a precondition for further knowing), may also find such a "displacement" or "refiguring" of epistemology promising.

In an age like ours, one of the great challenges is in discerning what might commend the Christian faith to anyone. In our current context epistemological arguments count neither for nor against the Christian faith. Why, then, should anyone not already predisposed to pay attention to the claims of the Christian faith care about it at all? My hunch is that we can rarely predict ahead of time what any person might find commendable about the Christian faith. Indeed, it may be that we unwittingly do violence to the other whenever we assume that we do know, since such a strategy too often domesticates the otherness of the other by transforming that person's alterity into a relatively safe abstraction. That is, once the person before you is not so

---

12. See, for example, Levinas's essay "Ethics as First Philosophy," trans. Seán Hand and Michael Temple, in *The Levinas Reader*, ed. Seán Hand (Cambridge: Blackwell, 1989), pp. 75-86.

much a person as she is a "Muslim" or a "Hindu" or an "agnostic," then we may find that we have less reason to listen carefully, since we may mistakenly believe that we already know what she thinks and what she needs to hear. Moreover, such labels, by neatly circumscribing the other's otherness, often make it more difficult for us to envision this person as a gift instead of as a threat.

My contention is that what is needed is not so much a basis for grounding such encounters but more a way of life that creates the space for such encounters. In other words, what we need is not so much a way of justifying ahead of time the likely contours of any such encounter, but rather a way of life that nurtures genuine face-to-face encounters. It may be that one of the most important services missiology can render in our current context is offering the resources needed to remain genuinely open to and open in such face-to-face encounters. The Christian tradition, particularly in its doctrine of the Trinity, may offer us one important resource not only for nurturing such encounters, but also for underscoring their vital importance.

The Uncontainable God:
Pre-Christendom Doctrine of Trinity

Frances Young

The great virtue of the way Lesslie Newbigin grounds mission in the Trinity is the fact that it highlights the priority of God. It is not just that "the goal of missions is the glory of God,"[1] but also that God is the one who acts, not the church — it is God's mission. Mission is the overflow of God's infinite love upon all creation, expressed in the incarnation and the outpouring of the Spirit.

This expression of God's love in the work of Christ and the Spirit means that Newbigin's trinitarianism works like that of the second-century theologian Irenaeus, who calls the Word and Spirit the two hands of God.[2] It is an "economic" trinitarianism; that is, it is focused on God's relationship with the world, grounded in the biblical story of creation, redemption, and sanctification.

In Newbigin's thought the theological undergirding of mission is made richer and deeper by its trinitarian thrust. An important challenge is offered to the dominant debates about strategies, objectives, and everything else that prioritizes what we do, or what the church does. We betray a lack of trust if we do not accept that God can look after the divine self. Our efforts to defend or promote God are a sign of doubt and lack of faith. Let God be God.

All this is important. But in fact, Newbigin's trinitarianism is not theologically developed. It is simply based on the fact of the incarnation and the dogma of the Trinity, taken to be evident in Scripture. However, the doctrine

---

1. Lesslie Newbigin, *The Gospel in a Pluralist Society* (London: SPCK; Grand Rapids: Eerdmans; and Geneva: WCC Publications, 1989), p. 180.
2. Irenaeus, *Adversus haereses* 5.1.3; 6.1.

of the Trinity as such is not transparent in the Bible. It emerged out of protracted internal debates in the church up to the fourth century. In taking further the theme of the doctrine of the Trinity and mission, what I have to say is premised on the proposition that there are important analogies between that period and our own, between the pre-Christendom and post-Christendom periods of pluralism.

Mission and the One God

The writings from early Christianity which most clearly engage in presenting the gospel in terms that non-Christians might grasp are the apologetic literature of the second century. This category includes the works of people like Justin Martyr, Athenagoras, Tatian, and Theophilus. The key point they make is that there is one God, who is the Creator of all; so there is one universe or cosmos, overseen by God's providence. God has oversight of everything, even seeing into the heart. God will judge all at the end. The Word of God has shown the Way by which people should live. This is a truth which makes demands on people and on their lifestyle.

What is noticeable in this message is its combination of challenge to then-prevailing views alongside appeal to common ground. The many gods and lords of the ancient world were attacked and firmly rejected. But contemporary interest in ethics provided the thrust of the message, grounded in a more dynamic monotheism than the rather vague theoretical picture of one underlying divine being found in then-current philosophies. Thus the key point lay in the proclamation of the unity of God as the source of all things, over against polytheism, idolatry, fatalism, astrology, and magic.

I would like to suggest that a radical recovery of this perspective is needed. We do not proclaim the sectional god of any group, nation, race, or religion, but the God of the whole universe. Let God be God. In our current context of pluralism we need a renewed sense of one universe to which we all belong, of one universal creation of which we are all a part, together with a recovery of trust in one God who holds all in being and love, the God who contains but is not contained.

Transcendence

God is not contained. The problem about the gods of the ancient world was that they were too intertwined with the world — divinized creatures, spirits

FRANCES YOUNG

of sacred groves and mountains, natural forces, even exceptional human beings. A very early philosopher, some five centuries before Christ, had suggested that human beings make gods in their own image — Ethiopians, for
example, make their gods black with turned-up noses, Thracians with red
hair and blue eyes — and if oxen or lions had gods they would be oxenlike or
lionlike. Xenophanes[3] anticipated Feuerbach, and we have his sayings because
they were preserved by the Christian, Clement of Alexandria. They were useful against idolatry, against projection of things with which we are familiar
onto the heavens.

At one time it was a theological commonplace to use the dynamic personal God of the Bible to challenge the so-called philosophical concept of
God supposedly imported by Greek philosophy. But the so-called philosophical concept of God was essential in the argument against idolatry, and had
roots in the Bible: "My thoughts are not your thoughts nor are your ways my
ways" (Isa. 55:8). The God of the Hebrew Bible was the unnameable one,[4]
whose face no one could see and live (Exod. 33:20). The transcendence of
God bespeaks not the Greek captivity of the church but a hallowing of God's
name. The early Christians insisted that biblical anthropomorphisms should
not be taken literally: reference to God's hands was a way of speaking of God's
activity, to God's eyes a way of describing God's oversight. Apophaticism, the
description of God by denying likeness to everything creaturely, the use of
negative attributes — invisible, immortal, indescribable, unknowable, infinite, and so on — all this kind of thing was about letting God be God, about
acknowledging God's otherness, about the fact that God, if God be God, is
not an object like other objects in the universe but the incomparable one, beyond language or thought.

That God could not be contained in the human mind, otherwise the divine would be less than that mind, was a crucial argument in the formulation
of the doctrine of the Trinity. In the fourth century the heretic Eunomius
wanted to define God as the one being that has never come into being (i.e.,
agenetos = ingenerate or unbegotten). Logically that meant the only-begotten
Son could not be God in the same sense as the Father — rather, here was a
distinct, derivative, and lesser being. Against him the Cappadocian Fathers
protested,[5] as did John Chrysostom, the most famous preacher of antiquity,

3. Fragment in Clement, *Stromateis* 5.14.
4. Already in reading the Hebrew Scriptures *Adonai* (= Lord) was pronounced rather
than God's name, and in the Greek of the Septuagint *kyrios* (= Lord) appeared wherever
God's name was inscribed in the Hebrew text.
5. The several volumes of Gregory of Nyssa's *Contra Eunomium* detail the argument,

the Syrian Ephraem, and many others: God is beyond definition. God cannot be contained. You cannot apply number to God and add up Father, Son, and Spirit to make three. God is one and indivisible, yet mysteriously Trinity. Trinitarianism won because of the argument that whereas we know something of God's "energies" or "activities," the divine essence is in principle infinite, therefore indefinable, uncontainable, unknowable, incomprehensible.[6] To speak of God as Trinity in this context was to refuse to define God's being and adopt the stance of proper creaturely humility and awe before the mystery of the divine.

At the same time, it is to affirm the doctrine of the essential Trinity, by contrast with the economic trinitarianism earlier attributed to Irenaeus and Lesslie Newbigin. It may be thought that the essential Trinity does not have much to do with mission and evangelism, being speculative dogma of interest only to abstract theologians. But at its heart this doctrine is really about an appropriate recognition of our creatureliness, about the quality of proper humility before the divine mystery. We should not presume to think that we know the whole truth. There is a proper place for a certain degree of agnosticism in the face of pluralism.

The mystery of the Trinity lies at the root of Eastern liturgies, liturgies which are still followed today in Eastern Orthodox communities but have their roots in the period of which I have spoken. I would like to suggest that Western theism is far more vulnerable to damaging critique than this trinitarian concept of God. Pure monotheism, expressed in the terms of philosophical theism, has encouraged Deism, turning God into the clever watchmaker

---

which was begun by his brother, Basil of Caesarea. These two, together with Gregory of Nazianzus, are the Cappadocians. For Gregory of Nyssa the journeys of Abraham (*Contra Eunomium* 2.84ff.) and Moses (cf. *The Life of Moses*) represented the willingness to set off into the unknown, raising one's conception as far as possible above the common bounds of nature, walking by faith and not sight. John Chrysostom preached a series of sermons, *On God's Incomprehensibility*, essentially against Eunomius, but also displaying the spiritual dimensions of the argument. Likewise, the many Syriac hymns and verse homilies of Ephraem include collections entitled *On Faith* and *Against Heresies* which emphasize the necessity of humility, given the way in which God is mediated through language and not known directly.

6. Gregory of Nazianzus, known as the theologian in the Eastern churches, preached *Five Theological Orations* that have become the standard of Orthodoxy. Here one finds a clear distinction between *theologia* and *oikonomia*, that is, between God as considered in terms of the divine essence and God as considered in relation to the world. The world is pervaded by God's *energeiai* — providential activities, revelation, incarnation, sanctification, etc., all of which are encompassed in God's *oikonomia*, which may therefore be known in some measure. But the subject matter of *theologia* is beyond human conception or speech, and only heretical busybodies attempt to speculate.

who simply set things going at the start, and also tends to create a God conceived by analogy with a monarch writ large — the superman (male, of
course!) or supertyrant, omnipotent, omniscient, omnipresent. Either of
these concepts of God is easily attacked. That the world fails to manifest the
qualities that would be expected if an all-powerful yet loving Creator were responsible for everything has not surprisingly attracted the full blast of modern atheism's arsenal of arguments. We could do with learning something of
the mystery of God's otherness which is celebrated in Eastern liturgies and
has a profoundly trinitarian basis. The critique of idolatry and a doctrine ensuring God's essential otherness are vital for the survival of theology. Mission
in the aftermath of atheism cannot do without the richer concept of God that
the Trinity affords.

God and the World: The Need for Theological Balance

Trinitarianism emerged as the Christian way of expressing God's being *in* the
world (immanent) but at the same time not *of* the world (transcendent). Both
these theological poles are essential; however paradoxical it may be, whatever
tensions are created, a proper balance between the two is fundamental. Let us
remind ourselves first of their significance for the doctrine of the Trinity.

Christology first grew roots in the compost of ideas drawn from antiquity's understanding of the world (we might call it ancient science). The
Greek word *logos* referred to the rationality behind what was spoken as well as
to the word itself. It was more or less synonymous with wisdom, with the
mind and reason, and in some philosophies it was used for the divine principle of order pervading the universe. The universe was susceptible to rational
inquiry precisely because it was constituted on rational principles, such as
mathematics, which could be recognized by the reason implanted in human
beings. In some Jewish texts, like the *Wisdom of Solomon*,[7] the divine wisdom
immanent in creation is vividly depicted in phrases that others (e.g., the
Stoics) used of this all-pervasive divine *logos*. This wisdom or *logos* both lay at
the heart of everything and was particularly evident among the sages of every
culture, among philosophers and prophets, and in their recorded words. For
Christians this cosmic Logos was embodied in Jesus Christ. The preexistent
Christ was God's own Logos, the divine Mind or Word, spoken out, as it were,

---

7. This book was written in Greek, probably a little before the time of the New Testament, and appears in the so-called Apocrypha (the intertestamental books printed in some
Bibles). See especially Wis. 7.

in the acts of creation and revelation. The one divine was both transcendent and immanent.

After the second century resolving the paradoxes of such a Christology would become a key doctrinal issue, but not yet. As we have seen, the apologists of the second century focused on the one God, and if any doctrine was controversial at that stage it was the doctrine of creation.[8] Like the writers of the New Testament, especially Paul and the author of John's Gospel, they saw no conflict between commitment to one God, the source and Lord of the universe, and to one Lord Jesus Christ who revealed God and the divine will for humanity. Logos theology was at first an entirely satisfactory expression of these convictions. It was the intentions in the mind of the one God which were genuinely expressed in the cosmic Logos and embodied in Christ.

At this stage the divine Spirit was identified as the inspirer of prophets and the sanctifying agent in the lives of Christians and the liturgies of the church. The Spirit was God's power at work in the world, and it would be much later before the truly divine individuality of the Spirit would be established. Trinitarianism was implicit rather than explicit. Yet both Logos and Spirit were genuinely of the one God, expressions of the immanent activities of the transcendent God within the world.

Subsequent debate would struggle with appropriate ways of spelling this out. But the important point is the balance between God's transcendence and God's immanence, between the presence of God in the world and that otherness of God that I emphasized earlier — God's hiddenness, the virtual absence of God from the world. This divine complexity finds balanced expression in the doctrine of the Trinity.

Fourth-century theologians, like the Cappadocian Gregory of Nyssa, would speak of trinitarianism providing a mean between monotheism and polytheism.[9] Why would one need such a mean? To answer that question requires a consideration of the theological difficulties of each stance. I have spoken already of the dangers of monotheism as they have become evident in the West. For Easterners, as we have seen, the problems focused on oversimplicity: if God is as it were a single, simple point, then God is easily definable and easily encompassed by a mind, even that of a creature. But they were also

---

8. I have argued elsewhere that it was in the second century, in the face of Platonism and Gnosticism, that the doctrine of creation "out of nothing" was fully articulated. See "*Creatio ex nihilo:* A Context for the Emergence of the Christian Doctrine of Creation," *Scottish Journal of Theology* 44 (1991): 139-51.

9. Gregory's *Great Catechism* sees heresy as slipping too far in the direction of either pagan polytheism or Jewish monotheism, and urges the need to establish the proper mean between them.

aware of the virtual inevitability of monism: everything too easily becomes God, and there is no distinction between Creator and creature. And that encourages pantheism, nature religion, and eventually falls into the same mire as polytheism, pagan idolatry which betrays an inability to distinguish between the divine and the creaturely. It was vital to recognize the contingency of creation. And the only way to do that was to hold the mean between polytheism and monotheism by affirming a trinitarianism that holds the balance between immanence and transcendence, absence and presence.

I suspect that we have a lot to learn from this in our engagement with the skepticism of the West. We cannot tackle postmodern Western culture by trying to resurrect a simplistic Father figure of a God who clearly failed to create a perfect world. Simone Weil[10] spoke of creation as an act of abandonment; only if the infinite God withdrew could there be space for anything to exist other than the divine. So, she suggested, the forsakenness of the cross is anticipated in that act of creative withdrawal. Paradoxically God is absent from the world yet present in the crucified Jesus. Somehow the core Christian story of atonement must inform every other doctrine. We need a God who is not contained but who somehow contains, holding things in loving embrace, never letting go, shouldering the heavy burden imposed by God's own creative act of withdrawal.

Christian history has demonstrated, I would suggest, that subtle balances constantly have to be struck in theology, keeping poles in play which seem in tension — even contradictory: Faith and works. Christ as human and divine. God as one and three. Does this mean that we should affirm, as Tertullian notoriously did, that we believe because it's absurd? Not quite, I suggest. Rather we struggle to express truths that transcend our minds and stretch our language. We admit our limitations, not in an anti-intellectual spirit, for as the church fathers would have affirmed, the *logos* or reason of the human mind images the *Logos* of the divine mind. But it is a created image or reflection, and as creaturely far from capable of encompassing the infinite divine. I suspect we need to recapture something of this theological humility as we face our pluralist world.

We also need to find a further delicate balance: between respect for others in a world of many faiths and conviction that ultimately there is one universe created by one God to which we all belong. The Fathers affirmed that in Christ God accommodated the divine self as far as possible to the human

---

10. Cf. my use of quotations from Simone Weil in *Can These Dry Bones Live?* (London: SCM Press, 1982, 1992), pp. 57-58. The quotations were drawn from *Gateway to God,* a selection from Simone Weil's writings edited by David Raper (London: Fontana, 1974).

condition: Ephraem[11] the Syrian poet depicts this rather tellingly in terms of someone trying to teach a parrot to speak and holding a mirror in front of his face so that the parrot would imagine it was conversing with one of its own kind. As the parrot barely has an inkling of human language and its meaning, so we are hardly capable of receiving God's attempted communication, let alone know the truth behind it. We may have proper confidence in what is revealed in Christ only as long as we recognize that inevitably God's truth is but dimly and inadequately grasped. We need to recognize with humility that we do not have a God's-eye view. That must mean admitting a kind of practical relativism. Yet we affirm one God who created one universe. Ultimately truth is not relative but universal. It's our knowledge of what is universal which is relatively limited. That balanced perspective is essential.

Conclusion

In Lesslie Newbigin's writings, appeal to the dogma of the Trinity has a christological focus: all the emphasis is on the fact of the incarnation.

In the light of discussion here, I would want to shift the emphasis in two ways: in the first place, so as to draw attention more firmly to God as Creator while holding in balance the paradoxical reality that, on the one hand, God is present and always ahead of us and, on the other, God is ever withdrawn, hidden, inaccessible, transcendent, and other; and secondly, so as to replace the emphasis on fact and dogma with a sense of vision, of invitation, of opening up to fresh possibilities. Should we not give an account of the *hope* that is in us, forgetting what is behind and straining toward what is ahead (Phil. 3:13)? It was from the latter Pauline phrase that the Greek Fathers developed the notion of *epektasis*, a kind of stretching of mind and heart that reaches ever onward in the desire to know and love the God that is beyond our understanding. That is the way to let God be God.

And after all, as Newbigin insisted, the goal of mission is God's glory. *Non nobis, domine, non nobis. . . .*[12]

---

11. *On faith* 31.6-7.
12. "Not unto us, O Lord, not unto us but to your name be the glory . . ." (Ps. 115:1).

SECTION 3

ENLIGHTENMENT, POSTMODERNITY, AND MISSION

The Church in the Postmodern Transition

George R. Hunsberger

I do not claim to be a scholar of postmodernism. But it is impossible to work at the missiological task of the church in the latter part of the twentieth century without engaging the visions and sensibilities of what is variously called postmodernity, the postmodern condition, or the postmodern transition. While Bishop Newbigin did not often speak directly of postmodernism or postmodernity, his last great project to invite a missionary encounter of the gospel with modern Western culture stood upon the ground of the emerging postmodern critique of the most fundamental confidences of the modern age. The perspective of cross-cultural missionary experience that he brought to the encounter only strengthened the postmodern texture of his vision.

What I do understand about postmodernity has been helped along by numerous colleagues who themselves have studied its philosophical assumptions and social characteristics at some depth. Many of these are colleagues in the Gospel and Our Culture Network in North America with whom I have worked to fashion a vision for the church in a post-Christendom as well as postmodern world. For many of us the encounter of the gospel with Western culture precipitates the question of the church as a central challenge, even in North America where churches seem to be doing so well. Whatever surface successes remain, the truth is that beneath that surface lies a severe crisis of meaning and identity. There is a churning quest for a rationale for being church, and a hunger for the experience of being the kind of church for which there is a compelling reason.

The themes of postmodern transition and ecclesial identity come together in a newly emerging movement among younger "Generation X" pastors and church leaders in the USA and Canada. This generation knows itself to be a generation formed within the postmodern condition, or as they prefer to call it, the postmodern transition.[1] They recognize more intuitively than the rest of us that "postmodern" designates a movement away from something and toward something else not yet present or identifiable. This is an on-the-way place for the culture, not an assured ending place. They know this to be liminal time.[2] In the midst of it, they have a keen sense that ministry and evangelism in this time involves a dialogue among church, gospel, and culture, a dialogue unlike any that has gone before. They have not been willing to accept the forms of church inherited from the Christendom- or Enlightenment-shaped world, not even the so-called contemporary or seeker-oriented church of the baby boomers which embodies the values of modernity that are now passing. This rising generation of leaders poses instead some fundamental questions about the nature of community and truth and mission. Their experience of Christian faith within the postmodern transition suggests that a contextual, missional ecclesiology must be at the center of the agenda for us all.

It is in light of these quests for knowing the meaning and vitality of the church that I have chosen to address "the church in the postmodern transition." This means that I am not so much looking at "Enlightenment, Modernity, and Postmodernity" from an historical or analytical point of view. Rather, I am addressing what I take to be a fundamental missiological challenge at the present time in view of that sociocultural heritage. By taking up the issue of an ecclesiology for such a setting, I hope to address some of the who, why, where, and how questions regarding the church's calling to be the sent people of God. I would like to do this by identifying three dynamics which I believe are made crucial for the church in light of the current moment, given what we inherit from the shaping forces of Enlightenment and modernity in the past and what faces us in the emerging postmodern present and future.

---

1. Jimmy Long's book *Generating Hope* (Downers Grove, Ill.: InterVarsity, 1997) shows the correspondence between the literature on postmodernity and that on so-called Generation X. Bringing the two analyses together forms the basis for his helpful proposals for ministry among a postmodern generation.

2. See Alan J. Roxburgh, *Missionary Congregations, Leadership, and Liminality* (Harrisburg, Pa.: Trinity Press International, 1997), for the use of liminality as a lens for interpreting the current cultural situation.

Truly the Community

I take the phrase from the title of one of Marva Dawn's books.[3] By it I mean to say that somehow the forms of church we have inherited have construed church in a very different way from being a community, and the recovery of being community is fundamental for the church at the present time. The newly arising generation certainly will not tolerate anything less. More than that, it is what we discover in the Scriptures to be the crucial element in the Holy Spirit's presence in the world, to fashion the church as "a body of people sent on a mission" (to borrow a phrase from David Bosch in a 1991 lecture series).

Such a vision has been thwarted and muted under other conceptions of church which have shaped how we do things. The subtle notion that the church is "a place where certain things happen" has held increasing sway since the time of the Reformation. In the American context this has persisted, but under forces peculiar to the USA this shaping notion has taken an additional turn, an economic one. Essentially, two hundred years of history have seen the churches shaped more and more around a conception of what a church is that is shared by people in churches as well as outside them: the church is "a vendor of religious services and goods."[4] The grammar of everyday conversation illustrates how deeply this is ingrained. In a recent newspaper article about one church's decision regarding its historic facility and a proposed rebuilding project, there is an example: "For others associated with Graafschap Christian Reformed Church, a church must pay the price to keep up with the times and better serve its congregation." Something called "church" has the function of serving something called "its congregation." In this vendor model, members of the congregation are reduced to consumers of services, staff and leaders are the production managers and sales force, the goal becomes member (a.k.a. customer) recruitment, and the gospel becomes a commodity needing to be appropriately packaged and marketed. The rela-

---

3. Marva J. Dawn, *Truly the Community: Romans 12 and How to Be the Church* (Grand Rapids: Eerdmans, 1992). The original title, *The Hilarity of Community: Romans 12 and How to Be the Church*, was changed to the current title in 1997.

4. For a more complete survey of the way this has emerged and the consequences of it, see George R. Hunsberger, "Sizing Up the Shape of the Church," in *The Church between Gospel and Culture*, ed. George R. Hunsberger and Craig Van Gelder (Grand Rapids: Eerdmans, 1996), pp. 333-46, and Darrell L. Guder, ed., *Missional Church: A Vision for the Sending of the Church in North America* (Grand Rapids: Eerdmans, 1998), especially chap. 4. See also Philip D. Kenneson and James L. Street, *Selling Out the Church: The Dangers of Church Marketing* (Nashville: Abingdon, 1997).

tionship between a church and its members is shaped around a pattern of vendor-consumer, provider-client relationships.

Here, I believe, is where we have inherited some of the harshest consequences of the Enlightenment. Critics of post-Enlightenment modernity, including Newbigin, have noted many of its features that beg for the gospel's missionary encounter: its confidence in autonomous human reason, its belief in the individual as the unit of identity and survival, its dichotomy between public facts and private opinions, and its reliance on effect and progress as the validation of what is right and true. But in modernity it is also the case that the rationalization of social systems and the process of routinization within social institutions have had a profound effect on the forms of church we inherit, and this needs as radical an engagement. Recent sociological interpretation of the history of churches in America suggests that the same rational choice theory which explains economics explains also the experience of churches.[5] As has been the case in other arenas as well, the economic part of life has come to define a whole range of institutions and organizations, not merely the commercial ones. The church is among them.

So the question is, What is the church? Is it an entity that exists for its members, to nurture their faith and give opportunities for their service? Or is it the members themselves who exist for the purposes God has in mind for them? Between the two views there lies a deep gulf. At present it is the first that defines the church and sets in motion its patterns of language and practice. But the church's birthright, possessed by all the people of God, is that it is a divinely called and sent community.

Several aspects of a reemerging vision for being truly the community have begun to take shape.[6] First, to be community means to possess a collective discipleship. The normal habit of speech, teaching, preaching, and even group Bible discussion is to emphasize the way biblical texts challenge and nourish growth in each individual's relationship with God and response to the gospel. In contrast to this the church is called into being to be a discerning community which receives the scriptural text as addressed to it corporately, which seeks the mind of the Spirit for its corporate calling and mission, which moves as one body in its expression of the gospel. The church is not a mere collectivity of individual disciples but together is a follower of Christ, in

---

5. For a defense of this line of interpretation, see Roger Finke and Rodney Stark, *The Churching of America, 1776-1990: Winners and Losers in Our Religious Economy* (New Brunswick, N.J.: Rutgers University Press, 1992).

6. The following three aspects of community, along with several others, are more fully developed in George R. Hunsberger, "Features of the Missional Church: Some Directions and Pathways," *Reformed Review* 52, no. 1 (autumn 1998): 5-13.

whose calling each one participates. The individual is not lost, but rather found, in its bondedness within the community.

Second, to be community means to gather for worship together. As a friend of mine has put it, worship has become a substitute for the church. Worship is something one goes to, something provided by professional staff. To be community again will invert this pattern. The church is the community. Worship is something that community does.

This makes a difference in the character of worship. It has the quality of being gathered up out of the collective praise and adoration and confession and pleading and hearing and responding of the community. This will mean, of course, a shift from professional planning and production toward worship that is the fruit of the work *(leitourgia)* of the laity to give expression to their praise. Persons of the community gifted for the kind of leadership that sees, values, empowers, and puts to voice the praise of the whole people will guide the shape and expression of the worship moments in the community's life.

Third, to be community means to remain community while scattered. The question, Where is your church? requires a better answer than the geographic location of the facility. Where are the people who are that community? Where are they working, living, playing? Essential to a notion of community is a new recognition that the missional placement of a congregation lies precisely within the workplaces and multiple social worlds the people inhabit day to day. And with that comes a new appreciation that when separated to all those daily worlds, the community is still a community, bound the same way to each other and responsible together to be a community that gives expression to the gospel. The church that is truly the community will be one in which there is a seamless harmony between its gathered moments and its scattered ones.

It is obvious that the portrait of community given here requires a serious and sustained critique of clericalism and a reversal of its manifestations in the life of churches that are now essentially "owned" by the clergy. Bishop Newbigin himself flagged this issue as one of the most crucial for the church living beyond Christendom, but this has tended to be missed by most of his readers.[7] New images and practices of leadership will have to emerge in which leaders find the formation and discipling of the community to be the first priority. What is needed is leadership that is an extension of the community, not a displacement of it.

---

7. Lesslie Newbigin, *Foolishness to the Greeks: The Gospel and Western Culture* (London: SPCK; Grand Rapids: Eerdmans; and Geneva: WCC, 1986), pp. 141ff.

Community of the True

If this rising generation is one hungry for connection, as so many have observed, it is also eager to find meaning. The acid test for people who claim to offer it is authenticity. It is not enough for the church merely to be community for people, hungry as they may be for even the most minimal sort of human connection. As David Lowes Watson has observed, the intimacy experienced in the small-group movement has the potential to be a mere "spiritual amphetamine," producing an immediate high but offering no sustaining life.[8] His own efforts to cultivate Covenant Discipleship Groups on the pattern of John Wesley's class meetings strike the necessary chord: "Christian Formation through Mutual Accountability."[9] The challenge is to be a community that bears the shape of the gospel, that is molded by the Spirit to represent distinctly the regime of God. The vision is to be genuinely Christian community.

I express that with the language of truth, but prefer to speak of being a community of the "true," a community that is "true to the truth." To say it this way is to stress that it is not a matter of holding the truth as a body of ideas, espoused, affirmed, and defended. But it is to embody a pattern of thoughts, language, and practices that is true to the truth that is Jesus the Christ.

I am using the term "true" here in the same sense that a carpenter might use it about the wall of a building when measured against a plumb line to determine whether it is vertically true. To say that a wall is vertical does not mean that the wall is the standard for being vertical. Rather it means that it corresponds to that standard which its builder has intended it to reflect.

There are distinct ecclesiological and missiological reasons for speaking in this way. It is a more modest way of understanding Christian identity to recognize that truth can never be so fully and rightly grasped that what is expressed is that truth. Not only the spirit of the postmodern age but the spirit of the cross-cultural missionary warn us to be humble about it. But having said that, it is still inescapable that Christian faith understands there to be truth, however inadequate is our way of comprehending it. Christians do believe (to use a phrase from the television program *The X-Files*) that "the truth is out there." That is, much as we must come to agree with the postmodern critique of modernity's confidence in reason, and the postmodern assertion that there is no one rationally defensible version of the truth and that all our

8. David Lowes Watson, *God Does Not Foreclose: The Universal Promise of Salvation* (Nashville: Abingdon, 1990), pp. 30-31.
9. David Lowes Watson, *Covenant Discipleship: Christian Formation through Mutual Accountability* (Nashville: Discipleship Resources, 1991).

claims to know it and efforts to state it are particular and provisional, nevertheless it is inherent to Christian faith that something is believed with "universal intent" and believed to have correspondence to some truth that actually is so.

This ultimate conviction of Christians is rooted in the incarnation. Wherever else *The X-Files'* search may take agents Mulder and Scully — investigating extraterrestrials, examining the paranormal, etc. — Christian faith is birthed by the presence among us at one time and place of one who embodied in himself the "truth that is out there." It is embodied and imbedded "in here" within the path of normal experience in an incarnation of the truth. He was the incarnation of the divine person. He said of himself, I am the truth.

The church knows that it does not embody the truth in the same way that Jesus is the truth. So while we do not claim for our creeds and actions that they are the truth, yet by embodying what is true to that truth, in all the particularity inherent in our doing so, we do claim that they correspond to the truth, which is the person Jesus. On that basis and against that standard, our creeds and actions are open to testing by all who observe and listen.

The recovery of the church's identity as community of the true rests on three perspectives about truth. First, truth is personal. If Jesus embodied it in his incarnation, truth is personal because he is that truth. In relationship and the revealing of a person to another it is known. Here is drawn into the picture the personal dimension of knowing which Michael Polanyi depicted and which Newbigin affirmed so often, owing in no small measure to the influence of John Oman in his theologically formative years. Oman had stressed the personhood of God, and Newbigin found that to provide a bedrock perspective for all his subsequent work.

Under the Enlightenment the West experienced a profound liberation of human reason. To speak of revelation does not deny the fruit the Enlightenment has produced nor that human reason is a source of the knowledge of truth. But it is to say that knowledge from human reason is always partial, and more than that, it is vulnerable to the bias and design of the interpreting human person or community. The postmodern hermeneutic of suspicion, which suspects all claims to knowing truth as expressions of a will to power, plays into this picture of things as a warning against confidence in the promise of human rationality.

Truth, if personal, is known in the relationship of persons. Here Newbigin's phrase about the revealing of God which comes to us in the form of Scriptures captures something important: the Bible is "that body of literature which — primarily but not only in narrative form — renders accessible to us the character and actions and purposes of God."[10] God as personal can and does act and choose the time and place of those actions, and those actions are that by which and in which God's character and purposes become known to other persons. In the end we are reminded that truth is then not some static, objective thing existing independently somewhere, but it is wrapped up in a willing, acting divine person.

Second, truth is perspectival. This is different from acknowledging that our knowing is always partial, or tainted. It surely is both. But to say that truth is perspectival is to affirm that it is inherent in the circumstances of life, created as they are by the one who is the truth, that human existence is by nature particular, contextual, and relational, and all knowing is relative to the language and culture creations that human societies establish, adapt, and transmit. Perhaps the point Newbigin made in *Foolishness to the Greeks* puts it most emphatically: "Neither at the beginning, nor at any subsequent time, is there or can there be a gospel that is not embodied in a culturally conditioned form of words. The idea that one can or could at any time separate out by some process of distillation a pure gospel unadulterated by any cultural accretions is an illusion."[11]

Here it is the vantage point of those who have experienced the missionary encounters of the gospel with the world of diverse human cultures that has companionship with postmodern sensibilities. Claims to truth beyond the particularities that shape all human life are relativized in both views. But in neither is there a necessary absolute relativity (which would be a contradiction in terms, at any rate). Rather, the relativity of knowing forces a communal and dialogical approach to all truth seeking. For the church as community of the true, that means at least two things: being true happens in mutual accountability between communities of the true, and being true happens in the conversation with persons beyond the Christian community at the frontiers where Jesus as the truth is becoming known.

Third, truth is practiced. To objectify truth is to distance oneself or one's community from personal responsibility. Truth not lived, meaning that it is not believed with the will, can hardly claim to be truth. Philip Kenneson makes this point well in his essay entitled "There's No Such Thing as Objective Truth, and It's a Good Thing, Too!"[12] The church's vision of truth must

10. Newbigin, *Foolishness to the Greeks*, p. 59.
11. Newbigin, *Foolishness to the Greeks*, p. 4.
12. Philip D. Kenneson, "There's No Such Thing as Objective Truth, and It's a Good Thing, Too!" in *Christian Apologetics in the Postmodern World*, ed. Timothy R. Phillips and Dennis Okholm (Downers Grove, Ill.: InterVarsity, 1995).

mean that the verbs "believe" and "obey" become synonyms once again, as they were for the writer to the Hebrews and for Jesus himself. Only a practiced truth bears the stamp of authenticity and livability. In the postmodern transition, people do not look for better (objective!) arguments about God's presence or purposes, but they look for demonstrations of it being lived in terms of contemporary life.

In Missional Relationship

The church is not merely a community, nor is it enough for it to be a distinctly Christian community whose life and character increasingly correspond to the truth. It is a sent community. Its very presence as a distinct community is part of that for which it is sent, so even its attentiveness to being truly the community and the community of the true begins to fulfill its missional character. But it is called and sent to be present within the flow of the world's life, and in its life, deeds, and words to represent there the regime of the goodness of God.

Newbigin's conception of mission and of the church as missionary by nature takes on graphic form in his phrase "the congregation as the hermeneutic of the gospel."[13] Here he illustrates that the church is not merely an agency of volunteers for certain tasks of mission. Rather, its very being is the lens through which people view and comprehend the gospel. For the church, this raises the importance of the challenges of community and truth already mentioned. And it means for any particular church that the ongoing dialogue between the gospel and the culture of which it is a part goes on most deeply and sharply precisely within that church. This inward dialogue between the gospel and the community's culture, Newbigin would frequently say, is logically prior to the outward one in which the church is engaged with its world.

But outward it does and must become, and apart from that its own inward dialogue will be impossible. The church which is the fruit of the conversion encounter of the gospel with its particular culture is made by that encounter to be the demonstration of the life the gospel offers and the conversion it challenges. Out of that wellspring of its transformed life comes its deeds in response to the vision of justice and peace which the gospel announces to be the intention of God for the world. Out of it comes also the clear and joyous announcement of the knowledge of God found in the person

13. Lesslie Newbigin, *The Gospel in a Pluralist Society* (London: SPCK; Grand Rapids: Eerdmans; and Geneva: WCC Publications, 1989), pp. 222-33.

103

of Jesus the Christ. This holistic mission of life, deed, and word comprises the identity — the missional identity — of the church today. The post-Christian age awaits such a visible demonstration, tangible expression, and clear articulation of the gospel.

When talking about the way the church's calling sends it to re-present the reign of God, the eschatological dimension of it cannot be far away. The sent community is in a very real sense a precedent community, one which shows the intrusion of God's future. The missionary and eschatological qualities of the church have always been closely joined in Newbigin's thought. This was in evidence in his early, but still fresh, portrait of the church in *The Household of God*.[14] The church in this precedent sense is the foretaste community, a harbinger of the coming springtime, a herald of what is on the way.

The missionary and eschatological way of the church will need to be re-learned. The long history of Christendom, including the recent phases of it as the functional reality in societies for which the legal forms have ceased, taught us to think in other terms. Now, without props from the social order and without a set role to play as its chaplain, whole new possibilities open up for the reemergence of the Western church's missionary identity.

But there are many potential pitfalls, most of all the multiple forms of the temptation to seize again some way of being for the society its orienting vision, to regain in subtle ways the lost position that so long gave the church large measures of power and privilege. It is here that I question the wisdom or appropriateness of speaking, as Newbigin tended to do in his later years, about the way "the gospel as public truth" might be envisioned to have bearing on the forms of contemporary secular societies. The phrase itself, it seems to me, has several potential points of reference in light of the whole of Newbigin's work. If by "the gospel as public truth" he means that the gospel is fundamentally a news report, an announcement of the public events of God's actions as they have their center in the life, death, and resurrection of Jesus, and if he means to assert that those events are decidedly world news bearing significance for the whole of the world's life and are thus not to be relegated to the religion page, then his assertions must be taken with seriousness regarding the forms of Christian life and community and witness such a news report implicates. Such a report is to be embodied and portrayed in the public life of the Christian community, and testimony to it given in affirmation and critique among the powers of the world. In these respects the phrase is an

---

14. Lesslie Newbigin, *The Household of God* (New York: Friendship, 1954). See chap. 5, "Christ in You, the Hope of Glory," and chap. 6, "Unto All the Nations."

important one, and one which has continuity with major themes throughout Newbigin's writings.

But if he means by it that the Christian vision is to be commended as a proposed basis for the unity and coherence of today's secular society, as the vision which alone is capable of giving the grounds for proper tolerance of all religions and a foundation for relating together the plural peoples of the society, then it seems to me that this moves once again in the direction of a certain kind of Christendom arrangement, albeit in a new form. On those occasions when Newbigin in fact made just this sort of move (and I can think of three such occasions in the USA in the 1990s when I myself was present), there were fundamental questions not answered. On what basis might, or could, the Christian vision be embraced or adopted by today's secular, pluralist Western societies? For a variety of reasons, Christians might want that or seek it, and might believe that it would be in the best interest of the society to do so. But why, on its principles, would or could the society choose to take the Christian vision as the basis for its unity and coherence? Unless, of course, it came to be converted to Christ, who is the center of the vision, in vast numbers!

To imagine that is to show the problem with the proposal. It suggests that a society might embrace the Christian vision as its basis quite apart from adherence to and allegiance toward Jesus the Christ. To imagine such a thing would be nonsensical, from the point of view of today's Western societies as well as that of the Christian faith. This, it seems to me, was precisely the problem with Christendom in the end, that finally the society had the shell of the Christian faith's perspective and ethos while no longer holding its essential faith. To use Max Weber's image, the gate to the iron cage was then flung open and has been ripped from its hinges. There's no putting it back. The captives are loose, and they won't be coming back to rebuild the cage.

For the church to return in spirit or form to a kind of relationship with the wider society that is rooted in the memory or remnants of Christendom will be to forfeit the next stage of its calling. A missional relationship implies life as a "parallel" community.[15] Such a community is not allergic to being a community of affinity with its surrounding communities, sharing common aspirations and quests as a people. Neither is it allergic to being a community of distinction from its surrounding communities, marching to the beat of a

---

15. This phrase was suggested by Mary Jo Leddy at a conference of the Gospel and Our Culture Network in North America in March 1996. The papers of the conference, including the one presented by Leddy, are published in *Confident Witness — Changing World*, ed. Craig Van Gelder (Grand Rapids: Eerdmans, 1999).

drummer who sometimes says dance when there is despair, sometimes says mourn when there is glee, and sometimes says refuse when all others move toward the destruction of life and hope.

Conclusion

In this postmodern transition, I have suggested, these three features will be required of the church: that it be truly the community, that it be a community of the true, and that it live in missional relationship with the world where it lives. The Spirit, I believe, moves us to such a journey and goes with us on the Way.

Churches and Postmodernity:
Opportunity for an Attitude Shift

Lynne Price

Before responding to some of the important issues George Hunsberger has raised for our consideration, I would like to tell you about some of the participants driving to the colloquium. They had an hour or two to spare and decided to take the countryside route but found themselves lost in a web of lanes, going round in circles. Being theologians, accustomed to hermeneutical circles, they didn't panic but kept driving around. At last they came across a farmer and asked him the way to Birmingham. The farmer paused, then answered, "I wouldn't start from here if I were you!"

The purpose of this story is to introduce at the outset my reservations about Lesslie Newbigin's approach to contemporary mission, especially in his writings from the publication of *The Other Side of 1984* onward. Newbigin's negative, adversarial appraisal of Enlightenment rationality and its alleged responsibility for the failure of Christian mission in Western culture;[1] his dogged attempts to extract a unified theology from the Bible;[2] his related defense

---

1. It is instructive that in his preliminary draft of *The Other Side of 1984* Newbigin omitted any positive appraisal of the Enlightenment. In the published edition three paragraphs have been added acknowledging its role in removing "barriers to freedom of conscience and intellectual enquiry," "against the resistence of the churches," ending "much cruelty, oppression and ignorance" (pp. 15-16). Rather important afterthoughts, one might consider, in an analysis of the role of reason in culture.

2. Hunsberger writes in "The Missionary Significance of the Biblical Doctrine of Election as a Foundation for a Theology of Cultural Plurality in the Missiology of Lesslie Newbigin" (Ph.D. diss., Princeton Theological Seminary, 1987), "In all of his ad hoc, biblical theology, Newbigin shows the capacity to maintain cogency and coherence. He works to establish a unified view of things" (p. 64).

of dogma as truth, something given which must be assented to;[3] and his insistence on "the gospel as public truth" in societies which are religiously and culturally diverse[4] are the areas where I consider his writing particularly problematic. It is here in this cluster that I find myself going round and round the web of lanes, locked inside a tightly controlled, white, Western-conceptual, male-dominated, authoritarian church compound with little traffic between it and the continuing life of the world. We can indeed be tempted, as George Hunsberger has elsewhere noted that others have been, "to see in Newbigin's proposals an accommodation either to a residual Christendom model or to a ghettoized sectarianism."[5]

This critical course is not undertaken lightly, nor without due regard for Lesslie Newbigin's considerable achievements as an ecumenical statesman in India, with the IMC and the WCC, which are well known and will no doubt be given proper attention by other speakers. However, he himself has described his experience at the local congregational level at the beginning of his career in India as that of an "old-fashioned district missionary" under the British Raj, "monarch of all I surveyed and telling everybody else what to do." From 1980 to 1988 he was minister of a small URC church in Winson Green, an urban priority, ethnically diverse area of Birmingham, where, he remarked in an address given in 1985, he was "beginning to learn what he ought to have learned at the beginning." He described "a very, very loyal congregation of white, aging people . . . trying to minister to a local area where it is not just thistles and tin cans but is mostly Hindus, Muslims and Sikhs."[6] I find these comments by Newbigin very telling and very disturbing.

It is partly because of a different set of experiences — as a laywoman, a qualified social worker who has always lived in Britain, a Methodist who has worked with Roman Catholics at the grassroots level and with people of other faiths in this wonderfully diverse city, who has enjoyed the benefit and challenge of the insights of colleagues from all over the world — that I would not

---

3. See particularly *The Gospel in a Pluralist Society* (London: SPCK; Grand Rapids: Eerdmans; and Geneva: WCC Publications, 1989).

4. See particularly *Truth to Tell: The Gospel as Public Truth* (Grand Rapids: Eerdmans; Geneva: WCC Publications; and London: SPCK, 1991).

5. Hunsberger, "The Newbigin Gauntlet: Developing a Domestic Missiology for North America," in *Church between Gospel and Culture*, ed. George R. Hunsberger and Craig Van Gelder (Grand Rapids and Cambridge, U.K.: Eerdmans, 1996), p. 12.

6. Newbigin Papers, SOC, Box 10. Doc. "Does Society Still Need the Parish Church?" (typescript of taped address given by Lesslie Newbigin on 5 November 1985 at the Centre for Exploration in Social Concern).

choose to start from where Newbigin left us.[7] It is partly as a missiologist of a different generation, who has learned much from more recent theological approaches to Christian life and witness — black, Asian, interfaith, process, liberation, and feminist — which actively seek to relate faith to the realities of life and are not afraid to engage in dialogue with "outsiders" to help reassess thinking and action.

Responding to George Hunsberger's paper, I consequently want to affirm his move toward a "more modest way of understanding Christian identity" which recognizes that truth can never be fully expressed, but suggest it does not go far enough, indeed cannot go far enough while bound to Newbigin's one-sided assessment of contemporary society and the theological and ecclesial package he sets over and against it.[8] Once it has been acknowledged, as George Hunsberger has done, that truth is embodied in a person and can only be known by personal knowing, that truth is perspectival (and I think that does make it partial), and that truth is something which is lived, not an objective argument, then there are so many difficulties about claiming the church as the "community of the true" that we would do better to drop it.

An Attitude Shift

I propose we make an attitude shift and aim for honesty and integrity instead. This demands a radical move away from confusing an idealistic picture of Christian community with the reality and toward a more reciprocal, dialogical relationship with the life of the world. The reality is that Christian discipleship, individually or in community, is a pilgrimage journey toward loving God with hearts, souls, strength, and mind, our neighbors and ourselves, full of failures as well as successes, dark nights as well as bright mornings. The reality is that Christianity is diverse — Christians hold different beliefs; interpret various parts of the Bible differently; give different interpretations and weight to affective, intuitive, and conceptual experiences; worship in different ways. Christians kill each other, kill others, are pacifists,

7. On the interfaith work in Birmingham, see Lynne Price, "Inside Out," *Mission Outlook* (Quarterly Review of the Pontifical Missionary Union) (autumn 1993): 12-14. "Who Is the Stranger?" *Connect* (April 1993): 10; "Step on the Way: The NEXUS Initiative of the British Province," *SVD Word in the World* (1993/94): 159-60. Also Lynne Price, *Interfaith Encounter and Dialogue: A Methodist Pilgrimage* (Frankfurt am Main: Peter Lang, 1991).

8. For a further critique of Newbigin, see Werner Ustorf, *Christianized Africa — De-Christianized Europe?* (Seoul: Tyrannus, 1992), chap. 8, "A Partisan's View: L. Newbigin's Criticism of Western Culture."

support or oppose forms of fascism or communism, support the IMF, criticize the policies of the IMF, and so on.

Aiming for honesty and integrity demands a radical attitude shift to a dialogical engagement within and outside the churches, in which practice and reflection are open to modification. "Faithful uncertainty" is the term I use to describe an appropriate Christian attitude, and have elsewhere used the life and work of the late British evangelist and pioneer in relating psychology, religion, and healing, Rev. Dr. Leslie D. Weatherhead, to demonstrate that this is a workable model for today. To Weatherhead, accepting the gift of the transforming friendship of Jesus meant faithful engagement in the complexities of life without having answers to all the questions about God, the universe, and everything. He recognized that the implications were subjectivity, inconsistency, plurality, networking across boundaries, and the questioning of "orthodox" belief. He advocated for all Christians, not just leaders, constant revision of thinking and action in the light of new experience of God and new information about the world.[9]

An Attitude Shift within the Churches

Within the churches it is particularly important that when we white Westerners address our own context, we do so remembering that we are part of the world church and of racially and culturally plural societies. There are more non-Western Christians than Western Christians in the world today, and they will increasingly shape the theological discourse of the future.[10] Pentecostalism with its black, oral, and catholic roots and in all its current manifold forms (classical, African-initiated churches, the charismatic movement, and so on) is the fastest-growing branch of Christianity.[11] White,

9. Lynne Price, *Faithful Uncertainty: Leslie D. Weatherhead's Methodology of Creative Evangelism* (Frankfurt am Main: Peter Lang, 1996).

10. See, for example, Andrew Walls, "Christianity in the Non-Western World: A Study in the Serial Nature of Christian Expansion," in *Studies in World Christianity*, vol. 1.1 (1995): "Perhaps the most striking single feature of Christianity today is the fact that the Church now looks more like that great multitude whom none can number, drawn from all tribes and kindreds, people and tongues, than ever before in its history. Its diversity and history lead to a great variety of starting points for its theology and reflects varied bodies of experience. The study of Christian history and theology will increasingly need to operate from the position where most Christians are; and that will increasingly be the continents of Africa, Asia, Latin America and the Pacific" (p. 24).

11. Walter Hollenweger, *Pentecostalism: Origins and Developments Worldwide* (Pea-

Western, mainstream Christianity can no longer maintain that it is normative for all Christians, and we are moving slowly, if reluctantly, beyond cross-
cultural mission to inter- and intracultural mission, that is, to the place
where we recognize, in practice and reflection, that we all need each other
for mutual enrichment and correction.[12] George Hunsberger, commenting
that Newbigin did not often speak of postmodernity, has made an important
point. Newbigin's approach to biblical authority, interpreted by some as
precritical fundamentalism;[13] his attitude to syncretism;[14] and his resistance

---

body, Mass.: Hendrickson, 1997), esp. chaps. 3 and 12. Newbigin is often credited with being
among the first to recognize the significance of Pentecostalism in his 1952 Kerr Lectures,
published in 1953 by SCM Press as *The Household of God: Lectures on the Nature of the
Church* (chap. 6). However, Martin Robinson writes, "At this particular time, Newbigin was
unaware of the existence of Pentecostal churches and he was not referring to the Pentecostal
denominations so much as a deeper stream within the history of the church" (*To Win the
West* [Crowborough: Monarch, 1996], p. 149).

12. On intercultural theology, see Walter Hollenweger, for example, *Erfahrungen der
Leibhaftigkeit: Interkulturelle Theologie* (Munich: Chr. Kaiser Verlag, 1979); "Intercultural
Theology," *Theology Today* 43, no. 1 (April 1986): 28-35. Having regard for mission history is
also important. Whatever the most recent writings of acknowledged experts like Lamin
Sanneh, with the influence of Newbigin, might say about the positive benefits of some "unin-
tentional and unpremeditated consequences of practice and conduct" of previous missionary activities for colonial peoples (Lamin Sanneh, *Encountering the West: Christianity and the
Global Cultural Process: The African Dimension* [London: Marshall Pickering, 1993], p. 18),
many of those ministering and reflecting in the postcolonial countries today do not share
this somewhat indecent rush to paper over the legacy of dependency, degradation, and, on
occasion, near annihilation. See, for example, Section III, "Facing Some Realities in Africa,
Asia and Latin America," in *Mission Matters*, ed. Lynne Price, Juan Sepúlveda, and Graeme
Smith (Frankfurt am Main: Peter Lang, 1997). See also Ellis, n. 20 below.

13. Newbigin in a letter to Professor Caird, 30.3.83, Newbigin Papers, SOC, Box 5. In
this letter Newbigin asked Prof. Caird for assistance with the question "How does, or should
the Bible function in guiding Christians to make the right decisions in their involvement in
public life?" Newbigin wrote that responses to his paper "The Other Side of 1984" had been
positive from laypeople but more critical from theologians, and that "I have been presumed
to have fallen back into a pre-critical fundamentalism of which I think I am not guilty." He
subsequently extensively rewrote the relevant section for the published edition.

14. Newbigin acknowledged that "there is a sense in which Christianity must always
be syncretistic" but wanted "criteria for responsible judgement" in a letter to Walter
Hollenweger (28.12.94) in response to the latter's contribution, "Towards a Pentecostal
Missiology," in *Many Voices in Christian Mission: Essays in Honour of J. E. Lesslie Newbigin,
World Christian Leader*, ed. T. Dayanandan Francis and Israel Selvanayagam (Madras: Chris-
tian Literature Society, 1994). Hollenweger, in part of his reply (25.1.95), wrote, "Responsible
syncretism is not learned by learning a few criteria. It is rather learned like playing the violin.
One goes to the maestro. . . . Our maestros are the biblical authors. They show us standards

to interfaith dialogue against the pressing concerns of his Asian colleagues[15] have strong echoes of the church's resistance to the Enlightenment and of the negative aspects of the colonial missionary period carried over into the postmodern transition.

An Attitude Shift toward Those Outside the Churches

Dialogue with those outside the churches is also vital for helping Christians to discover, or rediscover, what mission, being channels of God's love to the world, involves. For example, awareness of the need to care for the environment which sustains us all was hardly given any attention before other communities and action groups brought it to the fore in recent decades. Natural theology, exploring the immanence of God, which was almost totally ignored in traditional theism with its stress on transcendence, has not had a high profile during the modern period.[16] It has been argued that the church has in practice desacralized the natural world.[17] Instead of constant moaning about

---

and patterns. That is why we learn Greek and Hebrew, the art of exegesis so that we get a glimpse of their craftsmanship, their workmanship, their method on how they transform pagan material so that it becomes transparent for the Kingdom of God." Copies of the letters in the possession of Lynne Price, courtesy of Walter Hollenweger.

15. Newbigin's views on interfaith encounter and dialogue differed substantially from those of many of his Asian colleagues. In his personal report on the fifth WCC assembly at Nairobi in 1975, addressing the debate of the document "Seeking Community: The Common Search of People of Various Faiths, Cultures and Ideologies," in the Newbigin Papers, SOC, he wrote, "there was a well-orchestrated concert of Asian voices protesting against the European timidity which prevented Asians from getting on with the sort of dialogue which was a necessity of life for the Asian churches. In the face of this barrage the Europeans . . . kept quiet and the Report was adopted. It was a most unsatisfactory situation as the real theological issues had not been clarified and the debate had been conducted on the basis of an emotional confrontation between Europe and Asia rather than on a penetrating analysis of the issues." The story continued, as correspondence with Professor Johannes Verkuyl in 1988 reveals, with a concerted effort to influence international ecumenical discussion on interfaith relations along the line taken by Hendrik Kraemer in 1938, through their speaking and writing opportunities. Verkuyl, in response to a question from Newbigin, tried without success to find any younger theologians, Protestant or Catholic, in the Netherlands who could "carry on the torch of Kraemer" (letter dated 29 August 1988). Kraemer's book *The Christian Message in a Non-Christian World* was published for the IMC Tambaram Conference.

16. See, for example, John Macquarrie, *In Search of Deity* (London: SCM Press, XPress Reprints, 1993), chap. 1; first published 1984.

17. See, for example, Sallie McFague, *Models of God: Theology for an Ecological, Nuclear Age* (London: SCM Press, 1987); Anne Primavesi, "The Part for the Whole? An Ecofeminist

the New Age movement, we should be alerted to our own failings and do something about them.

My second example of the need to listen to others cuts even deeper. Marc Ellis, a Jewish writer, in his book *Unholy Alliance,* explores the ongoing reality of atrocity in the history of the Jewish and Christian religions.[18] Michael Taylor has described Ellis's book as "brilliant and bleak."[19] It is. Because, convincingly rejecting the easy get-out that events such as the Holocaust in Germany, Latin America after 1492, Palestine, Bosnia, and Rwanda are merely aberrations, Ellis asks whether they are so intrinsic to Judaism and Christianity that any future of these religions is questionable without radical change.[20] (We could also add the chilling escalation of violent hatred in the United States emanating from the white supremacy movements which merge Christian identity with political ideology.)[21] Ellis comments, after his consideration of contemporary theological writings addressing atrocities, that many of those burdened by the knowledge of the religious legitimation of atrocity are drawn to silence, as Dietrich Bonhoeffer was in his *Letters and Papers from Prison,* following Christianity's complicity with Nazism.[22]

In the section "In Missional Relationship" in his paper, George Hunsberger affirms Newbigin's conviction that the dialogue between gospel and culture goes on inside the church before it goes on outside. I would suggest, rather, that the dialogues cannot be separated sequentially; they happen simultaneously because that is how Christians have to live. To use a favorite postmodernism, we have a both/and, not an either/or, situation. It is in interaction that we find out what living a life of faith means. We are in an ongoing,

---

Enquiry," *Theology* (September/October 1990): 355-62. We could also note the current popular interest in so-called primitive religions and cultures such as North American Indian and New Zealand Maori, which, after near annihilation, are considered by many to have something to offer on this subject.

18. Marc H. Ellis, *Unholy Alliance: Religion and Atrocity in Our Time* (London: SCM Press, 1997).

19. Michael Taylor, review of *Unholy Alliance,* by Marc H. Ellis, *Theology* (May/June 1998): 205-6.

20. "In relation to Auschwitz, 1492, and the Palestinians, perhaps it can be said . . . that there is no assertion of religion and religious life, no tribunal, agreement, or ceremony, no ecumenical dialogue *ex post facto* that is free of its origins — that is free of its barbarism. When the historical event is over, we are left with speeches and agreements that again silence the victims, even and especially as the victors preach about the immense wealth bequeathed to them" (Ellis, p. 86).

21. "Everyman Special: Heart of Darkness," television documentary, BBC 1, 25 October 1998.

22. Ellis, p. 193.

dynamic engagement with the Bible, tradition, our life context, and our relationship with God through Jesus Christ.

Conclusion

An attitude shift along the lines I have briefly proposed moves us away from concern with our own identity and importance and toward a missionary engagement with life which operates more faithfully, humbly, and adventurously. We can, like Peter, in the process of evangelism, be moved to change our practice and our understanding of the gospel. I close with a quotation from Walter Hollenweger, former professor of mission here in Birmingham, who draws on his own innovative evangelistic experience with culturally contextual Bible studies during his time with the WCC and at the German Kirchentag, and currently in several European countries through his participatory biblical dramas with music, song, and dance. It catches something of the attitude shift and also the necessary corresponding theological shift. "If we are prepared to include in our understanding of the Spirit, the Spirit as giver of life, then this will have important implications for mission and evangelism. If the Spirit is in all people, we can invite whoever is willing to co-operate with us 'for the common good.' They can co-operate in our churches whether they are baptised or not, whether they sign our credal statements or not, because we know that the Spirit is poured out on all flesh."[23]

---

23. Walter Hollenweger, "All Creatures Great and Small: Towards a Pneumatology of Life," in *Strange Gifts? A Guide to Charismatic Renewal,* ed. David Martin and Peter Mullen (Oxford: Blackwell, 1984), p. 53. See also Hollenweger, *Pentecostalism,* chap. 17, and *Geist und Materie: Interkulterelle Theologie III* (Munich: Chr. Kaiser, 1988).

Mission in the West: On the Calling of the Church in a Postmodern Age[1]

J. Andrew Kirk

Introduction

The primary aim of this paper is to stimulate thinking on a complex set of cultural, social, and mission issues which are causing many Christians, myself among them, much perplexity at this time. I will present the subject by means of a number of short theses, which I will then elaborate briefly. The hope is that what Hercule Poirot (in the detective novels by Agatha Christie) calls "the little grey cells" will be spurred on to acts of imagination and inventiveness. I do not dare to claim any special insight or wisdom. I am as puzzled as most about which forms of mission might be truest to the gospel and most appropriate to the composite reality of the West today.[2]

Two obvious notes of caution should be sounded at the beginning.

1. This paper was given originally at the annual meeting of the Swedish Ecumenical Council in Malmo, April 1998, and subsequently expanded. It is included here as a contribution to the continuing discussion (after Newbigin) of a missionary encounter with Western society and culture.

2. A thoroughgoing discussion of the West would require a multidisciplined approach which should include at least the following disciplines: cultural studies, philosophy, economics, sociology, religious studies, ethics, aesthetics, media studies, and missiology. These are implied in this brief overview of the situation, but none of them are developed in depth. I have not discussed the significance of referring to one of the extremities of the Asian landmass as "the West." This concept, which began to take shape from 1492 onward and has been profoundly shaped by Europe's imperial and colonial contact with other continents, is problematical. At the turn of the second millennium, it might be worth considering exchanging the Greenwich Meridian and Date Line, so that Europe and the USA become the East (or even the Orient!).

First, the theme is immense and only in the first stages of being explored; therefore, not too much should be expected in one paper. My task will be fulfilled if I can provoke others to continue studying these matters themselves and experiment with new kinds of missionary activities in a new millennium. Secondly, the West is not a neat, homogeneous unity. I speak out of my limited British experience, which may differ in important particulars from other parts. I hope, nevertheless, that my description of our Western societies and the dilemmas faced by the church in carrying forward its mission in this context may have enough resonance with other people's experience for communication to be fruitful.

The Missionary Imperative

Without a strong sense of vocation to a missionary task, the church cannot be either apostolic or catholic.

The church's self-understanding and sense of identity (its ecclesiology) is intrinsically bound up with its call to share and live the gospel to the ends of the earth and the end of time. It lives "between the times," a period of discovering and rediscovering what it means to do mission "in the way of Christ." Mission is always undertaken with "a view to," in the double sense of a vision and a purpose, Christ's restoration of all things (Acts 3:21).

Today in the West, in particular, the church needs to recapture a joyful confidence in the power of God and the truth of the gospel, though without displaying a forced triumphalism. Although it must be thoroughly immersed in both the celebrations and pain of the world, it needs to keep its gaze unwaveringly fixed on Jesus Christ, "the author and perfecter of our faith" (Heb. 12:2).

Unless it takes the risk of cutting the many cords that continue to bind it to structures, traditions, strategies, and policies now quite obsolete, the church will not only continue to die but will thoroughly deserve to do so. Time has almost run out. A moribund church in the West is an acute embarrassment to Christians elsewhere, as it gives the lie to the optimistic expectations of two hundred years of missionary endeavor in other parts.

There is a sense in which the only other "missionary" force in the field is that of consumerism — "shop till you drop," "shop around the clock," or, in the words of the motto of the duty-free shop in Amsterdam airport, "see, buy, fly."[3] It is part of the evangelistic task of the church to seek to persuade a gen-

---

3. I would distinguish between bodies with the (proactive) missionary intent to persuade people to believe and act on fundamental convictions (in this case, that the yearning to

eration, whose identity is tied up with the urge to consume, that increasing acquisitions are an illusory reflection of the good life that is reflected in the anticipated messianic banquet.

The West as a Missionary Context

We have definitively come to the end of a long association between Christian beliefs and moral teaching and the personal and social life of Western people.

It is partly a definition of the contemporary meaning of the West (insofar as it manifests secular tendencies) that, for most practical purposes, its peoples live as if God did not exist, or exists only on the margin of life; as Lesslie Newbigin has often repeated, in current Western discourse God is not admitted to the public square. We live in the full flowering of secular assumptions, some of whose characteristics we will outline below.

At this point it is also interesting to note that certain forms of secularity are by no means incompatible with a multiplicity of "spiritualities." Indeed, there are even moves to define spirituality in such a way that somehow it becomes a "value-free" basis for morality, but one deliberately distanced in a pluralist age from any specific religious content. It is presented as a kind of universal intuition or spiritual essence that exists without a name both prior to and above religious beliefs, customs, and rituals.[4]

The Contours of the Missionary Context

In this section I wish to look at the most formative influences that have shaped, and continue to shape, Western societies. My inquiry accepts the validity of both a Weberian and Marxist approach to social analysis, that is, one that allows the place of both the power of ideas and the power of productive forces in the initiation of change.

---

be happy can be fulfilled by the ability to purchase a large range of goods and services) and those, like the proliferating varieties of spirituality, which seek (reactively) to alleviate the consequences of a profound spiritual malaise. For a powerful critique of the personal and economic consequences of "the aesthetic of consumption," cf. Zygmunt Bauman, *Work, Consumerism, and the New Poor* (Buckingham: Open University Press, 1998).

4. Yet another variation, perhaps, of Schleiermacher's "intuition of the infinite" or immediate perception of the interrelatedness of all things in the universe; cf. Nancey Murphy, *Beyond Liberalism and Fundamentalism: How Modern and Postmodern Philosophy Set the Theological Agenda* (Valley Forge, Pa.: Trinity Press International, 1996), pp. 22ff.

1. In the realm of ideas, we continue to be the heirs of a profound shift of perceptions that had its roots in the Renaissance.

The "modern" world is built on humanist assumptions. The father of humanism is Giovanni Pico della Mirandola (1463-94), who, in his celebrated book *Oration on the Dignity of Man,* began the long modern Promethean journey of stealing fire from the gods: "You may by your own free will trace the lineaments of your own nature. . . . We have made you a creature of neither heaven nor of earth . . . in order that you may, as the free and proud shaper of your own being, fashion yourself in the form you may prefer."[5] Man (for in the context it is appropriate to be gender specific) is the measure of all things. He is the only being in the universe with a mind that has the potential to fathom all mysteries. He no longer accepts any reality in the world beyond his own experience and reasoning about it. Using the logical device of Occam's razor, he endeavors always to find a naturalistic explanation for all events.

Moreover, against medieval asceticism he has discovered (or rediscovered) pleasure as the goal of existence. The desires of the body may be satiated, because the body is under the sole jurisdiction of the individual who inhabits it. Moreover, one day it will disintegrate and, at that point, life will end in oblivion. With the removal of a belief in an eschaton of judgment and accountability, there is no need to prepare for the future. Therefore, live for the present and maximize its enjoyments.

Naturally there is much more to the Renaissance than these paragraphs suggest. However, the pull of humanist assumptions and the push of the pleasure principle have had a profound effect on the shaping of the culture of the West.

2. In the realm of material forces, we continue to be the heirs of the scientific and technological revolutions that began in the seventeenth and eighteenth centuries.

The major consequence of the remarkable discoveries of the last three centuries is that we now live in a completely different relationship to the natural world. Invention and systematic experimentation have liberated us from the domination of the cycle of nature. Nature is now bent to do our will; we use it instrumentally as a means of satisfying our need for convenience. Knowledge of the natural world is demonstrated to be sound by the test of utility, that is, the ability to harness theoretical knowledge for practical uses. Perhaps it might be true to say that an ever present skepticism about the abil-

---

5. Quoted in David Cooper, *World Philosophies: An Historical Introduction* (Oxford: Blackwell, 1996), p. 231.

ity to know anything, which is the reverse side of all claims to universal validity, has been held at bay by the sheer practical brilliance of technological innovation.

According to the ideology of laissez-faire capitalism, the "consumer," whether of the latest collections from the top fashion houses or from the top manufacturers of military hardware, reigns supreme in a free market of willing buyers and sellers. The exchange of commodities is what makes the world go round. When purchasing stops, the result is economic catastrophe.

3. Only knowledge of a scientific nature is universal; being intrinsically accessible to all, it is not dependent on context, culture, tradition, belief, or individual personality.

The assumption that nothing should be believed that cannot be demonstrated by universally valid empirical methods of testing (evidentialism) is deeply embedded in Western consciousness. These beliefs alone, it is emphasized, are not open to reasonable doubt. They should, therefore, command universal assent; everything else is speculative — mere opinion.

The scientific principle of access to knowledge, enshrined in the methods of experimental verification and falsification, is a powerful egalitarian force against the privileged claims of religion, idealist philosophy, or ideology to esoteric knowledge. By way of refining this widely held conviction, one ought to say that evidentialism has been tempered in recent years by a recognition that matters of epistemology are a trifle more complex than this. Thus, even scientific knowledge is dependent on the presumption of the truth of nonempirical constructs, accepted in the first instance as a priori assumptions.[6]

Nevertheless, modernity is far from dead. Perhaps more sober and less extravagant claims are now made for the possibility of arriving at a "grand theory of everything" (Stephen Hawkins). And yet, there are experienced scientists who still entertain the hope that one day it will be achieved.

4. Freedom is the most highly prized value for Western people.[7]

At one level freedom experienced as an expansion of choice and increased leisure is the result of technological innovation and the accumulation of wealth. Choice comes through an ever widening variety of goods and ser-

---

6. Cf. Stephen Davis, *God, Reason, and Theistic Proofs* (Edinburgh: Edinburgh University Press, 1997), pp. 78-96.

7. Cf. J. Andrew Kirk, *The Meaning of Freedom: A Study of Secular, Muslim, and Christian Views* (Carlisle: Paternoster, 1998).

vices.[8] Labor-saving devices decrease the amount of time to be spent on basic living.

Attitudes to work have profoundly changed. In the Christian tradition work represents the human response to the cultural mandate (Gen. 1–2). Through work human beings glorify God by exercising their individually created gifts and abilities to grow into full human personhood. In the Marxist tradition work (as long as it is not experienced either as exploitation or drudgery) is the means by which human beings recover their "species-being." In modern parlance, however, work is equated with employment, whose chief purpose is to supply us with sufficient disposable income, and therefore choice, to consume.[9] (In the UK, the famous Cartesian aphorism is sometimes paraphrased to read, *Tesco ergo sum* — Tesco is the largest chain of supermarkets in the country!)

5. *Western culture is characterized most fundamentally by its unresolved[10] dualisms.*

These dualisms are found in a number of stark oppositions:

• between understanding how things function and what they mean;
• between the many and the one, that is, between the apparently unconnected multiplicity of particular objects and a framework which makes sense of them as a unified whole;[11]
• between fact and value, that is, between what is the case and what ought to be the case;
• between the subject and the object, that is, between the "decentered" self and the reality of an external world.

8. The advent first of cable and now of digital television shows both the extent of theoretical choice and its practical absurdity. As one cannot watch fifty channels simultaneously, nor video them for future viewing, more means less: knowing what one might enjoy, but cannot, leads to a wholly artificial sense of deprivation.

9. Cf. Bauman, *Work*, pp. 23-41.

10. As long as the prevailing worldview of a culture is explicitly or implicitly humanist, the dualisms are intrinsically irresolvable.

11. Some advocates of postmodernity attempt to portray dissonance and unconnectedness as positive steps in the overcoming of the sterile rationalism of the modern project; cf. Zygmunt Bauman, *Postmodern Ethics* (Oxford: Blackwell, 1993), p. 6; cf. also Colin Gunton, *The One, the Three, and the Many: God, Creation, and the Culture of Modernity* (Cambridge: Cambridge University Press, 1993); Carver T. Yu, *Being and Relation: A Theological Critique of Western Dualism and Individualism* (Edinburgh; Scottish Academic Press, 1987).

6. The major effect of dualism is the inability to distinguish between reality and fantasy.

There is a sense in which the image has become all-powerful. Fundamental uncertainty about the means of being able to differentiate between an imaginary and real world has led to the belief that implicit to being human is the freedom to create our own worlds. The ubiquitous advertising industry has seized on this state of affairs to insinuate for us desirable, designer images (e.g., in clothes and holiday fashions), which it presses us to accept.[12] If a grasp of reality is no longer possible, then everything can be simulated. And perhaps it no longer matters very much what is real and what is not, as long as the experience is satisfying.[13]

The loss of a given reality gives rise, then, to the creation of individual realities (what is "true for me"). For many, at least while blessed with health and wealth, the chief end of human life is the maximization of happiness or pleasure. Psalm 121:1-2 is parodied in the following way: "Where does my help come from? My help comes from . . . heaven (cosmic forces found within) and earth (technocratic rationality)." Hedonism (the immediate gratification of the senses and appetites) is perhaps the oldest philosophy of all: "good for food, pleasing to the eye and desirable for gaining wisdom" (Gen. 3:6); "there is joy and revelry . . . let us eat and drink . . . for tomorrow we die!" (Isa. 22:13).

Yet we cannot leave the subject without quoting a penetrating aphorism that helps give some perspective to a seemingly insatiable appetite for the superficial in contemporary culture, from the "father" of postmodernity, Friedrich Nietzsche: "the modern human being has created happiness and blinked." In the same vein Francis Fukuyama, in his celebrated "Hegelian" tour de force, *The End of History and the Last Man*,[14] often uses the word "banal" of his liberal democratic, free-market "utopia."

7. In terms of Greek mythology, the context of the Western world is a combination of Prometheus (autonomous science), Apollo (the principles of order, harmony, and aesthetic perfection),[15] and Dionysus (the pleasure principle).

As long as Western people accept the autonomy of any aspect of life and refuse to countenance the possibility of a source of truth external to the natu-

---

12. Cf. Celia Lury, *Consumer Culture* (Cambridge: Polity, 1996), pp. 40-51.

13. Frederic Jameson, "Postmodernism and the Market," in Slavoj Zizek, *Mapping Ideology* (London: Verso, 1994), speaks of "the consumption of the very process of consumption itself, above and beyond its content and the immediate commercial products" (p. 293).

14. Francis Fukuyama, *The End of History and the Last Man* (London: Hamish Hamilton, 1992).

15. Of which the latest and most dangerous may be "designer babies."

ral world, including their own psyches — that is, as long as they begin from the indubitability of naturalism as a necessary presupposition of existence — they will never discover the fundamental purpose of life. Starting from human experience alone, there is simply no means of holding together an explanation for both material existence and the sense human beings have that they are unique creatures in the universe.

Contemporary spiritualities, arising out of the exploration of inner experience or the mystical conjunction of natural forces, are not ways out of the dilemma of naturalism, only an extension of it. Unless a realm of existence distinct from the natural world is an objective reality, we are still confined in a one-dimensional world. Perhaps for this reason, in the continuing dialogue between science and theology, the question of God's action in the world is again being taken seriously in such theories as "top-down causality" and "emergent properties."

The Effect of the Western Context on the Life of the Church

1. The church is no longer considered the guardian of absolute ethical values.

Morality is conceived as being independent of religious belief, in the sense that a nonreligious person can lead an upright life and religion is no guarantee of ethical integrity. The secular view is that right and wrong are largely a matter of self-evident values, to be judged by the consequences of actions and to be implemented through a reciprocal care for the welfare of the other. In fact, what we see is a kind of inherited conventionalism in which society sticks to the known, until such time as determined pressure groups can persuade legislators and others that change is necessary.

Where the ethical teaching of the church (e.g., in the areas of marriage, divorce, human sexuality, gambling, human fertilization, and embryo experimentation) still appeals to notions of intrinsic right and wrong, it is rejected as dogmatic, arbitrary, or oppressive. Our culture is largely utilitarian in its approach to morality. A meaningful dialogue between those who believe that moral action is based on a given moral order and those who believe that everything is yet to be discovered is extremely difficult; the presuppositions are too far apart.[16]

---

16. Alasdair MacIntyre, *Three Rival Versions of Moral Enquiry* (London: Duckworth, 1990), believes that different systems of thought are not necessarily incommensurable and untranslatable "because exposure to debate may reveal that one of the contending standpoints fails in its own terms and by its own standards," and therefore "one party can emerge as undoubtedly rationally superior" (p. 5).

2. The church's message, structures, and ritual have become culture-bound.

Generalizing rather broadly, it appears that what the church is about either belongs to a premodern worldview and set of customs or is indistinguishable from the latest humanist philosophies or the most recent ethical opinions of political correctness. In other words, the church is somewhat inept in its attempts to inculturate its beliefs and practices, tending to swing between the extremes of conservative reaction and a fashionable progressive radicalism. In neither case is due justice done to the creative tension that ought to exist between the givenness and universality of the gospel and the particularity of ever changing contexts. In practice this is no easy task. Neither the gospel nor culture is asceptic; there will be both integration and conflict.

3. The church is seen as another institution that purveys goods and services in a competitive market.

The belief system and practices of Christian faith are now viewed as simply alternatives among a plethora of new and old spiritualities, therapies, counseling advice, and contemplative practices that claim to be able to put one in touch with one's authentic self or some kind of cosmic consciousness. Western people on the whole reject what they consider the strange beliefs and practices of world religions. Nevertheless, they latch onto the prevailing mood that each of them, in some way, is a valid alternative path to truth and wholeness for those who find them meaningful and consoling.

4. Attendance at church is seen as one leisure activity among many others.

In spite of a cultural perception that technology enables time to be saved, everyone everywhere is increasingly conscious of a lack of time. We live in a thorough time paradox: that which enables time to be more rationally apportioned (e.g., the ever present motorcar) also increases the number of projects we seek to engage in (e.g., the round of activities that parents believe are necessary for their children). It is no surprise, therefore, that people genuinely believe that they do not have time to go to church, or are too exhausted come Sunday to wake up early once again. (Incidentally, why do churches persist with their main weekly services on a Sunday morning? It seems somewhat culturally perverse.) Today's generation divides its time among a number of pursuits which either exclude or give a very low priority to formal worship.[17]

17. Of course, there are a number of other reasons for nonchurchgoing: for example, a view that the church preaches moralism; arcane rituals and practices; a lack of identity with the worshiping community; unhappy childhood experiences; a belief that the need for worship is a sign of weakness and immaturity.

123

5. Christian identity is no longer a matter of birth and geography.

The territorial nature of the Christian faith in the West is seriously undermined by, among other things, the notable decline in infant baptisms. Many parents (easily a majority in the UK) no longer see any necessity in having the baby "christened/Christianized." It appears to be no longer necessary to secure one's national identity to be marked with the sign of the cross in infancy. Belief is thought to be a matter of intimate, personal conviction. At the same time, baptism seems to give a finality to faith which is contradicted by the postmodern tendency to "serialize" experience, that is, to hold convictions only so long as they fit with a current lifestyle. How, then, it will be asked, can anyone commit a youngster to one particular set of beliefs for the rest of his or her life? The common expression that one should be free to make up one's own mind (have control of one's own destiny) is often the illogical response to the call to bring up children in the Christian faith.

It would be a mistake to imply that these trends are all negative. They are certainly a challenge, not least when Christians may not be aware of how much patterns of belief and lifestyle are changing and what is the significance of the change for the Christian community.

Reinventing a Missionary Church

In the light of the analysis so far, what does faithfulness to mission in the way of Christ require? Perhaps we could try to answer by setting up a kind of ends-means audit: What is the church's end or purpose? What are the most effective means, consonant with those ends, for fulfilling its mission? What hinders achievement of the ends?

1. The mission of the church could be described in four key affirmations: to be holy, to serve the neighbor in need, to communicate the good news of Jesus Christ, and to be salt and light in society.

However the church defines its mission, it is vital that, both in theory and practice, it keeps the different aspects in balance.[18] It must have an understanding which does equal justice to its priestly, servant, evangelistic, and

---

18. Cf. J. Andrew Kirk, *What Is Mission? Theological Explorations* (London: Darton, Longman and Todd, 1999). In this book, among other matters, I attempt to argue against all reductionist missiologies — whether of the left, right, or center, whether of liberals, radicals, conservatives, evangelicals, traditionalists, Catholics, charismatics, or any other group — that is any account of mission which seeks to marginalize one or more of its aspects.

prophetic nature. On the one hand, the sharing of a message of good news does not have integrity unless the community that proclaims it also lives it in practice. On the other hand, the message states that the community always proclaims from a position of being *simul justus et peccator,* not from a position of perfection, the implication being that it does not have to attain complete consistency between belief and action before it evangelizes.

2. For each aspect of its mission, the church needs to find suitable means that are culturally appropriate and congruous with the message it professes.

It pursues holiness through worship and prayer, both individual and corporate, and by a daily renewed resolution to a life of disciplined purity in every kind of relationship. Its service to the disabled, abused, inadequate, lonely, and distressed may well mean that its members sacrifice a legitimate lifestyle in order to give their time to caring and hospitality, and to demonstrating that life does not consist in the abundance of possessions. There will be a need for some members to be trained in counseling and the resolution of conflict, and for the whole community to put aside resources for meeting specific, otherwise unattended, needs.

To fulfill its evangelistic calling, the Christian community must understand how people are shaped and affected by the culture that surrounds them. There is no mission without paying attention in detail to the questions of communication. Likewise, there is no evangelism unless the bearers of the gospel believe in its truth and power. There has to be a recovery of confidence in the story of Jesus' life, death, and resurrection as the God-given way in which people's full humanity is restored to them, while at the same time being sensitive to the postmodern criticism that this appears to imply a will-to-power, dominance, and control.[19] Of course, evangelism is a sensitive issue, but to suggest that Christians should not call people to turn to Jesus Christ from whatever other "religious" beliefs they may hold is implicitly to turn the church into a religious sect. Moreover, it is surely historically inept to suggest that Christians should not seek to evangelize people of "other faith," for if the early church had stuck to such a proposal, Christians would not be here today to debate this issue!

Being salt and light in society means that the Christian community encourages its members to seek positions in society (e.g., in political life, the civil service, medicine, business, education, scientific research) which enable

---

19. Cf. Anthony Thiselton, *Interpreting God and the Postmodern Self: On Meaning, Manipulation, and Power* (Edinburgh: T&T Clark, 1995), pp. 3-39; Martyn Percy, *Power and the Church: Ecclesiology in an Age of Transition* (London: Cassell, 1998).

them to demonstrate again the meaning of the vocation to serve. At the same time, they may be in a position to influence decision-making processes in ways which can reflect the life of the kingdom of God.

3. For the church to be effective in the fulfillment of its mission in the West, it needs to address and, where possible, resolve those matters that hinder its effectiveness.

The complexity of life and the speed of change may lead the church to a fear of losing control, which is then translated into an immovable attachment to traditional forms and structures, unattractive and irrelevant to outsiders. The church often appears to be committed to wrong priorities. Prayer, for example, is relegated to the margins of its activities, while enormous time and energy are spent on maintaining a number of projects which perpetuate the church as an institution but do not energize the church as mission. Committees come to take the place of commitment to the living God.

We Christians in the West are deeply committed to our comfortable lifestyle. We find all kinds of plausible reasons why we do not have the time or ability either to respond to people in need or to share the gospel with those who do not know it. We are, quite possibly, full of fears deep down: the fear of making mistakes, because we lack an understanding of adequate methods of handling difficult people and situations; the fear of seeming intolerant, dogmatic, and insensitive; the fear of being unable to respond to people's questions and their objections to Christian faith, and therefore of being made to look like a fool; and finally the fear of isolation and misrepresentation if we stand publicly for the values of honesty, integrity, and openness. Many of the assumptions of the postmodern West are hostile to the Christian way of viewing life, and rather than be exposed as a small minority in a sea of indifference or antagonism, we keep our heads down, we keep ourselves to ourselves. Possibly one of the main difficulties the church in the West has in fulfilling its missionary calling is that it has lost "the art of witness." Either Christians are nervous about or unskilled in testifying to the living reality of God with us.

Finally, unresolved disputes among Christians about important beliefs and moral issues do not help our ability to be credible. It would be a legitimate question for any non-Christian to ask of a Christian: Which version of the faith do you represent? Of course, there are matters about which the church needs to take time to come to a mature judgment, which should not be foreclosed too quickly. However, there are other questions about which the church should have a settled opinion, given the message it lives by, even if its opinion is not popular with certain sectors of the population. Sometimes, on both sides of an argument (say about the status of homosexual relationships), theological conviction and pastoral sensitivity are confused. Just because pastoral care becomes so problematical in certain instances, some Christians are tempted to modify beliefs while others seem to indicate that, once the theology is sorted out, the pastoral needs will take care of themselves.

Clearly, mission is seriously compromised in a community divided against itself. Even if some issues seem so intractable that no amount of conversation and debate seems able to bring them closer to a resolution, the way we Christians handle disputes among ourselves is an important sign, or countersign, of the reality of the gospel. After all, one of the most powerful and attractive images of the church in the New Testament is that of a reconciled community, built on the same foundation and without walls separating different peoples: "God's purpose was to create in himself one new person . . . thus making peace, and in this one body to reconcile . . . them to God through the cross, by which he put to death their hostility" (Eph. 2:15-16).

There is a strong argument in favor of affirming that the church's most powerful tool for communicating the gospel is its inner and outer life in which it manifests a real restoration of human community through a self-sacrificing, compassionate concern for the well-being of all the members; such concern, of course, should overflow to others, especially those whom society excludes. If a postmodern age is marked by an endless plurality of discordant beliefs and lifestyles, true life in Jesus Christ is more likely to be recognized visually than aurally.

The church's supreme task is to begin to move from a dysfunctional to a functional (in function of its mission calling) institution. Probably this is the most difficult challenge it faces. How, in practice, in a fragmented, highly mobile, eclectic society, can a meaningful community identifying with its local situation, and which is reconciled, reconciling, and deeply caring for others, be created and sustained? Most of the other activities in which it is involved pale into insignificance beside this one.

The Emerging Christ of Post-Christian Europe

Werner Ustorf

Introduction

In writing this paper on the image of Christ in the context of post-Christian Europe, two considerations, though seemingly rather different at first glance, have been uppermost. One is the observation that the history of the global expansion of Christianity shows on the Christian side — though there are well-known exceptions, such as the missionary activity of the church of the East (the so-called Nestorians) — a readiness for *coercion* and sometimes *violence*, which is surprising given that God's love for, and his salvation of, humankind is certainly the core message of Christianity. I do not claim here that the Christian tradition necessarily has a more negative record than other religions, but, being part of this tradition myself, this aspect naturally concerns me. And in this I am not alone. Among some of the more evangelical circles in the West, for example, a new form of Christian apologetic blames the European Enlightenment for the collapse of Christian virtue.[1] In their perspective it is not Christianity itself which is the cause of misery and violence, but the captivity of the church to the cultural norms of liberalism, which has remodeled Christianity as a tool of the bourgeois-capitalist project of world hegemony. The mission carried out in this period is declared to have been

---

1. Cf., for example, Lesslie Newbigin's position, most explicit in his work *Truth to Tell: The Gospel as Public Truth* (Grand Rapids: Eerdmans; Geneva: WCC Publications; and London: SPCK, 1991); also Lamin Sanneh, *Encountering the West: Christianity and the Global Cultural Process: The African Dimension* (Maryknoll, N.Y.: Orbis, 1993); Sanneh, *Religion and the Variety of Culture: A Study in Origin and Practice* (Valley Forge, Pa.: Trinity Press International, 1996).

through and through Christendom mission,[2] that is to say, it was more an expression of modern Western civilization (or its repetition in religious language) than its conscience, "its prisoner rather than its prophetic reformer."[3] Justified as this position may be in terms of a necessary Christian self-critique,[4] it has to be acknowledged that what K. Madhu Panikkar has called the "Vasco da Gama epoch of Asian history"[5] dates back to 1498, while the Columbus project of conquering the "New World" had already started by 1492. The propensity for violence within Christianity is therefore historically anterior to the Enlightenment. It would be rather hard to explain the atrocities committed toward the Jews and Muslims during the Crusades, between 1096 and 1270, by way of "modern" or "liberal" influences. The history of the church from the fourth to the eighth centuries presents a similarly questionable picture, with a record of aggression and extinction vis-à-vis the non-Christians that has led the historian Ramsay MacMullen to the conclusion that the victory of Christianity over paganism was achieved to a large extent by coercion and persecution, organized by the state church, the Christian mob, and violent monks, and using methods ranging from iconoclasm to fines, and from murder to, *nota bene,* crucifixion.[6] The historical evidence

2. "Christendom" (in Latin: *corpus Christianum*) refers to the identity (or at least to a considerable overlap) of religion (church), culture, state, and territory; in brief, to the expansion of the Western Christian world.

3. Willem A. Visser 't Hooft, "The Significance of the Asian Churches in the Ecumenical Movement," *Ecumenical Review* 11 (1959): 365-76. Willem A. Visser 't Hooft was then the general secretary of the World Council of Churches (Geneva).

4. This critique is shared by John Hick, though leading to a different conclusion: "secular modernity has transformed the outlook of most of the Christian world, rather than that Christianity has out of its own rather distinctive religious resources introduced these modern liberal values into Western culture. Indeed during much of the greater part of its history Christianity has been neither democratic, nor liberal, nor science-oriented, nor historically-minded or individualistic in the modern sense." Cf. his "Towards a Universal Declaration of a Global Ethic: A Christian Comment," in *Theoria (Praxis: How Jews, Christians, and Muslims Can Together Move from Theory to Practice),* ed. L. Swidler (Louvain: Peters, 1998), pp. 229-33, here 229. I am most grateful to John Hick for having read a previous version of this paper. In his comment he pointed out the necessity of being critical even of one's own critique. To follow this advice will take longer than the writing of a paper.

5. K. Madhu Panikkar, *Asia and Western Dominance: A Survey of the Vasco da Gama Epoch of Asian History (1498-1945),* 2nd ed. (London, 1954), pp. 375-457, which is the section on Christian mission. This period was defined as extending from 1498 to 1945. Following E. Troeltsch, Panikkar defined Christian mission as a religious movement accompanying the West's aggressive economic, military, and political expansion. This attempt at spiritual conquest was declared to have failed once and for all.

6. Cf. his *Christianity and Paganism in the Fourth to Eighth Centuries* (New Haven and

available so far is at least sufficient to question the assumption that "alien" or "exterior" elements were responsible for the dark side of church and mission history. This being so, it may be necessary to ask whether the destructive elements involved came from the very center of the Christian tradition itself. And if this is the case, they need to be addressed in order to overcome them. At the center of the Christian tradition, however, is the figure of Jesus Christ himself. A further question must therefore be asked: Does Christianity, at least its European branch, have a problem in interpreting the central figure of its tradition?

The second consideration which has influenced my paper is the following: there is a widespread agreement, a common "negative theology" as it were, among the thinking believers of many religions that infinity and formlessness,[7] and therefore nondefinability, is one of the attributes of God, or of the Ultimate Reality, and that even the most central symbols of a religion cannot exhaust this.[8] The absolute is radically different from the relative. I would agree and argue that, on the other hand, there is also a "negative anthropology" in that the human longing for the Ultimate Reality is no less enigmatic and perhaps no less insatiable than God is inexhaustible;[9] in brief, that the relationship has the structure of *unitas oppositorum:* God's infinity is an inversion of the nondefinability of the human, and vice versa. Since the days of Ludwig Feuerbach, the one cannot be thought of without the other. For us there is no God *an sich,* but rather our perception of "us" and "God" in opposition. It is a matter of historical experience that the Christian may encounter "Christ," the Buddhist awake to the "Dharma," and the Muslim submit to "Allah," which means that the relationship is usually conditioned by factors of

---

London: Yale University Press, 1997), particularly the first two chapters on persecution (of the pagans).

7. The infinity of God's being is a concept not found in the Judeo-Christian Scriptures, but a predication used by some of the church fathers (Eastern and Western) and medieval theologians (such as Aquinas). It rests on an Aristotelian theory of act/potency or on a Platonic version of participation. Cf. Leo Sweeney, *Divine Infinity in Greek and Medieval Thought,* 2nd ed. (New York and Bern: P. Lang, 1998).

8. On the Christian side, this warning has been expressed throughout the life of the church, particularly in relation to its most complex symbol, the Trinity. Nicholas of Cusa (following thoughts expressed by Dionysius the Areopagite) stated in his *De docta ignorantia* (1.88) of 1440 that God in his infinity is neither Father, nor Son, nor Spirit. Within Christianity, John Hick is one of the eminent scholars continuing this line of thought; in fact, his understanding of religion is based on this; cf. his *An Interpretation of Religion: Human Responses to the Transcendent* (London: Macmillan, 1989).

9. Cf. Ulrich Schoen, *Bi-Identität. Zweisprachigkeit, Bi-Religiosität, doppelte Staatsbürgerschaft* (Zürich and Düsseldorf: Walter, 1996), p. 171.

time and place.[10] This has been acknowledged in various ways.[11] In this paper I shall assume that there is a (religiously and culturally) conditioned "medium," or a "field of contact," between human insatiability and divine inexhaustibility, and that it is located within the limits of personal human experience. This mutually dynamic field of contact is generating a creative tension (leading to a transition from one's religious ego to the encounter of one's true self, e.g., to the "Christ in me") and sometimes a destructive tension (reinforcing one's captivity inside the ego). It can also lead to the emergence of new images of the divine, that is, to religious innovation. To describe the "field of contact" means in principle to think what is unthinkable and to say what is ineffable and then to "weight" the relationship in favor of the "human" side of the equation.

The theological term for the resolution of the tension is "mediation." Mediation, within the Christian tradition, is the function of Jesus Christ, and the christological dogmas thus engendered are descriptions of the mediation process.[12] It is a fact, however, that today Jesus Christ is experienced among

---

10. Seiichi Yagi describes this connection in "Christ and Buddha," in *Asian Faces of Jesus*, ed. R. S. Sugirtharajah, Faith and Cultures Series (Maryknoll, N.Y.: Orbis, 1993), pp. 25-45: here 36, as follows: "the cognition of the ultimate in the person encountered is mediated by the awareness of the same reality in the person who encounters."

11. Yagi, starting from Gal. 2:19-20 (relating to the dialectics of Paul "being in Christ" and "Christ being in Paul"), developed an anthropological-theological theory (covering both Buddhism and Christianity) postulating the existence of a "frontal structure" mediating the "ego" and the "self" (the human and the divine). Sharply separated and, in principle, each other's opposites, both centers form at the same time a unity. The christological dogma, it seems, has been anthropologically democratized or universalized. Cf. Yagi, *Die Frontstruktur als Brücke vom buddhistischen zum christlichen Denken* (Munich, 1988); my thinking is developing along somewhat similar lines to that of Yagi's, but more time and help is required for a fuller exploration of his ideas, particularly the process by which the potentiality of the divine ("primary contact") becomes actuality and reality ("secondary contact") only in the human center.

12. Augustine, the African church father of the fourth and fifth centuries, emphasized in his *City of God* (11.2) that mediation works only when the very same person "is at once God and man." For him, only one (perfect, i.e., in Augustine's terms: sinless) person fulfilled this criterion, Jesus. Logically, the incarnation of the divine in the human can indeed be reserved exclusively to the unique theanthropos — thus excluding the many and making Jesus Christ the only mediator for all time. However, the other side of this mediational *unitas oppositorum,* namely, the incarnation of the human in God, logically cannot have any other object than God himself. The incarnation of the human in God, then, is no less paradoxical than the inverse; it is hardly ever reflected upon, but it opens fresh possibilities for theological thinking in terms of God's accessibility. Augustine himself is a case in point: already in his *Confessiones* (9.23-25: the vision at Ostia, described in Neoplatonist terms) he suggested the

131

the world's cultures in rather different ways.[13] It is not difficult to conclude that different images of Christ relate to the different needs they are expected to satisfy. When a religious tradition is crossing cultural boundaries, undergoing historical change, or experimenting with alternative avenues of faith, needs and questions will arise which are different from the ones addressed in the past. I believe that Christianity in Europe is currently passing through such a period of deep transition. The question of mediation or, in D. Bonhoeffer's words, of "who is Christ for us today" is still very much alive.

These two elements in the perception of contemporary European reality — the issue of aggression used in Christian history and the need for a rethinking of the question of Christ (mediation) — are not unrelated. In this paper I will argue that the disestablishment[14] of the tradition of Jesus Christ is not simply negative; it can offer the prospect of additional avenues for an understanding of mediation that may, in turn, contribute to the formation of new, life-oriented models of Christian spirituality and mission. That is why these avenues ought to be explored. To express the argument positively, the question is whether peaceful and nonaggressive forms of Christianity and mission are related to a particular configuration of the divine/human field of contact, creating a critical awareness also of the dark side of one's spirituality.[15] This is an alternative way of approaching the same issue.

Christianity in Europe: A Disestablished Tradition

I would now like to present a tentative sketch of how I see the religious topography of Europe. I am not discussing the value, say, of the secularization hypothe-

---

possibility of a general access to God by claiming to have achieved direct (i.e., nonmediated, in the double sense of "beyond words and images" and "without Christ's intervention") experience of God. Direct access to God (for the "purified" soul) is explicitly confirmed in *City of God* (11.2) as a possibility for humanity, *post Christum*.

13. There has been, since the days of H. Richard Niebuhr's *Christ and Culture* (New York: Harper and Bros., 1951), and due (in large measure) to the diversity of interpretations that is now acknowledged in the postcolonial period of Christian history, a comprehensive ecumenical debate on the diversity of Christologies, that is, on the different images and theological understandings of Christ. For the Asian continent see Sugirtharajah, *Asian Faces of Jesus*.

14. I have borrowed the term "disestablishment" from James W. Heisig (Nanzan Institute for Religion and Culture, Nagoya) and his very interesting article "Christianity Today: The Transition to Disestablishment," *Inter-Religio* 30 (1996): 63-79.

15. I have tried to address the dark side of missionary spirituality in "What If the Light in You Is Darkness? An Inquiry into the Shadow Side of the Missionary Self," in *Mission und Gewalt*, ed. U. von der Heyden and J. Becher (Stuttgart: Franz Steiner, 2000), pp. 139-52.

sis, or of pluralism and postmodernist paradigms, and I am also not commenting on declining church attendance or the presence of immigrant religions. All these are very important questions, but far too large to deal with in such a brief sketch.[16] My ambition is simply to summarize my encounters with people, "religious" ones and self-declared "nonreligious" people, over the last couple of years; and that means that I can speak with no other authority than my own. The most important feature of Europe's religious landscape, in my perception, has been its transformation, and this transformation has affected the way the quest for mediation itself has been expressed. The ways of expression are indeed so various that old terminological habits of classification, like "secular" and "religious," become less and less helpful. The religious dimension is present in nearly all spheres of so-called secular life, and vice versa. My impression is that words like "secular" and "religious" have increasingly become language fossils, terminological survivals of the power games of previously dominant groups: the established churches and the culture of agnostic liberalism, which are both currently losing their power to control minds. I would confirm Heisig's statement that even among Christians, established Christianity is regarded "as too narrow a receptacle for the religious consciousness of today."[17] That, however, has created a somewhat ambiguous situation: on the one hand, people are now free to regain their religious initiative and live it in places not controlled by religious institutions; on the other, we have the propagandists of capitalist corporatism, who are only too keen to exploit the religious longing and take over the place which church and liberalism have vacated.[18] In this context I have repeatedly heard considerations like the following:[19]

a. People, despite the negative media coverage of established Christianity (e.g., the purely self-interested church that is out of touch with the pres-

16. For the British context, the one I have been living in for the last eleven years, two books are to be recommended: Steve Bruce, *Religion in Modern Britain* (Oxford: Oxford University Press, 1995) (following the secularization hypothesis); Grace Davie, *Religion in Britain since 1945: Believing without Belonging* (Oxford: Blackwell, 1994) (as the subtitle indicates, Davie is exploring new avenues of interpretation).

17. Heisig, p. 65.

18. See John Ralston Saul, *The Unconscious Civilization* (London: Penguin Books, 1998); also Stephen Pattison, *The Faith of the Managers: When Management Becomes Religion* (London: Cassell, 1997).

19. I have excluded from these considerations those minorities who cling to different versions of the claim to have "privileged knowledge" — the radical exclusivists on the Christian side and the radical humanists on the atheist side. They do not attract many followers, but they do exist and have more influence on the public debate than their numbers would suggest.

ent; the ordained minister as a fraudster, a pedophile, at best a friendly idiot), still expect the church to give guidance in matters of daily life; they expect solidarity, and they do still hold Jesus in high regard. However, the Christian tradition is no longer felt to be "true" in the sense of propositional sentences about "what is the case." The dogmatic package is seen more as an attempt to "circumcise" illegitimately the contemporary world. The "truth" of Christianity is not expected to emerge in sentences and words, but in the testimony of one's life and also, perhaps foremost, in that of the church's.

b. The texts of the Bible have lost their privileged position in Europe's cultural and religious life. Other texts have come in and found a home. All texts, however, religious or not, tend to be seen as products of culture and history; in short, as myth. Why then should the myth of a certain period of history and of a particular culture be of more importance than today's myths? Many people question the right of the past to rule over the present.

c. There is a sort of popular revolt against the image of a God who is detached from the world and from life (a prisoner of the established church, of sacred texts and doctrines, as it were). There is a remarkable desire to become an active counterpart of God, not a spectator or a passive object that has to be ransomed. With this goes a further desire, namely, to search right into the center of one's being for the place where there is unity of life and death, and a reunification with the source of life. The examples of direct experiences, qualified as numinous, are countless. What is their message? It is, formally at least, I think, a double message: the "kingdom of God is within us," and secondly, people are no longer prepared to believe, especially if that means they have to force their souls into a belief which is not their own. They want, so to speak, to "feel the presence of God" and to be able to love God in every single movement of their heart.

d. The countermove, perhaps less frequent though, is a methodology of permanent skepticism toward one's own motivations, constructions, and even experiences. The verdict of this methodology is ultimately defeating. It says: How can we believe that the human being is made in the image of God if there is evidence that God is made in the image of the human being? Whenever the conflict is resolved in favor of one side only, feeling God right in one's heart or being rigorously agnostic, great psychic energies will be required to keep the dangerous opponent at bay.

My interpretation of these few impressions is fourfold. (1) There is a sizable population that does not engage in religious activities at all (such as the group of young white working-class men); however, in times of real crisis this does not prevent them from reconnecting themselves to the Christian tradition. The church for them is an option, a fallback position when the times get really hard.[20] Then (2) we have a group embracing happily the various options the so-called new religions have to offer. Central here is direct experience. This can indeed transform the selfish individual (the form of human survival fitted to a capitalist economy) into a person who is truly for others, but it can also increase the scope of narcissistic delusion. The most problematic aspect of this group is a rather frequent misunderstanding of religion as a means not to overcome but to reinforce the religious ego. The ego's craving for the certainty of salvation makes the transition to self-cognition virtually impossible. This criticism, of course, needs to be applied in some measure to the other groups as well. There is (3) a religious consciousness that regards itself as Christian without participating in established Christianity. It is a kind of individual attachment to Jesus as one's central symbol, without necessarily being attached to the dogmas about Jesus and to the institution that controls these dogmas. We have arrived at the one-person church, so to speak, a kind of selective Christianity (deselected have been: institutionalization, dogmatism, and aggressiveness) that in terms of numbers may be much bigger than the forms of established Christianity it coexists with. Finally, (4) there are what I would call the interreligious pilgrims, usually starting from within Christianity but prepared to explore alternative ways and even to question the primacy of Jesus Christ. They are creating "space" within their religious thinking and their lives for the presence and the message of another religion, and are therefore on the way toward religious bi-identity (which is not equal to forsaking one's religion). In all these cases the issue of mediation turns up in a different and often acute way.

A Disestablished Jesus Christ

It is the merit particularly of John Hick to have taken seriously the transformation of the religious topography in the West and to have searched for answers to questions asked in this time of "post-Christianity." Hick, as one of the most tenacious of thinkers, urges us to take on board the proposition that people do not accept any religious "message" unless it is embodied and made

20. Cf. Grace Davie's study of the Hillsborough football disaster (1989, when ninety-five fans were crushed to death), "Believing without Belonging: A Liverpool Case Study," *Archives de Sociologie des Religions* 81 (1993): 79-89.

visible in life. One of his latest books, *The Metaphor of God Incarnate*,[21] is about Christology. I find his arguments most helpful in sharpening up the theological issue of mediation. Hick does not question the idea of an incarnational Christology as such. In fact, he says Jesus was a man "who was exceptionally open to the divine presence and who thus incarnated to a high degree the ideal of human life lived in response to the Real."[22] What he questions is what he calls "the scandal of restricted access, or of limited revelation," particularly the story of God the Son descending from heaven to earth in order to die in atonement for the sins of the world and to found the church. Instead he takes Jesus as his spiritual guide, not as his God. In fact, Jesus — among the many great spiritual leaders — is (or was up to now) for Christians the principal guide for living and the supreme revelation of an ultimate transcendent reality.[23] In this perspective the traditional christological dogma of a total interaction of the divine and the human in Christ, Jesus Christ fully God and fully man and, as such, the uniquely complete and final self-revelation of God to humankind, appears to be a metaphorical truth only, albeit an "excellent" one. But its character is mythological, not ontological or propositional, and its function lies in touching our poetic and creative side, inviting our imaginative and emotional responses to the experience of transcendence that the myth itself tries to address. In finding their appropriate response and living it accordingly, promises Hick, Christians "are rightly related to the Real itself."[24] In terms of our four classifications mentioned above, Hick would perhaps belong to the third and fourth groups.

This is an interesting attempt at answering the question of mediation. But, in this particular case, it neglects the possibility that our poetic and emotional needs are not necessarily responding to God (the Real), but, as has been mentioned earlier, could instead be part of a purely human monologue. For Christians God's incarnation in Jesus is a received and established tradition, a brand name, as it were, and even as a metaphor is to some degree protected from being questioned. Should we, for example, declare a largely forgotten and therefore "unprotected" figure such as the saintly Apollonius of Tyane[25]

---

21. John Hick, *The Metaphor of God Incarnate* (London: SCM Press, 1993).

22. Hick, *Metaphor of God Incarnate*, p. 152.

23. Hick, *Metaphor of God Incarnate*, pp. 162f. Hick, in a letter to the author (September 1998), writes: "Christians have been (or were up to now) formed by Christianity. Christianity has created them in its own image, so that it fits them and they fit it." Today, however, Hick continues, Christians can live within the overlapping influences of several religions "without any sense of contradiction."

24. Hick, *Metaphor of God Incarnate*, p. 161.

25. Apollonius of Tyane/Cappadocia (d. in Ephesus in 97 C.E.), philosopher and be-

our metaphorical agent of mediation, the suspicion would be more general, particularly among Christians. The problem seems to be that the man from Nazareth, to use the language of business, is not sold at a true market price. He has been made artificially expensive and prestigious (like a top perfume from Paris). There is still in Hick's book the echo of the "Son of God" image: in spite of his purely human status, Jesus is still depicted in a romantic, that is, immaculate, perfect, and in fact superhuman, way. This Jesus, in his perfection, is mythological and not one of us. This, however, has, as we will see, consequences for his mediating powers.

An alternative "European" image of Christ, taken from a paper hardly noticed by the theological establishment, is found in Stephen Pattison's "The Shadow Side of Jesus."[26] Pattison observes that even recent scholarship, such as that of Vermes and Sanders,[27] and, I believe, we could now add the names of John Hick and, in order to include Japan, Katsumi Takizawa,[28] has, in attempting to set Jesus in a cultural, philosophical, and historical context and at the same time trying to make him "more human," fallen victim to the long-standing tendency of portraying him as a sort of hero of the human race. Jesus is depicted as an essentially admirable and innocent man leading a life showing no trace of personal negativity. The *raison d'être* of this idealized image, however, is to distinguish and in fact to save and exonerate Jesus from the responsibility for the catastrophes and dark side of the history of established

---

liever in Helios, had written a biography of Pythagoras, his philosophical father. A contemporary of Jesus, he had been to Asia Minor, Egypt, Babylon, and India, where he learned Brahmanic doctrines. A nonviolent vegetarian and itinerant teacher, he was known for his miracles, especially for exorcisms and resurrections; some called him "God" (which he detested). At the beginning of the third century, Philostratus had written a "Life of Apollonius of Tyane," and a number of letters from the hands of Apollonius have also survived. Materials from these texts, related to New Testament texts, are reproduced by K. Berger and C. Colpe, eds., *Religionsgeschichtliches Textbuch zum Neuen Testament* (Göttingen: Vandenhoeck & Ruprecht, 1987), pp. 55, 62, 108, 113, 127, 131.

26. Stephen Pattison, "The Shadow Side of Jesus," *Studies in Christian Ethics* 8, no. 2 (1995): 54-67. S. Pattison has also commented on one of the drafts of this paper. I am indebted in many ways to him. It goes without saying, however, that I am fully responsible for the picture I have drawn. Pattison is professor of practical theology at the University of Wales, Cardiff.

27. G. Vermes, *Jesus the Jew* (London: Fontana, 1976); E. P. Sanders, *Jesus and Judaism* (London: SCM Press, 1985).

28. Cf. his article "'Rechtfertigung' im Buddhismus und im Christentum," in *Das Heil im Heute. Texte einer japanischen Theologie*, ed. Theo Sundermeier (Göttingen: Vandenhoeck & Ruprecht, 1987), pp. 181-96. Takizawa describes Jesus as a flawless, perfect man, though being a (one) model only of the "secondary contact," that is, the awakening of the human being to the "primary" presence of God — not as the unique mediator of salvation.

137

Christianity. It is quite surprising that even Friedrich Nietzsche, not known to be a friend of Christianity, made the statement that "in principle, there was only one Christian, and he died on the cross!"[29]

To counter this tendency, Pattison argues that Jesus' very life and teaching also had a dark, a shadow, side, and that this side, as well, was and is "incarnated" in the church; in other words, Jesus was, and still is, coresponsible for what came after him in the church. In this light Pattison's argument could be regarded as an introduction to a "revisionist" historiography of Christianity, thus responding to the problem of the questionable historical record of the church. But it is also responding to the issue of mediation, for he says: "if Jesus was truly human he cannot have been so unlike me and my contemporaries that he did not have a shadow or negative side to his life and work." Pattison calls this his hermeneutical principle of partial analogy.[30] He reassures us of his conviction that the points he makes about Jesus could be made equally about other figures of that period and, indeed, about those who were to come later. Jesus was not special — that is precisely the point. Why, then, would one wish to focus on Jesus? The answer at first glance seems to be a practical one. Those who happen to belong to church and Christianity were forced to address the question because this tradition has a tendency to keep contemporary Christians "in a position of passive dependence on an omnipotent, all-good person, Jesus, who will do his perfect work of salvation without humans having to take responsibility for themselves and their world." And then the rationale is spelled out: "De-idealising Jesus is vital if Christians are to empower themselves in his name. Integrating the man Jesus and the church is also important if we are to come to maturity and not to covertly idealise the former while overtly despising (i.e. negatively idealising) the latter."[31]

The implicit hypothesis, I believe, seems to be even wider and at least twofold: firstly, that a Christian's reality is somehow bound up with the reality of Jesus, and that the fault line of the human/divine contact in Jesus is for some reason essential to a Christian human/divine configuration today. Whether this reason is purely historical and cultural, or whether there is more to it, must be left open. Secondly, it is assumed that the wrong sort of Christology will prevent Christians from achieving maturity and coming to terms with reality. I take these phrases to point to what I earlier referred to as mediation.[32]

---

29. Nietzsche, *Der Antichrist* (Munich: Goldmann, [1888] 1964), p. 41.

30. Pattison, "Shadow Side of Jesus," p. 56.

31. Pattison, "Shadow Side of Jesus," p. 57.

32. It is interesting that Heisig in the essay quoted above also gives "religious maturity" a prominent place in his vision of the future of Christianity.

Pattison, in an intra-Christian and perhaps iconoclastic approach, I think, is dealing with a fundamental question of contemporary Western culture. I am interested in this side of his argument, which I will portray in more depth now, leaving aside his methodological, exegetical, and historical considerations.

As humans we have a shadow side, the metaphor for our destructive potential. Our potential for good, for creation and love, cannot be truly liberated if our "shadow," hatred and evil, is ignored or repressed and therefore excluded from our self-awareness. A "full human personality"[33] is grounded on the acceptance and the integration of both potentials — that is the basic framework of Pattison's anthropology, and it functions as a torch in the search for the humanity of Jesus. It is clear that mediation here is expressed in psychodynamic terms, which is another form of a symbolic understanding of the mediation process. The quest for new models of understanding mediation is precisely, I think, what is going on currently in Western culture. So, how far was "Jesus" successful in becoming a full human personality? As said before, I am not analyzing the exegetical validity of the argument,[34] but rather the structure of the image of mediation Pattison is offering.

As a participant in a world where evil spirits and demons were believed to cause all sorts of misfortunes and illnesses, Jesus acted prominently as a healer and exorcist.[35] But in doing so, he not only underlined the power of the imminent kingdom of God, he also reconfirmed the existence of demonic forces and contributed actively to the sustenance and growth of the discourse of evil: no salvation without demonology! These demonic and dualistic elements of Jesus' ministry have contributed to the church's inability to face the evil within its own walls. A similar interrelationship is also discernible between offering salvation and creating fear. The God of the New Testament is not just the father in the parable of the prodigal son: Jesus also announced threats of eternal punishment[36] and repeatedly presented God as a judge or destroyer: a capricious despot.[37] In relation to this image of God, Feuerbach (and Job, for that matter) is still winning the argument. The mechanism of creating fear is used to support the idea of salvation in general, and its ur-

---

33. Pattison, "Shadow Side of Jesus," p. 58.

34. John Hick, in the letter quoted above, has drawn my attention to the fact that we have little assured knowledge about Jesus. Therefore, "N.T. passages suggesting his dark side are just as suspect as those about his light side!"

35. E.g., Mark 1:32; 3:10; Luke 11:14-23. I must mention in passing that Pattison is aware of the exegetical problems of recovering "the teachings" of Jesus, and that the biblical texts show us an image of Jesus worked over in the interest of the church.

36. E.g., Matt. 5:22; 8:12; 22:13; Mark 9:46.

37. E.g., Matt. 5:44, 48; 10:28; 18:8f.; 19:21; Luke 12:40.

gency in particular. Logically, of course, the construction of any idea of salvation, hope, and faith can only work if the contrasting elements of destruction, fear, and doubt are constructed as well. Here again, Pattison says, Jesus, the man, seems to be helping "to create the problem which it is claimed that he solves or saves people from." Problematic also is the ethical radicalism of Jesus, as expressed in the Beatitudes. The ideal of perfectionism leaves little space for negative emotions and in fact oversimplifies the ambiguous process and the dilemmas of reaching ethical judgment (in Jesus' teachings even thoughts can become "sinful"!). His followers then are not really invited to come to terms with themselves (and mature), but are required to deny their self and exchange it for the one offered by Jesus, leading to a secondhand identity.[38]

Socially this had important consequences. Jesus left obscure what living in the kingdom of God might mean. His social and political thinking seemed to be vague and without a specific program, since all this was left in the hands of God. All earthly regimes, basically, were a sort of provisional waiting hall, with the better world just around the corner. This Pattison calls "the politics and social policy of chaos," and it was further nourished by the social divisiveness Jesus introduced. There was a shadow side to the possibility of universal inclusion in the kingdom of God opened up by him, namely, the exclusion of outsiders. Outsiders would be judged without mercy, and they were those who did not repent and did not accept the message. This would explain why Christians often seem to be better at hate than love.[39] The dynamics of inclusion and exclusion, which in church history took on pernicious and violent forms, were set up by Jesus himself. In fact, Jesus introduced additional conflict, division, and violence into society. "You do not get crucified for being nice to little children" is Pattison's argument.[40] In other words, Jesus' violent death was perhaps caused by the considerable aggression he himself had helped to arouse.

As I said before, it was not Pattison's aim to create a full image of Jesus. The positive and creative aspects of Jesus' life, ministry, and teaching, particularly his option for the marginalized, are explicitly acknowledged. What

38. Mark 8:34b.

39. Cf. Elaine Pagels, *The Origins of Satan* (London: Penguin Books, 1996). S. Pattison, in recommending this book in a letter to the author dated 15 September 1998, writes: "I have lately become very conscious that Christians pour out love and affection to a disembodied God who officially lacks emotions and needs while they often deprive their fellow human beings, who do need them, of these things, meting out bile and hatred on some groups with as much enthusiasm as they are soft on God."

40. Pattison, "Shadow Side of Jesus," p. 62.

Pattison went for was to show the humanity of Jesus by focusing on the hardly ever acknowledged shadow side of his life. But this he did from a very specific perspective — he was searching within the Christian story for ways to integrate light and shadow within ourselves. What then did he find? Jesus was scandalously human, just like the rest of us. The profile of this man is that of a spirit-filled, charismatic figure; chaotic and creative, integrative and dis-integrative, powerful and confused, loving and guilty. The benefit of this "de-idealization" of Jesus and his teaching is that it puts the onus for acting mor-ally and salvifically on human beings now. The work of salvation has to be done by ourselves, and that means living with the knowledge that all our at-tempts to do this will cast a shadow just like Jesus' attempts at doing it did. This insight, with its acceptance of failure and therefore the necessity of for-giveness, Pattison describes as "Christian maturity, wisdom and integration" — this is a specific definition of mediation, but for me it contains the formal structure of the general working of mediation.[41] And indeed, the last sen-tence of Stephen Pattison's paper opens the arena of church and Christianity to humanity as such, offering the de-idealized memory of Jesus as a universal, and therefore missionary, potential for salvation.[42]

I will now try to interpret the mediational structure I believe to have found in this image of Christ. The first observation which springs to mind is that a particular facet of incarnational Christology is still extremely relevant here: the assumption that a real encounter of the divine and the human hap-pened in Jesus. However, important modifications have been made. One is that because this encounter partly failed in Jesus (see above), it can now be described as an encounter which becomes the aim of every human being's life. That is the universal aspect of the story of Jesus. The other modification is that the divine also turns up in the differently expressed language code of modern psychology ("integration," "maturity," "reality"). The divine, funda-mentally, is addressed in a *theoaphatic* way (literally, speechless with regard to God).[43] The "scandal of restricted access" (Hick) is overcome, for the de-

---

41. This is not to be taken as some sort of pre–World War I liberal progressive opti-mism, but — given the collapse of optimism and the belief in science — a rather sober or chastened form of Christian-humanistic realism.

42. "Possibly in this affirmation of reality lies potential for salvation and integration for the church, for humanity, and, not least, for the memory of the man, Jesus, himself. Jesus can grow up to be regarded as a recognisable human adult instead of an unnatural, irrespon-sible childlike visionary who is incredibly, not to say pathologically, innocent" (Pattison, "Shadow Side of Jesus," p. 66).

43. Pattison acts in fact like "his" Jesus when he asks his readers to accept the psychodynamic interpretation of the self, because those who do not accept it would run the

idealized Christ is no longer *the* mediator, though he still continues to mediate a message of salvation. All this reflects quite well some of the transformations of the religious topography of Europe that I mentioned earlier. Pattison brings together past and present in Christian interpretation, puts them on an equal footing, and enables contemporary Christians and others to address in their own way the question of maturity or mediation. The widespread feeling that the kingdom of God has to be sought within us is acknowledged. Even more, he tries to overcome the European or Western experience of non-mediation by transforming logos Christology into the interpretation of the *logos* made flesh in every process of growing to maturity. However, as is the case with the kingdom of God, which Jesus did not define, so the name of the God who is active here remains obscure. This God does not show his face, except in the depth and the ramifications of basically broken life stories. The place where we may come to know the divine is inescapably tragic. There seems to be no other way to come to know God than through vulnerability and suffering.

Conclusion

The disestablishment of Jesus Christ (not his "rejection," and neither the "reinstatement" of yesterday's image of Jesus nor the "import," as it were, of a foreign one) in post-Christian Europe is, as we have seen, currently — and differently from the sixties, when only a few "progressive" theologians addressed the issue[44] — happening across the board, from intellectuals to so-called ordinary people. What is being rejected is the allegedly timeless interpretation of Christ controlled by institutionalized Christianity (which is now in rapid decline). Pattison, and Hick as well, offer a contemporary European variation of a religio-cultural adaptation and transformation of the tradition of Christ. I do not claim that the image they are drawing is fully representative for post-Christian Europe, but it certainly belongs to a broad trend which seeks a reappropriation of the Jesus tradition, and which is happening largely

---

danger of failing in their attempts at integrating their respective light and shadow sides. This is structurally not so far away from a more biblical formulation, like "following Christ and taking up one's own cross," because the cross symbolizes precisely the definitely nonperfect, dark side of our life. All this I say in order to support Pattison's approach as a possible way of expressing our search for mediation in a language and in images we have access to today.

44. The following two books had a wide circulation in Britain: John A. T. Robinson, *Honest to God* (London: SCM Press, 1963), and Leslie D. Weatherhead, *The Christian Agnostic* (London: Arthur James, [1965] 1989).

outside the established church. I do think it is in its respective way "true" or honest to its context — it is the "people," not the professionals of the established church, who have formulated this new interpretation of Jesus Christ (new religious knowledge). In their attempt to express within the realities of their own lives the *unitas oppositorum*, that is, the nondual divine-human field of contact, they are not betraying but are reformulating the tradition in the interests of life.[45]

This image of Christ tells us that a distinction has to be made between the general mission of God and Christ's mission as its symbol and incarnation (historical manifestation). The story of Jesus had and still has a decisive and universal impact, in that it carries the struggle for a spirituality of love, peace, and justice into world history. Jesus is still an important pointer to the transcendent. However, God's loving but hidden presence is reflected and confirmed in all the various and diverse processes (incarnations) of salvific mediation (maturity) across the centuries, and through all the cultures and religions, without ever exhausting his presence. Mediation cannot take place outside human experience (i.e., as God's/Christ's work only, or as something ready-made that exists externally and waiting only to be "internalized"); it arises as existential knowledge in the process of knowing, and in the knower. Given this, mediation works on a local, cultural, or religious basis; it speaks "dialect," to use an ecumenical phrase. Human insatiability, and therefore also error and misery, come into the picture (also in relation to Jesus) because the occurrence of true mediation is more the exception than the rule. Often it is misunderstood; taken as a mechanical process; only partly, or not at all, achieved; and then, historically, creating less "salvation" than new problems. It is quite impossible to say at this stage whether the religious transformation of Europe will lead to the one or the other.

Nevertheless, I do see some signs of hope in this European process of the disestablishment of Christianity and its central symbol. It means perhaps to return in this regard to the first followers of Jesus, who were Jews. To put it in Christian terms: Christianity cannot save anybody, only God can. Jesus taught us to pray — not to him, but to God (the Lord's Prayer). Historically, the exclusive divinity of Jesus Christ, and with it the idea of divine atonement,

---

45. I would distinguish this rather sharply from the aggressiveness and madness of certain forms of ethnicist religion. An example of such a religion is the racially motivated Deutsche Glaubensbewegung, created by Jacob Wilhelm Hauer, a former missionary from Basel, in 1933. Hauer, also professor of Indology at Tübingen University, collaborated with Hitler and, himself being a prominent member of the SS, regarded it as his most important recruitment area; cf. Hauer's *Deutsche Gottschau. Grundzüge eines deutschen Glaubens,* 2nd ed. (Stuttgart: K. Gutbrod, 1934).

is one particular cultural (the Hellenistic) option. In other words, it would be possible to talk of the reestablishment of the disestablishment of Jesus Christ. If God is active in the process of awakening us to maturity, then Hick's interpretations, or Pattison's psychodynamic interpretations are valid descriptions of salvation. By the same token, other models of mediation, originating in other religions, can be looked at as offering alternative ways of mediating the salvific divine-human encounter.

It seems that the disestablishment of Jesus Christ is generating (for European Christians) new space to inherit the treasures of other religions as a matter of faith and practice, and to overcome the heritage of anxiety and aggressiveness. This would alter very much the format and structure of Christian mission, from one of confrontation to bridge building; that is, to a new form of a composite, bireligious, or plurireligious awareness, opening the possibility for Christians to convert to Buddhism or Islam, for example, and for Buddhists or Muslims to convert to Christianity; all of them without giving up their respective primary religious orientations (though acknowledging that our sacred texts are in need of constant reinterpretation). To me it seems that currently, and not just in the Christian tradition, a new perception and a new vision of reality are in the making. This vision involves a rethinking of spirituality, that is, of the image of God and of humanity and of the way we and the forthcoming generations want to live on this planet. Christian mission ought to be at the forefront of this process of mutual conversion and the recognition of each other's scriptures as chapters of an unfinished book. For Christian mission the challenge is no longer territorial or geographical, it is cosmic, it is to make a real contribution to the reconciliation and unification of all things. Christian mission can do this by becoming a guest first, then a friend, and finally a partner for life in the mission of other religions and also of (agnostic) humanism. Christianity, once disestablished, is not about itself and not about Christianizing the world. It is about sharing the fullness of life on this earth, about love and reconciliation, community and peace, justice and service *(kerygma, koinonia, diakonia)*. To risk a dangerous formulation: a disestablished Christian spirituality would have failed if it were to lead us to "God"; we need a spirituality that turns us into bridge builders or, in the words of Ulrich Schoen, "dividuals": split or composite personalities, but at the same time "individuals," attempting to bring together what is separated.[46] This missionary spirituality would lead us to our fellow human beings.

46. Schoen, pp. 170-73.

Enlightenment, Postmodernity, and Mission

Andrew Walls
Transcribed by Thomas F. Foust

For many years Lesslie Newbigin has been recognized above all as a prophet to the West — an interpreter of the gospel in relation to Western culture and of Western culture in relation to the gospel. But his prophetic calling arose from his days as a serving missionary. And there is a literary path from *South India Diary* to *Foolishness to the Greeks*. As editor of the *International Review of Missions*, he steadfastly rejected the removal of the *s*, holding that missions was the true topic of the journal. And the modernizers could not achieve its deletion except with his departure.

It was as a missionary that he viewed Western Christianity and Western culture. Perhaps like many another returning missionary, he never fully recovered from the culture shock of reentry. He analyzes his own culture as only someone can who has been used to analyzing somebody else's. In the final section of *Foolishness to the Greeks*, he lists seven conditions for what he calls a "missionary encounter with our culture." The fifth of these is "help in seeing our own culture through Christian minds shaped by other cultures." We need their witness to correct ours, as indeed they need ours to correct theirs. At the moment our need is greater, for they have been far more aware of the dangers of the syncretism of an illegitimate alliance with false elements in their culture than we have been.

His scriptural basis for this is Ephesians 3, and his understanding of the ecumenical movement is with reference to the world Christian family. Current abuse of the World Council of Churches (*Foolishness to the Greeks* was based on lectures given at Princeton in 1984) he attributes to resentment at the threat it poses to Western complacency. Thirty years ago, he continues, "the ecumenical movement was perceived as the worldwide triumph of our kind of Christianity. The colored and colorful representatives of the Asian and the African churches were hailed and photographed as trophies of our missionary success. Today the Ecumenical Movement is perceived as a threat, and the theologies coming out of the younger churches call our own certainties into question."[1]

In what follows I would like to explore this from a somewhat different point of view. Newbigin latterly was concerned with mission to the West and with a cultural history of the West and especially the Enlightenment, to which he attributed the Western failure to recognize the gospel as public truth. He was more concerned with modernity than with postmodernity, and with the world church principally as a potential source of renewal for Western Christianity. I propose that we consider the world church in relation to the situation of Christianity as a whole at this time, and consider the processes Newbigin analyzes so vividly in relation to the history of Christianity as a whole.

What he is documenting is the recession of Christianity in the West, a process of decline not more rapid than the Christian decline in central Asia in the face of the Mongol invasions, but much more rapid than that in the Middle East following the rise of Islam.

But this process has gone hand in hand with a substantial accession to Christianity — an accession to which the missionary movement to which Newbigin belonged was an important, though not the only, contributing factor. The most striking difference between Christianity at the end of the nineteenth century and at the end of the twentieth is in the cultural and demographic composition of the Christian church. At the end of the nineteenth century, well over 80 percent of the people in the world who called themselves "Christians" lived in Europe or North America. That is, Christianity began the twentieth century as essentially a Western religion. There were important Christian communities elsewhere, but the dominant influences were those of Europe and North America, which set the norms and the standards for what Christianity would be like.

At the end of the twentieth century, between 50 and 60 percent of those who called themselves "Christians" lived in Latin America, Africa, Asia, or the Pacific. What is more, that proportion is steadily rising. Every year there are fewer Christians in Europe and North America and more in the southern continents. Since they already constitute more than half the world's Chris-

---

1. Lesslie Newbigin, *Foolishness to the Greeks: The Gospel and Western Culture* (London: SPCK; Grand Rapids: Eerdmans; and Geneva: WCC, 1986), p. 147.

tians, if present trends continue, at some point in the twenty-first century they will constitute two-thirds of them. That is, Christianity enters the twenty-first century as a mainly non-Western religion. There are now many centers of Christian discourse. And in most of them the most pressing issues are neither of the Enlightenment nor of postmodernism. Christian faith is in constant interaction with older realities. Among the major discourses is that of Latin America, where in addition to processes which recall many features of sixteenth-century Europe in both its Catholic and Protestant reformations, one increasingly realizes the issues that are arising from indigenous culture, indigenous religion, indigenous identity. They occur, perhaps in more crucial form than they have ever done since that same sixteenth century.

The other really large Christian discourse is that of Africa, where a theological process is reassessing the relation of Christ to the African past, which the Ghanaian theologian Kwame Bediako sees as parallel to the theological process by which Justin and Clement and the others looked at Christ's relationship to the Greek past.

Among religious influences in Africa is the explosion in urban areas of charismatic and radical evangelical Christianity which has often outflanked the older independent churches with their alternative models of the church. The heart of African identity is not to be found in white robes and traditional drumming, but in the open frontier between the natural and the spiritual worlds in which spiritual powers, whether actuated by spiritual entities or human malice or neglected family or social duty, are active. And this can be combined with expertise in the latest sound systems and films and cassettes. The charismatic and radical evangelicals who at first sight appear so contrary to African culture are in fact using the same maps of the spiritual world as the older independent churches, even if they color them differently.

The remarkable fact is that though Christianity came to Africa, at least in its missionary expression (if we are looking at Ethiopia, there is a different story), mediated through Enlightenment sources and enmeshed in the great Enlightenment program of education and health provision, the present strength of Christianity in Africa is due to its capacity to be independent of the Enlightenment worldview. Enlightenment-conditioned theology never touched a large section of the world in which African Christians lived. For many today Christ is now filling the unoccupied sectors of that world through rereadings of Scripture by hosts of people who never realized they were theologians.

We have no time to consider adequately the other discourses — the neglected one of the Pacific, for instance, or that huge Asian one which is still more neglected because it is not seen as a whole. By that I mean the complex which for lack of a better term I call the "Himalayan Arakan." A Christian chain that starts in Nepal passes through northeast India, where there are Indian states with Christian majorities, across into Myanmar, up into southwest China, down into Thailand, through the Malaysian forest, into Indonesia. Here we often have Christian majorities in ethnic minorities, so that Christianity is one feature in the constitution of identity. Taken together this forms a very sizable segment of the Christian world. And all this without mentioning the special cases: the Indian mainstream, perhaps the most testing environment the Christian faith has yet had to live in; and China, where we have only recently begun to realize how significant the Christian population is; and the overseas Chinese population of Southeast Asia with its very considerable Christian element.

The question of Enlightenment and postmodernity will not therefore be the most prominent of the issues in the realms of discourse that make up the Christian world in the twenty-first century and constitute its most dynamic sectors. The principal constituents of Christian development are likely to come from the ancient cultures of Africa and Asia, and the backcloth of that development may be war, perhaps genocidal war; hunger; epidemic, natural disaster; environmental degradation; and unrelenting poverty.

Such things have formed the background to the development of Christian discourse before. But the multiplicity of Christian discourses across the world is something new, at least in its extent and potential. It is appropriate to return to Newbigin's citation of the epistle to the Ephesians, an epistle bursting with excitement at the novelty of the unexpected extent of the people of God. Not one race, but two. And two races, who for centuries had not been able to share a meal together, were partners around the table. And the completeness of Christ's body depended on the two. And the fullness of Christ's stature was reached only when the two races, with their separate inheritances and cultures, were gathered into him. It was a shining vision and it had its fulfillment, but that fulfillment was local and temporary. In a generation or two the church became as overwhelmingly Gentile, and in the eastern Mediterranean as overwhelmingly Hellenistic, as in the beginning it had been overwhelmingly Judaic. The conditions of our own day, where different Christian discourses subsist in ancient cultures, have potentially re-created the situation of the epistle to the Ephesians, but in a more dazzling complexity than the first century ever knew. No discourse is complete in itself. Only as the separate cultural inheritances come together in Christ is the full stature of Christ revealed. None can attain it on its own.

Newbigin saw in the variety of the world's churches the corrective that the Western church needed. A postmodern reading could take the separate

Christian discourses as severally authentic and valid. Surely Newbigin's instinct was right. These are not alternative versions of Christianity, but complementary expressions. It is only together that we reach the full stature of Christ.

Can we, however, go further? World Christianity in itself has no existence except in an infinite number of specific segments of social reality. There should, however, be some things which one can say covering them all. The historic pattern of Christian expansion has been serial rather than progressive. Islam can make a much better claim than Christianity to progressive expansion, to a continuing passion of geographical advance, to maintenance of the allegiance of territories and communities which accept it. Christianity does not have the Islamic resilience. Christian history is a series of advances and recessions. What is more, decline is a built-in feature of Christian history, decline in the areas of apparent strength. But decline at the center is accompanied by growth at the periphery. So that representative Christianity, what one might call the normative, creative Christian centers, at any given time changes its geographic and demographic focus. There is no single culture area that owns Christianity and shapes it, but rather a succession of different culture areas. This in turn leads to another generalization: that Christian history depends on a series of cross-cultural diffusions because of its inherent fragility and vulnerability. Its very continued existence as a significant factor in the world depends on its demonstrated ability to cross cultural frontiers. A third generalization follows, that Christian history demonstrates a series of extended processes of cultural interaction which often prove to be transformative of Christianity itself. Each period of interaction with a new tradition of thought and life produces a new agenda, a new set of questions, which can be answered only in terms of that tradition. And since the figure of Christ is at the heart of the Christian affirmation, these ultimately resolve themselves into questions about Christ.

We have become accustomed to a set of parameters for Christianity fixed by the Jewish, Hellenistic, and barbarian traditions that have shaped European history. Christianity is currently being reshaped by its now well established encounters with the traditions of Africa, Asia, native America, and the Pacific. Our common area of interest is the fact that the laboratory in which Christianity is being renewed and reshaped with new materials of Christian thought, Christian theology, is still open.

The preexisting materials are what makes theology. One remembers that pregnant observation of Origen: "How is it," he says, "that Israelites were able to make the cherubim in the wilderness? Where did the gold come from for the pot of manna? The answer is that they had spoiled the Egyptians. It was Egyptian gold that provided the symbols of the presence of God, and the tabernacle was hung with Egyptian cloth. It is the business of the people of God," he says, "to take the things of the heathen world and to fashion from them things for the worship and glorification of God."

If Origen is right that it is Egyptian gold that is to be used for the adornment of the tabernacle, then it is those same presuppositions, that same intellectual framework, which is turned toward Christ. And it seems to me that this actually happened with the Enlightenment. There was a Christian appropriation of the Enlightenment which was not all a betrayal of Christian faith. It was an indigenization of Christianity in Western terms. It was syncretistic. (Syncretism is somebody else's indigenization, is it not? Nobody ever actually says, "I am a syncretist." It is always something that somebody else does. It is like a sect. Nobody actually belongs to a sect. Only other people belong to sects.) But certainly it involves a mixture of materials. Again, if conversion is a matter of direction rather than content, turning the material toward Christ, then we may have something which allows for both a Christian Enlightenment and a Christian post-Enlightenment.

Response to Questions after Paper Was Given

It seems to me that the process of modernization does not necessarily produce modern worldviews. The missionary movement tried very hard to produce modern worldviews at a time when these appeared to be completely consistent with Christian faith and an outcrop of a Christian doctrine of progress. It rationalized witchcraft, it rationalized the forces of evil which were so important in African life. It did not remove witchcraft beliefs, it merely left large areas of African life untouched by a theology which spoke of Christ. It meant that there were areas in which Christ did not come, could not come.

Now this was inevitable. We can only work in the universe we've got. I am myself a lost child of the Scottish Enlightenment, and feeling very lost at the moment. But it seems to me that in what is happening within African Christianity, for instance, those open spaces left vacant by the older theology are being peopled. There are emerging theologies which take account of African worldviews. The African Independent Churches were first in the field because it was semiliterate people that felt the pressure heaviest. The pioneer theologians were semiliterate people because such people were living in both worlds. Building cities, using machinery, driving cars, people in the urban situation do not put the diviner out of business. He gets more business than ever: there are far more things to go wrong. All sorts of other parts of the traditional universe may collapse. Your link with the ancestors may be weakened because you are away from ancestral land and so on — all sorts of complications come in. But you are living in a world with an open frontier between the natural and the spiritual world. And there is crossing and recrossing of that frontier all the time.

The Enlightenment universe posits a sharp line between the natural world and the phenomenal world and the spiritual world. In its rationalistic form the frontier is closed off altogether: the spiritual world either does not exist or there is nothing we can know about it. In Christian forms of the Enlightenment there are recognized crossing places: incarnation, resurrection, prayer, and so on. But theology is a matter of policing that frontier. There are other universes in which the frontier is wide open. And a different theology emerges as a result. And to implement the theology, Christ has to fill the scene as people see the scene if it is to be truly Christian.

The nature of conversion is not a matter of content, but of direction, not of substituting something new for something old, not about adding something new to something old, but about reordering the elements that are already there so that they face toward Christ. Christian history takes its significance from the totality of cross-cultural expressions, not from any one of them, and from the totality of historical expressions, not from any one of them. Christianity is of its essence incremental and cross-generational; a multireel cinema film, not a studio portrait. It's also evident that built-in cultural diversity, the absence of a preset pattern, the fact that the norm is not the proselyte but the convert (going back to that initial crucial decision in Acts 15 to abandon the proselyte model which had been in use so long), involves a factor of risk and uncertainty, of discovery and exploration. The development of Christian patterns of thought and life, theology and praxis, depends on this process of exploration with the attendant risks and uncertainty. It is the fruit of that early Christian decision to take the risky uncharted path of the convert rather than the safe predetermined path of the proselyte, that decision to leave the new Christians with liberty under the guidance of the Holy Spirit.

It is also worth considering the relationship of the evangelical revival itself to the Enlightenment. And perhaps evangelicalism had a particular place in the construction of Enlightenment religion. It provided a religious resolution of an Enlightenment crux: individual consciousness and identity. Evangelical religion was able to reconcile a Christianity which in Europe had been historically corporate and communal with the Enlightenment insistence on personal responsibility. And because of its distinction between nominal

Christianity and real Christianity, it could do so without destroying the corporate expression of Christendom which was part of European identity. Evangelical religion, which is so important in the missionary movement itself, seems to me to have a part in the building up of a Christianity that made its peace with the Enlightenment. For although Lesslie Newbigin sees it as the great enemy, in fact the theology of modern Western Christianity has been indigenized to the Enlightenment. And possibly, evangelicalism gave Christendom a second wind and enabled it to survive the Enlightenment. It produced a very confident form of religion, a form which reaches its sharpest expression in someone like Alexander Duff, who is absolutely confident as he faces the powers of India in a universe of knowledge of which the Bible is the center and the sun, and in which politics and economics and the natural sciences all have their proper place that comes from the rational Calvinist model he had learned at Saint Andrews.

Lesslie Newbigin's Epistemology:
A Dual Discourse?[1]

Thomas F. Foust

Western culture is facing an epistemological challenge. The epistemological attempt, born out of the Enlightenment, to discover universal truth through reason alone has been abandoned. One of the distinguishing marks at present is the persistent assault on foundationalism, especially, since Lyotard,[2] in its meta-narrative form. Newbigin was not silent in this debate, and he argued that the parochial stories of humanity combine into one grand narrative encompassing all people of all times. This essay will limit its attention to a brief examination of Newbigin's epistemology, in which I find a "dual discourse" or "internal dialogue." My aim is to highlight one area from within Newbigin's epistemology that seems to need further attention and exploration for discussion.

Any discussion of epistemology in connection with Newbigin[3] ushers in

1. This essay, which was a discussion paper for one of the workshops of the "After Newbigin Colloquium," is more fully developed in chapters 2 and 3 of my doctoral thesis at the University of Birmingham. I am deeply indebted to Prof. Dr. Werner Ustorf for the conversations that gave the impetus to this paper.

2. Jean-Francois Lyotard, *The Postmodern Condition: A Report on Knowledge,* trans. Geoff Bennington and Brian Massumi (Manchester: Manchester University Press, 1984).

3. One recent study that gives attention to Newbigin's epistemology is the doctoral work of Jukka Keskitalo at the University of Helsinki: Jukka Keskitalo. "Kristillinen usko ja moderni kulttuuri: Lesslie Newbigin käsitys kirkon missiosta modernissa länsimaisessa kulttuurissa" (Finnish). Th.D. thesis, University of Helsinki, 1999. This was published in 1999 by Suomalainen Teologinen Kirjallisuusseura in Helsinki. A ten-page summary in English is available from the author entitled, "The Christian Faith and Modern Culture: Lesslie Newbigin's View of the Church's Mission in Modern Western Culture."

the philosophy of Michael Polanyi, whose book *Personal Knowledge* was published in 1958.[4] At least as early as 1966 Newbigin was well versed in Polanyi's
epistemology and had incorporated it into his own philosophy and theology.[5]
One finds extensive use of Polanyi in many of Newbigin's writings through the
years and in all his discussions on epistemology up to and including his last
writings.[6] Literally Newbigin utilized Polanyi's epistemological approach
shortly after its publication and never deviated from using it.

Newbigin followed Polanyi in arguing that since Descartes, we in Western culture have been seduced by the idea that there is a kind of knowledge
that cannot be doubted and that involves no personal risk. Like Polanyi,
Newbigin employed Augustine's assertion *Credo ut intelligam,* "I believe in
order to understand," in his epistemological claim that there is no knowledge
without faith, in order to emphasize the character of the knowledge to which
one is personally committed and upon which his or her professional reputa-
tion is at stake.[7] Polanyi argued from the perspective of scientific investiga-

4. Michael Polanyi, *Personal Knowledge: Towards a Post-Critical Philosophy* (Chicago:
University of Chicago Press, 1962). For an excellent popular survey of Polanyi and his ideas,
see Drusilla Scott, *Everyman Revived: The Common Sense of Michael Polanyi* (Chippenham,
Wiltshire: Antony Rowe, 1985); Richard Allen, *Polanyi* (Claridge Press, 1990); and more sub-
stantially, Harry Prosch, *Michael Polanyi: A Critical Exposition,* SUNY Series in Cultural Per-
spectives Press (Albany: State University of New York Press, 1986). Interestingly Drusilla
Scott rejects Prosch's interpretation of Polanyi. See Scott's article in *Convivium,* no. 24
(March 1987).

5. See Lesslie Newbigin, *Honest Religion for Secular Man* (Philadelphia: Westminster;
London: SCM Press, 1966), pp. 188ff.

6. See, for instance, the following books of Newbigin's: *The Other Side of 1984: Questions for the Churches* (Geneva: WCC Publications, 1983), pp. 17-27; *Foolishness to the Greeks:
The Gospel and Western Culture* (London: SPCK; Grand Rapids: Eerdmans; and Geneva:
WCC, 1986), pp. 65-94; *The Gospel in a Pluralist Society* (London: SPCK; Grand Rapids:
Eerdmans; and Geneva: WCC Publications, 1989), pp. 27-51; *Truth to Tell: The Gospel as Public Truth* (Grand Rapids: Eerdmans; Geneva: WCC Publications; and London: SPCK, 1991),
pp. 15, 18-20, 29-32, 41-59; *Proper Confidence: Faith, Doubt, and Certainty in Christian Discipleship* (Grand Rapids: Eerdmans, 1995), pp. 39-64, 75-76.

7. Newbigin used or referred to this quotation frequently. For instance, see *Pluralist
Society,* pp. 27-51; *Truth to Tell,* pp. 19-20, 29; *Proper Confidence,* pp. 48-50; et al. Newbigin
is of course adhering to Polanyi on this point. Polanyi asserted that modern men and
women are unprecedented as the past few centuries have led to completely new understandings of the whole cosmos and have enriched us mentally and morally to an extent unrivaled
by any other period of human history. Astounding achievements have been possible because Western culture's "incandescence had fed on the combustion of the Christian heritage
in the oxygen of Greek rationalism, and when this fuel was exhausted the critical framework
itself burnt away. . . . we must now go back to St. Augustine to restore the balance of our

tion. He used Augustine to assert that there is no knowledge without faith.[8] From this perspective Polanyi contended that all scientists had to operate out of a tradition of guidelines and limits that are accepted in faith. This tradition provided a set of assumptions that are not questioned but are accepted in faith. Rational doubt about a proposition could only be entertained on the basis of some belief which, at that moment, one did not doubt.

However, "faith" may be a misnomer for Polanyi and Newbigin.[9] For Polanyi this set of guidelines has presuppositions, some demonstrable and some not, and all of them, when taken together, constitute tacit knowing. This is not so much "faith" as it is "accepted understandings," which is some-thing other than a biblical understanding of faith.[10] And of course, this raises questions for Newbigin's epistemology.

There is validity in recapturing what Newbigin calls "Augustine's post-critical philosophy" for our postmodern context. Postmodernism has correctly alerted us that the attempt born out of the Enlightenment to discover universal truth through reason alone fails. But this has led many postmodernists to aban-don belief in universal truth because they are convinced that there are nothing

---

cognitive powers. In the fourth century A.D., St. Augustine brought the history of Greek philosophy to a close by inaugurating for the first time a post-critical philosophy. He taught that all knowledge was a gift of grace, for which we must strive under the guidance of ante-cedent belief: *nisi credideritis, non intelligitis* (from St. Augustine, *De libero arbitrio*, Book I, par. 4: 'The steps are laid down by the prophet who says, "Unless ye believe, ye shall not un-derstand"'). His doctrine ruled the minds of Christian scholars for a thousand years. Then faith declined and demonstrable knowledge gained superiority over it" (see Polanyi, pp. 265-66).

8. Polanyi uses the terms "faith," "trust," "belief," and especially "fiduciary" in refer-ence to this point.

9. Marius Felderhof touches on this point in his brief article, "*The Other Side of 1984: Some Epistemological Queries,*" *Selly Oak Journal*, no. 2 (January 1985). But, as Newbigin points out in his rejoinder, Felderhof likens Polanyi's "fiduciary framework" and Newbigin's "faith" to Nicholas Wolterstorff's "ultimate certitude" concept, and this misses the funda-mental point, for "ultimate certitude" is an eschatological notion. See Newbigin's response in the same issue, p. 34. Also see Nicholas Wolterstorff, *Reason within the Bounds of Religion* (Grand Rapids: Eerdmans, 1976; 2nd ed. 1984). Still, the essential consideration remains: what Newbigin means by Christian "faith" is something other than what Polanyi intends by "faith" and "fiduciary framework."

10. See, for instance, Dennis Lindsay's study on biblical faith. Dennis Lindsay, "Mobi-lising the Church for Mission," *European Journal of Theology* 6, no. 2 (1997): 147-55. At pres-ent Lindsay is expanding his ideas presented in the article in a monograph on a biblical theol-ogy of faith. He reminds us that a biblical understanding of faith must be understood in terms of "engaging with God" in reference to active participation in the work and purpose of God on the part of the believer.

more than conflicting and incompatible local narratives.[11] In this intellectual environment science is cast into the same boat that the humanities have been in during the modern period, that of uncertainty and unreliability. Reasons are being suggested to doubt the claims of science to objective truth, and cultural relativism is now being applied to the once exempt sciences. In this setting two noteworthy features come together: an attack on the legitimacy of epistemology and its replacement with a form of pragmatism.

However, as Colin Gunton argues, this postmodern shift toward pragmatism is giving priority to practice over truth, and this "derives from the same tendency to the divinization of the human that underlies the modern reassertion of Hellenism against Judaeo-Christian tradition. It represents a shift of the image of God from divine knowledge to a divine agency, and it is more dangerous still, for in it 'we are being said to be not so much like God as a replacement for God . . . no longer a spectator, but a being that actively creates, or shapes, its own world.'"[12]

One of our debts to Newbigin is his insistent reminder that history derives its meaning not from forces within it, but from the goal which has been promised by God and has as its central clue the crucified and resurrected Christ.[13] And, as Stanley Grenz asserts, this story is the story of God's action in human history and is centered in the person Jesus Christ, who is God's Son. This particular narrative is objective precisely because its center has come from *outside* this world into human history in terms understandable by all people. It is in this sense that all interpretations may be measured by the story of God's action in Jesus of Nazareth as it transcends (is outside) them all and is, ultimately, the truth for all women and men of all times.[14]

But when Newbigin follows Polanyi's use of Augustine and the Isaiah 7:9 text, "Unless you believe you will not understand," not only is there difficulty between Polanyi's and Newbigin's concepts of faith, but Newbigin and Polanyi are also presenting an incomplete understanding of Augustine on this

11. Such as Michel Foucault, Jacques Derrida, Richard Rorty, and others.

12. Colin Gunton, *The One, the Three, and the Many: God, Creation, and the Culture of Modernity: The 1992 Bampton Lectures* (Cambridge: Cambridge University Press, 1993; reprint, 1994), p. 111. Gunton was quoting from Edward Craig, *The Mind of God and the Works of Man* (Oxford: Clarendon, 1987), p. 32. Interestingly Gunton asserts that Rorty's postmodernist position is a movement coming from "the image of God exercised in reason to that realized in action." Thus, Gunton argues, Rorty belongs in the very tradition he affects to repudiate.

13. Newbigin, *Pluralist Society*, pp. 103-15.

14. Stanley Grenz, *A Primer on Postmodernism* (Cambridge, U.K., and Grand Rapids: Eerdmans, 1996), pp. 1-10, 45-49, and 161-74. Newbigin maintained this same argument often in his writings.

point. Augustine did not assert that there is no knowledge without faith. He held that a certain amount of rational evidence for Christ is necessary before one believes, but after one believes it, one can then go on to find new reasons to believe. Augustine is a moderate fideist and not a fideist as Newbigin and Polanyi suggest.[15] Norman Geisler states that reason initially precedes faith for Augustine for several purposes: (1) reason helps one judge whether authority is credible; (2) reason precedes faith in reality, not in time; (3) reason tells us that it is reasonable to believe what we cannot ascertain by reason; (4) reason helps us understand the contents of what is to be believed; (5) reason helps us believe what we cannot see; (6) reason removes objections to belief; and (7) reason, persuaded by evidence, can call one to faith. But, Geisler continues, while Augustine holds that reason precedes initial faith, Augustine also asserts that: (1) faith precedes full understanding; (2) faith rewards reason with clear understanding; (3) reason is adequate to demonstrate God's existence; (4) reason confirms faith with evidence; (5) faith is more profound and transcends reason; (6) faith and reason complement each other; and (7) faith and reason can be used to show truth in an extraordinary manner.[16]

Nevertheless, to defend his Augustinian position of *Credo ut intelligam,* Newbigin called upon Alasdair MacIntyre's argument in *Whose Justice? Which Rationality?* In using MacIntyre, Newbigin argued that the rationalism of modern culture is dependent on a particular tradition of human reasoning and that there is no critical act possible except when a set of beliefs is accepted acritically. Newbigin rejected the concept that there is an objective truth available to humans in a series of propositions independent of contingent events in history and to which we do not have to commit our whole lives.[17]

---

15. Byron Lambert first brought this to my attention. Personal letters, interviews, and related telephone interviews with Byron C. Lambert, Hagerstown, Ind., 6-7 March 1997 and 18 March 1998.

16. Norman Geisler, ed., *What Augustine Says* (Grand Rapids: Baker, 1982), pp. 13-31. M. J. Charlesworth stresses that "Augustine himself does not distinguish formally and explicitly between the different functions of 'understanding' in relation to faith. But we can at least say that, while he is anxious to safeguard the autonomy of faith by means of the 'crede ut intelligas' formula, he is equally anxious to affirm the possibility of rational speculation about God prior to and independently of faith in God. . . . Augustine did not want to be a 'rationalist' denying the proper autonomy of faith, any more than he wanted to be a naïve fideist denying the autonomy of reason, and the strain represented by 'crede ut intelligas' and that by 'intellige ut credas' exist together in his thought in an unresolved or ambivalent state." See M. J. Charlesworth, introduction in *St. Anselm's "Proslogion" with "A Reply on Behalf of the Fool" by Gaunilo and "The Author's Reply to Gaunilo,"* translated with an introduction and philosophical commentary by M. J. Charlesworth (Oxford: Clarendon, 1965), p. 28.

17. Lesslie Newbigin, *Truth and Authority in Modernity,* Christian Mission and Mod-

Newbigin stated that MacIntyre demonstrates that "it is an illusion to suppose that there is available to us some kind of pure rationality existing in a disembodied state and therefore capable of passing judgment on all the various ways of grasping truth developed in particular socially embodied traditions of rational discourse."[18] In other words, Newbigin maintained that reason always "operates within a specific tradition of rational discourse, a tradition that is carried by a specific human community. There is no supracultural 'reason' that can stand in judgment over all particular human traditions of rationality. All reason operates within a total worldview that is embodied in the language, the concepts, and the models that are the means by which those who share them can reason together."[19]

The rational discourse of the Christian community finds its clue in those events that form the substance of the biblical narrative and in the subsequent experience of those who have done the same. Returning to MacIntyre's argument, Newbigin contended that "no critical act is possible except on the basis of a whole complex of beliefs which are assumed a-critically as the grounds on which one can criticize the belief under discussion."[20] This unquestioned, complex, and accepted set of beliefs is the product of a particular socially embodied tradition of reasoning and becomes the ground upon which one can criticize a specific belief under discussion.

However, Newbigin's utilization of MacIntyre's claims may be questioned on grounds similar to those Mary Clark offers in regard to MacIntyre. Clark acknowledges that for Augustine Christ is the one "who makes possible not merely the illumination of minds to know the partial truths but the very seeing of God." But she disagrees with MacIntyre, and hence Newbigin, on the distinction between knowledge and faith within Augustine's teaching.[21]

---

ern Culture series, ed. Alan Neely, H. Wayne Pipkin, and Wilbert Shenk (Leominster, Herefordshire: Gracewing; Valley Forge, Pa.: Trinity Press International, 1996), p. 81.

18. See Newbigin, *Pluralist Society,* p. 82. Also see the writings of Alasdair MacIntyre. Especially see *After Virtue* (London: Gerald Duckworth, 1981) and *Whose Justice? Which Rationality?* (London: Gerald Duckworth, 1988). Further see Newbigin, *The Gospel and Our Culture,* Mission Today Pamphlet no. 47 (London: Catholic Missionary Education Centre, 1990).

19. Newbigin, *Truth and Authority,* p. 52. Thus, for Newbigin, even though the Christian faith is rooted in one strand of the whole human story, this does not invalidate its universal claims. It shares this feature with every other form of rationality. Consequently, Newbigin submitted that from the Christian perspective, all nations are invited to find the clue to understanding the world, not in some eternal truths of the philosophers, but in the biblical story.

20. Newbigin, *Pluralist Society,* p. 82.

21. Mary T. Clark, *Augustine,* Outstanding Christian Thinkers Series (London: Geoffrey Chapman, 1994), pp. 22-23.

Clark submits that MacIntyre is implying that there is no distinction within Augustine's teaching of what can be known by human reason and what must be accepted on faith when MacIntyre asserts that the totality of Augustine's thought must be believed to understand any part of it. Her argument, which maintains that this misunderstands Augustine, rests on a variety of reasons: (1) Augustine praised the Platonists for intellectually discovering the goal of human aspirations; (2) question 48 of Augustine's *Eighty-three Different Questions*, in which Augustine raises the question of what can be believed, could have saved MacIntyre from his "unwarranted generalization"; and (3) Augustine often referred to a priori truths as being in the memory.[22]

Thus an epistemology with its base primarily built on the Augustinian principle *Credo ut intelligam* is tenuous at best. And, as discussed above, faith in Christ is not coterminous with a set of accepted presuppositions or accepted understandings. Additional clarification is needed between Polanyi's use of the terms "faith" and "tacit knowledge" and Newbigin's appeal for faith in Christ as the starting point for a new rationality to usher in a missionary encounter with Western culture. It is in this tension, or internal dialogue, between knowledge and faith in Newbigin's epistemology, as found in these two areas, that one finds a significant key to his theology and what I call a "dual discourse." And it is this issue of dual discourse or internal dialogue that I want to bring to this workshop for discussion, as I find that this dialectic process has worked its way through all of Newbigin's theology. Let me demonstrate.[23]

In Polanyi's scientific world of theory, there was the demand for verification (as was true with the old logical positivists)[24] among scientists. Therefore all that Polanyi could do was demonstrate the limitations of their own (scientific) worldview and show how little could be proved from their working assumptions. The consequence of utilizing this approach in religious or humane studies, as Newbigin has done, is of course cultural relativism. That is, we are limited to seeing the world through the spectacles we have inherited or have chosen, which of course was one of Newbigin's tenets. But this makes all absolutes empty and all beginnings arbitrary. Thus it is not possible to know where

---

22. Clark, pp. 22-23.

23. To stimulate discussion, one illustration will serve our purpose, especially as we are primarily examining Newbigin's epistemology in this paper, and that only briefly. But this same internal dialectic process may be found throughout Newbigin's theology; hence, many examples could be offered. See my own doctoral research for other examples.

24. Such as those of the "Vienna Circle," Moritz Schlick, Rudolph Carnap, Friedrich Waismann, Herbert Feigl, Otto Neurath, and Kurt Gödel. And, although he was not a member of the circle, Ludwig Wittgenstein's early writings, or the "old" Wittgenstein, could also be included in this list.

to begin. As Sartre and the other existentialists insisted, we are doomed to be free as our own gods. Consequently, while this may free us from the tyrannies of science, as Polanyi and Newbigin hoped to do, it also fixes more deeply every discipline of the humane or supernatural in relativism.

Therein lies the internal dialectic for Newbigin as he, on the one hand, affirms the postmodern tenet that reality will be understood differently by each knowing person that encounters it and, hence, ends up with cultural relativism. But on the other hand, he departs from the postmodern insistence — and therefore from his relativist position — that this therefore means that there is no one meaning of the world. For Newbigin also makes the claim that there is a transcendent reality central to the whole and that Christians have been let in on this "open secret" now. But it is only in the end that the Christian perspective of reality will be shown to be the truth.

Newbigin asserted that the Christian story is "objective" truth, as it comes from *outside* this world, but it will not be *proved* to be so until God gives his verdict at the end. Until that time Christians may appeal to the gospel of Jesus Christ with confidence, as they believe it to be the truth and demonstrate that truth in their lives individually and collectively. But the claim to objective truth does not follow from Newbigin's epistemological beginning.

At the heart of this issue is how one must ultimately understand Newbigin. To approach Newbigin's theology from a purely scholastic standpoint will result in misunderstanding him. One may best understand his thought processes from a scriptural standpoint. In this respect he thought "from above." Newbigin's thinking may be described similarly to the way Hans Küng describes Karl Barth's thinking.[25] Newbigin began with what he perceived to be the real, the factual, the concrete, with what he believed was from God and his revelation in Jesus Christ. His overriding interest was from what he held to be the factual and historical, which contained the essential and the immutable, the abstract and the universal. Thus he emphasized act, event, and reality. Consequently he gave little regard to systematizing his theology. His concern was more as a missionary activist than as an academic or theologian.[26]

But this is in contrast with Newbigin's epistemological approach "from below," in which he followed Polanyi. It is here that we may find the key to Newbigin's dual discourse. On the one hand, Newbigin always argued that we

---

25. Hans Küng, *Justification: The Doctrine of Karl Barth and a Catholic Reflection*, trans. Thomas Collins, Edmund E. Tolk, and David Granskou (Philadelphia: Nelson, 1981), pp. 3-5. For a discussion from Newbigin's perspective on Barth's passionate attack on natural theology, see Newbigin, *Truth and Authority*, pp. 60-88, esp. 67ff.

26. The notable exception between Newbigin and Barth is that Newbigin did not reject completely all thinking "from below," as Barth did with regard to natural theology.

are all limited in our knowledge and that there is no privileged position for knowing that is above all others. We must therefore pursue truth from that perspective (epistemology from below). All that we know is from an historically limited perspective (cultural relativism). This means that we must think from the context of an historically determined human position. On the other hand, Newbigin also held that Christians had been given the ultimate meaning to the universe in the person Jesus Christ and that Scripture was testimony to that fact (thinking from above). While the verification of the truth as found in Jesus Christ will not be revealed fully until the end of human history, we have been given the meaning in the person of Jesus Christ as revealed in Scripture. Consequently when the position of thinking from below brings difficulties to Newbigin's position, he can (and does) simply move to the thinking-from-above perspective to solve the historical dilemma he faces without necessarily noting he has done so. Thus he does not stay in the thinking-from-below position — even though he states that that is the only position from which we can know — to face his problems from that position. This thinking "from above" approach led Newbigin to have limited appreciation, and even some aversion, to what he saw as thinking "from below" (thinking that begins "from below" to fashion reality out of possibilities or potentials).

But this dialectic should not be too surprising for us since epistemologically for Newbigin it was the debate itself that was fundamental along with the publication of what was discovered anew from the deliberation. And if controversy was the result, then so be it. Friends, colleagues, and rivals of Newbigin's will quickly recall his custom of taking up an opposing position in conversation for the purpose of fully testing an idea. This characteristic is sometimes present in his writings as well. It is likely that this was a carryover from his theological training days, but it was also certainly influenced by his epistemological approach in that it was in and through the public debate that ideas and knowledge would gain strength and authority through the verification of others or would be diminished when sufficiently challenged in the arena of public debate. This was, of course, a Polanyian concept. The end result was that Newbigin was less concerned with producing a systematic theology than with making his thoughts accessible to a wide audience for the purpose of determining their merit and for adding to the authority of the tradition in which he saw himself.

This dual discourse in Newbigin's epistemology works its way through his theology and allows him to move from one position to the other without notice to his reader, carrying on two discourses concurrently.[27] For example,

---

27. I am not referring to changes in Newbigin's theology or epistemology. Certainly

this is why Newbigin must argue for eschatological verification even though at the same time he contends for objective truth that insiders (believers) can know.[28] This is also likely why Newbigin has such a wide appeal to theologians from widely different (e.g., rationalist and fundamentalist) positions, why it is often difficult to criticize him, and why he does not fit theologically into any one "camp." It also means that when Newbigin typically makes theological or doctrinal claims, one will regularly find a parallel discourse. Thus to understand Newbigin, the whole dialectic must be considered. The claim here is that there is more to Newbigin's theology and epistemology than many people think. He was provocative even within his own theology and epistemology, which I identify as an internal dialectic or a dual discourse. While Newbigin's ad hoc epistemological approach served a useful purpose for him, he has left those of us who follow some epistemological work to do.[29]

---

these exist between his earlier and more recent writings. For instance, Newbigin's shift in approaching missions from a christocentric to a trinitarian position; cf. *One Body, One Gospel, One World* of 1958 with *The Open Secret* of 1978 gives rise to distinctions in his thought. However, it is not these changes that are the issue. The dual discourse or internal dialogue within Newbigin may be understood as a dialectic move within Newbigin's thought and writings that swings from one position to another without indication. To understand Newbigin one must grasp this dual discourse within his thought.

28. Newbigin's best explanation for this particular tension is found in *Pluralist Society,* pp. 103-15, esp. 104-9.

29. The purpose of this essay, as one of the papers given in a workshop of the "After Newbigin Colloquium," is to stimulate discussion in relation to one aspect of Newbigin's theology. From my own perspective the resolution of Newbigin's dialectic may be permissible when it is understood as an "eschatological epistemology," a phrase that came from a conversation with George Hunsberger. Newbigin's epistemology has a presuppositional approach in that he has foundations that cannot be proven. But he does not follow it through like a typical presuppositional approach. By its very nature an eschatological epistemology must, in the end, be agnostic when confronted with the empirical demand. For instance, both Gabriel Fackre and George Hunsberger have identified Newbigin as an "eschatological agnostic" (i.e., maintaining "an intentional silence") on the question of the salvation of those who do not know Jesus Christ. See Gabriel Fackre, "The Scandals of Particularity and Universality," *Mid-Stream* 22, no. 1 (1983): 32-52, and George Hunsberger, *Bearing the Witness of the Spirit: Lesslie Newbigin's Theology of Cultural Plurality,* Gospel and Our Culture Series, ed. Craig Van Gelder (Grand Rapids: Eerdmans, 1998), pp. 225-34. Newbigin's epistemology is not thoroughly presuppositional; rather, it is eschatological. And this arises from the fact that Newbigin's theology should be understood primarily as pastoral or didactic, not as academic or theological. Many have made this point — even Newbigin himself more than once — and Jenny Taylor echoes this in her essay within this collection. Consequently one may best understand Newbigin's thought processes from a scriptural standpoint, and in this respect he thought "from above."

SECTION 4

GLOBALIZATION AND THE GOSPEL

The Globalization of Poverty
and the Exploitation of the Gospel

K. P. Aleaz

It is the contention of this paper that if globalization in terms of the free-market economy[1] started in the eighties of the last century, a globalized gospel may have to be envisaged as five hundred years old, as old as colonialism, and that the gospel according to Lesslie Newbigin is only a twentieth-century manifestation of it. But at the same time, globalization today can further the cause of a globalized gospel in a drastic way because globalization in terms of the free-market economy simultaneously can mean globalization of a particular culture and its values, including a particular religion, namely, Christianity. It is a second contention of the paper that if globalization along with economic growth achieves globalization of poverty, the globalized gospel today is a poverty-stricken gospel as it perverts the gospel of God in Jesus for all of humanity into a sectarian expression of it. The quest of the paper is to identify a way out from this perversion. In the first section of the paper a Third World perspective on globalization is highlighted. The second section is on the gospel in the context of globalization. Our concluding observations, in the third and final section, are presented in relation to the thought of Lesslie Newbigin.

---

1. For a study on globalization, cf. E. Kofman and G. Youngs, eds., *Globalization: Theory and Practice* (London: Pinter, 1996); A. Hoogvelt, *Globalisation and the Postcolonial World: The New Political Economy of Development* (London: Macmillan, 1997). For the impact of globalization on the present author's country, cf. N. Vinayakam, ed., *Globalisation of Indian Economy* (New Delhi: Kanishka Publishers, 1995); G. Dietrich, *The Impact of New Economic Policy on Women in India and Feminist Alternatives* (Bangalore: ECC, 1997).

K. P. ALEAZ

A Third World Perspective on Globalization

The present international situation of globalization is marked by the domination of the ideology of the free-market economy. The market with its sole criterion of economic growth determines policies regarding other economic goals like liquidation of mass poverty, economic welfare and eco-justice, and policies regarding directions in social, educational, and cultural life. It is the ideology of the market that has been enforced globally, through the International Monetary Fund (IMF), the World Bank (WB), and the World Trade Organization (WTO), by the economic powers in the unipolar world.[2] The market economics of the G7-TNC-IMF-WB-WTO combination dominates, through their "global governance," not only the political UN but also the UN special agencies for social development and justice like the International Labor Organization, UNESCO, Food and Agricultural Organization, commissions of human rights, women's development, indigenous people, etc., for their goal of economic growth.[3]

However, the fact is, globalization along with economic growth achieves globalization of poverty. This is because in the new economic policy of globalization and liberalization, the function of the state is only just to make the climate safe for the market and withdraw almost completely from the realm of economic goals such as liquidation of poverty and unemployment, distribution of welfare, narrowing the gulf between the rich and the poor, people's participation in the economic process, accountability of economic centers to the people, and economic self-sufficiency. Here it should be clearly identified that the market is not concerned with these economic goals,[4] and therefore globalization of poverty is the result. The ideology of the free market further globalizes pollution of soil, air, and water. It leads to the exploitation of the natural resource base of the country, especially of forest and sea, and this has disastrous consequences for tribals, scheduled castes, traditional fisherfolk, and such other groups who depend on them to eke out a living. They are also torn away from their natural roots as well as from their community and cultural ties, and thus the social objectives of the people are destroyed for the sake of economic growth.[5]

Since the disintegration of socialist regimes in 1989, the free-market

---

2. M. M. Thomas, *The Church's Mission and Post-Modern Humanism: A Collection of Essays and Talks, 1992-1996* (Tiruvalla: CSS; Delhi: ISPCK, 1996), p. 93.

3. Thomas, p. 39.

4. Thomas, p. 38.

5. Thomas, p. 39.

ideology has dominated the world, and the Third World countries have fallen into line. For example, India launched its "New Economic Policy" in 1991. But many of our Indian academics are today looking forward to an alternative paradigm, the base of which has to be the movements of peoples who are the victims of globalization.[6] The people's movements of Dalits, tribals, fisherfolk, and women in India may be too feeble politically, but it is possible that such movements acquire a transnational character because the problem we encounter in globalization is worldwide. Vandana Shiva says:

> We are really living through a period in which brute force of a tiny exploiting group of people is disrupting all social and ecological structures of the world. It seems to be not just for making money. I think it stems from a level more primitive than that. It seems to be a brute force that is connected to a fear of everything that dares to be alive. In the face of that brute force we will continue to celebrate our freedom, to dare to strive for justice.[7]

M. M. Thomas, the Indian theologian, gives the following exhortation:

> The present anti-people State with its policy of globalisation giving itself up to the profit-orientated market economy and to the ideology of high-technology development under the auspices of the multinational corporations from outside and inside which are free to exploit nature and people, has to be fought. But we should work for a people-oriented state while doing so.[8]

K. C. Abraham is of the view that the process of globalization is inevitable, and hence the valid question is how we orient the forces of globalization for the furtherance of justice. We should seek a new global solidarity of the victims of the present system to build a just global order. An alternative development paradigm supported by an alternative vision of human bond to one

---

6. Thomas, pp. 38-39, 97. R. Kothari, A. Sen, A. Nandy, V. Shiva, C. T. Kurian, and M. A. Oommen are some of these Indian academics. For the writing of some of these see, for example, Amartya Sen, *Beyond Liberalisation: Social Opportunity and Human Capability* (New Delhi: Institute of Social Science, 1994); C. T. Kurian, *Global Capitalism and the Indian Economy* (New Delhi: Orient Longman, 1994). Tracts for the Times 6.

7. Vandana Shiva, "People's Power Expropriated," in *The People vs. Global Capital: The G7, TNCs, SAPs, and Human Rights. Report of the International People's Tribunal to Judge the G7, Tokyo, July 1993* (Tokyo: Pacific Asia Resources Center, 1994), p. 82.

8. Thomas, p. 82.

another and to the earth should emerge from the experience of the poor and the marginalized.[9]

The Gospel in the Context of Globalization

Theology can be pressed into service toward building a just global order and thus counter the globalization process. Theology should emerge from the experience of the people, and contextual theology is an effort to ground theology in the immediate experience of the oppressed and suffering people.[10] An organic holistic model of reality has to be conceived[11] side by side with the conviction that plurality is an essential aspect of the global as it provides the space for different identities to grow in dialogue.[12] There is radical interrelatedness and interdependence of all the plurality in creation. As radical interrelatedness is the characteristic of reality and therefore of the divine, openness to the other becomes the essential mode of response to God.[13] Our struggle against globalization today has to be for open communities; a community of communities is the question. The core of our vision has to be a community of communities that accepts a plurality of identities in a nonthreatening and mutually affirming way.[14] If globalization means globalization of a particular culture and its values, including a particular religion, namely, Christianity, then instead of a community of communities it gives rise to fundamentalist trends not only in Christianity but also in other religions. Globalization thus becomes a theological concern. To quote S. J. Samartha:

> In our time, attention is drawn almost exclusively to the economic dimensions of globalisation — globalisation of the market, including extensive discussions on GATT and the Dunkel proposals. This is of course important and cannot be neglected. However, it is unfortunate that its religious and cultural dimensions are almost wholly forgotten. The mass

9. K. C. Abraham, *Liberative Solidarity: Contemporary Perspectives on Mission* (Tiruvalla: CSS, 1996), pp. 150-52.

10. Abraham, p. 152.

11. Abraham, pp. 152-53.

12. Abraham, p. 150.

13. Abraham, p. 154.

14. Abraham, p. 154; cf. S. J. Samartha, *One Christ — Many Religions: Toward a Revised Christology* (Bangalore: SATHRI, 1992), p. 13. The phrase "a community of communities" was first used in recent years at the Colombo multilateral dialogue organized by the WCC in April 1974. Cf. S. J. Samartha, ed., *Towards World Community: The Colombo Papers* (Geneva: WCC, 1975), p. 120.

media is very much involved in the globalisation of a particular culture and its values. Christianity and Islam have manifested globalising ambitions throughout their respective histories. This continues even to this day. The fact that one aspect of Hindu fundamentalism is an angry rebellion against this oppressive religious and cultural globalisation, and is a fight to safeguard and preserve their own religious faith and cultural values, gets no attention whatsoever in Christian circles. Should not this dimension enter into the discussion . . . with theological not just political concern?[15]

The lesson Christians have to learn in the context of an awareness of the interrelatedness and interdependence of reality is to discard all trends of exclusivism of globalization in Christian theology. There is a need to evolve a new perspective on Christology avoiding "christocentric universalism"; "Christ-in-relation" is perhaps a better way of affirming the trinitarian concern of the process of transformation and renewal. A spirit-filled theology will be more open, creative, and responding to the pathos of people and their striving for liberation.[16] The significance of Christ lies not in christological formulation, but in his unique combination of suffering and hope at the cross.[17]

In order to overcome the religio-cultural exclusivism involved in globalization, our struggle should be for a new global order through the mobilization of the resources of all religious traditions. That is to say, from exclusivism we have to progress to pluralistic inclusivism in theology of religions through dialogical theologies for the relational convergence of religions. Pluralistic inclusivism inspires each religious faith to be pluralistically inclusive; that is, on the one hand each living faith is to become truly pluralistic by other faiths contributing to its conceptual content, and on the other hand inclusivism is to transform its meaning to witness the fulfillment of the theological and spiritual contents of one's own faith in and through the contributions of other living faiths.[18] The Christian pilgrimage is progressive integrating of the truth that is revealed to others in one's own experience of the story of Jesus. Christians have to identify the glorious ways in which God's

---

15. S. J. Samartha, "The Causes and Consequences of Religious Fundamentalism," in *Fundamentalism and Secularism: The Indian Predicament*, ed. A. Nehring (Madras: Gurukul, 1994), p. 30.

16. Abraham, p. 154.

17. Abraham, p. 154.

18. K. P. Aleaz, *Theology of Religions: Birmingham Papers and Other Essays* (Calcutta: Moumita Publishers and Distributors, 1998), pp. 168-99.

revelations are available to them in other religious experiences which can help in their experience of new dimensions of meanings of the gospel of God in Jesus.[19]

Rather than evaluating other religious experiences in terms of preformulated criteria, we have to allow ourselves to be evaluated by them in our understanding of the gospel. They in the Holy Spirit will provide us with new meanings of the person and function of Jesus, rather than we dictate it to them always. From the particular Jesus of fundamentalism we have to come to the universal Jesus,[20] avoiding christocentric universalism. The universal Jesus belongs to the whole of humanity in the Holy Spirit. How can we arrive at an authentic understanding of Christ and the Christian gospel? is the basic question. Who decides the content of the meaning of Christ and the gospel? is the fundamental question. The meaning of Christ and the gospel have to emerge in the process of an intercultural, interreligious communication. Nobody is giving the Christian missionary the authority to decide what is the content of an "authentic gospel." In the Asian context of an integral relation between religion and culture, there is no way of minusing the religion from culture and inculturating the Western cultural gospel in the illusion that it is *sui generis*.[21] People from diverse religio-cultural backgrounds will, in terms of their contexts, decide the content of the gospel.

In such a creative vision the gospel is not preformulated but is always in a process of formulation. The particular context will decide the content of the gospel. The process of hermeneutics or understanding and interpretation is the key issue here. It is the hermeneutical context or the contextual socio-politico-religio-cultural realities which decide the content of our knowledge and experience of the gospel. Knowledge is formulated in the very knowing process, and understanding the gospel of God in Jesus is a continuous, integrated, nondual, divine-human process. We cannot accept some timeless interpretation from somewhere and make it applicable to our context. Understanding and interpretation belong exclusively to us and our context, and there is the possibility for the emergence of new meanings of the gospel in the process of this.[22]

19. Cf. K. P. Aleaz, *An Indian Jesus from Sankara's Thought* (Calcutta: Punthi Pustak, 1997).

20. K. P. Aleaz, *The Role of Pramanas in Hindu-Christian Epistemology* (Calcutta: Punthi Pustak, 1991), pp. 99-100.

21. Cf. K. P. Aleaz, "Hope for the Gospel in Diverse Religious Cultures: A Response to the Salvador Conference on World Mission and Evangelism," *Asia Journal of Theology* 11, no. 2 (October 1997): 263-81.

22. K. P. Aleaz, *The Gospel of Indian Culture* (Calcutta: Punthi Pustak, 1994).

Knowledge of the gospel is an immediate existential knowledge by the knower, the content of knowledge itself being formulated in the very knowing process. Here it should be noted that the current theological concepts of adaptation, indigenization, inculturation, and contextualization are an outcome of a defective hermeneutical principle. In reality, in our understanding process there exists nothing externally ready-made that can be adapted, indigenized, incultured, or contextualized, and no gospel externally ready-made that can be adapted, indigenized, incultured, or contextualized.[23] Rather the content emerges from the context. The perspective of inculturation has its basis in inclusivism in theology of religions. Perhaps there is a need to go beyond the approach of inclusivism to that of pluralistic ratification of the defects and dangers of globalization.

In order to overcome the dangers of religious globalization, religious pluralism has to be taken seriously; in which case, mission cannot be understood and practiced as one-way proclamation by one particular community to the rest of the world.[24] S. J. Samartha explains:

> Christians indeed have "a story to tell to the nations." But do not neighbours of other faiths also have their own stories to tell the world? Mission cannot be seen as the numerical expansion of one particular religious community leading to a corresponding diminution of other communities. The word "mission" itself, because of its colonial associations, may have to be abandoned. If mission is understood as sharing in the continuing work of God (speaking in Theistic terms) mending the brokenness of creation, overcoming the fragmentation of humanity, and healing the rift between humanity, nature and God, then possibilities of co-operation should be welcome. Such co-operative efforts are already going on between different communities in some parts of the world. The Church's mission then is not to seek its own expansion but to seek first the kingdom of God, to promote and practise the values of justice and peace, truth and love which have been decisively revealed to Christians in the life and work, the death and resurrection of Jesus Christ.[25]

Moreover, we need not envisage a dichotomy between witness and dialogue, which view may put limitations to both. For the very witnessing, dialogue is needed because what we witness itself is a product of dialogue. It is the new insights received from other religious experiences in dialogue which

---

23. Cf. Aleaz, *An Indian Jesus from Sankara's Thought.*
24. Samartha, *One Christ — Many Religions*, p. 13.
25. Samartha, *One Christ — Many Religions*, pp. 13-14.

decide the content of what we witness.[26] We may say that dialogue to begin with gives rise to further dialogue for mutual enrichment and relational convergence of religions.[27]

Concluding Observations in Relation to the Thought of Lesslie Newbigin

A globalized gospel from a Christian missionary in reality can be the most sectarian gospel, and it is time for us to see the content of the gospel as propagated by Lesslie Newbigin in the light of what has been said above. According to Newbigin,[28] the Christian message for the whole human race is that in Christ, once for all, the total rebellion of the human race against its Maker is unmasked, judged, and forgiven. The cross simultaneously reveals the measure of our sin against God as well as the measure of God's love for us. He had a strong conviction about "the finished work of Christ," about the centrality and objectivity of the atonement accomplished on Calvary. The source, cen-

26. Cf. K. P. Aleaz, *Dimensions of Indian Religion: Study, Experience, and Interaction* (Calcutta: Punthi Pustak, 1995).

27. Cf. K. P. Aleaz, *Jesus in Neo-Vedanta: A Meeting of Hinduism and Christianity* (Delhi: Kant Publications, 1995).

28. Cf. Lesslie Newbigin, *The Gospel in a Pluralist Society* (London: SPCK; Grand Rapids: Eerdmans; and Geneva: WCC Publications, 1989), pp. 12, 86, 97, 121, 151-53, 163-64, 166, 169; *Truth to Tell: The Gospel as Public Truth* (Grand Rapids: Eerdmans; Geneva: WCC Publications; and London: SPCK, 1991), pp. 33-34, 37-39, 59-60, 72, 80, 87-88; *Foolishness to the Greeks: The Gospel and Western Culture* (London: SPCK; Grand Rapids: Eerdmans; and Geneva: WCC, 1986), pp. 18, 88-89, 90, 94, 123, 136, 140, 148-49; *The Other Side of 1984: Questions for the Churches* (Geneva: WCC, 1983), pp. 27, 50-54, 63; *Unfinished Agenda: An Autobiography* (Grand Rapids: Eerdmans; London: SPCK, 1985), pp. 30-31, 39, 57-58, 127-28, 143, 231, 244-45, 254-55; *The Finality of Christ* (London: SCM Press; Richmond: John Knox, 1969); *Mission in Christ's Way: Bible Studies*, WCC Mission Series no. 8 (Geneva: WCC Publications, 1987), p. 40; *Is Christ Divided? A Plea for Christian Unity in a Revolutionary Age* (Grand Rapids: Eerdmans, 1961), p. 32; *A Faith for This One World?* (London: SCM Press, 1961), pp. 38-41, 70-71; *A South India Diary* (London: SCM Press, 1951), pp. 115-16; *The Reunion of the Church: A Defence of the South India Scheme*, rev. ed. (London: SCM Press, 1960), pp. 89-90; *Journey into Joy* (Madras: CLS; Delhi: ISPCK, 1972), pp. 38-39; *Your Kingdom Come: Reflections on the Theme of the Melbourne Conference on World Mission and Evangelism, 1980* (Leeds: John Paul the Preacher's Press, 1980), p. 41; *The Household of God: Lectures on the Nature of the Church* (London: SCM Press, 1953), p. 137; *Sin and Salvation* (London: SCM Press, 1956), pp. 56-91; *The Good Shepherd: Meditations on Christian Ministry in Today's World* (Madras: CLS, 1974), p. 15; *The Open Secret: Sketches for a Missionary Theology* (Grand Rapids: Eerdmans; London: SPCK, 1978), pp. 172, 185-87, 190-91, 197-99.

ter, and goal of history is Jesus, the incarnation of the Logos. Jesus is the Lord and Savior of the world, and there is no other name. This faith is not founded on any supposedly more ultimate principles. Rather, according to him, God's revelation in Jesus Christ is the starting point, the foundation. It is only in the light of Jesus that both the world religions and the whole structure of modern science will ultimately be seen for what they truly are. Surely it is time for us to reformulate such a "gospel according to Newbigin" while paying homage to the integrity and sincerity of that great soul. The globalized gospel instead has to become localized. The gospel has to emerge from the hermeneutical context, from the experience of the oppressed and suffering people due to globalization on the one hand, and from the diverse, enriching religious experiences of humankind on the other. The gospel has to be the gospel of interrelatedness in a community of communities in terms of pluralistic inclusivism, rejecting both exclusivism and inclusivism. From the particular Jesus of fundamentalism we have to come to the universal Jesus who belongs to all of humanity, avoiding christocentric universalism. People from diverse religio-cultural backgrounds will, in terms of their contexts, decide the content of the gospel, and if that is allowed to happen, mission ceases to be a one-way proclamation and witness and dialogue become mutually enriching endeavors. The poverty-creating globalization and the poverty-stricken globalized gospel, both these, stand rejected here.

Globalization and the Gospel: A Muslim View

Mahmut Aydin

In this paper, first of all, I would like to stress how globalization has contributed to the dawn of a new age in our relationship with people of other faiths, and then I would like to come back to Aleaz's paper by highlighting its main points from a Muslim point of view. In doing so, my main objective is to discuss how globalization can be used as a tool to develop a suitable environment for our relationship with people of other faiths by rethinking our own traditional beliefs which seem to be problematic for that relationship. Within this objective my starting point in this paper is the new global situation and the new demands it presents for our relationship with people of other faiths.

As is well known, in our postmodern world, which has become a "global village" where religious and cultural pluralism seem to be an inescapable reality, we are witnessing the beginning of a new age in our relationship with people of other faiths. A number of significant factors have contributed to this development, among them an explosion of knowledge about various religious traditions, developments in the scientific study of religion, and the personal contacts between followers of different faiths due to travel opportunities, massive immigration from east to west, and dialogue meetings.[1] The renowned historian of religion W. Cantwell Smith in his *Faith of Other Men* (1972) highlights this new situation as follows:

1. For these factors see Alan Race, *Christians and Religious Pluralism: Patterns in the Christian Theology of Religions* (London: SCM Press, 1983), pp. 1ff.; John Hick, *The Rainbow of Faiths* (London: SCM Press, 1995), pp. 12-13; Daniel B. Clendenin, *Many Gods, Many Lords: Christianity Encounters World Religions* (Grand Rapids: Baker, 1995), pp. 18-29; Charles Kimball, *Striving Together: A Way Forward in Christian-Muslim Relations* (Maryknoll, N.Y.: Orbis, 1991), pp. 48-56.

The religious life of mankind from now on, if it is to be lived at all, will be lived in the context of religious pluralism. This is true for all of us: not only for mankind in general on an abstract level, but for you and me as individual persons. No longer are people of other persuasions peripheral or distant, the idle curiosity of travellers' tales. The more alert we are, and the more involved in life, the more we are finding that they are our neighbours, our colleagues, our competitors, our fellows. Confucians and Hindus, Buddhists and Muslims are with us not only in the United Nations, but down the street. Increasingly, not only is our civilisation's destiny affected by their actions; but we drink coffee with them personally as well.[2]

This new awareness of other cultural and religious traditions has forced one person to reconsider the religious status of the other by asking the following questions about the absolutist claims of his/her faith. "If God is the God of humanity and has a universal will to save mankind, why is the true religion, the right approach to God, confined to a single strand of humanity, so that it has not been available to the great majority of the thousands of millions of human beings who have lived and died from the earliest days until now? If God is the Creator . . . and [Sustainer] of all, can God have provided true religion only for a chosen minority?"[3]

These questions can be seen as creating a positive environment for a fruitful interreligious dialogue. As is well known, human society today is witnessing the beginning of the end of the age of cultural and religious isolation. People previously isolated one from another by distance, culture, and language are becoming increasingly aware of each other's customs and ways of thinking. Also, a constant stream of journals, books, films, documentaries, and international conferences keeps the human race abreast of news and events from around the world. Similarly, the scientific and technological achievements of this past century, as much as they have altered the pattern of everyday living, have had no effect more profound or far-reaching than the development of global awareness. This situation is inevitably creating a climate conducive to a full understanding of what is meant by "human solidarity."

Also, the independent histories and religious traditions of nations and civilizations, past and present, are being forged into something new: an integrated world history. Consequently, ancient views and traditional beliefs are being seriously questioned because, as Alan Race states, "changing patterns of

2. Wilfred Cantwell Smith, *The Faith of Other Men* (New York: Harper Torchbooks, 1972), p. 11.

3. John Hick, foreword to *Meaning and End of Religion*, by Wilfred Cantwell Smith (Minneapolis: Fortress, 1991), p. vi.

175

mobility have shattered older conceptions of the religious history of the world which viewed the faiths as confined, culturally and geographically, within particular boundaries. Personal contact between men and women from different cultures and faiths, at work or in a neighbourhood, is becoming increasingly commonplace. But with the technological revolution in travel and communications the meaning of neighbourliness now has a global application."[4]

Thus the world "is becoming a global village where personal contact between persons of different religious and cultural affiliations" is commonplace. Also a wealth of knowledge has accumulated about different faiths; the days of religious and cultural isolationism are at an end. In this process many creative intellectuals argue that the future of one faith's theology lies in the encounter of that faith with other faiths.[5]

After this introduction of the issues, I would like to come back to Aleaz's paper. In its first part Aleaz points out the negative effects of globalization on the Third World countries in terms of the free-market economy. In doing so he indicates that when we are speaking of globalization, we need to take into account how it has been used as a tool to exploit underdeveloped countries by economically and politically powerful states. In this point he seems to be quite right, because through the globalization process underdeveloped countries are totally and completely dominated by the financial institutions and global markets of the developed countries. As a consequence of this, the gap between the rich and the poor countries has become greater by the latter not having access to key factors of production such as capital.[6]

In the second part of the paper, Aleaz tries to develop a new theology in order to move away from the idea that globalization means globalization of a particular culture and its values. By doing this, contrary to Bishop Lesslie Newbigin, he argues that the core of our vision has to be a community of

---

4. Race, pp. 1-2.

5. In recent years increasing numbers of creative Christian theologians have argued that the future of Christian theology is very much dependent on the relationship between the Christian faith and the other faiths. See Race, pp. ix-x; Hans Küng, *Christianity and World Religions: Paths of Dialogue with Islam, Hinduism, and Buddhism* (Maryknoll, N.Y.: Orbis, 1993; first published 1986), p. xiii; Frank Whaling, *Christian Theology and World Religions: A Global Approach* (London: Marshall Pickering, 1986), pp. 5ff.; David Tracy, *Dialogue with the Other: The Interreligious Dialogue* (Grand Rapids: Eerdmans, 1990), p. 90; Smith, *Faith of Other Men*, p. 133.

6. K. C. Abraham, "Socio-Political Pluralism and Global Solidarity," in *Peace for Humanity: Principles, Problems, and Perspectives of the Future as Seen by Muslims and Christians*, ed. Andreas Bsteh (New Delhi: Vikan Publishing, 1996), pp. 229-45.

communities that accepts a plurality of identities in a nonthreatening and mutually affirming way.[7]

This idea of Aleaz challenges Christians more than Muslims, since the idea that globalization means globalization of a particular culture and its values seems to be compatible with the teaching of the first book of the Bible, which indicates that the human community was created as a single community (Gen. 1:1). But it seems to be contradictory to the Qur'anic teaching, which is strongly pluralist. Not only is it pluralist, but it repeatedly lays its emphasis on pluralism. The Qur'an teaches Muslims two things. First, it reminds Muslims that Allah is not the Lord of one nation or one religious community but the "Lord of the worlds" (Q. 1:1), and he created different nations and different communities in this world. In this issue the Qur'an emphasizes that "if God had pleased He would have made you a single people, but He might try you in what He gave you, therefore strive with one another to hasten to virtuous deeds . . ." (Q. 5:51). Secondly, it urges Muslims to respect the otherness of the other by repeatedly saying that each one has his own religion and his own ways of worshiping God (Q. 5:48). Concerning this point, the renowned Muslim scholar Hasan Askari comments that "as there are varieties in human language and culture, there are also varieties in religion, not an artificial variety, but rather spontaneous variety, 'needs to be explored.'"[8] During our exploration of variations in religion, Askari states, the Qur'an does not indicate that the beliefs of one follower of a religious tradition should be exchanged for those of another. On the contrary, it emphasizes that whatever beliefs they have, they should not commit the ultimate sacrilege of absolutizing them.[9] For no religion and no revelation can be the only and the final or the exclusive or inclusive word of God in the sense that it confines who God is, since this sort of absolutism and exclusivism would be idolatry, as Cantwell Smith states.[10]

Unfortunately, this pluralistic perspective of the Qur'an has been narrowed by Muslims claiming the necessity of globalization of the Muslim *umma*. But today our world as a global village has made it obvious that Mus-

---

7. K. P. Aleaz, "The Globalization of Poverty and the Exploitation of the Gospel," pp. 165-73 above.

8. Ataullah Siddiqui, *Christian-Muslim Dialogue in the Twentieth Century* (London: Macmillan, 1997), p. 113.

9. Siddiqui, p. 114.

10. See Paul F. Knitter, *Jesus and the Other Names: Christian Mission and Global Responsibility* (Maryknoll, N.Y.: Orbis, 1996), pp. 38-40; Wilfred C. Smith, "Idolatry: In Comparative Perspective," in *The Myth of Christian Uniqueness,* ed. John Hick and Paul F. Knitter (London: SCM Press, 1987), pp. 53-68.

lims cannot think of their *umma* as an isolated community, since it is no longer a geographical entity, no longer one nation because there is no longer a nation whose citizens are all Muslims. This situation urges followers of various religions to enter into dialogue with each other in order to remove barriers and increase the amount of good in the world by a free exchange of ideas.

When we evaluate Aleaz's paper in the light of this pluralistic vision of globalization, it would be accurate to conclude that his paper is inspired by the idea of seeking a way out from the negative effects of globalization in terms of the free-market economy and religious exclusivism, and toward establishing a harmony among world religions. While doing this, he suggests a move away from Christian exclusivism, which means globalization of Christian faith and Western culture, to religious pluralism, which regards Christian faith and Western culture as one among many faiths and cultures. In order to reach this objective, he maintains, Christians need to take the following three major steps.

First, he suggests that Christians move away from an exclusivistic understanding of the status of Jesus to a pluralistic one. He says the traditional christological formulations which hold Jesus as the absolute savior apart from whom there is simply no salvation, should be reconsidered in order to make the globalization process a suitable tool for better relations with people of other faiths. By doing this, he rejects exclusivism and inclusivism by developing a new phrase, namely, "pluralistic inclusivism." It seems to me that what Aleaz means by this term is a kind of inclusivism that he has rejected, since he suggests that Christians shift from a particular Jesus to the universal Jesus who belongs to the whole humanity in the Holy Spirit. Thus, as long as Christians continue to announce Jesus as a universal figure for all humanity in terms of his function, we cannot speak of a pluralistic Christian theology of religions. In this point I would like to ask in what way Jesus is universal. Is it the way he is the decisive and normative revelation of God for all people, or the way he is a decisive and normative revelation of God only for those who accept him and follow his message? It seems to me that as long as Christians continue to announce Jesus as a universal figure for all humanity in terms of his function, we cannot speak of a pluralistic Christian theology of religions. In order to rescue us from this dilemma, it would be better to understand the Christ event by relativizing it. This means that Jesus is the unique and normative revelation of God for those who follow his way, not for those who follow other ways.[11] So, in a globalized world, the duty of adherents of different reli-

11. Concerning different understandings of the uniqueness and normativeness of Jesus Christ, see L. Swidler and P. Mojez, eds., *The Uniqueness of Jesus: Dialogue with Paul Knitter* (Maryknoll, N.Y.: Orbis, 1997), pp. 79-84.

gious traditions should not be to claim the superiority of their own religious tradition as an a priori entity, but to show in practice how much their faith brings liberation to the poor and how much it contributes to the development of the common good.[12]

Secondly, Aleaz maintains that the content of the gospel should be determined by taking into account the religio-cultural backgrounds of the people to whom it is proclaimed. This implies that the content of the gospel differs from one culture to another. This idea could be argued appropriate for the Christian scripture, whose content emerged in the process of an intercultural, interreligious communication after Jesus. But it is definitely not suitable for the Muslim scripture, whose content was revealed to the prophet Muhammad directly from God and written down in his lifetime. It seems to me that there is a danger in this idea for committed Christians. For this sort of idea could increase their anxieties by leading them to be alienated from their faith. Because of this danger, it would be more accurate to say that the interpretation of the text, not its content, depends on which context that text is proclaimed in. This means that people from diverse cultural backgrounds can understand or interpret the text in the light of their context. In this sense the globalization process cannot be used as a tool to globalize one interpretation of the text, since as Aleaz rightly maintains, "we cannot accept some timeless interpretation from somewhere and make it applicable to our context."[13]

As a third step to move away from the dangers of religious globalization and to adopt religious pluralism, Aleaz suggests not understanding and practicing mission as one-way proclamation by one particular community to the rest of the world. This point is very significant indeed. For if we want to avoid the globalization of a particular religious tradition, we need to abandon all kinds of tools which give way to this idea. Also, for a genuine and fruitful dialogue people from different religious traditions need to leave aside all kinds of tools which seem to impose their own religious particularity on others or

---

12. This idea reminds us of Hans Küng's first criterion, the general ethical criterion of the *humanum*, which he employs to evaluate religions. This criterion seeks to evaluate religious beliefs, practices, and values on the basis of their adequacy to promote the human good and the humanization of humanity. To this criterion, if one religion offers an ultimately comprehensive meaning of life and death; proclaims a highest, indestructible value; sets unconditionally binding standards for our behavior and suffering; and shows the way to a spiritual home, then this means that the dimension of the true and the good, the meaningful and the valuable, merge together in that religion. Hans Küng, "What Is True Religion? Toward an Ecumenical Criteriology," in *Towards the Universal Theology of Religions,* ed. L. Swidler (Maryknoll, N.Y.: Orbis, 1986), pp. 231-50.

13. Aleaz, p. 170 above.

to try to convert others to their faith. Instead, they should assume mutual witnessing. This means that in the dialogue process people should share their own good news with others as well as be ready to share the other's good news. By taking this point into account, we can easily assume that neither the traditional Christian understanding of mission nor the traditional Islamic understanding of *da'wah* has this function, since both have the idea that only they have a story or message to tell to the nations. So in our globalized world the traditional Christian understanding of mission and the Islamic understanding of *da'wah* should move away from trying to convert the other to their own faith to mutual transformation toward the Transcendent Reality.

In the light of the above accounts, I would like to conclude my response to Aleaz's paper by making the following comments concerning the contribution of globalization to the development of a new global order of our postmodern world.

First, globalization enables us to meet and enter into dialogue with people of other faiths and allows us to see and experience the intrinsic value of their religious traditions. As Smart states, the future of religions lies in a dialogue in which followers of various religious traditions will be asked neither to give up nor to compromise their deeper values. But they can still hold to the complementary hypothesis as the framework for a specific global ideology.[14] So, in a globalized world, the duty of adherents of different religious traditions should not be to claim the superiority of their own religious tradition as an a priori entity, but to show in practice how much their faith brings liberation to the poor and how much it contributes to the development of the common good. For all religious traditions provide different liberative elements in order to liberate oppressed and poor people.[15]

Secondly, the globalization process should not be seen as a tool to persuade others of one's own beliefs but as a tool to enable discussion, to make one's beliefs intelligible to those who want to try to understand, and reciprocally to take a genuine interest in the beliefs and practices of the others, to try to learn about them to correct prejudices and grow in emphatic understanding.

Thirdly, globalization which is understood by taking into account the

14. Ninian Smart, *Choosing a Faith* (London: Boyars, 1995), p. 103.

15. See Knitter, "Towards a Liberation Theology of Religions," in *Myth of Christian Uniqueness*, pp. 178-200; Knitter, *One Earth, Many Religions: Multifaith Dialogue and Global Responsibility* (Maryknoll, N.Y.: Orbis, 1995); A. Asgar Engineer, *Islam and Liberation Theology: Essays on Liberative Elements in Islam* (New Delhi, 1990); Farid Esack, *The Qur'an, Liberation and Pluralism: An Islamic Perspective of Interreligious Solidarity against Oppression* (Oxford: Oneworld, 1997).

necessities of pluralism provides the notion of self-identity. Whenever there is an attempt to impose globalization from above, it leads to primordialization from below. If we try, for example, to make a particular culture or religious tradition a globalized culture or religious tradition through globalization, it is bound to lead to religious exclusivism in which there is no room for those who belong to other religious traditions apart from the globalized one.

Briefly, in my opinion, if we want to live together with people of other faiths peacefully without being imperialistic, triumphalistic, and exclusivistic by establishing a harmony among world religions, we need to see globalization as a tool which provides an equal opportunity to followers of every religious tradition to express their differences.

The Gospel as Authentic Meta-Narrative

Charles R. Taber

The term "globalization" has been a buzzword in certain circles for well over a decade, but its meaning is not always as precise as one could wish. It may, for instance, be used purely descriptively of any or all of a number of processes — cultural, political, and above all economic — going on in today's world, in which case it falls in the semantic domain of such other terms as "global village," "systems theory," and "system-theory."[1] It is also used in a prescriptive or even hortatory manner, as when theological institutions are adjured to globalize their curricula.[2] What all these usages have in common is a sense that somehow the whole world is being brought closer together, for good or ill; that vast distances and immemorial barriers are being overcome; and that, willy-nilly, human groups and persons are being placed into increasingly intense relationships. In such a situation, perhaps the most conspicuous tension is that between local freedom to be different and global pressure to conform to a single pattern. Peoples who not long ago did not even suspect each other's existence, and who more recently represented for each other the remote and the exotic, today interact daily in the world's commercial and political arenas. And the sad experience is that growing proximity creates growing pressure, friction, and conflict at least as easily and as often as growing concord and harmony.

The chief mechanisms of the relentless globalization — in the descrip-

---

1. See S. K. Sanderson, *Civilizations and World Systems* (Walnut Creek, Calif.: Alta-Mira, 1995), and various writings of Immanuel Wallerstein and Fernand Braudel.
2. See Alice Frazer Evans, Robert A. Evans, and David A. Roozen, eds., *The Globalization of Theological Education* (Maryknoll, N.Y.: Orbis, 1993).

tive usage, as systems theory and system-theory in their somewhat different ways correctly insist — are the mechanisms of the production, trade, and consumption of commodities. System-theory in particular argues that traffic and trade on a continental scale date back to remote prehistory, as evidenced by archaeological findings. But in the modern world the emergence, first, of economically self-contained colonial empires (the mercantilist model), then of the post–World War Two global economy, has created a new system of extraordinary scope, complexity, and power from which no one is exempt. Inevitably, beginning in prehistory, along with trade has also always come mutual cultural influence and cultural change.

There is a substantial body of literature addressed to the noxious, even demonic dimensions of some of these processes. The ruthless incorporation of small preliterate societies through colonial conquest for economic profit and political power in the imperial systems of yesterday has been analyzed with great penetration and denounced with eloquent passion, together with the cultural vandalism it entailed. Today it is the global extension of this kind of domination, exploitation, and pauperization of the world's powerless populations by the affluent minority that is addressed with equal fervor, especially by Christians.[3] But, as Meeks points out, Christians have not been guiltless in these processes.

It is in this context of debate and critique that the prescriptive use of "globalization" must be assessed, especially as it concerns the church and its institutions, and above all the way the church relates to the world's structures of political and economic power. The issue, moreover, is significant not merely at the level of acts and actions, but at a very fundamental level of beliefs and self-image. In this vein several writers in *The Globalization of Theological Education* point out both the necessity and the potential perils of globalization.[4] It is not too much to say that globalization is necessary for the very salvation of churches in the affluent world, to call them to repentance and transformation.[5] The perils that potentially threaten the Third World if Christian globalization fails to be implemented, or if it is implemented in ways reminiscent of the older colonial patterns, cause many Third World persons to view the whole idea with caution if not with fear: "For many years, talk of love, peace, and reconciliation formed the basis of white Christians'

---

3. M. Douglas Meeks, "Global Economy and the Globalization of Theological Education," in *The Globalization of Theological Education*, pp. 247-61.

4. Evans, Evans, and Roozen, eds., *The Globalization of Theological Education.*

5. Cf. Robert J. Schreiter, "Globalization as Cross-Cultural Dialogue," in *The Globalization of Theological Education*, pp. 122-33.

political defense of the status quo [in South Africa]";[6] and a few pages later: "The church cannot simply view itself as an agent of change in South Africa. It is itself an object of change."[7] In other words, we, the Western church, and not only in South Africa, find ourselves deeply implicated, sometimes unconsciously but really, by the abuses of a world in which we are far too much at home, and our brothers and sisters are hopeful but not altogether sure that we can free ourselves from that bondage.

I suggest that there are three ways of conceiving of and dealing with globalization: the modern way, the postmodern way, and — if I may so express it in a shorthand manner — the "gospel" way, with which Lesslie Newbigin emphatically associated himself, as can be seen even from some of his titles: *One Body, One Gospel, One World* (1958); *A Faith for This One World?* (1961); *Is Christ Divided?* (1961); *The Finality of Christ* (1969). I will attempt briefly to sketch each of these in turn.

The Modern Perspective

In the modern perspective, as a number of scholars have pointed out,[8] the concept of globalization (though not the term itself, since "universal" was the term of choice) was one of the essential and constituent components of the modern agenda. The fundamental unity of the human race was postulated over against the localisms and particularisms of the past (and also of romanticism), and that universalizing concept in turn gave birth to such subsidiary concepts as "universal grammar" by the scholars of Port Royal in seventeenth-century France, the "universal rights of man [*sic*]" in the eighteenth century, the "psychic unity of mankind [*sic*]" so dear to the evolutionary founders of anthropology in the nineteenth century, and the "universal" laws of economics today. Ironically, even the rhetoric of universal human rights, to say nothing of the other notions mentioned, tended to exert in practice a ruthlessly homogenizing effect on societies and cultures as it was disseminated across the world in the colonial era. Today it hardly needs mentioning that the homogenizing impact of the West on the rest of the world is driven chiefly by the forces of the global market, with its messianic illusions and false

---

6. Itumeleng J. Mosala, "Commentary: A Place for Reconciliation," in *The Globalization of Theological Education*, p. 271.

7. Mosala, p. 273.

8. Cf. Christopher Lasch, *The True and Only Heaven* (New York and London: Norton, 1991), pp. 124-26.

salvific claims. In many quarters in the West, the collapse of Marxism in Eastern Europe has had as its chief effect to foster the disastrously unfortunate notion of the inevitability and infallibility of free-market forces to solve all problems.[9] We are currently seeing the fallout of this in Russia.

The moderns at their idealistic best desperately wanted to overcome the destructive effects of the divisions and particularisms of humankind and create one world of peace and order. After all, the terrible wars of religion and various wars of national aggrandizement were very vivid in their memories. But precisely because of those wars of religion, they saw faith in God as a divisive rather than a unifying factor. So they aspired to reap the fruits of faith in God on their own without God. But the human predicament, as Genesis 3–4 points out with devastating simplicity and profundity, begins precisely at the point where God's rule is rejected in the name of human freedom. The human declaration of independence from God leads automatically to either anarchy (Hobbes's "war, as of every man, against every man"; cf. Cain and Abel, Gen. 4) or the rule of the stronger over the weaker (cf. Adam and Eve, Gen. 3). The problem of any human dream of order, local or universal, apart from the rule of God, is this: if God is not acknowledged to be in charge, then someone else is. Whether one is talking about a monarch or a corporate CEO; about an oligarchy, a patriarchy, a gerontocracy, a bureaucracy; or even the tyranny of "the market," the dilemma is the same. It has exercised thinkers from Hobbes to George Orwell and Aldous Huxley, and was best formulated by Lord Acton in the nineteenth century: "Power corrupts, absolute power corrupts absolutely." And if one looks at attempts to ground power and authority in "the people" (Locke, Rousseau, Jefferson, et al.), the result is also deeply disappointing: whether in the Marxist version of lockstep collectivism or in the "liberal" version of an ad hoc assortment of free individuals, "the people" all too easily lend themselves to the tyranny of the majority or to manipulation by demagogues. Newbigin was entirely right when he affirmed that "There is no place at which mankind can receive the gift of unity except at the mercy-seat which God has provided."[10] This theme recurs in Newbigin's writings.

Though I intend to discuss the "gospel" perspective at some length below, it is necessary to mention here that the missionary movement of the last five centuries, as the current truism correctly insists, emerged and flourished in precisely the modern climate of thought: the idea was increasingly domi-

9. Cf. Meeks, p. 250.

10. Newbigin, *Is Christ Divided? A Plea for Christian Unity in a Revolutionary Age* (Grand Rapids: Eerdmans, 1961), p. 9.

nant that all human beings were, at least potentially, equal and alike, and that differences were imputable to delays in evolution, or perhaps to the "evils" of non-Christian religions; thus the agenda to Christianize and "civilize" concurrently. Actually, as I tried to point out in an earlier work,[11] the missionary movement operated with an often unrecognized tension between the modern agenda and the gospel agenda, and not a few missionaries from time to time gave expression to a gospel attitude in conscious contrast to the modern attitude. The picture was a mixed one indeed. But Newbigin's judgment is unfortunately accurate, and not only in the past: "There is one way by which the effort has been made to bridge the gulf between the particular and the universal . . . , the way of colonialism. . . . It is tempting to apply the same kind of thinking to the claim that Jesus Christ is universal Lord."[12]

At any rate, through the colonial system and the market, even more than through the work of Christian missionaries, the West came to be ever more powerfully influential and even in some cases determinative in the rest of the world, leading inevitably to various movements of political and religious protest and reaction: nationalism and national independence, religious reform and resurgence. Comparable movements of economic protest, on the other hand, have been very scarce: to my knowledge no one, with the exception of Gandhi, has actually proposed an alternative economic system.

The Postmodern Perspective

The postmodern model, fundamentally, is the rejection and the negation of the modern model because the latter is said to be inherently and invincibly tainted by coercion and violence.

Interestingly enough, the reaction against the homogenizing impact of Western culture and related understandings of the Christian gospel was expressed very early in the religious domain, conspicuously in the 1893 Parliament of Religions in Chicago. Under the charismatic influence of Vivekenanda, a strong pressure for religious egalitarianism and relativism swept the assembly and was expressed in its reports. World War One and its demoralizing impact on the West added to the loss of conviction in the Western missionary movement, finding expression, for instance, in the Report of the Laymen's Enquiry on Re-Thinking Missions (Laymen's Foreign Missions

11. Charles R. Taber, *The World Is Too Much with Us* (Macon, Ga.: Mercer University Press, 1991).

12. Newbigin, *The Good Shepherd* (Grand Rapids: Eerdmans, 1977), p. 123.

Enquiry, 1932), edited by W. E. Hocking of Harvard.[13] So in a sense, ironically, some Christians were "postmodern" before the postmoderns, perhaps because they had a bad conscience about having been on the cutting edge of the religious version of the modern project. Christians are, after all, supposed to have tender consciences.

Later, cultural anthropology, at least in the English-speaking world, picked up various philosophical strands from the heritage of Rousseau and the romantics, and reacted against racism and cultural arrogance by proposing cultural relativity, and therefore the imperative to respect and appreciate non-Western cultures.[14] But no one in fact took cultural relativity to its logical conclusion; there were always limits insisted upon, if only to exclude Hitler's "final solution" from acceptance as a mere eccentricity of German culture. But it is hard to find solid foundations for this instinctive judgment, since cultural relativity denies universal ethical standards. The judgment seems in fact to rest upon an unacknowledged residue of Judeo-Christian faith. Some anthropologists, notably Bronislaw Malinowski, went so far as to argue that "a culture" was a *sui generis*, closed, self-contained reality, so that comparisons and generalizations across cultures were illegitimate, and cultural change became highly problematical.[15] The sociology of knowledge further undermined the self-confidence of modern epistemology, and also played hob with ethics.[16]

It was left to the postmodernists of several stripes to complete the job. Carrying the "critical method" (Descartes et al.) and the "hermeneutics of suspicion" (Nietzsche, Marx, Freud, et al.) to their logical conclusion, they applied these methods with devastating effect to the modern vision itself, undermining all the epistemological confidence, not to say arrogance, of that perspective. The postmodernists are right, after all, to identify and denounce those many situations in which reality, especially social reality, as well as right and wrong have been defined and legitimated by an exercise of power rather than persuasion. But they, together with their master Nietzsche, shared a passionate hostility toward Christianity, and so found themselves unable to con-

13. Laymen's Foreign Missions Enquiry, *Re-Thinking Missions* (New York and London: Harper and Bros., 1932).

14. Cf. Franz Boas, *Race, Language, and Culture* (New York: Macmillan, 1940), and Melville Herskovits, *Cultural Relativism*, ed. Frances Herskovits (New York: Vintage Books, 1973).

15. Bronislaw Malinowski, *Argonauts of the Western Pacific* (London: Routledge, 1922).

16. Cf. Peter L. Berger and Thomas Luckmann, *The Social Construction of Reality* (Garden City, N.Y.: Doubleday, 1966).

struct any positive approach to either modern epistemology or modern ethics. They came to emphasize that knowledge, belief, and values on the part of persons and groups were inevitably determined by the person's or group's position in the hierarchies of the world, so that in the end defining "reality" became an exercise in sheer power. Milbank argues persuasively that postmodernists, whatever their differences, share in common three dominant concepts: "a historicist 'genealogy,' . . . an 'ontology of difference' . . . and 'ethical nihilism.'"[17] What he means is that the postmodernists deny that anything might be permanent or universal in human experience, that the differences between persons and groups override commonalities, and that there is no foundation for any substantive ethics beyond the will-to-power. "No universals are ascribed to human society save one: that it is always a field of warfare."[18] But postmodernism, it seems to me, by discrediting modernity, does demonstrate the bankruptcy, indeed the folly, of modernity's attempt, alluded to above, to reap the fruits of the gospel while denying its roots.

In other words, over against the ruthless pressure of the modern agenda to obliterate differences in the interests of "order," "harmony," and above all "rationality," the postmodern agenda in its more extreme forms turns all differences into occasions for raw competition and conflict, with no resolution except by means of superior force. The fruit of such an approach can be seen in today's Middle East, the former Yugoslavia, and in other places; and, for that matter, in the inner cities of much of the Western world. Or, to put the matter in a quite different perspective, more in keeping with postmodernism's own self-understanding, letting all the differences express themselves conflictually is merely unmasking and eliminating all efforts, notably those of the modern West, to create "one world" of peace and order, since these efforts are totalitarian in their essence.

Some postmoderns, notably Rorty, are sometimes said to be more optimistic and pragmatic. No one should doubt Rorty's goodwill in this regard, but his proposal fatally lacks any dynamic spiritual power by which it might be translated into reality in the world. This is exactly the same weakness that characterized Adam Smith's "invisible hand" that would somehow transform the sum of individual selfishness into the common good, as well as Marx's notion that the elimination of classes would somehow create a new, good humankind. But both structures and persons are warped by sin, and both need to be addressed transformatively at the same time.

Is there no way out of the impasse? No way to avoid the chaos and vio-

---

17. John Milbank, *Theology and Social Theory* (Oxford: Blackwell, 1990), p. 278.
18. Milbank, p. 282.

lence of allowing all differences to express themselves and confront each other on the one hand, or the iron tyranny of an imposed order on the other? I suggest that the gospel offers an alternative image of globalization, one which admittedly is not given very visible expression in today's church but which Lesslie Newbigin argued for with passion and cogency.

The Gospel Perspective

I suggest, in fact, that the gospel of the kingdom of God is the only valid universal meta-narrative, the only one which is not ruthlessly homogenizing and totalitarian, because it is the only one based on self-sacrificing love instead of worldly power, the only one offered by a king on a cross, the only one offered by a conquering lion who turns out to be a slaughtered lamb (Rev. 5:1-10). This is the guarantee that it is not totalitarian. Pentecost, if correctly understood, is the guarantee that it is not homogenizing.

I begin with an observation: the accusation that A is "imposing" the gospel on B is credible only when A wields noticeable coercive or manipulative power over B. Though the apostles were indeed accused of "turning the world upside down" (Acts 17:6), and though they did in fact express total confidence in the truthfulness and universality of their message, no one in the New Testament imagined that they were "imposing" the gospel on anyone; the notion would have been simply ludicrous, given the obvious powerlessness of the apostles in the world's terms. The only power they had was, quite literally, the intrinsic persuasive power of the gospel.

But they nevertheless had a breathtakingly universal, global perspective and ambition. The New Testament is filled with expressions that make this abundantly clear: "all nations/Gentiles" (*panta ta ethne,* Matt. 28:19; Mark 13:10); "the whole creation" (*pase te ktisei,* Mark 16:15); "the ends of the earth" (*eschatou tes ges,* Acts 1:8); and in a single passage, both "the whole world" and "all nations" (*hole te oikoumene* and *pasin tois ethnesin,* Matt. 24:14). The unambiguous and unequivocal belief of the church in the apostolic age was that sin and condemnation were panhuman (Rom. 1:18–3:20), and that God's salvific intention through Jesus Christ was likewise panhuman (e.g., Rom. 5; 1 Tim. 2:4; passim). Later arrogant distortions of this conviction, such as Cyprian's *extra ecclesiam nulla salus;* Augustine's misuse of Luke 14:23, "compel them to come in";[19] and the conquest-and-conversion pattern established

---

19. See David J. Bosch, *The Transformation of Mission* (Maryknoll, N.Y.: Orbis, 1991), p. 219.

by Charlemagne and applied by various others, including the *conquistadores* in Latin America, have made us nervous about making much of this apostolic conviction, and all too ready to see it as a pious overstatement. We have been led by this nervousness to overstate the admitted degree of "imposition" of the gospel in the modern missionary era. But it would be dishonest exegesis and hermeneutics to deny that it was the apostolic conviction, and that this conviction is transparent in the New Testament. They were also convinced that through them God was creating a new thing: a single body comprising all those of whatever social or geographic origin who decided to follow Jesus. As Newbigin put it, "The fellowship created by the Holy Spirit is both local and universal. . . . But God's love embraces the whole world, and that fact must find expression in the form of the Christian fellowship."[20]

But how did the New Testament church implement its vision? We might correctly answer, "With great difficulty and pain!" I have already pointed out that one advantage it had over the modern church is that it had no worldly power to abuse. But Gonzalez and Gonzalez give us an important clue to kick off our discussion: "According to the book of Acts, the very first action of the Spirit upon the nascent Christian community was to globalize theology. . . . Contrary to what is often claimed, the story of Pentecost is not the undoing of the multiplicity of languages stemming from Babel, but rather the demonstration that a multiplicity of languages and cultures does not necessarily lead to division and confusion."[21]

Gonzalez and Gonzalez go on to describe the growing recognition in the earliest church of the implications of this liberating insight. But they also trace the steady pressures in subsequent centuries toward uniformity in language, liturgy, and doctrine, culminating in episodes like the Council of Trent and the modern cultural imperialism of many missions. This initial clue is nevertheless strong enough to permit Alice Frazer Evans and her colleagues, in the introduction to their book, to argue that "For the Christian church, 'globalization' is the late twentieth-century equivalent of Pentecost."[22] I would more cautiously say that it can become that if properly understood and carried out. But is this possible, given present power relations in the world? Schreiter points out that the business world today talks of globalization, but that this represents "the same old pattern of domination under new

---

20. Newbigin, *One Body, One Gospel, One World: The Christian Mission Today* (London and New York: IMC, 1958), p. 23.

21. Justo L. Gonzalez and Catherine G. Gonzalez, "A Historical Survey," in *The Globalization of Theological Education*, p. 13.

22. Evans, Evans, and Roozen, p. 1.

terms" because "the discourse must be carried out in English, . . . it assumes the mobility in time and space powered by telecommunications and air travel, and . . . the terms of negotiation and resolution emanate from North Atlantic culture."[23]

Can today's church do better? Schreiter argues that globalization, in the form of cross-cultural dialogue, can accomplish two important things: "First of all, it challenges the sometimes subtle and unconscious discourses of power and ethnocentrism that underlie honest attempts at mission, dialogue, and a justice praxis. . . . Second, cross-cultural dialogue deconstructs the powerful, dominant culture in a special way . . . , challenging a powerful culture to give over its sense of control, commit its trust, and suffer a disorienting cognitive and emotional dissonance that can lead to transformations."[24]

But are we really ready to "relinquish power and . . . [to] be led through [our] vulnerabilities to conversion"?[25] Observation leads one at best to a cautious "perhaps." Meeks points out the difficulties: "The ominous fact of which North American Christians are only barely conscious is that the church itself is also more or less governed by the market logic. Even our church institutions, including the seminaries, have joined the move from traditional accountability to accountancy. . . . The great task facing the church toward the next century is how and where to find the actual free space in our market society to become the *oikonomia tou theou*. No other question is so urgent for the globalization of church and seminary."[26]

Or, as Newbigin put it, "It is true, alas, that Christians have often been guilty of pride and intolerance. But pride is not an inevitable concomitant of a belief in the uniqueness of Christianity. . . . If I believe that God really did send his Son into the world to die for me and all men, I am bound to say that that message is incomparable and final. And if I understand it rightly, it means the end of all my pride."[27]

Conclusion

To summarize: our problems include, as I see it, the following: (a) our own captivity, mental and institutional, to the patterns of either modernity or

---

23. Schreiter, p. 124.
24. Schreiter, p. 124.
25. Schreiter, p. 129.
26. Meeks, p. 256.
27. Newbigin, *A Faith for This One World?* (London: SCM Press, 1961), p. 42.

postmodernity, or some confused mishmash of these, as opposed to the gospel perspective; (b) a long history of mediocrity and failure, often masked as triumph, that has made both some of us and many of our brothers and sisters outside the West pessimistic about the possibility of change; and (c) on the part of others of us, a complacency with our present affluence and power and a corresponding unwillingness to give them up, or a frank indifference to the problems of the rest of the world.

But for those Christians, including us in the West, who truly want to move beyond present frustrations, is there any hope of contributing to solutions instead of perpetuating problems? I would not presume to offer, in the triumphalistic Western mode, a few simple steps to solve all the problems, since that very mentality is a major part of what we are trying to get past. But I offer the following few tentative suggestions:

1. Humankind is one, not only as an amazingly homogeneous biological species but as a single race with a single history. System-theory, as we have seen, affirms this by highlighting the ways in which human groups have interacted since the dawn of prehistory. Scripture also affirms it, but adds that that universal history is marked not only by happenedness but also by purpose, meaning, and a goal, just because it is God who is the most active agent in it, as Newbigin pointed out: "History, therefore, is not the story of the development of forces immanent within history; it is a matter of the promises of God. History has a goal only in the sense that God has promised it."[28] And the most decisive events, the most decisive acts of God in history, have to do with the coming of Jesus, his life, his death, and his resurrection.[29]

2. One facet of that unity is fallenness and sin. No account of the human condition which does not take this fact seriously into consideration merits a second glance. It is this fact which makes all purely human efforts at unity futile, regardless of their sincerity.[30] As Newbigin wrote, "The gospel is good news at this point because Christ has overcome the power of sin and death,"[31] and, he correctly implies, no other agency has done so or could do so.

3. Religions give expression to the best insights and impulses of human persons and societies, but also to their futile efforts at self-salvation. At this point Newbigin takes an almost Barthian position, the starkest expression of which is perhaps the following: "If the Bible is our guide, we cannot exclude

28. Newbigin, *The Gospel in a Pluralist Society* (London: SPCK; Grand Rapids: Eerdmans; and Geneva: WCC Publications, 1989), p. 103; see also p. 91.

29. Newbigin, *Pluralist Society*, p. 94.

30. Newbigin, *A Faith?* pp. 68ff.

31. Newbigin, *Foolishness to the Greeks: The Gospel and Western Culture* (London: SPCK; Grand Rapids: Eerdmans; and Geneva: WCC, 1986), p. 136.

the possibility that precisely religion may be the sphere of damnation";[32] and again, "It is precisely at points of highest ethical and spiritual achievement that the religions find themselves threatened by, and therefore ranged against, the gospel."[33] But this is not, he emphasizes in many places, to denigrate the genuine moral and spiritual insights and experiences of the devotees of other religions; nor is it in any way to presume to decide who will be "saved" in the end, since that is God's prerogative alone. And, he insists, "There is something authentically Christian in an attitude of humility in the presence of other faiths."[34]

4. The divisions — "race," ethnicity, nationality, class, caste, sex — which set persons and groups at each other's throats are some of the best evidence of the radical nature of sin in the world, and of the desperate need for some basis of reconciliation, since, as things are at present, they can be suppressed only by force (Hobbes). We have seen how the modern agenda ruthlessly obliterates difference where it can, and how the postmodern throws up its hands and lets all parties fight it out.

5. For Newbigin — and I agree with him fully — the only answer is in the gospel of the reign of God. Just as the biblical story gives the only diagnosis of the human condition which is profound enough, so it gives the only remedy which works. But for it to work properly, as God intends it to work, it must be offered under certain conditions:

a. It must not be associated with any form of worldly power in the hands of its advocates, since, as we have seen, such power distorts the gospel and is, or is read to be, unavoidably coercive or manipulative.

b. It must invite the persons who respond into the community of faith, which is universal, and accept any and all who will come. It is precisely in that fellowship that the pilot program of God's ultimate intention for the world is demonstrated: "The basic reality is the creation of a new being through the presence of the Holy Spirit. This new being is the common life *(koinonia)* of the church";[35] and "The Church is a congregation, set to draw all men of whatever kind into one family."[36]

c. It must lead its advocates and converts to appreciate, to learn from,

32. Newbigin, *The Finality of Christ* (London: SCM Press; Richmond: John Knox, 1969), p. 43.

33. Newbigin, *The Open Secret: Sketches for a Missionary Theology* (London: SPCK; Grand Rapids: Eerdmans, 1978), p. 193.

34. Newbigin, *The Finality of Christ*, p. 15.

35. Newbigin, *One Body*, p. 20.

36. Newbigin, *Honest Religion for Secular Man* (Philadelphia: Westminster; London: SCM Press, 1966), p. 111.

and even to celebrate each other's differences of perspective rather than to suppress them. The unity to which the church is called, and which is in fact God's gift to the church, is not uniformity: "Properly speaking, the Church is just the people of God, just humanity remade in Christ. It should therefore have as much variety as the human race itself."[37] New believers in each culture must be accorded the greatest possible freedom to discover — or invent — culturally appropriate ways to express their response to the good news. In fact, the specific formulations by which the gospel is communicated must be discovered in dialogue with the new hearers so as to respond as specifically as possible to the existential questions which give expression to their own form of "lostness," and so as to capitalize as fully as possible on the valid insights they already have. This is, after all, exactly what the writers of the various books of the Bible did in their own days. Paul, for instance, did not mechanically repeat himself in each context, but addressed each context in its specificity, even at the risk of apparently contradicting himself.

d. It must be exclusively under the rule of God, exercised by the crucified Son, through the Holy Spirit, working through human messengers who have forsaken all pretense to authority. For authority does not belong to human beings; nor do we claim finality for Christianity itself, since it is the religion developed by human beings in response to the revelation of God in Christ; we claim finality for Christ alone.[38] "To claim finality for Christ is to endorse the judgment of the apostles that in this life, death, and resurrection God himself was uniquely present, and that, therefore, the meaning and origin and end of all things was disclosed."[39]

37. Newbigin, *A Faith?* p. 82.
38. Newbigin, *The Finality of Christ,* p. 72.
39. Newbigin, *The Finality of Christ,* p. 76.

Globalization, Gospel, and Cultural Relativism

Robert M. C. Jeffery

We are dealing with an ill-defined term, which is now coming into common use. Globalization, according to Richard Bliese, refers to "both the compression of the world as a whole and the intensification of consciousness of the world as a whole."[1] While the general impact of this cannot be denied, it might be a question as to whether it has fully impacted on the ordinary person in any culture. For instance, an Englishman staying in America and reading the *New York Times* might wonder whether England actually existed at all! There is a new sort of technological colonization, not distinctively Western, which sweeps us all along. It has the effect of putting all countries on a much more equal footing than has ever happened before. Technology is no respecter of racial or tribal barriers.

Alongside this we note the phenomenon, first noticed by Teilhard de Chardin,[2] that as the world gets smaller there is a strong attempt to reassert the local, the tribal, and the distinctive culture, albeit in a different form. (This was one of the main themes of Dr. Anthony Giddens in his 1999 Reith Lectures.) Globalization thus does not undermine distinctive cultures; rather it gives them a new significance. There is more pressure to assert the local and the distinctive. This will have an effect on expressions of religion, and Mr. Taber is right to assert that we are all being changed by the process. However, he offers no real definition of globalization nor of colonization. Indeed, one

1. Richard H. Bliese, "Globalisation," in *Dictionary of Mission*, ed. K. Muller, T. Sundermeler, et al. (Maryknoll, N.Y.: Orbis, 1997).
2. See Teilhard de Chardin's *Le Milieu Divin* and other books. There is plenty of food for thought in these writings for globalized spirituality.

criticism of Taber's paper is that he has too narrow a view of colonization. There is a tendency to concentrate on the effect of British colonialism of the nineteenth century. But that is very different from the Spanish, French, or Portuguese colonialism from the sixteenth century onward. Nor should we forget the insidious impact of American colonialism through direct rule or "banana republics" since the Second World War. Nor is it self-evident in many of these cases that colonial rule actually meant "globalization" or acculturation. India did not become Western; Taiwan has remained within Chinese culture. It is also clear that much of the affirmation and humanization of communities under colonialism was done by the Christian missions and not by the colonial powers.

The question is how we react to this situation. Mr. Taber suggests three perspectives, and the one he commends he calls "the gospel perspective," having dismissed the other two. I am not sure that these are all the options, nor do I think there is any such thing as *the* gospel perspective. There will be many responses to globalization, and they will relate to whatever is the local cultural expression. For instance, Bliese argues that religion will give a traditional, a revisionist, or a prophetic response to globalization, and each may have in it elements of the gospel. For the gospel is always in tension with the world, and in any situation will want to say a yes and a no to what it encounters.

Before looking at this more closely, I wish to question one of Mr. Taber's unspoken presuppositions, which would also be Newbigin's. It is the issue of cultural relativism. "How," I once asked Lesslie Newbigin in a letter, "are we to handle the cultural conditioning of the New Testament itself?" I did not receive a reply. The New Testament worldview is not ours. In every age and culture we are engaged in a process of translation, which is implicit in the nature of our faith. The question is well posed by Dennis Nineham in these words: "What exactly members of biblical cultures understood themselves to be doing when they carried out the rites described by the Hebrew and Greek words usually translated as 'sacrifice' is far from clear; so is the meaning they attached to the terms somewhat misleadingly translated in English versions as 'Son of Man' and 'kingdom of God' and what would it have been like to live expecting the end of the world at any moment, as New Testament Christians did?"[3]

Nineham goes on to ask how we are to approach the use of the historical-critical method in understanding the biblical texts. We cannot just accept the texts as they are unless we adopt a strongly Barthian position, which is what Newbigin did. The trouble is that such a position does not resolve the

---

3. Dennis Nineham, "Cultural Relativism," in *The Dictionary of Biblical Interpretation*, ed. R. J.Coggins and J. L. Houlden (London: SCM Press, 1990), pp. 155-59.

question of the cultural conditioning of the Bible; it simply sidesteps it. I am not willing to reject the historical-critical approach to Scripture. It is one of the good fruits of the Enlightenment, and central to making the gospel credible. We see this also in Mr. Taber's use of the Acts of the Apostles, which simply accepts the rather glamorous views Luke gives us, rather than looking at what lay behind them. Mission is exactly this process of translation in relation to other cultures. This process does not mean accepting the cultures as they are, but probing their roots and relating them to our understanding of the gospel. This will lead to a diversity of expression. Christians can never jump clear of the cultural conditioning in which they live. Nor should they. It is part of the nature of an incarnational gospel that this is not possible. The trouble is that Barthianism stands over against cultures and societies. Tillich's theology of correlation is more helpful because it presupposes a linkage between gospel and culture.

An essential expression of the gospel is one of openness to all we encounter. This has been well expressed by Kenneth Cracknell in his book *Justice, Courtesy, and Love*.[4] He analyzes the approach of theologians and missionaries to people of other faiths between 1846 and 1914. He finds that the data collected in preparation for the 1910 Edinburgh Conference reveals a very open approach to other faiths. This had all but vanished under the influence of Dr. Hendrik Kraemer and his Barthian colleagues by the time the matter was considered at Tambaram in 1938. Cracknell quotes Wesley Ariarajah, that those contributing to Edinburgh were willing to "examine other faiths at their best and as they receive expression in the life of true believers in those faiths."[5] So these pioneers were able to understand other religious traditions on their own terms. They were able to grasp "the meaning behind the formulations and the spiritual search which lay behind them."[6] Thus doctrinal formulations and belief systems were not ruled out as hostile or incompatible with the message of the gospel. To talk of "the gospel perspective" or indeed of "the gospel as public truth" undermines this essentially Christian position.

I wish to look at two other aspects of Mr. Taber's paper in the light of these remarks. When we read in the Great Commission that the disciples are sent into all the world, what does that mean? The world as we know it or the world as they knew it? Are we really saying that the function of the church is

---

4. K. Cracknell, *Justice, Courtesy, and Love: Theologians and Missionaries Encountering World Religions, 1846-1914* (Epworth Press, 1995).
5. Cracknell, p. 285.
6. Cracknell, p. 285.

to bring everyone in the whole world into its fold? Or are we to see the church as a representative and vocational body whose function is to declare the universal application of gospel insights to the world? Is the church a representative body, or more than that? Certainly there has been a tradition which has maintained this other view. A view that seeks to reassert the dominance of Christendom seems doomed to arrogance and failure. Fortunately, or not, a globalized society is unlikely to be willing to accept a new Christendom.

Secondly, let us look at the Acts account of Pentecost. It may well be right that the action of the Spirit can be seen as a globalization of theology. People hear the gospel in many languages, but is this all that is meant? It is a significant fact that it is at this point that Christianity is very different from some other faiths. Often they are limited by having a special language in which the faith is expressed.[7] This has never been the case for Christianity. Mission and translation go hand in hand. The strong attachment of other religions to the language of their scriptures contributed to their being seen as less universal than Christianity. The processes of mission and translation are intermingled. This goes right back to the Septuagint and the Vulgate. Even in a globalized world there will be vastly different cultural expressions of Christianity. There is a need for truly cross-cultural dialogue, as Schreiter has expressed it.

We have learned that openness, love, humility, suffering, and vulnerability will be marks of the gospel. I would be more positive about an approach to mission that was open to our vulnerabilities than Mr. Taber seems to be. David Bosch, in a very moving essay reflecting on Endo's book *Silence*, calls for Christians to be victim missionaries rather than exemplar missionaries. Paul himself, in Corinthians, stresses the fragility and weakness of the missionary. Bosch quotes Desmond Tutu: "I fear that we have all been so seduced by the success ethics that we have forgotten that in a very real sense the church was meant to be a failing community." So he concludes that "A church which follows the model of the victim-missionary is one that is called to be a source of blessing to society without being destined to regulate it. It knows that the Gospel ceases to be Gospel when it is foisted upon people."[8]

When we look at a globalized society, that is a very important insight. If there is a gospel model, it lies somewhere here. The trouble with the quota-

---

7. See Willard G. Oxtoby, "Telling in Their Own Tongues," in *Concilium*, no. 1, issue on "The Bible as Cultural Heritage" (1995), published by SCM Press and Orbis. The whole issue is highly relevant to this theme.

8. D. Bosch, "The Vulnerability of Mission," in *New Directions in Mission and Evangelism 2*, ed. J. A. Scherer (New York: Orbis, 1994), p. 85.

tion from Lesslie Newbigin, just before Taber's conclusion, is that statements like that do not express the victim missionary model to which we are called. In spite of admitting the dangers of pride and intolerance, that is exactly what is communicated to other cultures.

So I agree that the gospel must not be associated with any form of world power. I do believe that in every culture we have to work out the process of translation of the gospel in ways that will make it meaningful in each culture. I also think there is a proper place for the search for a global ethic, which is put before us by Hans Küng and those who work with him. The statement made on a global ethic by the Parliament of the World Religions has nothing in it which is contrary to the gospel. It would provide a firm agenda for Christians in every place to work out with people of other faiths the significance of living in a global village with people of other faiths.[9]

Stephen Toulmin has a very profound analysis of our postmodern situation in his book *Cosmopolis*.[10] He argues that the way forward lies in the following:

- The return to the oral. We have to look at the rhetoric we use, and it always relates to its context, be it global or national.
- The return to the particular. We have to deal with distinctive problems rather than abstract theories. This is where our dialogue with different cultures is essential.
- The return to the local. We have to take anthropology seriously and consider what is distinctive about each culture.
- The return to the timely. We have to tackle the real issues before us, like ecology, AIDS, etc. — the matters that are really before us. In an evolving world we have to be adaptable.

These "returns" need to take place in every distinctive culture. So I go along with Bliese when he points out that in the global culture, religion is on the increase and we have to face a major dialogue with other religions. The naming of God in a global culture will be linked to the theological issues in relation to soteriology. The gospel makes sense only if it fulfills a redemptive purpose for the world. This will be fruitful in relation to global ethics and a common approach to tackling the problems which lie before us. But there will be no one solution. Toulmin quotes Walter Lippmann: "To every human problem there is a solution that is simple, neat and wrong," and then com-

9. See especially *Yes to a Global Ethic,* ed. Hans Küng (1995).
10. S. Toulmin, *Cosmopolis* (Chicago: University of Chicago Press, 1990).

ments: "The seduction of High Modernity lay in its abstract neatness and theoretical simplicity; both of these features blinded the successors of Descartes to the unavoidable complexities of concrete human Experience."[11]

It is that very complexity which leads me to think that there is no one solution to our reaction to globalization. Taber makes too simplistic a jump from globalization to "the kingdom of God." The active reign of God is not to be equated with a world church or a return to Christendom. We are involved in a long process of translation and of reacting to global and local issues in a way that opens us up to the future as "victim missionaries." So we are called to share in the agonies of the world and to seek with other faiths ways of working for a global ethic. This will inevitably involve us in much greater co-operation with, and understanding of, other religions. A firm stand on the uniqueness of Christ will be unhelpful. There are many expressions of Christianity, which understand the uniqueness of Christ in different ways. We have to reassess the Laymen's Enquiry of 1932.[12] The issues of globalization drive us back to Hocking's idea of a process of mutual learning among faiths and cultures leading to a reconception, which preserves the best.[13] We are learning that Kraemer did us a grave disservice.

11. Toulmin, p. 201.

12. See Prof. W. Ustorf's inaugural lecture at Birmingham. A much more radical view is expressed in David Krieger, *The New Universalism* (New York: Orbis, 1991).

13. See J. Macquarrie's comments in *Twentieth Century Religious Thought* (London: SCM Press, 1963).

Gospel, Authority, and Globalization

David Kettle

The great question is not really as to the seat of authority, but as to its nature.

P. T. FORSYTH[1]

As Western society has changed from premodern through modern to "postmodern," so within it authority has changed. I want to sketch this change and the issues it raises today for non-Western traditional societies in the face of globalization. I shall then consider the nature of authority as it is experienced in the gospel of Jesus Christ, and suggest a line of thought on how the gospel speaks to these issues. I hope that my merely programmatic account may offer some leads on the issues involved.

Within traditional societies around the world, explicit formal authority has played a key part. The authority exercised by elders over a community, by families over their members, by social conventions and by sacred writings and stories has been integral to the fabric of such society. This authority and the social structures associated with it have been seen as part of an organic whole which is normative, and which is often explained and validated in religious terms.

Europe's forms of traditional society have been dissolving for hundreds of years. During this time modern processes have worked to subvert Christendom and its medieval synthesis (for when we think of the modern period, we must surely think of processes under way, although these may not necessarily lead in a coherent direction or to a sustainable outcome). These processes have accelerated dramatically in recent decades. Globalization is part of

---

1. P. T. Forsyth, *The Principle of Authority* (Independent Press, 1913), p. 10.

this, which accelerates the same processes in non-Western cultures. The acids of modernity supplemented by the dissolving agent of "postmodern" relativism make a corrosive mix, which drips from legislative instruments increasing the scope of property rights and securing a global free market, and from the intimacies of the Western media penetrating homes throughout the world. Current social changes are disorienting enough for those of us who live in the West, though we face them having long lived with the progress of the modern from which they have taken wing; how much more disorienting are these changes for traditional societies.

The place and nature of authority have been changing in Western society since the beginning of the modern period. Most obviously, the domain of individual autonomy has greatly enlarged. At the same time, the West has seen the slow marginalization of Christian belief as now a private value and no longer a publicly acknowledged truth, with today many established public values fading in the same way. We have to ask: As globalization proceeds, will the modernization of non-Western traditional societies bring the same marginalization of Christian belief — even in societies where the church is strong today? Clearly it is not for the sake of the West alone that Christians address the question of authority.

Christians and Authority

Christians do not find the question of authority an easy one. For example, in the context of Anglican–Roman Catholic talks in the 1970s and early 1980s, it was the topic of authority with which the Anglican–Roman Catholic International Commission struggled longest and hardest. Michael Ramsey, to whom these talks were dear, with hope found in this struggle "a moving impression of integrity and perseverance which makes the authors resemble Jacob wrestling until the break of day."[2]

When Lesslie Newbigin and others planned the national Swanwick Consultation held in 1992, eight topics were chosen for inclusion in a volume of preparatory study material. The material on each topic was to be written following a seminar on the subject. Newbigin wrote later, "It was both disappointing and very significant that the only one of these eight seminars which proved entirely sterile was the one on authority." He continued, "It seemed wrong to proceed with the conference if there was no point at which the question of authority could be discussed. In the end it was decided that I should

2. Michael Ramsey, "Rome and Canterbury," *Theology* (May 1982): 164-58, here 166.

write a short paper which would define the central thesis which the conference should address, namely that the Gospel is public truth."[3]

Later, characteristically, Newbigin returned again to what he saw as a key issue, writing the book *Truth and Authority in Modernity*.[4] At the beginning of the modern period, the memory of religious wars coupled with the growing obsolescence of many established social structures and norms contributed toward suspicion of authority. What could be trusted as a guide for the future? Where was confidence to be invested? Descartes had proposed the thinking self as a starting point for sure knowledge. John Locke had distinguished sure knowledge from belief: sure knowledge was evident to all by the light of universal reason, whereas belief involved faith in a particular external authority. Here an epistemological basis was provided upon which other people, doubtful of belief and of authority, would attempt to build a future by the light of reason alone.

Newbigin rejected the views of Descartes and Locke that there was certain knowledge to fall back on, knowledge not entailing faith. He argued that all knowledge entails faith. Even the act of questioning authority is grounded in premises which are, in this act, themselves authoritative for us, and entail our faith. It emerges that the modern suspicion of authority involves, among other things, a shift in authority, but with the important feature that the new "authority" now operative is unacknowledged as such. Newbigin saw this new authority — the authority of autonomous reason — as rival to the final authority of God's act in Christ. For his own part he bore witness eloquently to the latter; he urged that the authority of God's act in Christ was grounded in itself, there being no higher authority; and he invited trust in this authority.

From Premodern to Modern

Let us trace a little further what has happened to authority in Western society. I want to start by noting a standard definition of authority and the questions it raises.

"Authority" has been defined as "rightly held power." But this immediately raises the question: From where, in this context, do we get our understanding of "right"? There is a danger that authority may, through a process

3. Lesslie Newbigin, *Unfinished Agenda: An Updated Autobiography* (Edinburgh: Saint Andrew Press; London: SPCK; and Geneva: WCC Publications, 1993), p. 254.

4. Lesslie Newbigin, *Truth and Authority in Modernity*, ed. Alan Neely, H. Wayne Pipkin, and Wilbert R. Shenk, Christian Mission and Modern Culture Series (Valley Forge, Pa.: Trinity Press International; Herefordshire, U.K.: Gracewing, 1996).

of normalization, become self-legitimating, so that it simply defines "the right" for those who exercise it and those over whom it is exercised, and the whole is self-enclosed, circular, and relative. Such self-legitimating authority is power operative through unreflective personal assent. This is a danger in all authority (we need follow Foucault no further than this).

The danger of circular self-legitimation is inherent in traditional societies where the relative stability of social order from generation to generation strongly encourages acceptance of the way things are as a "given order." However, there is no warrant for identifying traditional societies as such with self-enclosed, self-legitimating authority. There is within them scope for accountability to a divine source. Classically, the Davidic kings are understood in the Bible as authorized by and accountable to God, whose prophets could press such accountability. Later, medieval Christendom similarly affirmed the divine right of monarchs, whose accountability to God could be pressed by church leaders.

Conversely, the danger of self-legitimating authority has not been absent from modern societies; witness the appearance during the modern period of absolute monarchies and totalitarian regimes driven by revolutionary ideologies. This danger is also present in a new form, as I shall argue, in some "postmodern" developments.

Within modern society as it has developed, suspicion of authority has encouraged the view that if authority is to be granted to people or institutions, it must be legitimated outside of itself by appeal to the good as it is known to universal reason. This has provided foundations for democracy — and also, in principle, for revolution.

Thus within modernity there has remained room for formal authority to be exercised by (for example) the government, military, police force and judiciary, and the professions of education and medicine. But such formal authority has been in the wider context of an implicit belief in the good as it is known to human reason. This context has been deliberately nurtured by setting out to make people civilized, educated, and cultured, so that they may participate dutifully in public life and serve the public good. And all the while, science has offered the hope of extending the material power to achieve good. Taken together, these have spelled widespread confidence in progress.

From Modern to "Postmodern"

Times have moved on. What I have just described sounds distinctly old-fashioned today. For some, what had been held to be universal good is now seen increasingly as a set of values and beliefs private to particular Europeans, maintained through an unwarranted exercise of power. For many other people these beliefs and values have lost their authority, and they are simply confused. Perhaps the only securely legitimate authority today is that which exists to protect the autonomy of individuals. Unfortunately this can get exercised in a very authoritarian fashion.

We are at a vulnerable moment in Western culture. Religious beliefs and, increasingly, beliefs about truth and goodness are often today suspect as mere bids for power. And the vision (no doubt observed more often in the breach) of common participation in the pursuit of truth and goodness is being displaced by something else which needs to be a matter of concern. It is being displaced by two utterly separate, self-enclosed, self-legitimating authorities, in symbiotic relation. These may be labeled the "narcissistic self" and the "system."

The narcissistic self is dominated by a decision against the world as reliably offering meaning and purpose in which we may personally share, and a decision for living instead by reference to fleeting impulse in pursuit of a self-image. Consumerism is fueled by this pursuit. Accounts of narcissism and its dynamics in Western culture today can be found in, for example, Christopher Lasch,[5] Richard Sennett,[6] David Riesman,[7] and Charles Taylor.[8]

"Systems" get described in the language of science, but they do not represent scientific endeavor as such. Science brings knowledge which sometimes can be used as a means to an end but claims no authority to dictate ends, whereas systems apply science within a self-enclosed logic in which means and end merge. For example, in warfare and in business there is a systemic compulsion to pursue every possibility insofar as it may yield an advantage or competitive edge which turns the system into an end in itself.

Neil Postman has coined the term "technopoly" to denote technology as a system which has become an end in itself;[9] Jacques Ellul has described how this system can take on the religious authority once possessed by the natural world in traditional societies, being apprehended with the same awe as sacred and normative.[10]

5. Christopher Lasch, *The Culture of Narcissism* (New York: Norton, 1979).

6. Richard Sennett, *The Fall of Public Man* (New York: Knopf, 1977), see esp. chap. 14.

7. David Riesman, *The Lonely Crowd* (New Haven: Yale University Press, 1961); see esp. his account of the "other-directed" chaacter type.

8. Charles Taylor, *The Ethics of Authenticity* (Cambridge: Harvard University Press, 1992), chap. 6.

9. Neil Postman, *Technopoly: The Surrender of Culture to Technology* (New York: Knopf, 1992).

10. Jacques Ellul, *The Technological Society* (New York: Knopf, 1964).

Where there is a plurality of systems bearing upon the same situation which can check each other, the danger of self-legitimating systems is somewhat mitigated. It is of moral concern today that one particular system has in recent decades been gaining ground as "the bottom line" to which we defer in all things. This is the economic system — which is of course a major source of the momentum of globalization.

It is important to note that neither a narcissistic image nor the "system" invokes the language of authority. Compelling narcissistic images are intimated to us seductively, while the system demands that we defer to it as simply the bottom-line description of "the way things work." But nobody ever tells us (yet) that we have a serious formal duty to ourselves, or to the system. Yet the commands are there, and they need to be that much more of concern because their operation is unacknowledged.

We see here a development beyond the tension in modernity between the autonomy of the individual and the authority of the state. On the one hand, the autonomy of the modern individual, grounded ultimately in the cultural formation of personal moral integrity, is in the decentered narcissistic self subverted by submission to the fleeting impulses of the present moment. On the other hand, the authority of the modern state, upheld ultimately by individuals and put in place to enable corporate action at a national level, gives way to a system spanning nations and accountable to none because (as it claims) it depends on no bestowed authority but simply describes "the way things work" in the world. In this way the domain where public truth and the public good have been pursued — a shared endeavor directed ultimately toward a common purpose — is being displaced by a different kind of space where purely private choices are made in a vacuous public space framed by the system. The only values which remain public here are the atrophied values of citizenship required by life in this space.

Do we see here, in the symbiosis of the narcissistic individual and the system, a final resolution of the earlier tension between individual and state? By no means. As in the previous stages of modernity, what we see here is not a stable state of affairs but rather processes under way which do not necessarily have any coherent direction or sustainable goal. A reminder of this is the growth of single-issue crusades. When life is drained of meaning, the escape from anomie offered by crusades acquires strong appeal. "Mini-ideologies" come to be pursued with fundamentalist fervor. These buck the reduction of values to private choices and of truth to what the system dictates, and they look set perpetually to create mischief for the "postmodern" symbiosis.

It is into this postmodern world of the self-enclosed consumer and system, in which both religion and much that has been regarded as public truth and public good are marginalized as private values, that globalization draws non-Western cultures today.

The Good News of the Authoritative Act of God in Jesus Christ Today

Let us now reflect upon the gospel, the good news of the authoritative act of God in Jesus Christ, and consider how it bears upon this situation.

We have seen that when Lesslie Newbigin set about commending the truth and authority of God's initiative in Christ, he did so by first rejecting John Locke's distinction between knowledge (evident to reason) and belief (involving faith).[11] All knowledge, he says, entails faith. The general failure to appreciate this within modernity has rendered suspect not only religious but also moral understanding, as the role of faith in these becomes evident. The result has been a gradual erosion of the public claim of religious and moral understanding and its relegation to the private realm, where it no longer invites critical engagement.

Heard within the frame of modernity itself, of course, the claim that all knowledge entails faith sounds like a denial that there is any such thing as knowledge; rather there is only a range of beliefs which come to be treated as authoritative.

Newbigin has broken with the terms of modernity, however. He takes Locke's basic distinction between knowledge and belief, reason and external authority and claims to set it within a new context. This new context is, first, the authority of God's act in Christ, and secondly, an appreciation of rationality as a living, changing, historical, and cultural phenomenon. Let us take the second of these first.

Rationality as Historical and Cultural

Modernity has been associated with a belief in ahistorical, universal rationality. Now this belief is at its most plausible in the logical manipulation of straightforward propositions within established theoretical frameworks. Now it is clear enough that in the case of a straightforward theoretical proposition,

11. Lesslie Newbigin, *The Other Side of 1984: Questions for the Churches,* Risk Book Series, no. 18 (Geneva: WCC, 1983), p. 21; and Newbigin, *Truth and Authority in Modernity;* see also the argument in chap. 3 of *The Gospel in a Pluralist Society* (London: SPCK; Grand Rapids: Eerdmans; and Geneva: WCC Publications, 1989).

"seeing (its truth) for oneself" and "believing (its truth) on authority" are two distinct alternatives. But it is another thing to claim that these are, in every case, distinct conceivable options. This would be implicitly to claim for oneself, in respect of every truth claim, a vantage point from which to survey and from which seeing (the truth of it) and believing (the truth of it) are contingent possibilities.

Now this claim may be challenged as reductive from two points of view. First, although modern reason for its own part tends to find authoritative truth in general, lawlike propositions, questions of truth are wider than these terms allow. Truth includes the substance of particular, unique acts of personal and moral discernment; it includes our knowledge of other persons; and crucially, it includes the gospel, which emphatically cannot adequately be framed in these terms. Thus Newbigin opposes synthesizing the biblical testimony "into a series of propositions which can be solidified as 'revealed truth' to be set against the kind of knowledge which is available through the study of nature and its laws."[12] The gospel is irreducibly a matter of testimony to the gracious action of God. It cannot be accommodated to the theoretical framework of modernity.

The second challenge to Locke is this: When any such framework is itself upheld, it is upheld as a matter of faith. It belongs to a tradition of rationality. Newbigin draws upon the work of Alasdair MacIntyre and Michael Polanyi to discuss the historical nature of rationality.[13] Human reasoning is to be acknowledged as a shared cultural endeavor involving an irreducible polarity of commitment and discernment, faith and questioning. Authority too is implied in such commitment and faith, of course, although this does not necessarily take the form of authority invested in a definable set of presuppositions.

---

12. Newbigin, *Other Side of 1984*, p. 49. It is precisely at this point that Stephen Williams's criticism of Newbigin fails (Williams, *Revelation and Reconciliation* [Cambridge: Cambridge University Press, 1995]). Williams criticizes Newbigin (following Polanyi) for seeing the modern rejection of Christ as deriving from epistemological doubt, when it derives as much from the moral rebellion of autonomy. However, Newbigin himself incorporates the latter within his understanding of doubt. He cites the older Christian view of doubt as "something evil, something of which the symbol was the sin of Adam and Eve in doubting the goodness of God's prohibition. . . . according to the biblical story, the primal sin . . . was the willingness to entertain a suspicion that God could not be wholly trusted" (*Other Side of 1984*, p. 19). This doubt clearly represents more than doubt toward a set of revelatory propositions. Newbigin is concerned to resist the "traditional dichotomy between reason and revelation" (*Pluralist Society*, p. 61) which is associated with this understanding of revelation, and which allows a wedge to be driven between "epistemological doubt" and "the moral rebellion of autonomy" in the first place.

13. See esp. Newbigin, *Pluralist Society*, chaps. 3-5.

208

In this new context it becomes clear why, as a methodology, the modern tradition of doubting belief and questioning authority is an inadequate means of finding out truth. There is no solid core of knowledge to be exposed by scraping away the accretions of "faith." Rather, unremitting suspicion leaves nothing intact (except, finally, the immediate authority of fleeting impulse and image). Kant's summons "dare to know" dissolves into an excuse for paying attention "when it suits," and his summons to responsibility into an excuse for irresponsibility. It is this subverting process which has accelerated in the West in recent decades.

To say that all knowledge is embedded in traditions of rationality is not necessarily to leave us carried by the tides of relativism, our search for truth aimless. That concern for truth remains which has impelled the modern wariness of mistaken belief and ungrounded authority. What does not remain is the modern assumption that one always has a superior vantage point (in "universal rationality") from which to question any particular belief. Certainly the possibility must remain, in any given case, that one advances the truth by questioning a particular belief from a different vantage point. But a second and crucial possibility arises, that this particular belief exposes and questions our own (perhaps unrecognized) presuppositions and faith commitments or challenges our unreflective captivity to narcissistic images.

Openness to this second possibility is required if rationality is ever to be more than relative. It is required above all if we are ever to be open toward "absolute truth" or "final authority," whatever these might signify in this new context.

All the above remains liable to interpretation, of course, within the frame of the modernity itself. When this happens, the claim to set the contrast between knowing and believing in a new context gets resisted, and is interpreted in a way which still presupposes this contrast. In particular, the meaning of questioning and of faith may, despite every effort to challenge this, be reduced to the meaning these have when their object is a straightforward theoretical proposition. This leaves an unresolved conflict with the testimony of final authority as found in God's act toward us in Christ rather than in the theoretical framework of modernity.

Authority as It Is in Christ

And so we are brought to the first and fundamental feature of the new context in which Newbigin sets the contrast between knowledge and belief, questioning and faith: the context of God's initiative in Jesus Christ. How are we to understand authority and truth as we find them here? Let us approach the biblical testimony from this viewpoint.

Central to the biblical testimony was Jesus' own message, in word and action, of the in-breaking kingdom of God, the authoritative rule of God pressing close. And the source of Jesus' embodiment of and testimony to the kingdom of God was God's own authority, or power of agency. In turn, the whole intention of Jesus' parables and his healings was that people should see and believe for themselves in the authority of God active in himself, and in faith allow the kingdom to find its embodiment in them. This was the kind of authority, the kind of power, God exercised in Jesus Christ, in his ministry and then finally and consummately in his death and resurrection: it was the authority of divine grace.

The contrast could not be greater between this kind of authority and the kind of limited authority exercised by a modern specialist in a theoretical field. When a specialist tells us what is the case, this exercise of authority is commonly limited to answering a question we bring, in terms we can understand without first needing to see for ourselves what the specialist sees, and without the specialist having the intention of leading us to see this truth for ourselves. By contrast, the authority of God exercised in Jesus is the kind of authority which shows itself by how it gets us wrestling in the first place with deep religious, personal, and moral questions — and leads us to see and understand truth of this nature for ourselves.

Thus, while the authority of God active in Jesus is God's authoritative act upon us, equally it entails a most lively, self-involving act on our part. This is a matter of our active participation with Christ in God's initiative toward us, inaugurating his kingdom. Ours is a doxological act in which, by God's grace, we offer up to God the whole meaning of our world, to be made new. "All that he has, all that he is, he gives; all that we have, all that we are, he takes." In this we do not finally lose our selves and our particularity — God's authority does not obliterate these — but rather we receive them newly transformed from God.

Again, if this is our deepest, most demanding act of obedience, it is nevertheless an act of freedom and not of compulsion. As Gerhard Ebeling writes, "The believer has always owed his faith to a miracle, to a radical change of mind which overwhelms him." And having described what this involves, he writes, "all this, as it happens to the believer, is genuinely *self-evident*. He does not give his assent to it because his heart is forced and broken, but because it is set free and made whole."[14]

Given its empowering character, how is the authority which is active in

14. Gerhard Ebeling, *Introduction to a Theological Theory of Language* (London: Collins, 1973), p. 18.

Jesus experienced as final? Its finality is related to Jesus' urgent summons to his followers to join him in seeking and seeing the will of a good God at work to fulfill his purposes through his own senseless execution. Anticipating this execution, Jesus faced the limitless outrage of sin and the final mockery which this apparently makes of God's good purposes. In it God's authority or power of agency seems finally defeated. And yet, here there lies a profound secret: the true authority of God now shows itself precisely as by grace Jesus perseveres in seeking and seeing for himself, in his own execution, God's good purposes precisely to forgive the limitless outrage of sin.

This is the secret consummated in the resurrection of Jesus. The authority of God to bring limitless freedom and wholeness is here revealed. Having first empowered Jesus, God now calls us to find the same empowerment through him, and become in turn living witnesses to the empowering authority of God among other people.

Responding to this, a person is drawn into an act of witness to God which was first Jesus' own witness. So it is that in the New Testament God's action toward us in Christ is described as a *mysterion*, a secret disclosed to us personally in that initiative itself (Mark 4:11; Matt. 11:25-27; 1 Cor. 2:7). Our relationship to Jesus binds us closely to him through God's initiative in him. Saint Paul describes the closeness of this relationship in various terms: he speaks of the Spirit of Christ dwelling in us (Rom. 8:9-11); and of us living "in Christ" (many passages), putting on Christ (Gal. 3:27), belonging to the body of Christ (1 Cor. 12:12f.), and sharing for ourselves in his sufferings, death, and resurrection (Rom. 6:3-8; 8:17). Saint John similarly writes of our calling to "dwell in" Christ as he dwells in the Father's love, and links this to witness (John 15:4-10; 17:20-26).

This "open secret" of God's empowering, authoritative action in Christ is revealed only insofar as we allow this action to become the formative center of our lives and of the world we inhabit, as we indwell the testimony of Christ, of the Scriptures and the church. In this action of God authority has a distinctive nature which, belonging to that action, we may know only as we allow it to shape our lives.

What Will It Mean to Witness to the Gospel in the Setting of Globalization?

We have considered briefly what kind of authority it is that we discover and "own" in the gospel as final authority and therefore as shaping our understanding of all authority. Given this context, what will it mean to witness to the gospel in the setting of globalization, particularly as this beckons individuals in traditional societies into the "postmodern" world?

Above all I think we must emphasize that the nature of divine authority in Christ, which empowers personal seeking and seeing at its most vital and self-involving, affords a new context for the "modern" vision of personal autonomy. On the one hand, it affirms the right of the individual to question traditional authority; on the other hand, it finds the basis for this not in the natural possession of autonomous reason, but in the higher authority of God in Christ which empowers questioning and reasoning at its most vital. And this difference has profound consequences — including, paradoxically, greater freedom precisely to appreciate the authority of tradition.

At this point the ambiguity of the modern vision is exposed. Insofar as it is led by a certain theoretical understanding of autonomy, it is vulnerable to the postmodern turn, and moral vitality of address dissolves in the domination of the narcissistic self on the one hand and the system on the other.

On the other hand, modernity has moral resources within it which are more open to authority as this is found in God's action in Christ. The relation of these resources to Christian faith is admittedly a complex question which would lead us into debate concerning such matters as how Christian faith has, by figures in both the Renaissance and the Enlightenment, been implicitly affirmed or denied, and the question when this has corresponded with or contradicted the explicit affirmation or denial of this faith; how we should appraise vis-à-vis Christian faith such matters at the beginnings of the modern period as the status of moral reasoning, suspicion of authority, and responses to the prospect of a new age with an unknown future; and issues arising from the diverse strands within modernity.

What is hardly disputable is that the worst tendencies toward relativism are mitigated where personal moral formation such as that pursued in modernity has equipped individuals to make good choices. Without this background of moral formation for the right exercise of freedom, individuals in traditional societies (like the new young generation in the West, lacking such moral formation) are more vulnerable to co-option by a postmodern world as their traditional world dissolves.

By way of a concluding proposal, I suggest that we might fruitfully enlarge discussion of these matters by drawing on and developing David Riesman's account of changes in the place of authority in traditional, modern, and postmodern societies.[15] Rather than describing these changes in terms of the changing offices, beliefs, and practices to which authority is granted, he has

---

15. Riesman, *The Lonely Crowd*.

described them in terms of changes in the "character-type" of individuals within these societies. These changes are, broadly speaking, from a "tradition-directed" through an "inner-directed" to an "other-directed" character today (the suffix "-directed" means "directed by"). His account reminds us that the changes in question involved changes in the nature of authority itself.

The tradition-directed person is found in traditional societies where there is relatively little change and individuals are largely constrained by and conform to the expectations of an established social order. The inner-directed person emerges in the West from the Renaissance onward. He/she has internalized, from elders at an early stage of life, beliefs and values which then guide him/her in the consistent exercise of a personal freedom which is beyond that available in traditional societies. Riesman offers here the metaphor of a gyroscope holding its own direction in a variable situation. The inner-directed person can be highly achieving and strongly individualistic. The other-directed person has been found increasingly since the 1950s in the United States and takes a lead from peers, watching for and following patterns of change among them with some anxiety. The metaphor Riesman offers here is that of radar.

Now Riesman's concern is sociological, rather than with first-order issues of truth and relativity in relation to authority. However, from the viewpoint of the tradition-directed person, it would seem that the other-directed person tends toward relativism; he/she identifies with whatever choices happen to be in vogue. Also, from the viewpoint of the other-directed person, it would seem that the tradition-directed person is rigidly constrained by external authority; he/she has relatively few choices.

The crucial question now arises, whether the inner-directed character is merely a transitional stage between these two things: a character embodying, partly, authority which in its internalization becomes little more than a set of programmed "choices," and partly freedom of choice which amounts to little more than the exercise of subjective preference.

I want to suggest another way of understanding, or at least developing the possibilities latent in, inner direction: a way which, by comparison with tradition direction and other direction, offers promising clues to what it might mean to live in the future by the empowering authority which is testified in the gospel of Jesus Christ.

Christian Inner Direction?

Briefly, we can conceive of a Christian inner direction which is in intention responsive to and responsible before God. This will entail, on the one hand, an appreciation and "interiorization" of the Christian heritage as witnessing to God, and correspondingly a retrieval of the importance of canon. Personal formation takes place here within the tradition of witness found in Jesus Christ, in the Scriptures and in Christian tradition.

Christian inner direction will entail on the other hand the discerning, free exercise of personal responsibility. This will involve creative participation in the renewal of public space and pursuit of the public good, now grounded in our responsibility before God.

Personal formation with its dual aspects of indwelling tradition and freely exercising responsibility will then take place within the church and within other mediating structures in society which are open to God. Such mediating structures will have a particular continuing role in traditional societies as these are faced with the pressures of globalization. On the one hand, they may help individuals who indwell tradition to form good moral judgments in the face of these pressures, and to discern and resist pressure from the "system" which works precisely to erode such mediating structures. On the other hand, they may help individuals who exercise personal responsibility to resist reduction of their autonomy merely to opportunities for narcissistic consumption.

In summary, then, I suggest that in our age the gospel invites a renewal of public space, and of the public good; but in their renewal these must be formed by the gospel of God's action toward us with the empowering authority of grace. Corresponding to this, the gospel invites a renewal of "inner direction" formed by the gospel and shaping people for responsible personal participation in the recovery of public space and of the public good. Together these invite a third renewal: that of mediating structures in church and society, formed once again under the gospel. To pursue renewal on these three counts will be to resist in a practical way the overweening demands of the narcissistic self and of the system, and to challenge them as distorting the proper polarity of self and world under God.

The renewal I have sketched is for both "postmodern" Western societies and traditional societies vulnerable to subversion by postmodernity through globalization. It is a renewal of public vision and of "inner-directed" character formation grounded in the gospel and lived out under the guidance of the Spirit. It embodies a hope for the empowering authority of God to be more fully realized in public society. Such is the church's task today, both in public society and in its own life: to sponsor the renewal of public space — even to *be* that space — under the authority and grace of God in Christ.

Lesslie Newbigin's Understanding of Islam

Jenny Taylor

Lesslie Newbigin's own self-understanding was as pastor and preacher, not as academic or even theologian. It is typical of the man — and indicative of his unfashionable "breadth" — that there were many things you could pin on him, but only the least pretentious stuck. He distrusted "expertise," which he believed bedeviled the academy and stripped thought of its humanity — and practiced what he preached. Endearing though this is, it makes the job of the researcher more difficult. "Lesslie Newbigin's Understanding of Islam" — a title that would no doubt have made him chuckle — is a tricky subject just because his modesty as a scholar meant he usually dispensed with the paraphernalia of scholarship. Only one of his most recent five books has an index — and that is his autobiography. One cannot simply trawl the indexes looking for "Islam" or "Muslims" or some such. He never addressed the subject head-on in a whole book — and indeed, his only specific writing on the subject was published posthumously, almost as if it were an afterthought in a life very much taken up with other matters.[1]

If this is so, it raises several questions. First, why would a missionary whose life was largely spent among Asians give so little evident thought to the world's only other great missionary religion? And secondly, why right at the end? And indeed, if he had thought and wrote so little on the subject, why is it worth pursuing in a paper for so eminent a collection as this?

Faith and Power: Christianity and Islam in "Secular" Britain, published in July, six months after his death in January 1998, sprang both from conver-

---

1. Lesslie Newbigin, *Faith and Power: Christianity and Islam in "Secular" Britain*, with Lamin Sanneh and Jenny Taylor (London: SPCK, 1998).

215

sations about recent persecution of Christians particularly in Iran — Newbigin was a friend of Hassan Dehqani-Tafti, former bishop in Teheran, whose son was murdered during the Iranian so-called revolution — and from the post-Rushdie furor. He had also met and been impressed by Yale's once-Muslim professor of missiology, Lamin Sanneh, during the Gospel as Public Truth consultation process — and discovered a soul mate. The mutual influence of those two great minds on each other will be a matter for historians of the world church. Sanneh, of a royal line of Senegalese scholars, acknowledges his own debt to Newbigin both in *Encountering the West* and again in a whole chapter of *Faith and Power*. There Sanneh identifies perhaps the signal truth about why Newbigin became interested in Islam when he did. "Newbigin offers encouragement to those who wish to seize the theological initiative . . . and in that respect his challenge to the modern West is no different in kind from that of Muslims. *Les extrèmes se touchent*."[2]

In other words, Newbigin singled out Islam per se instead of in the earlier generalized terms of pluralism, only because Islam was challenging the West — within the West. Newbigin was not interested in Islam as a *religion*. It was Muslims' anger with the West as a culture without legitimacy that fascinated him. They were being so very *public* about their beliefs when the church had become so obligingly private.

Although his principal concern in the twenty years after his return to Britain from Madras was mission to the *West*, he saw more clearly than most that the West's deep problems were affecting the rest of the world and would increasingly do so. He meant this not in terms of unjust global economic structures, for example, but more profoundly in terms of cultural integrity. "This culture has penetrated into every other culture in the world, and threatens to destabilize them all," he wrote in *The Other Side of 1984*.[3] Although this is not especially germane to his thinking about Islam, it is nonetheless indicative of his orientation. As I have said before, he was not so much interested in mission among Muslims or Hindus as in the corrosive mission that Western culture was so effectively doing for itself, and which he believed would reap the whirlwind. His analysis was being uncannily echoed by Muslims around the world. I single out just one illustration of this point. In 1977, papers of the First World Conference on Muslim Education in Mecca, held under the auspices of King Abdulaziz University, which I doubt

---

2. Lamin Sanneh, "Tolerance, Pluralism and Christian Uniqueness," in *Faith and Power*, p. 43.

3. Lesslie Newbigin, *The Other Side of 1984: Questions for the Churches*, Risk Book Series, no. 18 (Geneva: WCC, 1983), p. 23.

he read, parallel Newbigin exactly. They begin with the following poignant remark: "It can be seen that religious groups are no longer dominating the social scene in the West and hence all branches of knowledge have no central, integrating force."[4]

The writer goes on: "[I]f the intellectuals of the Muslim world do not stem the tide now by instilling Islamic concepts in all branches of knowledge and changing the methodology from unbridled questioning to the exploration of the significance of everything for the sake of understanding human life and External Nature, the time is not far away when the tide will sweep away even the bedrock on which the structure of Muslim society is based."[5]

The writer describes in Newbiginesque terms Western "brainwashing" and rootlessness and the bloodshed and bitterness in which a dual allegiance of educationists to Western and Islamic values in Turkey and Indonesia, for example, would inevitably result. The writer advocates the "extreme value to the whole western world of a radical new programme for the Islamisation of education which will build intellectual inquiry on the firm basis of a faith in divine revelation." Newbigin could hardly have put it better.

Newbigin had returned to Britain in 1974 to find himself, like so many Muslims, an outsider — a *religious* outsider in the West. As a stranger in the country, he could see more clearly than most of the inhabitants what was wrong. By the time of the writing of *The Gospel in a Pluralist Society*, published in 1989, his forebodings that Western liberalism would lead to global destabilization seemed to have found strident confirmation as reports of Muslim rioting and assassinations in reaction to the *Satanic Verses* began to come in from all over the world. True to prophethood, Newbigin was far more perturbed at the time by the reaction of his own tribe:

> As I write [he says], the press is full of the cries of outrage from Western liberal writers and critics in face of the Muslim reaction to Salman Rushdie's book *The Satanic Verses*. But it is doubtful whether these cries have behind them anything that can withstand the determined onslaught of those who hold firm beliefs about the truth. Freedom to think and say what you like will not provide the resources for a resolute grappling with false beliefs. The demand for freedom of thought and expression must itself rest on some firmly held belief about the origin, nature, and destiny

---

4. Syed Ali Ashraf, ed., *Crisis in Muslim Education* (a compilation of papers read at the First World Conference on Muslim Education, organized by King Abdulaziz University), p. 2.

5. Ashraf, p. 2.

of human life. If it has no such foundation it will prove powerless in the face of those who have firm beliefs about the truth.[6]

Contemporary Islam had, in Newbigin's view, unquestionably "firm beliefs" — albeit false ones. He admired that firmness while being astonished at the vulnerability of the West to its falseness.

In an angry six-point letter to the *Independent* newspaper published on 21 February 1989 and reprinted two years later by the Islamic Foundation in their *Sacrilege versus Civility* — a compendium of writings on the Rushdie affair — he sympathizes with Muslims "in their anger at what is perceived as blasphemy against God and his messenger." He likens blasphemy to the injection of "poison into public life" — a poison with more deadly long-term effects than anything offered by the drug merchants. He pointedly asserts that Christians "are not permitted to respond as the Ayatollah has done, because the centre of their faith is at the point where the Lord himself accepted death on a charge of blasphemy." Finally he lets off his sharpest barb, not at Rushdie, or Khomeini, or the book burners of Bradford, or the liberal intelligentsia who published blasphemous books — but at the church. "Whether the silence of contemporary British Christians in the face of blasphemy is due to an understanding of their faith, or to indifference, only God can judge."[7]

As Sanneh says, Newbigin and the Islamic Foundation *se touchent*. While being indicative of the very extremity of Newbigin's prophetic isolation within his own culture, these writings tell us little about whether Newbigin *understood* Islam. But his obvious sympathy with their critique of secularism — and its force — is instructive to us of the power of Islam to attract sympathy in some conservative Western quarters, who are nonetheless aware of its excesses elsewhere.

We must therefore consider Newbigin's earlier writing about Islam — or its lack — to put his later interest in Islam in perspective. And I believe we can conclude that this interest was in fact congruent merely upon Islam's relation to the impending *Western* "disaster" as he saw it. In 1978 he produced *The Open Secret*, which launched him as a missionary to the West, at the end of a career as one of the church's foremost ecumenists and ecclesiologists based, oddly, in the East. Published four years after his return to Britain from

---

6. L. Newbigin, *The Gospel in a Pluralist Society* (London: SPCK; Grand Rapids: Eerdmans; and Geneva: WCC Publications, 1989), p. 244.

7. L. Newbigin, letter to the editor, *Independent*, 21 February 1989, quoted in "*The Satanic Verses*: Blasphemy v. Freedom of Speech," in *Sacrilege versus Civility*, ed. M. Ahsan and A. Kidwai (Leicester: Islamic Foundation, 1991).

Madras, it is a most powerful and moving expression of his Christology. "The Christian goes to meet his neighbour of another religion on the basis of his commitment to Jesus Christ . . . ," he writes; "Jesus is for the believer the source from whom his understanding of the totality of experience is drawn and therefore the criterion by which other ways of understanding are judged." Newbigin, like Saint Paul, "resolved to know nothing except Jesus Christ and him crucified." From that unflinching standpoint he reviews — and demolishes — four kinds of theology of religions, including of course John Hick's (but this is not the place to go into that). Islam gets a solitary mention in this particular work — and that in regard to the Jerusalem Conference of 1928 which, in exploring the opportunities of pluralism, sought, he says, to affirm "values" in other religions as part of one truth. The majesty of God in Islam is cited in the conference report as its "value," though the "values" project as a whole gets the Newbigin thumbs-down since, he says, it doesn't actually work. The sum of the values in all the other religions does not equal the "value" in Christ, he points out, and indeed, turning to Christ often means renouncing the highest values of the tradition one leaves behind.[8] This is a somewhat trivial reference, but I mention it to indicate that once again Islam is referred to obliquely only in the context of some wider debate.

In *The Other Side of 1984*, written in 1983, Muslims get a mention along with Sikhs and Hindus as those who, along with believing Christians, are being forced in Britain's schools to learn about religion as an aspect of culture, not as a vision of truth.[9] He is deeply sympathetic here with religious migrants coping with the dishonesty of the British system that dragoons its victims into its own faith in irreligion while praising itself for its "impartiality."

Muslims get three mentions in a small book published by the Grubb Institute in 1988 to which Newbigin contributed the article "On Being the Church for the World."[10] There he writes amusingly of his ministry at a little URC church in inner-city Birmingham — a ministry accepted with gusto in 1980 at the age of seventy-one. "If you want to visit me you ask for Winson Green Prison and then look for the building just opposite, which Hitler unfortunately missed," he writes. The people who lived there were "all OHMS," according to the local policeman. "I thought he was saying something about the prison, and said 'what exactly do you mean?' He said, 'Only Hindus, Mus-

---

8. Lesslie Newbigin, *The Open Secret: Sketches for a Missionary Theology* (London: SPCK; Grand Rapids: Eerdmans, 1978), p. 194.

9. Newbigin, *Other Side of 1984*, p. 62.

10. Lesslie Newbigin, "On Being the Church for the World," in *The Parish Church?* ed. Giles S. Ecclestone (London: Mowbray, 1988), pp. 25-42.

lims and Sikhs.' So we have this situation of a loyal congregation of white ageing people, who, not of their own will, have been banished to the suburbs and do not have cars to travel in, trying to minister to a local area where it is not just thistles and tin cans but is mostly Hindus, Muslims and Sikhs."[11]

Muslims are still very marginal to Newbigin's view — marginal in society, and marginal to his thinking. This is reflected in another classic vignette, in the same essay, from his Madras days. Half the congregations in Madras had no buildings, he tells us. For twelve years he conducted all their services in the street.

He writes: "My picture of the church formed in those years is deeply etched in my mind, the picture of a group of people sitting on the ground and a larger crowd of Hindus and Muslims and others standing around listening, watching, discussing; and thank God, when one came back a few months later some of these would be in the group in the front."[12]

Muslims, therefore, on the fringes of "the group" or even in the wilderness, until their conversion, when they are restored by the "mysterious work of the Holy Spirit" to equality, when they are now "in front." It is almost a diagram of the perfect plural society.

Newbigin had some slight correspondence with one or two key Muslims in Britain during the next ten years. I remember him particularly pleased with his contacts with Shabbir Akhtar, a fiery young Bradford-based intellectual and fierce opponent of Western secular hegemony — until his comeuppance in Kuala Lumpur at the International Islamic University in Malaysia where he was officially ostracized for insisting his students question their teachers as he had been taught to do in his English education, and later resigned — but that was later.[13] His 1990 book *The Light in the Enlightenment: Christianity and the Secular Heritage*[14] Newbigin read, and according to Akhtar, reviewed sympathetically (though I have been unable thus far to trace the review). Akhtar told me recently that he admired Newbigin for his "firmness" — a word Newbigin had himself used of Muslims, as we have seen. (If I

11. Newbigin, "On Being the Church," p. 26.

12. Newbigin, "On Being the Church," p. 32.

13. See his revealing account of this episode in "Ex-defender of the Faith," *Times Higher Education Supplement*, 22 August 1997. He writes: "Most of the literature in the university library was in English . . . this modern movement of an endless intellectual curiosity about all things is one we owe to western man. Owing to the grammatical limitations of Arabic, it is impossible to express most philosophical claims with an acceptable degree of riguor and clarity. . . . Freedom is a precondition of profundity."

14. Shabbir Akhtar, *The Light in the Enlightenment: Christianity and the Secular Heritage* (London: Grey Seal, 1990).

were to begin a study of the correlates in the Newbigin and Islamic critiques of Western culture — I would begin here.)

But his firmness was hardening. In May 1995 he wrote to Lamin Sanneh, telling him of a paper he had written called "What Kind of Britain," based on a lecture he had given at Duke University in the States the previous autumn. In the letter he outlines his ideas for a book tackling the Weber fallacy of irreversible secularization and posing the question: "What would it mean to work and hope for a Christian society?" He says: "The Max Weber theory . . . is proving false. Religion is now a much bigger factor in world politics than it has been for 200 years. In particular, Islam — powerfully resurgent — offers a model for society (law, state, economics, culture, science) which challenges this view. Contemporary British society is incapable of meeting, or even of understanding this challenge — as the episode of the Satanic Verses demonstrated."[15]

He says he wants to write a book about it — but "this I cannot do, for I do not have the knowledge of Islam." He expresses his growing fascination with the centuries' long interaction between Christendom and Islam. He also sees "powerful forces and personalities (including the heir to the throne) acting to raise the profile of Islam among the major institutions of this country — which is beginning to seem like a viable alternative to the emptiness of the accepted idea of the secular society."

Faith and Power is what emerged from these early musings. We again see the ambivalence: concern for human beings whose innate religiosity is being squashed. And concern for a society which he believed was threatened by religious militancy as a result.[16]

In the very first paragraph of his introduction to the book, Newbigin commends the Muslim stance: "Muslims are now 'offering an all-embracing challenge to [the] legitimacy [of secular society],' something he describes as 'even more unexpected' than the post-war rise of Fascism and National Socialism."[17]

In the next chapter, commenting on the resurrection by Muslims of the concept of blasphemy, he writes: "The firmness of their stance contrasts with the relative timidity with which Christian leaders occasionally challenge the norms of British society. . . . Christians' protests can be ignored, not those of Islam."[18]

---

15. Private collection.

16. Newbigin was surely wrong to assume that the raising of the profile by officialdom of religious groups in Britain had more to do with filling any spiritual void than with the perplexing political logic of ethnicity in contemporary pluralist democracies.

17. Newbigin, *Faith and Power,* p. 15.

18. Newbigin, *Faith and Power,* p. 19.

And again:

> In our present situation in Britain where Christians and Muslims share a common position as minority faiths in a society dominated by the naturalistic ideology, we share a common duty to challenge this ideology, to affirm that it can only lead our society into disintegration and disaster, and to bear witness to the reality of God from whom alone come those "norms" that can govern human life, that *dharma* which can give order to the chaos of human passions. Here, Christians should be both encouraged and challenged by the much more vigorous testimony of Islam. . . . Christians have reason to be grateful to their Muslim fellow citizens for this service . . . the service of unmasking the folly that there is no objective reality, only "values."[19]

By the final section in the book, Islam has itself become the threat. "If the truth about the meaning and purpose of human life is something in principle unknowable, then there are no grounds for defending the liberal doctrine against any other doctrine of human nature and destiny. The helplessness of liberal societies in the face of militant religious fundamentalism amply illustrates this point. If the truth about these ultimate matters is unknowable, then there are no arguments except those of the gun and the bomb."[20]

Notice the language: helplessness, militancy; gun; bomb. There is a new edge of darkness to the man of blithe spirit who ten years earlier was writing merrily about Muslims and Hindus in the context of thistles and tin cans. They have emerged from the dusty pre-Rushdie streets and neglected wastelands at the very fringes of civilization to an overwhelming centrality where they threaten that civilization with guns and bombs. Society itself is now helpless, strangled by the weeds of its own inner contradictions, strewn with the litter of its falsehoods.

Islam is no alternative, however, since in the very next paragraph he writes of society's "gradual slide into moral anarchy" — against which, he says, "there are no barriers." Islam is not a serious option for a contemporary society, merely a symptom of its increasing disarray.

I have three observations to make from the foregoing.

First, Newbigin appears to equate militant fundamentalism with Islam. I believe he did so unconsciously — and it served his rhetorical purpose.[21] He had never studied the subject.

19. Newbigin, *Faith and Power*, pp. 22-24.
20. Newbigin, *Faith and Power*, p. 142.

Second, Newbigin was interested in militant Islam only as a *symptom of Western decay* rather than as a critique in itself.

Third, militant Islam held up for Newbigin a mirror image of the kind of religious activism that he believed faced the civilized world if it failed to shore up its Christian pillars. He saw what violent protest had achieved: the fatwa was like a hammer blow to a rotten plank: liberalism just caved in. I have researched the changed post-Rushdie criteria among secular publishers of religious books. One said: "Publishing houses don't want the aggravation. Any good controversial book about Islam wouldn't get published in Britain."[22] A writer I consulted who was commissioned by publishers Little, Brown, pre-Rushdie, to write a book about jihad for the popular market, afterward had his contract revoked on apparently spurious grounds.[23] Seventeen other British publishers also rejected it. It is now being published in the States by the only house that will touch anathematized religious controversies, Prometheus Books. The media had learned to be afraid. Words — for a while perhaps — matter after all.

Newbigin saw what Muslims themselves had seen: they had managed to change the intellectual tide. Journalist Fuadh Nahdi, editor of *Q News,* has said: "Muslim protest ended secular legitimacy to speak for religion."[24] Tariq Modood, a British scholar with a Muslim background, even calls for the maintenance of the established church to guarantee a place for the sacred — and hence for less than popular religious identities — in the public domain.[25] Indeed, much of the Anglican hierarchy has come to see itself in light of what an Anglican-sponsored research project analyzed it as, in a multicultural society: a "broker for faiths." Yet what alarmed Newbigin at the end was just this: that traditional Christian belief and practice were now so weakened that the church's domestication as a kind of wet nurse[26] for democratically unweaned religious

21. There is not the space to analyze a subject amply documented by Giles Keppel, Olivier Roy, and others, save to note what Modood says: "Islam is using any of the tools of ethnic identity to force its way into public consciousness." This does not mean the tools or those who wield them are necessarily Islamic. Others have amply written that the Islamic grudge against Western civilization is more a product of its marginalization from the dominant discourse due to its own self-induced and inbuilt economic and intellectual retardation, than from a true understanding of its own religiosity or of the West's ailment. Newbigin never discussed this fact.

22. *Dagens Nyheter* (Stockholm), 24 February 1998.

23. There was considerable publicity surrounding this case. See, for example, *Daily Telegraph,* 3 November 1997.

24. Unpublished interview with author, 13 February 1998.

25. A good summary of Modood's arguments is contained in his article "Establishment, Multiculturalism and British Citizenship," *Political Quarterly* 65, no. 1 (January-March 1994).

groupings might itself prove fatal. In one of the very last things he ever wrote, he said: "Chartered pluralism can only exist where there is a sufficiently large, vigorous and articulate Christian community to sustain the basis on which it rests. . . . if the recent erosion of Christian belief continues beyond a certain point it will become impossible to offer any alternative to the present dominant secularist ideology, since . . . this ideology is ultimately self-destructive, and the way would be open for other powerful or seductive alternatives."[27]

Conclusion

As I have hoped to show, Newbigin's target was not Islam itself, to which he barely gave a moment's thought, but his own coreligious. He was right in thinking that the church had failed to understand its own epistemological problem and allowed itself to operate by the culture's own meager substitutes for truth. This lack of understanding is amply reflected in the reviews of *Faith and Power*. Brian Pearce, director of the Inter Faith Network, was so angry with Newbigin's contribution to the book that he refused to review it for *Crucible*. Martin Forward in *Expository Times* believed it reflected "the baleful shadows of Barth and Kraemer," "substituting unexamined Christianity for unexamined secularism" and oddly accusing the authors of *Faith and Power* of "pietism." And Christopher Lamb, Anglican Interfaith secretary at Church House, somewhat patronizingly accused him in his old age of fighting yesterday's battles. "It is baffling to be told that Christians have to *enter* the public arena. My recent colleagues at Church House and CCBI have never left it."[28] The obvious retort hardly needs making.

As a bishop, it was always principally the inadequate response of the church to the growing cultural darkness that shocked and grieved Newbigin — and Islam's reaction to Rushdie went some way in his eyes to showing us up for what we are. We have perhaps moved on since then. There is growing sympathy for the church in government circles — and bishops are actively involved in inner-city policy making. Muslims lost a huge amount of liberal sympathy over this period, and the liberal hegemony got a very bloody nose. But the deeper "truth" questions which Newbigin cared enough to articulate at every level and at every opportunity have lost their most valiant champion — and the battle has barely begun.

26. Modood's expression is "mother hen primacy" (Modood, p. 66).
27. Newbigin, *Faith and Power*, p. 159.
28. In *Theology* (March/April 1999): 148.

SECTION 5

REPORT AND RESPONSE

A Response to the Consultation

Daniel W. Hardy

Being on the margin between different aspects of theology, and between theology and other disciplines, often helps develop a fresh perspective on the significance of what is said by different parties. I am accustomed to, and welcome, such marginality and the insight it can afford. In the case of this conference there has been a remarkable array of different vantage points associated in varying ways and degrees with Lesslie Newbigin's life and work, and their significance. The effect has been kaleidoscopic. There are too many, and complex, facets of theology and mission under consideration even to be able to respond to all of them. What I present to you, therefore, is a report and comments on some of the conference themes as they have appeared in the sections I have heard or the presentations I have read.

On the whole I shall not attempt to discuss the significance of Lesslie Newbigin, fine and good friend as he was, nor the implications of the papers for understanding him. This would simply be too complex. Besides, I think Lesslie would be the last person to want attention called to himself. The concern of his thought and of his very life was the gospel of Jesus Christ. Unlike so many, he exercised no proprietary rights on the deep insight into the gospel that he had. It was exactly this that freed him to engage with other people so thoughtfully and caringly, and to set in motion discussions that needed to take place without himself ever dominating them, although he might intervene to help them serve the gospel. I believe that this testified to a remarkable capacity that he had for immersing himself completely in the issues that needed to be addressed: a self-immersion in the issues opened by the gospel of Jesus Christ. Beyond that, which I regard as the most important feature of Lesslie Newbigin's life and work, I will not try to comment on him and what he stood for.

I would like to identify for attention four themes pervasively present during the conversations so far. Those I have chosen are loosely related to the organizing titles of the sections of the conference. There has been a very interesting discussion around these topics. Each has been quite illuminating in its own right and has merited concentrated attention. At times, however, I have found myself rather starkly disagreeing with some of what has been said, or wanting to extend it or modify it. These four topics are those I think especially require further comment. I will take them in no particular order of priority.

The significance for us of the Enlightenment and the postmodernity that displaces it has provoked lively discussion. It seems to me that the very liveliness of discussions about the Enlightenment and postmodernity on occasions like this testifies to something more fundamental happening in our situation today. By probing the benefits and problems of these movements, it seems to me that we are recovering something of the sense of the dynamic of history that was lost where the habits of the Enlightenment were dominant. The liveliness of the discussions today indicates something far more complex underlying them, which they somehow manage to avoid. What is that? It is the very sense of history and the complexities of change which — as I need hardly remind you — is one of the unique contributions of Hebrew civilization to our long-running Western and European and world civilization.

Clearly there is no easy way of summarizing the characteristics of the Enlightenment or postmodernity. But both respond to the complexities of historical movement by oversimplifying them. The Enlightenment and postmodernity are alike in one respect: they are reductive concentrations and oversimplifications of historical movement and change. In that respect they are quite remarkable.

We ignore both the Enlightenment and postmodernity at our peril. I suspect we will never have done with the Enlightenment, because it sponsors so much of the movement of modern industrial, business, economic, and social life; and all these reflect, and also perpetuate, Enlightenment thinking. In a curious way postmodernity appears to support some of the features of modern life stemming from the Enlightenment, for example, a supervening metaphysic of some kind. At the same time, it is a refusal of all those certainties that the Enlightenment had promoted. There is a great deal to be learned from the continuities and discontinuities of the two. This is not the place for extensive attention to the issues. I would only point out that each of the two — Enlightenment and postmodernity — is valuable for its achievements. But both are also profoundly problematic because they are reductive concentrations of the movement of history. We have to become accustomed to the fact

228

that they are beneficial and also highly problematic and probably will always remain so.

Our concern for the Enlightenment and postmodernity is important, however. The recovery of history by Christians may serve to reattach issues of Judeo-Christian faith to the dynamics of history. This is no easy task, for the history in which we now find ourselves is one of great complexity and change; and, in common with others, we don't quite know how to make sense of it, or of the implications of the gospel for it.

One of the ways Christians should not respond is by indulging in over-simplifications about Christian faith. Although it is somewhat dangerous to speak in these terms, the excessive reliance on a simple notion of "revelation" was probably the product of a seventeenth-century reaction to the Enlightenment, through which the source of Christian understanding was conceived as "given" for faith. In the form in which it is most commonly used today, "revelation" was therefore probably a Christian reaction to the Enlightenment. And as such, it employed the very oversimplifying that is characteristic of both Enlightenment and postmodern understanding; in effect, their oversimplification induces Christian understanding to do the same. Rather than indulging in such habits, we ought, in my view, to be relearning ways to deal with the complex fabric of world history, the fabric in which we are all engaged and to which both the Enlightenment and postmodernity bear inadequate witness. The issues of history, Enlightenment, and postmodernity, and how the gospel is interwoven with history, deserve much more attention: I think they will continue to be major features of the discussion about missiology.

Within this very large issue, we can now approach three constructive themes in the discussion. We have been witness, I think, to three kinds of struggle. I shall identify them very quickly and then say more about each one of them:

1. the struggle for a renewed life with God
2. the struggle for renewed value for the other and a renewed approach to the other
3. the struggle for how to be the church sent in the world

The Struggle for a Renewed Life with God

There was a very interesting paper given by Professor Kenneson early in the conference about the kind of understanding of God needed to sponsor real engagement with the other in the world. It dwelt a good deal on what has become a common theme in modern systematic theology; that is, the relationality of everything. (Notice, by the way, that I was pleading for a relational understanding of Enlightenment, postmodernity, and Christian faith.) Kenneson spoke of the relationality that is implicit in God and also in our life with each other.

In my view the modern discussion about relationality both in God and with others in the world rarely moves beyond a very static form of understanding. It needs to be enriched by a far deeper appreciation of the dynamics of God's life and of God's life with the world. This is the dynamic of the trinitarian life of God, and of God with the world, in creation, redemption, and eschatological fulfillment. Fully appreciated, this produces a very rich understanding of the trinitarian life of God which is itself in the trinitarian work of God for human salvation. If fully undertaken, this is a wonderful discussion, which consists in following in the dynamic of the self-giving of God fully present in the person of Jesus Christ and fully dispersed in the world through the power of the Holy Spirit. It is always a dynamic trinitarian view of God. Taken as such, it is one of the most important features of modern understanding for Christian faith. It is a form of "tacit knowledge," which speaks powerfully of the way God enriches our very life in the world through the complexity of his own agency maintaining himself in relation to the world. That is a very important strand in our discussion I hope will be taken a good deal further.

The Struggle for Renewed Value for the Other and a Renewed Approach to the Other

I believe this is a fundamental missiological discussion. This too needs to be seen in dynamic terms. There is a kind of sterility, I think, in some contemporary missiology where it simply talks about relations with the other. This is found even, I think, in such powerful thinkers as Emmanuel Levinas, with his highly developed understanding of being-for-the-other. The sterility I think arises from the same source as the sterility of that relational thinking in God that is so characteristic of modern theology; that is, that it is not sufficiently dynamic.

What we need — and can have — is a Spirit-led understanding of the trinitarian life of God that shows us how to be related to the lives of other people. What would that be? It would not only be the attempt to be "with" the other in the other's "otherness." It would be empathetically and sympathetically to enter into the existence of another person for the sake of the well-being of the other person. That well-being would be the God-given flourishing to which the gospel attests. This, however, would not be the gospel we bring to the other person, our telling of the gospel in such a way as to form the other person. It would be the gospel found by that other person as we are with him or her and are sympathetic to his or her well-being.

That is a kind of understanding capable of producing the same kind of dynamic that we find in the life of God in relation to others. Instead of simply "being with" other people in mission, as if mission were an aspect of our being, we would be those who are really sent: we go, we find, we receive, we suffer, we are patient with the other, we live in and with the other, within the other's existence, and with the other we learn — and relearn — the meaning of the gospel. And in relearning the meaning of the gospel with the other, we enable him/her to receive responsibility for the gospel, rather than ourselves taking responsibility for the gospel even with the other person. So the essence of mission would be the transference of the responsibility for the gospel to the other to whom we had gone. What I have been trying to hint at in saying this is the remarkable kind of dynamic that can be introduced into a missiological understanding through a renewed appreciation of the dynamics of the trinitarian God.

The Struggle for How to Be the Church Sent in the World

Are we to fall into the kind of "ecclesio-centrism" whereby we equate the church with God, as indicated in the paper by Peter Cruchley-Jones? Or are we to achieve another kind of understanding of the church in the world: the church sent into the world?

Before continuing, let me say that most of our discussions seem always to be permeated by an understanding of the church that is drawn primarily from the Reformed tradition. And it needs, actually, to be accompanied by another kind of understanding of the church that is found outside the Reformed tradition. It is the Reformed tradition, I think, that speaks of the church as being a God-constituted association, a God-constituted community of those who are true to Jesus Christ (as Professor Hunsberger described it), of those who are called by the Spirit into the reign of God. That is a very important and valuable understanding of the constitution of the church. But it has to be set alongside another understanding of the church which talks about the church as being realized in eucharistic worship, which in its full implications is perhaps not as familiar among us as it might be. When I speak of a church that is realized in eucharistic worship, I am talking about a church that finds itself through liturgical participation in the history of salvation. At each Eucharist the history of salvation is presented in a participatory form; and the church learns itself, finds itself, and is reconstituted as the body of Christ in that eucharistic liturgy. That needs to be set alongside the understanding of the formation of the church that comes from the Reformed tradition.

For both alike there is the question about how God moves and continues to move this church. Is it constituted in centrifugal acts of the preaching and following of the Word, or in centrifugal acts of eucharistic worship? Is it constituted as the embodiment of the community for the purposes of sending, or something still more centripetal? These are issues that still need to be considered much more fully. And after much of the conversation that I have heard here about the church, I find myself wanting to ask: How is this happening? How should it happen? And perhaps most of all: How should it happen in the world? For I keep hearing of a church that is somehow itself independent of the world and parallel to the world, even if also present in the flow of the world's life. But I don't hear any clear views of how these things are so, or of how the church is itself in its sending. How are we to be there in the world?

For my own part, I am strongly convinced that the world has its own vitalities conferred from the life of God. The vitalities of God are not to be found only in the church's life; they are to be found in many of the vitalities that have brought the world to its present position, for good or for ill. And whether the vitalities are those of poor communities in Latin America or Africa, or those of advanced Western civilization driving a rather questionable world economy, the fact is that there are vitalities in the world that are not of the church's making and with which the church needs to engage. And in fact, if we are going to engage effectively, if we are really going to be present in the flow of the world's life, we have to engage with those vitalities not as if they are somehow alien but as vitalities where the presence of God is already active. There is much more here that needs to be explored. How is the church to serve the world? And so my most fundamental questions are these: How is the church itself in its sending? And is the meaning of its sending only found when the world follows the source of its own vitality, the Spirit of Christ?

How is the church sent? How is the church a sending church? And how is it sent in the same way that the trinitarian God seems to be commending that we relate to others, by full immersion in the world's life? This will be full immersion in many things that are strange and difficult, and difficult to comprehend, but can be understood, and can be understood as the loci of the work of God if we are patient in doing so, and if we engage fully enough in the world as we do so.

Conclusion

These are some of the themes present with us. I hope we will continue with them and work intensively on them. In many respects, however, they are enduring questions that we will carry away from the conference and will need to continue to address in the years to come. That we will continue to do so will be our best testimonial to the life and work of Lesslie Newbigin.

Two Wonderful, Bewildering Days

G. Jan van Butselaar

In this symposium, "After Newbigin," we have lived two wonderful days full of new insights, new ideas, new inspiration. It certainly worked well to ask the contributors to this meeting not only to remember Lesslie Newbigin, but to see how to go from where he brought us. At the same time, they were two bewildering days: the enormous range of subjects, the quite different ways of treating the different themes of this symposium. If all this is inspired by Newbigin's thinking, it shows once more how big that small man was.

It is almost an impossible task to echo in a coherent way all that has been presented. When the invitation came to me to act as a rapporteur, I was quite happy: I did not have to produce a paper! But in the end, I am not so sure whether it might have been better to have written a paper with my own personal ideas, instead of engaging in this hazardous adventure. . . .

I would like to reflect on three topics that most frequently came back in our discussions:

1. How to understand the world of power?
2. How to understand the world of faiths?
3. How to understand the world of mission?

The world of power is the first one. "Globalization" has been one of the key words in the discussions of the past days. It should be noted that globalization is not only a negative phenomenon. It can also mean that we can be quickly informed about what is going on in other parts of the world, and with this we may feel coresponsible for global developments. Also, the fact that globalization may have its effects on local culture cannot only be seen as necessarily devastating. Culture is a dynamic entity, changing and being changed all the time by influences from inside and outside. Furthermore, the confrontation with globalizing systems can even strengthen the awareness of the value and richness of local culture.

But globalization can of course also function as a negative power. Then it becomes important to denounce the aberrations of such power, and to reflect on possible remedies against evils resulting from it. And there are plenty of evils. Several participants have pointed to the ill effects of the hegemony of the free market, of "faith" in unlimited liberalism. It became clear how all are horrified by the negative "products" of a world that is in the grip of these factors: growing poverty in the South, new poverty in the North, local wars in which all parties seem to be well provided by global arms dealers. What can our missiological answer be to that degrading situation? It has been proposed that we should work for the unity of all humanity, for developing global ethics, in close collaboration with other world religions. These are valid proposals. The evil is so strong that we certainly should try our best to use those ideas. But will they bear fruits that liberate the poor, that guarantee peace, that deliver justice? Newbigin, in his last speech in Holland (1996), made an important remark in this respect. He argued that if such a unity of all humanity is to be effective, we should be concerned about the question: What can be the center of such unity? For, he said, if this endeavor has not a clear center, or if it has the human self as center, it can quickly deteriorate into a new exploitation and manipulation: "[Such] human unity is the genesis of all the imperialisms of world history."[1] So the question is: What can be the center of such ethics, of such unity? For Newbigin, the answer was clear.

The second topic that came through in the last two days had to do with the world of faiths, the fact that there exists not just Christian faith but many more religious systems. In the popular understanding, relations between people of different religions involve fighting, verbally or even physically. That negative image confronts us with fundamental theological and missiological questions. Some heard in this symposium were: How to prevent Christian fundamentalism in relations with people of other faith convictions? How to prevent "totalitarian mission"? How to escape from the danger of feelings of superiority on the part of Christians vis-à-vis Hindus, Buddhists, Muslims, and others?

The questions were clear and relevant. Daring theological concepts were presented to ease the dialogue with people of other faiths — at least, that

---

1. L. Newbigin, "Vijfentwintig Jaar Zending," in *Pinstervuur in de "secular city"? (Jaarverslag Nederlandse Zendingsraad 1996-1997)* (Amsterdam: NZR, 1998), pp. 74-78.

was the expectation behind those concepts. But still, the evils formulated in the questions above are not so easy to exclude. It is clear that characteristics such as deep respect, careful listening, and expressed appreciation for the religious views of others are of course important conditions for the encounter between people of different faiths. But there is also a danger linked to these expressions; they can also hide a lack of real interest, a lack of real engagement with the fate of the other, with the fate of humanity. It should therefore be stated that true effective dialogue cannot be realized without a very firm faith commitment of the parties concerned, even to the point that they wish to convince, that they wish to convert the other. If such a faith commitment is present and can fully operate, something new, something unexpected can happen in the relations between people of different faiths.

The world of mission was in the forefront of presentations and discussions as much as the other topics mentioned. Important discoveries were made on the role of the trinitarian concept in mission thinking. It was made clear that a theology of dialogue does not necessarily exclude a trinitarian basis for mission, although Trinity then had to be interpreted in a (new) way. It was shown how the mysterious and irrational term "trinity" also might be of tremendous importance in order to save us from the pitfall of claiming to be able to explain God: he cannot be contained by us. Trinity helps us remember that.

A symposium that honors the legacy of Lesslie Newbigin, the reflection on the challenge of mission to the West, cannot but give much attention to the role of culture. It is important not to depict (post)modern Western culture in a purely negative way. Even missiologists cannot massively condemn the current Western culture and continue to live by its standards. Many new possibilities to reflect on the Christian faith are also provided in this culture, where spirituality has recently regained a place next to rationality.

But that mission to the West presents the church with new and difficult challenges is broadly recognized. For Lesslie Newbigin the whole struggle to regain missionary vision for Western culture started when General Simatupang from Indonesia asked him once: "Can the west be won?" Can the West be won; can the West be saved from murderous individualism and devastating fragmentization, from pure self-centeredness and from the denial that truth is worth looking for, that truth can be found? Or is truth only economic truth? If that is the case, truth is a shaky affair, as we are learning all the time through the developments of the world economy. Can the West be won? It cannot be won by copying the Christendom model — but Newbigin did not provide clear answers as to what could then be the new model. But this is sure: there is truth to tell. Truth, not as a cold rationalistic affair, nor as gunpowder for new religious warfare. But truth as an "eschatological conspiracy," as was said during past days, as engagement, as suffering, as love. Truth to offer and to receive. Truth through life stories of human beings, through the life-giving story of the gospel. Mission has to do with confronting others and being confronted with the truth.

If Newbigin had been present at this symposium and heard my reflection on it, he probably would have been irritated, and after a good joke he would have asked me: "How can you speak on these three fundamental questions for mission without even mentioning the name of Jesus Christ?" My face would have turned quite red, but I would probably have answered: "Well, Lesslie, people have heard that name so often, sometimes they stop listening once you quote his name — they think they know already what's coming. I am sure people can discover that name themselves. For if he is the Lord of the world and not just the tribal God of the Christians, we will not be able to go around him, but we will have to decide whether we want to follow him." Newbigin would probably have said then: "But you still have to name him, just in case Jesus wants to invite the other through you to take part in God's mission." He would have been right, of course.

Afterword

Michael H. Taylor

The healthiest place to start reading this book might well be Andrew Walls's reminder (chap. 14) that Christianity is no longer a Western religion. The majority of its members and the major issues it now faces are of the East and of the South, and of the poor. Given this perspective, some of the discussion in this varied and interesting collection of essays might seem relatively parochial, including those in the fourth and final section on globalization. They are not so much about the future mission of the world church as about the issues which confront the churches in western Europe and how they should respond to their inheritance as heirs not only of the gospel but of the Enlightenment and modernity, and as sojourners for the time being in a postmodern age. Parochial as they may be, the issues nevertheless remain important for Christians in the North, as they were for Newbigin, the missionary bishop returning from the East and the South. They ought to be important also for all who acknowledge the force of the ecumenical call, with which he was long associated, to mission in all six continents, Europe included!

One or two writers in this volume, while doubtless sharing the widespread admiration for Newbigin's penetrating and passionate contribution to missiology, reflect on his concerns but scarcely refer to him at all. Andrew Kirk, for example (chap. 12), sympathetic to Newbigin's approach, sets out to stimulate debate on a whole range of mission-related issues. Werner Ustorf (chap. 13) responds to Bonhoeffer's question "Who is Christ for us today?" in a way Newbigin would not have done, by proposing a "disestablished Jesus Christ." Most contributors, however, engage with Newbigin more explicitly. Not surprisingly they diverge from each other, sometimes quite sharply, in

238

the extent to which they agree or disagree with his opinion. This can be seen in three of the major discussions in the book.

First, there is a good deal of support for Newbigin's largely negative critique of modernity, calling for missionary encounters of a Christ-against-culture variety. George Hunsberger (chap. 10), who provides a useful thumbnail sketch of modernity, and Charles Taber (chap. 18), who is as despairing of postmodernity as of modernity, are of this view. Jenny Taylor, as far as I can judge (chap. 20), writing about Newbigin's understanding of Islam, and David Kettle (chap. 19), in his discussion of authority and his advocacy of "inner direction" formed by the gospel, share a similar perspective. Bert Hoedemaker, on the other hand (chap. 2), points to an affinity between Christianity and modernity, but also believes that Newbigin unwittingly remained trapped in the presuppositions of the latter. Lynne Price (chap. 11) openly warns against Newbigin's use of biblical authority as a bastion against what he sees as cultural breakdown in the West, while she herself calls for what she terms "faithful uncertainty."

Secondly, some writers (for example, Philip Kenneson in chap. 8) are inclined to go along with Newbigin's approach to the Trinity as a distinctive, given truth which determines, or at least provides a major source of insight into, our understanding of mission. Others see it more as one product of ongoing Christian reflection which, along with others, interacts with missiology. Colin Green (chap. 6) firmly supports Newbigin's view, while Perry Schmidt-Leukel (chap. 5), in sharp contrast, suggests that trinitarian ideas are neither definitive nor determinative, for they can be linked to all the main models of mission, whether exclusive, inclusive, or pluralist, some of which Newbigin would definitely have disavowed.

Thirdly, no one is likely to disagree that, as Christians, we learn about truth from the past, especially from the traditions which focus on Jesus Christ, but that we also have much to learn from outside those traditions and still more to learn in the future. The question is about where the balance lies. Tom Foust (chap. 15) suggests that the issue was not altogether resolved in Newbigin's own writings. He was certainly not simplistic, though he loudly and publicly insisted that the truth has been given to us in Jesus Christ. Andrew Kirk (chap. 12) and Jan van Butselaar (chap. 22) agree with Newbigin on this point. However, Kalarikkal Aleaz (chap. 16); Mahmut Aydin, not surprisingly, for he is a Muslim (chap. 17); and Lynne Price (chap. 11) take a very different view. Frances Young, in her discussion of trinitarian missiology (chap. 9), underscores the extent to which the doctrine of the Trinity witnesses to what we don't know as well as to what we do. She reminds us that it was itself the result of protracted debates and came to speak confidently of a God who is not confined but remains everywhere at hand to teach us.

The main purpose of the conference held in honor of Newbigin was not, however, to rerun debates such as these, important as they are, but to ask: Where do we go from here? It was called "After Newbigin"! Here the reader may well judge that this volume, on the whole, misses opportunities, especially if she or he is looking for strikingly new, or sweeping, or specific suggestions (although these may not be readily available to sojourners in postmodernity). Peter Cruchley-Jones (chap. 3) prefers to call the place "exile" and makes a striking plea, born of his own urban experience, not to lament a loss of power and status but to pray for this strange city we are in and seize the chance to find God there. Although there are numerous and laudable calls to live by our convictions and be genuinely open and receptive to people of other cultures and religious traditions (Aleaz in chap. 16 is quite radical at this point), not enough is said about what that could actually mean for the missionary church in the twenty-first century. Some want it to have more integrity as the harbinger of a new social order, while others find the notion of a "true church" a false start (for example, Hunsberger and Price). Yet others warn against a ghettolike existence for a church shaped by a different story and, like Newbigin himself, encourage it to make its presence felt in the marketplace and equip its members for their secular vocations (thus Michael Goheen in chap. 4). All this and much else is to be taken seriously, but it is not really breaking new ground.

My own sympathies, which are familiar, would tend to be with those who look for practical action in the face of growing poverty and conflict around the globe. I am surprised and disappointed, however, that this vision does not feature more prominently in a discussion on the future of mission. It is nearer to the agenda of the kind of church to which Andrew Walls has drawn our attention. It is in line with the New Testament Gospels' understanding of what lies at the heart of God's mission in Christ: good news to the poor. It recognizes what may well be the most serious test bed of truth (even though such a test may beg as many questions as it answers): not universal reason, nor empirical verification, nor the God-given absolutes of "fideism," nor private opinion, but whether it brings liberation to the poor and contributes to the development of the common good.

Such sympathies betray my own partiality, which, like everyone else's, arises from my limited experience and understanding and my particular interests and formation. It may be qualified and corrected by the partiality of others, but from it there is no escape. There may well be universal, even absolute truth, but to quote Frances Young, "It's our knowledge of what is universal which is relatively limited" — and I take the word "relatively" to be carefully chosen! These same sympathies (even prejudices), however, usefully demonstrate that a pluralist or relativist, like myself, can have firm convictions and commitment (Jenny Taylor usefully discusses "firmness" in chap. 20). I am biased, but I believe something, so it is not a matter of "anything goes."

A commitment in the immediate future to Christian action in the face of global poverty (linked to conflict, the environment, and much else) is wholly at one with at least part of what Newbigin meant by the gospel as public truth. The gospel must be in the midst of the world (as Goheen emphasizes in chap. 4), contributing to a global ethic and the construction of social, political, and economic policies, which will shape a more equal world in which all of us can, to echo Newbigin's words, freely love and be loved. The gospel is a public servant, not a private opinion. However, I personally differ from Newbigin in his confidence, not just in knowing what this gospel truth is, but in its ability to redeem and transform human life. I would give two reasons.

First, the connections between Christian "doctrine," general value statements such as that we are made to love and be loved, and detailed social policies are somewhat tenuous and complex. There are many considerations to take into account. There may be little direct, linear theological reflection between what we believe and what in our political and economic affairs we plan to do. We should therefore be cautious about making too many claims for the ability of gospel "truth" to be decisive or even highly informative for public policy. In this regard, it is instructive to be reminded by Duncan Forrester (chap. 1) that, although Newbigin was impressive in his use of the gospel to oppose what he saw to be destructive social policies, crying a plague on the houses of both Right and Left, he rarely if ever ventured into specific policy making.

Secondly, the assumption, held to by Newbigin and vigorously supported in some of these essays (by Charles Taber in chap. 18, for example), that the gospel deals with the sins of the world as no other agency can, is challenged at every turn by its apparent inability either to redeem our perverted wills or, as I would prefer to put it, strengthen our weakness and calm our fearfulness. (Lynne Price, in her plea for "reality" and her references to dark nights and Christian atrocities in chap. 11, and Werner Ustorf, in his comments on the negative record of Christianity in chap. 13, have recognized this.) As a result, we fail again and again to implement even our own more enlightened social policies. Why is this gospel seemingly made to promise so much more than it has delivered?

It would be wonderful to be able to commend a collection of essays which set out a clear agenda whereby the church in mission could become more effective for our good and our salvation in the world of today and tomorrow. Given the historical place and moment we are at, and mindful of Dan Hardy's warning (chap. 21) of the tendency to oversimplify, I do not complain unduly that this is not the case. Nevertheless, personally I would have welcomed a greater degree of astonishment that, if the gospel is as strong as a prophet like Newbigin suggests, after two thousand years of missionary endeavor, after Christendom, the Enlightenment, and modernity, it still leaves a divided, violent, and ambiguous world at much the same moral and spiritual level as it was. In the light of that astonishment I would have welcomed a greater determination to ask what such an apparent contradiction means for the understanding of our faith and a greater urgency to address the agenda of the "non-Western" church, largely made up of the poor. We understand enough about God's Christlike mission to know that our most pressing calling is to do just that.

After Newbigin: A Missiological Enquiry in Honour of Lesslie Newbigin

Programme for Sessions
2-3 November 1998 — Draft

MONDAY, 2 NOVEMBER 1998

9.00 OPENING REMARKS ————————————————————

Cadbury Hall

Platform: Werner Ustorf, Michael Taylor, Andrew Kirk, Colin Greene, Thomas Foust

9.30–11.00 SESSION I ————————————————————

Cadbury Hall
(Theme: *The Universal Church and the Ecumenical Movement*)

President: Duncan Forrester

(20 mins.) Speaker and rejoinder: Emilio Castro
Title: "The Universal Church and the Ecumenical Movement"

(15 mins.) Responder: Emmanuel Lartey

Selly Oak Methodist Church
(Theme: *Trinitarian Missiology*)

President: Allan Anderson

(20 mins.) Speaker and rejoinder: Philip Kenneson

Title: "Trinitarian Missiology: Mission as Face-to-Face Encounter"

(15 mins.) Responder: Israel Selvanayagam

11.15–12.45 SESSION II

Cadbury Hall
(Theme: *Enlightenment, Postmodernity, and Mission*)

President: Werner Ustorf

(20 mins.) Speaker and rejoinder: Andrew Walls
   Title: "Enlightenment, Postmodernity, and Mission"

(15 mins.) Responder: Hugh Montefiore

Selly Oak Methodist Church
(Theme: *Globalization and the Gospel*)

President: Andrew Kirk

(20 mins.) Speaker and rejoinder: David Kettle
   Title: "Gospel, Authority and Globalization"

(15 mins.) Responder: K. P. Aleaz

13.00–14.00 BUFFET LUNCH

Cadbury Hall

14.15–15.45 SESSION III

Cadbury Hall
(Theme: *The Universal Church and the Ecumenical Movement*)

President: Michael Taylor

(20 mins.) Speaker and rejoinder: Duncan Forrester
   Title: "Lesslie Newbigin as a Public Theologian"

(15 mins.) Responder: Jabal Buaben

Selly Oak Methodist Church
(Theme: *Enlightenment, Postmodernity and Mission*)

President: Aasulv Lande

(20 mins.) Speaker and rejoinder: George Hunsberger
Title: "The Church in the Postmodern Transition"

(15 mins.) Responder: Lynne Price
Title: Churches and Postmodernity: Opportunity for an Attitude Shift"

16.15–17.00 WORKSHOP I ————————————————

Cadbury Hall

President: Michael Taylor

(15 mins.) Speaker: Peter Cruchley-Jones
Title: "Entering Exile: Can There be a Missiology for 'Not My People'?"

17.00–17.45 WORKSHOP II ————————————————

Cadbury Hall

President: Werner Ustorf

(15 mins.) Speaker: Thomas F. Foust
Title: "Newbigin's Epistemology: A Dual Discourse?"

17.45–18.05 RAPPORTEUR ————————————————

Cadbury Hall

Daniel Hardy
Title: "A Response to the Consultation"

18.05–18.15 CLOSING REMARKS ————————————————

Cadbury Hall

Werner Ustorf

18.30 FREE TIME TO EXPLORE LOCAL EATING HOUSES ——————

20.00–21.00 INTRODUCTION TO NEWBIGIN PAPERS ——————

Cadbury Hall

President: Thomas Foust

Speaker: Dan Beeby

Title: "Personal Reflections"

TUESDAY, 3 NOVEMBER 1998

9.30–11.00 SESSION I ——————————————————

Cadbury Hall
(Theme: *Trinitarian Missiology*)

President: Israel Selvanayagam

(20 mins.) Speaker and rejoinder: Perry Schmidt-Leukel

Title: "Mission and Trinitarian Theology"

(15 mins.) Responder: Colin Greene

Title: "Trinitarian Tradition and the Cultural Collapse of Late Modernity"

Selly Oak Methodist Church
(Theme: *Globalization and the Gospel*)

President: Lynne Price

(20 mins.) Speaker and rejoinder: K. P. Aleaz

Title: "The Globalization of Poverty and the Exploitation of the Gospel"

(15 mins.) Responder: Mahmut Aydin

Title: "Globalization and the Gospel: A Muslim View"

11.15–12.45 SESSION II

Cadbury Hall
(Theme: *The Universal Church and the Ecumenical Movement*)

President: Dennis Lindsay

(20 mins.) Speaker and rejoinder: L. A. (Bert) Hoedemaker

Title: "Rival Conceptions of Global Christianity: Mission and Modernity, Then and Now"

(15 mins.) Responder: Eleanor Jackson

Selly Oak Methodist Church
(Theme: *Globalization and the Gospel*)

President: Hugh Montefiore

(20 mins.) Speaker and rejoinder: Charles Taber

Title: "The Gospel as Authentic Meta-Narrative"

(15 mins.) Responder: Robert Jeffery

Title: "Globalization, Gospel, and Cultural Relativism"

13.00–14.00 BUFFET LUNCH

Cadbury Hall

14.15–15.45 SESSION III

Cadbury Hall
(Theme: *Trinitarian Missiology*)

President: L. A. (Bert) Hoedemaker

(20 mins.) Speaker and rejoinder: Frances Young

Title: "The Uncontainable God: Pre-Christendom Doctrine of Trinity"

(15 mins.) Responder: Aasulv Lande

Selly Oak Methodist Church
(Theme: *Enlightenment, Postmodernity and Mission*)

President: Werner Ustorf

(20 mins.) Speaker and rejoinder: Denys Turner
  Title: "Enlightenment, Postmodernity, and Mission"

(15 mins.) Responder: Andrew Kirk

16.15–17.00 WORKSHOP I

Cadbury Hall

President: Andrew Kirk

(15 mins.) Speaker: Mike Goheen
  Title: "The Missional Calling of Believers in the World:
  Lesslie Newbigin's Contribution"

17.00–17.45 WORKSHOP II

Cadbury Hall

President: Philip Seddon

(15 mins.) Speaker: Jenny Taylor
  Title: "Newbigin's Understanding of Islam"

17.45–18.05 RAPPORTEUR

Cadbury Hall

G. Jan van Butselaar
  Title: "Two Wonderful, Bewildering Days"

18.05–18.15 CLOSING REMARKS

Cadbury Hall

Platform: Werner Ustorf, Michael Taylor

(Closes at 18.30 on Tuesday)

Bishop J. E. Lesslie Newbigin:
A Comprehensive Bibliography

compiled by Thomas F. Foust and George R. Hunsberger

A lifetime of Lesslie Newbigin's missionary engagement has left to us a rich and extensive testimony, enacted and spoken and written. In most of what he wrote he was putting on paper what he intended to say in some lecture or address he had been invited to give. And most of those occasions came about because of his personal engagement in issues critical to the moment, essential for the church's missionary engagement. In all of it, his was always an ad hoc theology, spoken to a time and place in the church's life as a community sent by the Spirit to bear witness to the reign of God in Christ.

This bibliography traces the several kinds of materials produced from this missionary life. There are of course the *published materials* (section A). In regard to those, the bibliography is extremely comprehensive, though undoubtedly not entirely complete in that Newbigin's writings have always tended to emerge and reemerge in print in a wide range of venues. A limited form of annotation is supplied for each item to indicate, so far as it is known, the setting in which an address or essay was first given and/or to trace the various forms and places in which materials have been republished, including translations into various languages. In most cases particular published materials are included in the listing only once, at the point of initial or primary publication. Revised editions of books have been listed a second time in those cases in which the revisions are substantive and of significant importance.

A number of *unpublished manuscripts* are referenced in section B. The selection is limited to those works deemed to be especially significant for Newbigin research. Many more materials exist in archival collections that are as yet not fully catalogued. At the head of the list, detailed information is provided regarding the relevant archival collections. The locations where particular items can be found are included in the annotations.

A great number of *audio and video recordings* of Newbigin's addresses are accessible from a variety of libraries. These are referenced in section C. While the list is considerable, it is undoubtedly well short of being comprehensive, given the number of institutional and personal recordings that surely must have been made along the way. Information about some of the places making these recordings available is given at the head of the list.

Each item in these first three sections is identified by a reference code that consists of the last two digits of the year of publication followed by up to four lowercase letters representing the first letters of the key words in the title. The materials are listed in chronological order by year within each section. Within each year they are listed in alphanumeric order by reference code which generally, but not always exactly, corresponds to the alphabetic order of the titles.

Section D provides an extensive list of *published reviews* of Newbigin's books. These are listed by book in chronological order. Section E adds a representative selection of books and articles in which there are critical *engagements with Newbigin's thought.* Most of these are published, but important studies (e.g., master's theses and doctoral dissertations) that have not been published are also included. These materials represent the leading edge of responses to Newbigin's challenging vision as well as a burgeoning scholarship on Newbigin's work.

Section F, the final section, identifies several *explicit expressions of the Gospel and Our Culture Movement* that have been spawned by Newbigin's work. Details for making contact with them are provided.

Contents

Abbreviations

BBC	British Broadcasting Corporation
CLS[I]	Christian Literature Society [for India]
CSI	Church of South India
CWME	Commission on World Mission and Evangelism
IMC	International Missionary Council
[I]SPCK	[Indian] Society for the Propagation of Christian Knowledge
NCCCUSA	National Council of the Churches of Christ in the U.S.A.
NCCI	National Christian Council of India
SCM [Press]	Student Christian Movement [Press]
URC	United Reformed Church
WCC	World Council of Churches
YMCA	Young Men's Christian Association

A. Published Materials

33svmu   "The Student Volunteer Missionary Union." In *The Christian Faith Today*, pp. 95-104. London: SCM Press.

37cfmw   *Christian Freedom in the Modern World*. London: SCM Press.

38cibc   "Can I Be Christian? — VIII." *Spectator* (6 May): 800.

38tns   *Things Not Shaken: Glimpses of the Foreign Missions of the Church of Scotland in 1937*. Unsigned. Edinburgh: Church of Scotland Foreign Missions Committee.

39le   *Living Epistles: Impressions of the Foreign Mission Work of the Church of Scotland in 1938*. Unsigned. Edinburgh: Church of Scotland Foreign Mission Committee.

42wig   *What Is the Gospel?* SCM Study Series, no. 6. Madras: CLSI.

44cg   "The Church and the Gospel." In *The Church and Union*, by the Committee on Church Union, South India United Church, pp. 46-59. Madras: CLSI.

44f   Foreword to *The Church and Union*, by the Committee on Church Union, South India United Church. Madras: CLSI.

45ofmi   "Ordained Foreign Missionary in the Indian Church." *International Review of Missions* 34: 86-94.

46ib   "I Believe." In *I Believe*, edited by M. A. Thomas, pp. 73-88. Madras: SCM Press. Address given at the Regional Leaders' Conference, Madras, December 1945.

46ibc   "I Believe in Christ." In *I Believe*, edited by M. A. Thomas, pp. 101-14. Madras: SCM Press. Address given at the Regional Leaders' Conference, Madras, December 1945.

46ibg   "I Believe in God." In *I Believe*, edited by M. A. Thomas, pp. 89-100. Madras: SCM Press. Address given at the Regional Leaders' Conference, Madras, December 1945.

47stba   "Some Thoughts on Britain from Abroad." *Christian News Letter*, 12 October, supplement no. 298.

48csu   "The Ceylon Scheme of Union: A South Indian View." *South India Churchman* (June): 162-63. Acknowledgment to the *Morning Star*, Jaffna.

48dacp   "The Duty and Authority of the Church to Preach the Gospel." In *The Church's Witness to God's Design*, Amsterdam Assembly Series, vol. 2, pp. 19-35. London: SCM Press; New York: Harper and Bros.

48hcsi   "The Heritage of the Church of South India: Our Presbyterian Heritage." *South India Churchman* (January): 52-54.

48rc   *The Reunion of the Church: A Defence of the South India Scheme*. London: SCM Press. Republished in a revised second edition in 1960. See 60rc.

50eea   "The Evangelization of Eastern Asia." In *The Christian Prospect in Eastern*

Asia: Papers and Minutes of the Eastern Asia Christian Conference, Bangkok, December 3-11, 1949, pp. 77-87. New York: Friendship. Republished in *International Review of Missions* 39 (1950): 137-45.

50lesi   "Lay Evangelism in South India." *World Dominion* 28: 215-17.

51cccw   "Comments on 'The Church, the Churches and the World Council of Churches.'" *Ecumenical Review* 3: 252-54.

51sid   *A South India Diary.* London: SCM Press. Republished in an American edition entitled *That All May Be One: A South India Diary: The Story of an Experiment in Christian Unity* (New York: Association Press, 1952). Also published as *Sydindisk Dagbok* (Stockholm: Gummessons, 1963), as *Christus in Zuid India* (Den Haag: Lectuurbureau NHK, 1959), as *Journées Indiennes* (Bâle: Editions de la Mission de Bâle, 1953), as *Südindisches Tagebuch: Erlebtes mit Menschen und Mächten* (Stuttgart: Evangelischer Missionsverlag, 1960), and as *Mestarin Askelten Tuntimassa: Lehriä Intian Päiväkirjasta* (Suomen: Lähetysseury, 1959). A revised English edition was published in 1960 by SCM Press, London. See 60sid.

51wich   "What Is the Christian Hope?" *Listener,* 20 September, pp. 464-65.

52clwc   "The Christian Layman in the World and in the Church." *National Christian Council Review* 72: 185-89.

52nch   "The Nature of the Christian Hope." *Ecumenical Review* 4: 282-84.

52ot   "Odd Theologians." *South India Churchman* (January): 2-4.

52rcg   Review of *The Communication of the Gospel,* by David H. C. Read. *International Review of Missions* 41: 526-28.

53afc   "Ambassadors for Christ." *South India Churchman* (August): 3-4.

53ccgc   "Can the Churches Give a Common Message to the World?" *Theology Today* 9 (January): 512-18.

53ch   "The Christian Hope." In *Missions under the Cross,* edited by Norman Goodall, pp. 107-16. London: Edinburgh House Press. Also published as "Die Christliche Hoffnung," *Evangelische Missionszeitschrift* 9 (1953): 132-39. Address given in 1952 at the Enlarged Meeting of the IMC at Willingen.

53gtsi   *Growing Together in South India.* Edinburgh: Church of Scotland Foreign Mission Committee.

53hg   *The Household of God: Lectures on the Nature of the Church.* London: SCM Press. The Kerr Lectures given at Trinity College, Glasgow, November 1952. An American edition was published in 1954 by Friendship Press, New York. Republished in a slightly revised edition in 1964 by SCM Press, London. Also published in a French edition entitled *L'Église: Peuple des Croyants, Corps du Christ, Temple de l'Esprit* (Paris: Delachaux et Niestle, 1958), a German edition entitled *Von der Spaltung zur Einheit: Ökumenische Schau der Kirche* (Basel: Basler Missionsbuchhandlung, 1956), a Spanish edition entitled *La Familia de Dios: La Naturaleza de la*

Iglesia (Mexico: Casa unida de Publicaciones, 1961), and a Chinese edition entitled *Shang-ti chia li ti jen* (Hsiang-kang: Chi-tu chiao fu ch'iao ch'u pan she, 1965).

53mc   *The Ministry of the Church, Ordained and Unordained, Paid and Unpaid.* London: Edinburgh House Press. Also published as "The Ministry of the Church," *National Christian Council Review* 73 (1953): 351-55.

54c   "Conversion." *Guardian* (Madras), 23 December, p. 409.

54lwlc   "The Life and Witness of the Local Church." In *The Church in a Changing World: Addresses and Reports of the National Christian Council of India, Gumtur, November 5-10, 1953.* Mysore: Wesley.

54pccc   "The Present Crisis and the Coming Christ." *Ecumenical Review* 6, no. 2 (January): 118-23.

54rgo   Review of *God's Order: The Ephesian Letter and This Present Time,* by John A. MacKay. *Theology Today* 10 (January): 543-47.

54wsot   "Why Study the Old Testament?" *National Christian Council Review* 74: 71-76.

55qutr   "The Quest for Unity through Religion." *Journal of Religion* 35: 17-33. The Hiram W. Thomas Memorial Lecture given at the University of Chicago on 12 August 1954. Republished in the *Indian Journal of Theology* 4, no. 2 (October 1955): 1-17.

56nms   "National Missionary Society." *South India Churchman* (January): 6-7. Address at a meeting of the Golden Jubilee Celebration of the National Missionary Society, Madras, November 1955.

56rll   Review of *Local Leadership in Mission Lands* [Proceedings of the Fordham University Conference of Mission Specialists, 23-24 January 1954], edited by J. Franklin Ewing. *International Review of Missions* 45: 225-28.

56ss   *Sin and Salvation.* London: SCM Press. Also published in 1957 by Westminster Press, Philadelphia, and in 1968 by CLSI, Madras. Published in a Spanish edition as *Pecado y Salvacion: Que Significan para el Hombre Contemporáneo?* (Buenos Aires: Methopress, 1964). First published in Tamil (preface dated 31 October 1954) in the Church of South India Tamil Theological Series. A majority of the manuscript was written by Newbigin in Tamil; the remainder of it was written in English and translated by V. Jeyaraj.

56vse   "Von der Spaltung zur Einheit." *Ökumenische Rundschau* 4, no. 2: 51-59.

56wgc   "The Wretchedness and Greatness of the Church." *National Christian Council Review* 76: 472-77. Sermon preached at the united service during the triennial meeting of the NCCI, Allahabad.

56wjc   "Witnessing to Jesus Christ." In *Presenting Christ to India Today,* by P. D. Devanandan, A. E. Inbanathan, A. J. Appasamy, and J. E. L. Newbigin, pp. 57-62. Madras: Diocesan, for CLSI. This was originally a sermon preached at the Synod Service on 12 January 1956.

57nuws   "The Nature of the Unity We Seek: From the Church of South India." *Religion in Life* 26, no. 2 (spring): 181-90.

57tfd   "A Time for Decision." In *Revolution in Missions,* edited by Blaise Levai, appendices. Vellore: Popular.

58acr   "Anglicans and Christian Reunion." *Theology* 61: 223-27.

58obog   *One Body, One Gospel, One World: The Christian Mission Today.* London and New York: IMC. The first portion (pp. 7-24) was published in *Ecumenical Review* 11, no. 2 (January 1959): 143-56. Also published in *La Mission Mondiale de l'Eglise* (Paris: Société des Missions Évangéliques de Paris, 1959), *En Udfordring til ny Taenkning om Kirkens Mission* (Copenhagen: Dansk Missionsrad, 1959), *En Värld, Ett Evangelium, En Kyrka* (Stockholm: Svenska Kyrkans Diakonistyrelses Bokförlag, 1959), *Das Eine Evangelium für die Ganze Welt* (Stuttgart, 1959), and *Die Eine Kirche — das Eine Evangelium — die Eine Welt: Die Christliche Mission Heute* (Stuttgart: Evangelischer Missionsverlag, 1961).

59guhc   "The Gathering Up of History into Christ." In *The Missionary Church in East and West,* edited by Charles C. West and David M. Paton, pp. 81-90. London: SCM Press. Address given in 1957 at the Ecumenical Institute in Bossey.

59lmc   "The Life and Mission of the Church." *Chaplain* 16, no. 2 (April): 37-43. Reprinted from *Episcopal Overseas Missions Review* (Epiphany 1959), which in turn was reprinted from *Dashran* (Journal of the SCM of India) 3, no. 2 (March 1958), an issue of the journal republished in book form under the title *The Life and Mission of the Church* (Bangalore: SCM of India, 1958).

59mek   "Mission und Einheit der Kirche." *Evangelische Theologie* 4 (April): 156-76.

59scmt   "The Summons to Christian Mission Today." *International Review of Missions* 48: 177-89. Address given at the Annual Dinner of the North American Advisory Committee of the IMC, New York, November 1958.

59wgdu   "Will God Dwell upon Earth?" *National Christian Council Review* 79: 99-102. Text of a sermon preached at the dedication of a chapel in a Christian college.

60bicu   "Basic Issues in Church Union." In *We Were Brought Together,* edited by David M. Taylor, pp. 155-69. Sydney: Australian Council for the WCC. Address given at the National Conference of Australian Churches, Melbourne, February 1960.

60bnfw   "Bishop Newbigin's Final Word." In *We Were Brought Together,* edited by David M. Taylor, pp. 128-30. Sydney: Australian Council for the WCC. Address given at the National Conference of Australian Churches, Melbourne, February 1960.

60bsft   "Bible Studies: Four Talks on 1 Peter by Bishop Newbigin." In *We Were Brought Together,* edited by David M. Taylor, pp. 93-123. Sydney: Australian Council for the WCC. Addresses given at the National Conference of Australian Churches, Melbourne, February 1960.

60csi   "Church of South India." Letter to the editor. *Faith and Unity* 5, no. 8: 24.

60gcw   "Die Gestalt der Christlichen Weltmission: Mission auf Ökumenischer Basis." *Evangelische Missionszeitschrift* 5 (October): 140-51.

60lmc   "The Life and Mission of the Church." In *We Were Brought Together*, edited by David M. Taylor, pp. 59-69. Sydney: Australian Council for the WCC. Keynote address at the National Conference of Australian Churches, Melbourne, February 1960.

60mcsi   "The Ministry of the Church of South India: A Letter from Bishop Lesslie Newbigin to Fr. Dalby, S.S.J.E." *Faith and Unity* 5, no. 7: 12-14.

60mm   "Mission and Missions." *Christianity Today* 4, no. 22 (1 August): 911.

60muc   *The Mission and Unity of the Church.* Grahamstown, South Africa: Rhodes University. The Eleventh Peter Ainslee Memorial Lecture, 17 October 1960. Republished in 1963 under the title "Is There Still a Missionary Job Today?" in *563 St. Columba: Fourteenth Centenary, 1963,* by Nora K. Chadwick, Lesslie Newbigin, and T. Ralph Morton (Glasgow: Iona Community Publications Department, for the Church of Scotland).

60pp   "The Pattern of Partnership." In *A Decisive Hour for the Christian World Mission,* by Norman Goodall, J. E. Lesslie Newbigin, W. A. Visser 't Hooft, and D. T. Niles, pp. 34-45. London: SCM Press. One of the John R. Mott Memorial Lectures at the Founding Assembly of the East Asia Christian Conference, Kuala Lumpur, May 1959.

60rc   *The Reunion of the Church: A Defence of the South India Scheme.* Revised edition of 48rc. London: SCM Press.

60rgpi   Review of *God's People in India,* by John Webster Grant. *International Review of Missions* 49: 353-55.

60sid   *A South India Diary.* Revised edition of 51sid, including a new foreword and epilogue. London: SCM Press.

60taii   *The Truth as It Is in Jesus.* Pamphlet. U.S.A.: North America Ecumenical Youth Assembly. Address given at a Faith and Order luncheon in San Francisco, December 1960.

60um   "The Unification of the Ministry." *Faith and Unity* 6: 4-10. Republication of 60rc: xx-xxvii, a portion of the introduction added in the revised edition of 48rc.

60whal   "The Work of the Holy Spirit in the Life of the Asian Churches." In *A Decisive Hour for the Christian World Mission,* by Norman Goodall, J. E. Lesslie Newbigin, W. A. Visser 't Hooft, and D. T. Niles, pp. 18-33. London: SCM Press. One of the John R. Mott Memorial Lectures at the Founding Assembly of the East Asia Christian Conference, Kuala Lumpur, May 1959.

61ec   "Ecumenical Comments." *Lutheran World* 8: 74-77. An invited response to an article by Peter Brunner entitled "The LWF as an Ecclesiological Problem," *Lutheran World* 7 (1960): 237ff.

61f   Foreword to *The Theology of the Christian Mission,* edited by Gerald H. Anderson, pp. xi-xiii. Nashville and New York: Abingdon.

61ftow   *A Faith for This One World?* London: SCM Press. Also published as *L'Universalisme de la Foi Chrétienne,* trans. C. Bodmer-de Traz (Geneva: Éditions Labor et Fides, 1963). The William Belden Noble Lectures given at Harvard, November 1958.

61icd   *Is Christ Divided? A Plea for Christian Unity in a Revolutionary Age.* Grand Rapids: Eerdmans.

61sic   "Sugar in the Coffee." *Frontier* 4 (summer): 93-97.

61uam   "Unity and Mission." *Covenant Quarterly* 19 (November): 3-6.

62bomm   "Bringing Our Missionary Methods under the Word of God." *Occasional Bulletin from the Missionary Research Library* 13: 1-9. Address at a mission consultation of the Presbyterian Church, U.S. Also published as "Gottes Werk in der Weltweiten Gesellschaft der Menschen," *Evangelisches Missionsmagazin* 106 (1962): 97-113.

62clu   "The Church — Local and Universal." In *The Church — Local and Universal: Things We Face Together, No. 2,* by Lesslie T. Lyall and Lesslie Newbigin, pp. 20-28. London: World Dominion.

62f/mm   Foreword to *Missionary Methods: St. Paul's or Ours?* by Roland Allen, American edition, pp. i-iii. Grand Rapids: Eerdmans.

62f/ue   Foreword to *Upon the Earth,* by D. T. Niles, pp. 7-8. London: Lutterworth.

62f/se   Foreword to *The Spontaneous Expansion of the Church,* by Roland Allen. Grand Rapids: Eerdmans.

62ghm   "Gemeinsames Handeln in der Mission." *Evangelische Missionszeitschrift* 19, no. 2: 91-95.

62jam   *Joint Action for Mission.* Geneva: WCC Commission on World Mission and Evangelism. Also published in *National Christian Council Review* 83, no. 1 (1963): 17-23.

62mdem   "The Missionary Dimension of the Ecumenical Movement." *Ecumenical Review* 14 (January): 207-15. Reprinted in *International Review of Mission* 70 (October 1981): 240-46. Published in French as "La Dimension Missionnaire du Mouvement Oecuménique: 3eme Assemblée du Conseil Oecuménique des Eglises, New Delhi, 1961," *Istina* 8, no. 4 (1963): 493-99 and in *Foi et Vie* 61, no. 3 (May-June 1962). The inaugural sermon given as general secretary of the International Missionary Council at the Act of Integration of the IMC and the World Council of Churches that took place within the opening session of the Third Assembly of the WCC on Sunday, 19 November 1961, at New Delhi. Available in audio recording (61mcwc).

62ommt   *The Ordained Ministry and the Missionary Task.* Pamphlet. Geneva: WCC.

62p   Preface to *Survey of the Training of the Ministry in the Middle East,* by Douglas Webster and K. L. Nasir. Geneva, London, and New York: Commission on World Mission and Evangelism, WCC.

62rdwm   "Report of the Division of World Mission and Evangelism to the Central Committee." *Ecumenical Review* 15 (October): 88-94.

63aik   "Auswirkungen der Integration in den Kirchen des Ökumenischen Rates." *Kirche in der Zeit* 18: 473-77.

63bp   "Benignus, Pierre, 1912-1963," coauthored with Charles Bonzon. Obituary. *International Review of Missions* 52 (October): 453-56.

63curm   *The Church's Unity in Relation to Its Missionary Task.* Atlanta: Board of Women's Work, Presbyterian Church, U.S. A message given at a Pre-Assembly Conference on World Missions and Evangelism, sponsored by the Board of World Missions and the Division of Evangelism of the Board of Church Extension, Presbyterian Church, U.S.

63dd62   "Developments during 1962: An Editorial Survey." *International Review of Missions* 52 (January): 3-14. Unsigned.

63en   "Editor's notes." *International Review of Missions* 52: 242-46, 369-73, 508-12. Unsigned.

63gdpt   "Gesta Dei per Tamulos." Review of *The Dispersion of the Tamil Church,* by N. C. Sargant. *Frontier* 5 (winter 1962-63): 553-55.

63gm   *Gottes Mission und Unsere Aufgabe: Treffpunkt 1963 Mexico.* Stuttgart: Evangelischer Missionsverlag.

63jsmc   "Jesus the Servant and Man's Community." In *Christ's Call to Service Now,* edited by Ambrose Reeves, pp. 23-33. London: SCM Press. Address given at the Student Christian Congress, Bristol, 1-6 January 1963.

63mend   *Mission et Église à New Delhi.* Paris: Société des Missions Évangéliques de Paris.

63mm   "The Message and the Messengers: Notes of Bible Studies Given at the Singapore Situation Conference (1 Cor. 1-4)." *South East Asia Journal of Theology* 5 (October): 85-98. Republished in *One People — One Mission,* edited by J. R. Fleming. The Bible studies were given at the East Asia Christian Conference in 1963.

63rtdt   *The Relevance of Trinitarian Doctrine for Today's Mission.* WCC Commission on World Mission and Evangelism Study Pamphlet no. 2. London: Edinburgh House Press. Republished in an American edition entitled *Trinitarian Faith and Today's Mission* (Richmond: John Knox, 1964). Also published as *Missionarische Kirche in Weltlicher Welt: Der Dreieinige Gott und Unsere Sendung,* Theologische Brennpunkte Series, Bd. 5. (Frankfurt: G. Kaffke, 1966). Republished as *Trinitarian Doctrine for Today's Mission,* with an introduction by Eleanor Jackson (Carlisle, Cumbria: Paternoster, 1998).

64ccre   "The Church: Catholic, Reformed, and Evangelical." *Episcopalian* 129: 12-15, 48.

64dp   "Die Pfingstler und die Ökumenische Bewegung." *Ökumenische Rundschau* 13, no. 4: 323-26.

64en   "Editor's notes." *International Review of Missions* 53: 248-52, 376-79, 512-17. Unsigned.

64fgam   Foreword to *God for All Men,* by Robert C. Latham, p. 4. London: Edinburgh House Press; New York: Friendship; and Geneva: WCC.

64fkwg   Foreword to *Key Words of the Gospel: Bible Studies Delivered at the Mexico Meeting of the World Council of Churches Commission on World Mission and Evangelism, 1963,* by Hendrikus Berkhof and Philip Potter, pp. 7-9. London: SCM Press.

64rsbm   Review of *The Spirit Bade Me Go: The Astounding Move of God in the Denominational Churches,* by David J. Du Plessis. Rev. ed. *Frontier* 7 (summer): 144-45.

64sy63   "Survey of the Year 1962-1963: By the Editor." *International Review of Missions* 53 (January): 3-82. Unsigned.

65fe1   "From the Editor." *International Review of Missions* 54 (April): 145-50. Unsigned.

65fe2   "From the Editor." *International Review of Missions* 54 (July): 273-80. Unsigned.

65fe3   "From the Editor." *International Review of Missions* 54 (October): 417-27. Initialed.

65hmmc   "The Healing Ministry in the Mission of the Church." In *The Healing Church,* pp. 8-15. Geneva: Division of World Mission and Evangelism, WCC.

65i   Introduction to *The Programme Fund of the Division of World Mission and Evangelism.* Geneva: WCC.

65ibin   "Introduction by Lesslie Newbigin." In *All Africa Conference of Churches.* Geneva: WCC.

65im   "Intégration et Mission." *Rythmes du Monde* (Brugge-Paris) 13: 139-47.

65ml   "Ministry and Laity." *National Christian Council Review* 85: 479-83. Summary of a talk given to the United Mission of Nepal at Kathmandu, March 1965.

65p   Preface to *The Healing Church,* pp. 5-6. Geneva: Division of World Mission and Evangelism, WCC.

65rets   Review of *Ecumenics: The Science of the Church Universal,* by John A. MacKay. *Princeton Seminary Bulletin* 59 (November): 60-62.

65staf   "Sänd till alla folk." Translated by B. Zackrisson. *Svensk Missionstidskrift* 53, no. 1: 1-10.

65sy64   "Survey of the Year 1963-4: By the Editor." *International Review of Missions* 54 (January): 3-75. Unsigned.

65thzh   "Technische Hilfe Zwischenkirchliche Hilfe und Mission." *Evangelisches Missionsmagazin* 109, no. 4: 241-51.

66c   "Conversion." *National Christian Council Review* 86: 309-23. Notes of an address given at the Nasrapur Consultation, March 1966. Republished in *Religion and Society* (Bangalore) 13, no. 4 (December 1966): 30-42 and in *Renewal for Mission,* ed. David Lyon and Albert Manuel (Madras: CLS, 1967), pp. 33-46.

66hrsm   *Honest Religion for Secular Man.* Philadelphia: Westminster; London: SCM Press. The Firth Lectures, University of Nottingham, November 1964. Republished in 1967 in Lucknow by Lucknow Publishing House. Also published as *Godsdienst in een Geseculariseerde Wereld* (Utrecht: Aula-Boeken, 1968), as *Una Religiona Autentica Per un Mondo Secolarizzato* (Assisi: Collana di Cittadella), and as *Une Religion pour um Monde Séculier* (Tournai: Casterman, 1967).

66sy64   "A Survey of the Year 1964-65." *International Review of Missions* 55: 3-80. Unsigned.

67cwm   "The Church in Its World Mission." In *Outlook for Christianity: Essays for E. A. Payne,* edited by L. G. Champion, pp. 109-18. London: Lutterworth.

67ggg   "Glory, Glory, Glory." *Lutheran Standard* (USA), 30 May, pp. 13, 16. Bible study on John 17 given at the 1966 meeting of the National Council of Churches of Christ of the USA, Miami Beach.

67hh   "The Hinge of History." *Lutheran Standard* (USA), 4 April, pp. 10-11. Bible study on John 17 given at the 1966 meeting of the National Council of Churches of Christ of the USA, Miami Beach.

67jwie   "Just Who Is the Enemy?" *Lutheran Standard* (USA), 2 May, pp. 12-13. Bible study on John 17 given at the 1966 meeting of the National Council of Churches of Christ of the USA, Miami Beach.

67pwmw   "A Point from Which to Move the World." *Lutheran Standard* (USA), 16 May, pp. 9, 30. Bible study on John 17 given at the 1966 meeting of the National Council of Churches of Christ of the USA, Miami Beach.

67rrlm   Review of *Repenser la Mission: Rapports et Compte Rendu,* Semaine de Missiologie, 35th ed. (Louvain, 1965). *International Review of Mission* 55 (July): 379-80.

67sfow   "The Spiritual Foundations of Our Work." In *The Christian College and National Development,* pp. 1-8. Madras: CLS.

67srd   "Strong Roots of Driftwood." *Lutheran Standard* (USA), 18 April, pp. 9-10. Bible study on John 17 given at the 1966 meeting of the National Council of Churches of Christ of the USA, Miami Beach.

68amim   "Anglicans, Methodists and Intercommunion: A Moment for Decision." *Churchman* 82 (winter): 281-85.

68bima   *Behold I Make All Things New.* Madras: CLS. Talks given at youth conferences in Kerala, May 1968.

68bsgn   "Bible Studies Given at the National Christian Council Triennial Assembly, Shillong." *National Christian Council Review* 88: 9-14, 73-78, 125-31, 177-85. Four studies given in October 1967. Republished in *Renewal for Mission*, ed. David Lyon and Albert Manuel, 2nd revised and enlarged ed. (Madras: CLS, 1968), pp. 192-213.

68coec   *Christ Our Eternal Contemporary.* Madras: CLS. Published in a Spanish edition as *Cristo Vive* (Buenos Aires: La Aurora, 1975). A teaching mission conducted at the Christian Medical College and Hospital, Vellore, July 1966. A prior undated edition was published by the C.M.S. Press, Kottayam (India).

68rtr   Review of *Theology in Reconstruction*, by T. F. Torrance. *Indian Journal of Theology* 17: 43-45.

68ske   "Sydindiens kyrka efter tjugo år: predikan hållen i S: t George-katedralen, Madras, på Sydindiska Kyrkans." Translated by A. Andrén. *Svensk Missionstidskrift* 56, no. 1: 9-16.

68wmc   "The World Mission of the Church." *South India Churchman* (September): 2-4.

69cmcu   "The Call to Mission — a Call to Unity." In *The Church Crossing Frontiers*, edited by Peter Beyerhaus and Carl F. Hallencreutz, pp. 254-65. Lund: Gleerup. A contribution to a collection of essays on the nature of mission in honor of Bengt Sundkler.

69cuww   "Church Union: Which Way Forward?" *National Christian Council Review* 89: 356-63.

69fc   *The Finality of Christ.* London: SCM Press; Richmond: John Knox. The Lyman Beecher Lectures, Yale University Divinity School, April 1966. Also given as the James Reid Lectures at Cambridge University. Published in Spanish as *Christo Valore Definitivo: Il Evangelo e le Religione* (Bologna, 1972).

69sfbs   *Set Free to Be a Servant: Studies in Paul's Letter to the Galatians.* Madras: CLS.

69wwfo   "Which Way for 'Faith and Order'?" In *What Unity Implies: Six Essays after Uppsala*, edited by Reinhard Groscurth, World Council Studies no. 7, pp. 115-32. Geneva: WCC. Also published as "Glauben und Kirchenverfassung vor Neuen Aufgaben," in *Christliche Einheit*, ed. Reinhard Groscurth (Geneva: WCC, 1969).

70bsl   "The Bible Study Lectures." In *Digest of the Proceedings of the Ninth Meeting of the Consultation on Christian Union*, pp. 193-231. Princeton: Consultation on Church Union. Lectures given in March 1970. Also published in four parts in *Mid-Stream* 9 (fall 1970): 193-202, 203-13, 213-27, 228-31.

70cu   "Co-operation and Unity." *International Review of Mission* 59 (January): 67-74. An excerpt of this article was published again within "A Review of the Review," *International Review of Mission* 76 (April 1987): 173-258 (the excerpt of Newbigin's essay is on pp. 222-24).

70esr   *An Easter Sermon on Romans 8:11.* Pamphlet. Vellore: A. H. Press. An Easter sermon given at Madras Cathedral in 1970 and again at Saint Johns, Vellore, in 1971.

70msc   "Mission to Six Continents." In *The Ecumenical Advance: A History of the Ecumenical Movement, Vol. 2, 1948-1968,* edited by Harold E. Fey, pp. 171-97. London: SPCK.

71c   "Conversion." In *Concise Dictionary of the Christian World Mission,* edited by Stephen Neill, Gerald H. Anderson, and John Goodwin, pp. 147-48. Nashville and New York: Abingdon.

71csc   "The Church as a Servant Community." *National Christian Council Review* 91: 256-64. Lecture given at the Consultation on Love and Justice in the World of Tomorrow, October 1970.

71jc   "Jesus Christ." In *Concise Dictionary of the Christian World Mission,* edited by Stephen Neill, Gerald H. Anderson, and John Goodwin, pp. 307-9. Nashville and New York: Abingdon.

71rsh   Review of *Salvation and Humanisation,* by M. M. Thomas. *Religion and Society* (Bangalore) 18 (March): 71-80.

71s   "Salvation." In *Concise Dictionary of Christian World Mission,* edited by Stephen Neill, Gerald H. Anderson, and John Goodwin, pp. 537-38. Nashville and New York: Abingdon.

71t   "Trinitarianism." In *Concise Dictionary of the Christian World Mission,* edited by Stephen Neill, Gerald H. Anderson, and John Goodwin, p. 607. Nashville and New York: Abingdon.

71uc   "Uniqueness of Christianity." In *Concise Dictionary of the Christian World Mission,* edited by Stephen Neill, Gerald H. Anderson, and John Goodwin, p. 620. Nashville and New York: Abingdon.

72amtj   "Address on the Main Theme, 'Jesus, Saviour of the World,' at the Synod Assembly of January 1972." *South India Churchman* (February): 5-8.

72bck   "Baptism, the Church and Koinonia: Three Letters and a Comment." *Religion and Society* 19, no. 1 (March): 69-90. An exchange of letters between Lesslie Newbigin and M. M. Thomas with a comment by Alfred C. Krass. Letter of 17 November 1971 ("18-11-71") by Lesslie Newbigin, pp. 75-84. Republished in M. M. Thomas et al., *Some Theological Dialogues* (Madras: CLS, 1977), pp. 110-44. Excerpts from the letters of Thomas and Newbigin were published in *Asia Focus* (Bangkok) 7, no. 4 (1972) and as "Salvation and Humanization: A Discussion," in *Mission Trends No. 1: Crucial Issues in Mission Today,* ed. Gerald H. Anderson and Thomas F. Stransky, C.S.P. (New York, Paramus, N.J., and Toronto: Paulist; Grand Rapids: Eerdmans, 1974), pp. 217-29.

72csit   "The Church of South India — Twenty-five Years After." *Christian Advocate,* 21 December, pp. 13-14.

72fcwp   "The Finality of Christ within a Plurality of Faiths." *Dialogue* 24: 15-19.

72foii   "Faith and Order in India Now." *National Christian Council Review* 92: 433-36. Guest editorial.

72hsc   *The Holy Spirit and the Church.* Madras: CLS. Addresses originally given at a convention in Madras, April 1972.

72jij   *Journey into Joy.* Madras: CLS; Delhi: ISPCK. Addresses given at the Christian Medical College, Vellore, October 1971. Republished in 1973 in an American edition (Grand Rapids: Eerdmans).

72kdg   "Kirche als Dienende Gemeinschaft." *Evangelisches Missionsmagazin* 116: 66-74.

72ldm   "Lettre de Madras." Translated from English by F. Cartan. *Communion* 26, no. 1: 4-6.

72sad   "The Secular-Apostolic Dilemma." In *Not without a Compass: JEA Seminar on Christian Education in the India of Today,* edited by T. Mathias et al., pp. 61-71. New Delhi: Jesuit Educational Association of India. Responses by Pierre Fallon, G. Casimir, and G. Soares, pp. 72-78.

72ssl   "Servants of the Servant Lord." *Vivekananda Kendra Patrika* (February): 153-55.

72tfyc   "Twenty-five Years of C.S.I." *National Christian Council Review* 92: 141-45.

72tfyo   "Twenty-five Years Old: How Fares the Church of South India?" *Presbyterian Life* (Philadelphia) 25, no. 9: 38-40.

73ccas   "The Churches and CASA." *National Christian Council Review* 93: 543-49. Paper written for the Consultation between CASA (Christian Agency for Social Action) and Heads of Churches at Delhi, September 1973.

73fsvu   "The Form and Structure of the Visible Unity of the Church." In *So sende Ich Euch: Festschrift für D. Dr. Martin Pörksen zum 70. Geburtstag,* edited by Otto Wack et al., pp. 124-41. Korntal bei Stuttgart: Evang. Missionsverlag. Also published in two parts as "The Form and Structure of the Visible Unity of the Church," *National Christian Council Review* 92 (1972): 444-51; 93 (1973): 4-18. Republished in *One in Christ* 13 (1977): 107-26.

73rcyc   Review of *Christ and the Younger Churches,* by Georg F. Vicedom. *Indian Journal of Theology* 22: 183-85.

73snhc   "Salvation, the New Humanity and Cultural-Communal Solidarity." *Bangalore Theological Forum* 5, no. 2: 1-11.

73tsb   "The Taste of Salvation at Bangkok." *Indian Journal of Theology* 22 (April-June): 49-53. A personal response to the Bangkok 1973 Conference of the Commission on World Mission and Evangelism of the WCC.

74cfm   "Christian Faith and Marxism." *Madras Christian College Magazine* (1974): 21-26. The substance of an address given to students at the Fellowship Breakfast organized by the Student Christian Movement of Madras Christian College, 11 February 1973.

74gs   *The Good Shepherd: Meditations on Christian Ministry in Today's World.*

Madras: CLS. Talks originally given to meetings of the clergy working in the Church of South India in the city of Madras. Republished in a revised edition in 1977 (Leighton Buzzard, Beds: Faith). See 77gs.

74ratd   "Reflection after Three Decades." *South India Churchman* (April): 2-3.

74lwc   "Living with Change." *Religion and Society* (Bangalore) 21, no. 4 (December): 14-28. Address given at a conference at Coventry Cathedral.

75aih   "Abiding in Him." In *Uniting in Hope: Reports and Documents from the Meeting of the Faith and Order Commission, Accra, Ghana (University of Ghana, Legon), 1974,* by John Deschner et al. Geneva: WCC.

75bwku   ". . . But What Kind of Unity?" *National Christian Council Review* 95: 487-91.

75rcdt   Review of *Crisis of Dependency in Third World Ministries,* by James A. Berquist and P. Kambar Manickam. *Religion and Society* (Bangalore) 22: 81-82.

75rcp   Review of *Canterbury Pilgrim,* by A. Michael Ramsey. *Ecumenical Review* 27: 171.

75rgcc   Review of *Great Christian Centuries to Come. Ecumenical Review* 27: 171-72.

75rilc   Review of *India and the Latin Captivity of the Church,* by Robin Boyd. *Scottish Journal of Theology* 28, no. 1: 90-92.

75rim   "Reflections on an Indian Ministry." *Frontier* 18 (spring): 25-27.

75vg   "Vollverbindliche Gemeinschaft: Die Oekumene muss sagen welche Einheit sie will." *Lutherische Monatshefte* 14: 611-13.

76aopa   "All in One Place or All of One Sort: On Unity and Diversity in the Church." In *Creation, Christ, and Culture: A Festschrift in Honour of Professor Thomas F. Torrance,* edited by Richard W. A. McKinney, pp. 288-306. Edinburgh: T & T Clark. A response to John Macquarrie, *Christian Unity and Christian Diversity* (London and Philadelphia: SCM Press, 1975). Republished in *Mid-Stream* 15 (October 1976): 323-41.

76cc   "The Centrality of Christ." *Fraternal* 177: 20-28. Address given at the Ministers' Session of the 1976 Assembly of the Baptist Ministers' Fellowship.

76cuan   "Christian Unity at Nairobi: Some Personal Reflections." *Mid-Stream* 15 (April): 152-62. Excerpts of this article were republished under the title "Nairobi 1975: A Personal Report," *National Christian Council Review* 96: 345-56 and *Faith and Unity* 20, no. 2 (1976): 27-32. Also published as: "Nairobi 1975: Ein Persönlicher Bericht," *Ökumenische Rundschau* 25, no. 2 (1976): 149-60.

76rnwc   Review of *New Ways for Christ,* by Michael Wright. *International Review of Mission* 65 (April): 228-29.

77bmm   "The Bishop and the Ministry of Mission." In *Today's Church and Today's World,* edited by J. Howe, pp. 242-47. London: CIO Publishing. A contribution to the preparatory volume for the Lambeth Conference, 1978.

77bpmi   "The Basis, Purpose and Manner of Inter-Faith Dialogue." *Scottish Journal of Theology* 30, no. 3 (June): 253-70. Originally prepared in November 1975 for the Lutheran Church in America, Division for World Mission and Ecumenism and distributed by them in pamphlet form under the title *Interfaith Dialogue* (New York: Lutheran Church in America, World Mission Interpretation, 1976). Reprinted in *Interreligious Dialogue: Facing the Next Frontier,* ed. Richard W. Rousseau, S.J. (Scranton, Pa.: Ridge Row, 1981), pp. 13-31. Published in 1977 in two German translations: "Christen im Dialog mit Nichtchristen," *Theologie der Gegenwart* 20, no. 3: 159-66, and "Dialog zwischen verschiedenen Glauben," *Zeitschrift für Mission* 3, no. 2: 83-98. Modified and republished as "The Gospel among the Religions," in *The Open Secret* (Grand Rapids: Eerdmans, 1978), chap. 10, pp. 190-206 (see 78os), and reprinted under that title in *Mission Trends No. 5: Faith Meets Faith,* ed. Gerald H. Anderson and Thomas F. Stransky, C.S.P. (New York: Paulist, 1981), pp. 3-19. Some paragraphs recur in *Christian Witness in a Plural Society.* See 77cwps.

77cc   "Christus en de Culturen." *Wereld en Zending* 6: 287-303. Republished in *Zeitschrift für Mission* 4 (1978): 134-49.

77cu   "Conciliar Unity: A Letter to the Editor." *South India Churchman* (March): 10.

77cwps   *Christian Witness in a Plural Society.* London: British Council of Churches. Also published as *Christliches Zeugnis in Einer Pluralistischen Gesellschaft* (Bern: Evangelische Arbeitsstelle Ökumene Schweiz, 1988). Paper presented to the Assembly of the British Council of Churches, April 1977. (Similar in content to 77bpmi but developed from a different starting point.)

77fcg   Foreword to *Christliche Gurus: Darstellungen von Selbstverständnis und Funktion indigener Christseins durch unabhängige, charismatische geführte Gruppen in Südindien,* by Werner Hoerschelmann. Frankfurt am Main: Lang.

77fmm   "The Future of Missions and Missionaries." *Review and Expositor* 74, no. 2 (spring): 209-18.

77gs   *The Good Shepherd: Meditations on Christian Ministry in Today's World.* Revised edition of 74gs. Leighton Buzzard, Beds: Faith. Foreword by the archbishop of Canterbury. Also published in America as *The Good Shepherd* by Eerdmans in Grand Rapids. Reprinted in a third edition in 1985 by Mowbray, London.

77mm   "Recent Thinking on Christian Beliefs: VIII. Mission and Missions." *Expository Times* 88 (June): 260-64. A review of mission theology from 1950 to 1976. Also published as "Recent Thinking on Christian Beliefs," *Sedos Bulletin* 8 (1978): 141-48.

77trsp   "Teaching Religion in a Secular Plural Society." *Learning for Living* 17, no.

2: 82-88. Address given at the annual general meeting of the Christian Education Movement. Republished in *Christianity in the Classroom* (London: Christian Education Movement, 1978), pp. 1-11, and in *New Directions in Religious Education,* ed. John Hull (London: Falmer, 1982), pp. 97-108.

77wilc   "What Is a 'Local Church Truly United'?" In *In Each Place: Towards a Fellowship of Local Churches Truly United,* by J. E. L. Newbigin et al., pp. 14-29. Geneva: WCC. Republished in *Ecumenical Review* 29 (April 1977): 115-28.

78caw   "Church as Witness: A Meditation." *Reformed World* 35 (March): 5-9.

78cc   *Context and Conversion.* London: Church Missionary Society. The 1978 CMS Annual Sermon, delivered at Saint Andrew's Church, Short Street, London, 4 December 1978, on the text 1 Corinthians 1:23-24. Republished in *International Review of Mission* 68 (July 1979): 301-12.

78cic   *Christianity in the Classroom,* by Lesslie Newbigin et al. London: Christian Education Movement. The lead essay by Newbigin is a republication of 77trsp.

78ctc   "Christ and the Cultures." *Scottish Journal of Theology* 31, no. 1: 1-22. Paper read to the 1977 Conference of the Society for the Study of Theology. Adapted as part of chap. 9 of *The Open Secret* (see 78os).

78mgz   "Maak u geen zorgen over zending maar over uw gemeente." *Kerkinformatie* 89. A summary of 79ttgv.

78os   *The Open Secret: Sketches for a Missionary Theology.* London: SPCK; Grand Rapids: Eerdmans. Republished in a revised edition in 1995. See 95os. Also published in a Korean edition entitled *Son'gyo sinhak kaeyo: Konggae toen pimil* (Seoul: Han'guk Sinhak Yon'guso, 1995).

78rd   Review of *Denominationalism,* edited by Russell E. Richey. *Ecumenical Review* 30 (April): 189.

78rfl   "The Right to Fullness of Life." In *A Vision for Man: Essays on Faith, Theology, and Society,* edited by Samuel Amirtham, pp. 339-47. Madras: CLS. A contribution to a collection of essays in honor of Joshua Russell Chandran on the occasion of his sixtieth birthday.

78rfmf   Review of *Faith Meets Faith: Some Christian Attitudes to Hinduism in the Nineteenth and Twentieth Centuries,* by Eric J. Sharpe. *Theology* 81 (March): 142-43.

78tiol   *This Is Our Life.* Leeds: John Paul the Preacher's Press. Moderator's address to the General Assembly of the United Reformed Church, Southport, 1978.

79atws   "Authority: To Whom Shall We Go?" Sermon preached on the text John 6:66-71 at Saint Mary's, the University Church at Cambridge, on 6 May 1979 under the general theme of "Voices of Authority." Published and distributed by the secretary, Saint Mary's, the University Church, Cambridge, CB2 3PQ.

79cjh   "The Centrality of Jesus for History." In *Incarnation and Myth: The Debate Continued*, edited by Michael Goulder, pp. 197-210. Grand Rapids: Eerdmans. Followed by a reply article, "Comment on Lesslie Newbigin's Essay," by Maurice Wiles, pp. 211-13.

79ltr   "Les temoins du royaume: l'Eglise." *Flambeau: Revue Trimestrialle de Theologie pour l'Ensignement de l'Eglise dans le Monde Africaine*, no. 55, (March): 276-80.

79nwwh   "Not Whole without the Handicapped." In *Partners in Life: The Handicapped and the Church*, edited by Geiko Müller-Fahrenholz, Faith and Order Paper no. 89, pp. 17-25. Geneva: WCC.

79pct   *Preaching Christ Today*. Birmingham, U.K.: Overdale College. The Eighteenth Joseph Smith Memorial Lecture, published as a pamphlet.

79rmer   Review of *The Meaning and End of Religion*, by Wilfred C. Smith. *Theology* 82 (July): 294-96.

79tewp   "Theological Education in a World Perspective." In *Ministers for the 1980s*, edited by Jock Stein, pp. 63-75. Edinburgh: Handsel. Republished from *Churchman* 93, no. 2 (1979): 105-15 with an introduction added. The substance of a paper given to the Conference of the Staffs of the Church of England Theological Colleges, 3 January 1978. Also published in *Ministerial Formation* 4 (1978): 3-10 and in *Missions and Theological Education in World Perspective*, ed. Harvie M. Conn and Samuel F. Rowan (Farmington, Mich.: Associates of Urbanus, 1984), pp. 3-18.

79ttgv   "Toespraak tot de gezamenlijke vergadering van de Synoden van de Nederlandse Hervormde Kerk en de Gereformeerde Kerken in Nederland op 22 November 1978 in De Blije Werelt te Lunteren." *Wereld en Zending* 8, no. 1: 96-109. Summarized in 78mgz.

80cwu   "Common Witness and Unity." *International Review of Mission* 69 (April): 158-60. Written for the Joint Working Group Study on Common Witness of the Roman Catholic Church and the World Council of Churches, Venice, 29 May–2 June 1979.

80htsh   "He That Sitteth in the Heavens Shall Laugh." In *Imagination and the Future: Essays on Christian Thought and Practice*, edited by J. Henley, pp. 3-7. Melbourne: Hawthorne.

80jws   "John W. Sadiq 1910-1980." *International Review of Mission* 69: 575-76.

80m80   "Mission in the 1980's." *Occasional Bulletin of Missionary Research* 4 (October): 154-55.

80pfnd   *Priorities for a New Decade*. Birmingham, U.K.: National Student Christian Congress and Resource Centre. Reprinted from *Reform* (United Reformed Church).

80sa   "South Africa: A Fabric of Fear and Hope." *One World* 62 (December): 10-11.

80ykc   *Your Kingdom Come: Reflections on the Theme of the Melbourne Conference on World Mission and Evangelism, 1980*. Leeds: John Paul the

Preacher's Press. Presented as the Waldström Lectures at the Theological Seminary of the Swedish Covenant Church, Lidingo, September 1979. Also published as *Sign of the Kingdom* (Grand Rapids: Eerdmans, 1981) and as *Låt Ditt Rike Komma* (Stockholm: Gummessons Bokförlag/ Musikförlag, 1980).

81ispr   "Integration — Some Personal Reflections 1981." *International Review of Mission* 70 (October): 247-55. Published along with a reprint of Newbigin's sermon at the Act of Integration of the International Missionary Council and the World Council of Churches (62mdem), pp. 240-46.

81mp81   *Perspectives Missionnaires 1981, No. 2: Articles on Melbourne 1980 and Pattaya 1980 Conferences.* Coauthored with Gottfried Osei-Mensah et al. Geneva: Perspectives Missionnaires.

81pc   "Politics and the Covenant." *Theology* 84 (September): 356-63.

81rrtg   Review of *Red Tape and the Gospel*, by Eleanor M. Jackson. *Churchman* 95, no. 3: 273-74.

82buc   "Bishops in a United Church." In *Bishops, but What Kind*, edited by Peter Moore, pp. 149-61. London: SPCK.

82ccee   "Cross-Currents in Ecumenical and Evangelical Understandings of Mission." *International Bulletin of Missionary Research* 6, no. 4 (October): 146-51. Responses by Paul G. Schrotenboer and C. Peter Wagner, pp. 152-54, and a rejoinder by Newbigin, "Lesslie Newbigin Replies," pp. 154-55. Also published as "Ontwikkelingen in Ökumenische en Evangelische Opvattingen over Zending," *Soteria* 1, no. 2 (1984): 34-40 and *Soteria* 1, no. 3 (1984): 30-36.

82eis   "L'Eglise de L'Inde du Sud." *Unity Chretienne* 65: 9-15.

82lhc   *The Light Has Come: An Exposition of the Fourth Gospel.* Grand Rapids: Eerdmans.

82lt   "Living Together." *Now* (Methodist Church Overseas Division, London) (June): 18-19.

82rbi   Review of *Beyond Ideology*, by Ninian Smart. *Theology* 85 (September): 381-83.

82rcl   Review of *Christ's Lordship and Religious Pluralism*, edited by Gerald H. Anderson and Thomas F. Stransky, C.S.P. *International Bulletin of Missionary Research* 6 (January): 32.

82rcoe   Review of *Conflict over the Ecumenical Movement*, by Ulrich Duchrow, translated by David Lewis. *Ecumenical Review* 34 (October): 428-30.

82tc   "Text and Context: The Bible in the Church." *Near Eastern School of Theology Theological Review* 5, no. 1 (April): 5-13. Written for the Festschrift in honor of Bishop Kulandran published in India in 1981 under the title *God's Word in God's World*, ed. D. J. Ambalavanar.

83cwr   "Christ and the World of Religions." *Churchman* 97, no. 1: 16-30. Written for a collection of reflections on the theme of the Vancouver 1983 WCC

Assembly, "Jesus Christ, the Life of the World." Republished in *Reformed Review* 37, no. 3 (spring 1984): 202-13.

83os84 *The Other Side of 1984: Questions for the Churches.* Risk Book Series, no. 18. Geneva: WCC. With a postscript by S. Wesley Ariarajah. Also published as *Verder dan "1984": Missionaire Confrontatie met de Moderne Cultuur,* with a foreword by Hendrikus Berkhof (Kampen: Kok, 1985), as *Med 1984 i Bakspejlet: Sporgemal til Kirkerne* (Hellerup: DMS Forlag, 1984), and as *Salz der Erde? Fragen an die Kirche Heute* (Neukirchen-Vluyn: Schriftenmissions-Verlag, 1985).

83rim "Renewal in Mind." *GEAR* (Group for Evangelism and Renewal in the United Reformed Church), no. 29: 4-7. Text of an address given at the Birmingham, U.K., GEAR Day, 26 February 1983.

83rmu Rejoinder to "Mission and Unity in the Missionary Ecclesiology of Max A. C. Warren," by Ossi Haaramäki. *International Review of Mission* 72: 271-72. Haaramäki's article is found in the same issue of the *International Review of Mission,* on pp. 267-71.

83up "An Unsystematic Postscript." In *Christian Initiatives in Community Education,* edited by Liz Ross, pp. 44-48. Birmingham, U.K.: National Centre for Christian Communities and Networks.

84bfu "The Basis and the Forms of Unity." *Mid-Stream* 23 (January): 1-12. The Second Peter Ainslee Lecture, given at the Council on Christian Unity luncheon, San Antonio, Tex., 24 September 1983. Published as a monograph as *The Basis and the Forms of Unity* (Indianapolis: Council on Christian Unity, 1984).

84bocm "The Bible and Our Contemporary Mission." *Clergy Review* 69, no. 1: 9-17. The Fourth Thomas Worden Memorial Lecture, given at the Upholland Northern Institute, 4 May 1983.

84ffem "Faith and Faithfulness in the Ecumenical Movement." In *Faith and Faithfulness: Essays on Contemporary Ecumenical Themes,* edited by Pauline Webb, pp. 1-7. Geneva: WCC. An essay in tribute to Philip A. Potter.

84sctb "The Sending of the Church — Three Bible Studies." In *New Perspectives on World Mission and Unity,* Occasional Paper no. 1, pp. 1-14. Edinburgh: Church of Scotland Board of World Mission and Unity. Addresses given at a Conference on World Mission and Unity, Edinburgh, November 1984.

84swme "Emilio Castro: Servant of World Mission and Evangelism." *International Review of Mission* 73 (January): 110. Remarks contained within an article by Johannes Verkuyl with contributions from a number of authors (pp. 106-17).

85cwbc "Can the West Be Converted?" *Princeton Seminary Bulletin* 6, no. 1: 25-37. Lecture given on 20 May 1984 and originally published by the Friends of Saint Colm's, the Education Centre and College of the Church of Scotland. Republished in the *International Bulletin of Missionary Research* 11

(January 1987): 2-7 and in the *Evangelical Review of Theology* 11 (October 1987): 355-68. Also published as "Kan västerlandet omvändas?" trans. L. Johansson, *Svensk Missionstidskrift* 78, no. 4 (1990): 11-25.

85fc   "A Fellowship of Churches." *Ecumenical Review* 37, no. 2 (April): 175-81.

85hiao   "How I Arrived at *The Other Side of 1984*." *Selly Oak Journal*, no. 2: 6-8. An introduction to a series of six responses to *The Other Side of 1984* (83os84). See also 85rtr.

85rhci   Review of *A History of Christianity in India: The Beginnings to* AD *1707*, by Stephen Neill. *Journal of Theological Studies* 36, no. 2 (October): 530-31.

85rrrs   Review of *Revolution as Revelation: A Study of M. M. Thomas's Theology*, by Sunand Sumithra. *International Bulletin of Missionary Research* 9 (October): 199-200.

85rtr   "A Response to the Responses." *Selly Oak Journal*, no. 2: 33-36. Newbigin's comments on the series of six responses to *The Other Side of 1984*. See also 85hiao.

85ua   *Unfinished Agenda: An Autobiography*. Grand Rapids: Eerdmans; London: SPCK. A revised and updated edition was published in 1993 (see 93ua).

85wscp   *The Welfare State: A Christian Perspective*. Oxford: Oxford Institute for Church and Society. The Gore Memorial Lecture given at Westminster Abbey in November 1984. Republished in *Theology* 88 (May 1985): 173-82.

86bep   "A British and European Perspective." In *Entering the Kingdom: A Fresh Look at Conversion*, edited by Monica Hill, pp. 57-68. Middlesex, U.K.: British Church Growth Association and MARC Europe.

86bvdw   "The Biblical Vision: Deed and Word Inseparable." *Concern* 28, no. 8: 1-3, 36.

86ep   "Ecumenical Pilgrims." *Catholic Gazette* (Catholic Missionary Society) 77, no. 2: 6-8. An abridged version of an address entitled "By Faith Abraham Obeyed . . . ," given at a celebration of the seventy-fifth anniversary of the Edinburgh 1910 World Missionary Conference.

86f   Foreword to *Redeeming Time: Atonement through Education*, by Timothy Gorringe, pp. ix-x. London: Darton, Longman and Todd.

86fg   *Foolishness to the Greeks: The Gospel and Western Culture*. London: SPCK; Grand Rapids: Eerdmans; and Geneva: WCC. The Benjamin B. Warfield Lectures given at Princeton Theological Seminary, March 1984. Also published as *Den Griechen eine Torheit: Das Evangelium und Unsere Westliche Kultur*, with a foreword by Gerhard Koslowsky (Neukirchen-Vluyn: Aussaat Verlag, 1989).

86wbp   "Witness in a Biblical Perspective." *Mission Studies* 3, no. 2: 80-84.

87mcw   *Mission in Christ's Way: Bible Studies*. WCC Mission Series no. 8. Geneva: WCC Publications. Also published in a Malayalam edition (Madras: CLS,

1988), as *Mission in Christ's Way: A Gift, a Command, an Assurance* (New York: Friendship, 1988), as *Mission in der Nachfolge Christi: Bibelarbeiten* (Hamburg: Evangelisches Missionswerk, 1988), as *Zending in het Voetspoor van Christus: Bijbelstudies* (Sliedrecht: Merweboek, 1989), as *En Mission Sur le Chemin du Christ: Perspectives Bibliques* (Aubonne: Editions du Moulin, 1989), and as *Mission pa Jesu Sätt: Bibelstudier* (Stockholm: Verbum Förlag, 1990). Excerpts published as "Sharing the Passion of Jesus," *Accent* (Auckland) 3, no. 9 (November 1988): 28. Originally given as Bible studies at the meeting of the Synod of the Church of South India in 1986.

87po   "The Pastor's Opportunities: VI. Evangelism in the City." *Expository Times* 98 (September): 355-58. Reprinted as "Evangelism in the City," *Reformed Review* 41 (autumn 1987): 3-8, and as chap. 5 in the book *A Word in Season*. See 94awis.

87rcc   Review of *The Catholicity of the Church*, by Avery Dulles. *Journal of Theological Studies* 38, no. 1 (April): 273-74.

87rcf   Review of *The Christ and the Faiths: Theology in Cross-Reference*, by Kenneth Cragg. *Journal of Theological Studies* 38, no. 2 (October): 585-88. Also published in *Selly Oak Journal* 7 (autumn 1987): 49-51.

87rjow   Review of *Jesus in Our Western Culture: Mysticism, Ethics, and Politics*, by E. S. Schillebeeckx. *Theology* 90: 472-73.

87rrcc   Review of *Risking Christ for Christ's Sake: Towards an Ecumenical Theology of Pluralism*, by M. M. Thomas. *Ecumenical Review* 39, no. 4 (October): 495-96.

87ww   "Witnesses to the World." *Christian* (U.K.), no. 1 (May/June): 5-8. Paper Presented to Partnership for World Mission and the Board for Mission and Unity in England.

88bcw   "On Being the Church for the World." In *The Parish Church?* edited by Giles S. Ecclestone, pp. 25-42. London: Mowbray.

88bisi   "Britons in India since Independence: An Individual Response." *Indo-British Review* 14, no. 1: 78-84.

88cfwr   "The Christian Faith and the World Religions." In *Keeping the Faith: Essays to Mark the Centenary of Lux Mundi*, edited by Geoffrey Wainwright, pp. 310-40. Philadelphia: Fortress; Allison Park, Pa.: Pickwick; and London: SPCK (1989).

88evcc   "The Enduring Validity of Cross-Cultural Mission." *International Bulletin of Missionary Research* 12, no. 2 (April): 50-53. Reprinted in *Ministry and Theology in Global Perspective: Contemporary Challenges for the Church*, ed. Don A. Pittman, Ruben L. F. Habito, and Terry C. Muck (Grand Rapids: Eerdmans, 1996), pp. 335-38. Excerpts published in *Together* (World Vision International) 20 (October-December 1988): 2-3. Address on 5 October 1987 at the service of dedication and inauguration of the new Overseas Ministries Study Center facility in New Haven,

Conn. Also published as chap. 10 in the book *A Word in Season.* See 94awis.

88hfff   "Human Flourishing in Faith, Fact and Fantasy." *Religion and Medicine* 7: 400-412. Address given in the summer of 1988 at a conference sponsored by the Churches' Council on Health and Healing under the theme "Towards Health in the 1990s." A brief excerpt appeared as "Human Flourishing in a World of Fantasy," *Health and Healing* 19 (summer, 6 September 1988): 4.

88idg   Interview in *Different Gospels: Christian Orthodoxy and Modern Theologies,* edited by Andrew Walker, pp. 30-41. London: Hodder & Stoughton.

88rds   "Response to David M. Stowe." *International Bulletin of Missionary Research* 12, no. 4 (October): 151-53. See Stowe 1988. Also see Charles C. West 1988 for his comments on both Newbigin's and Stowe's remarks.

88rsts   "Religion, Science and Truth in the School Curriculum." *Theology* 91 (May): 186-93.

88spts   "A Sermon Preached at the Thanksgiving Service for the Fiftieth Anniversary of the Tambaram Conference of the International Missionary Council." *International Review of Mission* 77 (July): 325-31.

88st   "The Significance of Tambaram — Fifty Years Later." *Missionalia* 16, no. 2 (August): 79-85.

89bfm   "Beyond the Familiar Myths." In *Gospel and Our Culture* (U.K.), no. 1 (spring): 2-3.

89crhr   "Culture, Rationality and the Unity of the Human Race." *Gospel and Our Culture* (U.K.), no. 3 (autumn): 1-2.

89fbr   "Freedom, Blasphemy, and Responsibility." *Gospel and Our Culture* (U.K.), no. 2 (summer): 1-2.

89gcwc   "Gospel and Culture — but Which Culture?" *Missionalia* 17, no. 3 (November): 213-15.

89gps   *The Gospel in a Pluralist Society.* London: SPCK; Grand Rapids: Eerdmans; and Geneva: WCC Publications. Also published as *L'Evangelo in una Società Pluralistica* (Torino: Claudiana, 1995). A series of lectures given at Glasgow University as the Alexander Robertson Lecturer for 1988.

89mcwc   *Mission and the Crisis of Western Culture: Recent Studies.* Edited by Jock Stein. Edinburgh: Handsel. The booklet includes an address to the annual conference of the German organization Arbeitsgemeinschaft Missionarische Dienste; an address at the service of dedication of the Overseas Ministries Study Center facility in New Haven, Conn., in 1987 (88evcc); and a talk given to an ecumenical group in Cambridge, England.

89m90   "Mission in the 1990s: Two Views." Coauthored with Anna-Marie Aagaard. *International Bulletin of Missionary Research* 13, no. 3 (July): 98-102.

89rltt   Review of *Living Today towards Visible Unity*, edited by Thomas F. Best. *Mid-Stream* 28 (January): 144-47.

89rmcu   Review of *The Myth of Christian Uniqueness*, edited by John Hick and Paul Knitter. *Ecumenical Review* 41, no. 3: 468-69.

89rpuj   "Religious Pluralism and the Uniqueness of Jesus Christ." *International Bulletin of Missionary Research* 13, no. 2 (April): 50-54.

89sv   "*The Satanic Verses:* Blasphemy vs. Freedom of Speech." *Independent Newspaper*, 21 February. Newbigin's was one of a number of letters to the editor contained in the article on the book by Salman Rushdie.

89vc   "Vision for the City." In *The Renewal of Social Vision*, edited by A. Elliott and I. Swanson, Occasional Paper no. 17, pp. 39-41. Edinburgh: Centre for Theology and Public Issues (University of Edinburgh).

90bgso   "The Bible: God's Story and Ours." *Reform* (January): 7. The first in a series of eleven articles.

90cbec   "The Church: 'A Bunch of Escaped Convicts.'" *Reform* (June): 6. The sixth in a series of eleven articles.

90chs   *Come Holy Spirit — Renew the Whole Creation*. Selly Oak Colleges Occasional Paper no. 6. Birmingham, U.K.: Selly Oak Colleges. Lecture given on 12 July 1990 to the Ecumenical Summer School at Saint Andrew's Hall, Selly Oak Colleges.

90ea   "Episcopacy and Authority." *Churchman* 104, no. 4: 335-39. A contribution to the Eighth Anglican Evangelical Assembly, High Leigh 1990, on the conference theme. Reprinted in *Liberate Oversight: Episcopal Ministry Today*, ed. G. Ogilvie, Grove Pastoral Series, no. 46 (Bramcote, U.K.: Grove Books, 1991), pp. 17-21.

90edcs   "Evangelisatie in de Context van Secularisatie." *Kerk en Theologie* 41, no. 4: 269-77. Published in English as chap. 13 in *A Word in Season* (94awis).

90f   Foreword to *Another Way of Looking: Helping You Challenge the Assumptions of Today's Culture*, by John De Wit, p. iv. Swindon, U.K.: British and Foreign Bible Society Publication. See De Wit 1990.

90fs   "The Free Society." *Gospel and Our Culture* (U.K.), no. 5 (spring): 1-2.

90goc   *The Gospel and Our Culture*. Mission Today Pamphlet no. 47. London: Catholic Missionary Education Centre. Talk given to the World Mission Conference of the National Missionary Council and the Conference for World Mission held at High Leigh in December 1989 under the theme "Doing God's Will in Our Plural Society."

90hs   "Holy Spirit: The Believers Strike Oil." *Reform* (May): 6. The fifth in a series of eleven articles.

90itac   "Is There Anyone in Charge Here?" *Reform* (March): 6. The third in a series of eleven articles.

90jelm   "Journeys End in Lovers Meeting." *Reform* (October): 13. The ninth in a series of eleven articles.

90le   "A Letter to the Editor: Reply to F. J. Balasundaram." *Bangalore Theologi-*

cal Forum 22 (June): 62-63. A reply to Franklyn Jayakumar Balasundaram's article, "The Voice and the Voices," *Bangalore Theological Forum* 21-22 (December 1989–March 1990): 94-139.

90mcpd   "Muslims, Christians and Public Doctrine." *Gospel and Our Culture* (U.K.), no. 6 (summer): 1-2.

90mmwc   "A Mission to Modern Western Culture." In *The San Antonio Report: Your Will Be Done: Mission in Christ's Way,* edited by Frederick R. Wilson, pp. 162-66. Geneva: WCC Publications. An excerpt of an address given at the 1989 WCC Conference on World Mission and Evangelism.

90obr   "Our Baptism Renewed in Bread and Wine." *Reform* (July/August): 18. The seventh in a series of eleven articles.

90qast   "A Question to Ask; a Story to Tell." *Reform* (November): 11. The tenth in a series of eleven articles.

90rm   "Religion for the Marketplace." In *Christian Uniqueness Reconsidered: The Myth of a Pluralistic Theology of Religions,* edited by Gavin D'Costa, pp. 135-48. Maryknoll, N.Y.: Orbis.

90sfmc   "Socialism, Free Markets and Christian Faith." *Gospel and Our Culture* (U.K.), no. 4 (winter): 1-2.

90tp   "The Threat and the Promise." *Gospel and Our Culture* (U.K.), no. 7 (autumn): 2-3.

90ttph   "This Is the Turning Point of History." *Reform* (April): 4. The fourth in a series of eleven articles.

90v84   "Verder dan 1984." In *Het Evangelie in het Westen: Nederlandse Reacties op Lesslie Newbigin,* edited by Martien E. Brinkman and Herman Noordegraaf, pp. 21-36. Kampen: Kok.

90wcm   "Worship — Cleaning the Mirror." *Reform* (September): 7. The eighth in a series of eleven articles.

90wdwm   "What Do We Mean by 'God'?" *Reform* (February): 7. The second in a series of eleven articles.

90xmgv   "An X-ray to Make God Visible in the World." *Reform* (December): 7. The eleventh in a series of eleven articles.

91bifr   "The Bible and Inter-Faith Relations." Coauthored with H. Dan Beeby. In *Using the Bible Today: Contemporary Interpretations of Scripture,* edited by Dan Cohn-Sherbok, Canterbury Papers Series, pp. 180-87. London: Bellew Publishers.

91cuhu   "Christian Unity and Human Unity." In *Tradition and Unity: Sermons Published in Honour of Robert Runcie,* edited by Daniel M. Cohn-Sherbok, pp. 220-24. London: Bellew Publishers.

91gpt   "The Gospel as Public Truth." *Gospel and Our Culture* (U.K.), no. 9 (spring): 1-2.

91md   "A Missionary's Dream." *Ecumenical Review* 43, no. 1 (January): 4-10. Also published as chap. 16 in *A Word in Season.* See 94awis.

91mipg   "Mission in einer Pluralistischen Gesellschaft." In *Ökumenische Theologie* in den Herausforderungen der Gegenwart: Lukas Vischer zum 65. *Geburtstag,* edited by Karin Bredull Gerschwiler et al., pp. 66-91. Göttingen: Vandenhoeck & Ruprecht. Also published in English as chap. 14 in *A Word in Season.* See 94awis.

91ndt "Niles, Daniel Thambyrajah." In *Dictionary of the Ecumenical Movement,* edited by Nicholas Lossky, José Míguez Bonino, John Pobee, Thomas F. Stransky, C.S.P., Geoffrey Wainwright, and Pauline Webb, pp. 729-31. Geneva: WCC Publications; Grand Rapids: Eerdmans.

91r "A Response." *Gospel and Our Culture* (U.K.), no. 10 (summer): 2-3. Response to an article by Fr. John Coventry, S.J., in the same issue which offered a rejoinder to Newbigin's article in the previous issue (91gpt). See Coventry 1991.

91rbn "Response from Bishop Newbigin." *Gospel and Our Culture* (U.K.), no. 8 (winter): 4. Reply to a response from Graeme Jackson to Newbigin's earlier article, "The Threat and the Promise" (90tp).

91stc "Speaking the Truth to Caesar." *Ecumenical Review* 43 (July): 372-75. Reprinted from *Truth to Tell.* See 91tt.

91tat "Theism and Atheism in Theology." *Gospel and Our Culture* (U.K.), no. 8 (winter): 1-2.

91tt *Truth to Tell: The Gospel as Public Truth.* Grand Rapids: Eerdmans; Geneva: WCC Publications; and London: SPCK. The 1990 Osterhaven Lectures at Western Theological Seminary, Holland, Mich., USA. Available in audio (90me/a) and video (90me/v) recordings.

91uo "Union, Organic." In *Dictionary of the Ecumenical Movement,* edited by Nicholas Lossky, José Míguez Bonino, John Pobee, Thomas F. Stransky, C.S.P., Geoffrey Wainwright, and Pauline Webb, pp. 1028-30. Geneva: WCC Publications; Grand Rapids: Eerdmans.

91uoa "Unity of 'All in Each Place.'" In *Dictionary of the Ecumenical Movement,* edited by Nicholas Lossky, José Míguez Bonino, John Pobee, Thomas F. Stransky, C.S.P., Geoffrey Wainwright, and Pauline Webb, pp. 1043-46. Geneva: WCC Publications; Grand Rapids: Eerdmans.

92cv "A Christian Vedanta?" Review of *A Vision to Pursue,* by Keith Ward. *Gospel and Our Culture* (U.K.), no. 12 (spring): 1-2.

92eh "The End of History." *Gospel and Our Culture* (U.K.), no. 13 (summer): 1-2.

92fal Foreword to *Angels of Light? The Challenge of New Age Spirituality,* by Lawrence Osborn, pp. viiff. London: Daybreak (Darton, Longman and Todd).

92fgoc Foreword to *The Gospel and Our Culture: The Gospel as Public Truth.* Documents of a National Consultation, the Hayes, Swanwick, 11-17 July 1992, organized by British and Foreign Bible Society and the Gospel and Our Culture. Swanwick: British and Foreign Bible Society.

92flc   Foreword to *Loosing the Chains: Religion as Opium and Liberation,* by J. Andrew Kirk, pp. vii-viii. London: Hodder & Stoughton.

92goc   "The Gospel and Our Culture: A Response to Elaine Graham and Heather Walton." *Modern Churchman* 34, no. 2: 1-10. Response to Graham's and Walton's article, "A Walk on the Wild Side: A Critique of the Gospel and Our Culture," *Modern Churchman* 33, 1 (1991): 1-7. See Graham and Walton 1991. See also John Reader's response to both articles (Reader 1993).

92gpt   "The Gospel as Public Truth." *Gospel and Our Culture Movement Supplement* (January): 1-2. Description of the purpose and thesis of the National Consultation of the Gospel and Our Culture Movement in association with the British and Foreign Bible Society, held in the Hayes, Swanwick, 11-17 July 1992.

92gpte   "The Gospel as Public Truth." Editorial. *Touchstone: A Journal of Ecumenical Orthodoxy* 5 (summer): 1-2.

92gpts   "The Gospel as Public Truth: Swanwick Opening Statement." In *The Gospel and Our Culture: The Gospel as Public Truth.* Documents of a National Consultation, the Hayes, Swanwick, 11-17 July 1992, organized by British and Foreign Bible Society and the Gospel and Our Culture. Swanwick: British and Foreign Bible Society. Plenary address. Available in audio recording (92gp/a).

92igpt   Introduction to *The Gospel as Public Truth: Applying the Gospel in the Modern World.* London: CENBooks. Introduction to a series of articles in the *Church of England Newspaper* on the Gospel and Our Culture Conference at Swanwick in 1992 on the theme "The Gospel as Public Truth."

92lwav   "The Legacy of W. A. Visser 't Hooft." *International Bulletin of Missionary Research* 16, no. 2 (April): 78-82. Also published in *Theologische Beitrag* 2 (1997).

92ras   "Reflections after Swanwick." *Gospel and Our Culture* (U.K.), no. 14 (autumn): 4.

92rnog   "Review of *No Other Gospel: Christianity among the World Religions* by Carl E. Braaten." *First Things* 24 (June-July): 56-58.

92rpuj   "Religious Pluralism and the Uniqueness of Jesus Christ." In *Many Other Ways? Questions of Religious Pluralism: Papers from a Symposium on Religious Pluralism Conducted by the Church Growth Research Centre McGavran Institute at the Gurukul Lutheran Theological College Chapel, Madras on 23 June 1990,* by M. Bage et al., pp. 69-80. Delhi: ISPCK, for the Church Growth Research Centre McGavran Institute, Madras.

92wj   "Whose Justice?" *Ecumenical Review* 44 (July): 308-11.

92wow   "Way Out West: The Gospel in a Post-Enlightenment World." *Touchstone: A Journal of Ecumenical Orthodoxy* 5 (summer): 22-24.

93cat   "Culture and Theology." In *The Blackwell Encyclopedia of Modern Chris-*

tian Thought, edited by Alister E. McGrath, pp. 98-100. Oxford, U.K., and Cambridge, Mass.: Blackwell.

93cfwk   "Certain Faith: What Kind of Certainty?" *Tyndale Bulletin* 44, no. 2 (November): 339-50. Lecture delivered to the Tyndale Fellowship Ethics Study Group, Cambridge, July 1993.

93ddad   *"A Decent Debate about Doctrine": Faith, Doubt, and Certainty.* A GEAR (Group for Evangelism and Renewal within the United Reformed Church) Booklet. Plymouth, U.K.: GEAR Publications. Presented to the Bromley District Council of the United Reform Church, July 1993, in response to Donald Hilton's address to the general assembly of the United Reformed Church as moderator.

93fdi   Foreword to *Dharma, India, and the World Order: Twenty-one Essays,* by Chaturvedi Badrinath. Edinburgh: Saint Andrew Press.

93kgoh   "The Kingdom of God and Our Hopes for the Future." In *The Kingdom of God and Human Society: Essays by Members of the Scripture, Theology and Society Group,* edited by Robin Barbour, pp. 1-12. Edinburgh: T & T Clark. Written in December 1987 to be presented to the "Scripture, Theology and Society" group that meets annually at Oxford University.

93p   Preface to *Towards the Twenty-first Century in Christian Mission: Essays in Honour of Gerald H. Anderson,* edited by James M. Phillips and Robert T. Coote, pp. 1-6. Grand Rapids: Eerdmans.

93pitc   "Pluralism in the Church." *ReNews* (Presbyterians for Renewal) 4, no. 2 (May): 1, 6-7.

93reit   Review of *Ecumenism in Transition: A Paradigm Shift in the Ecumenical Movement?* by Konrad Raiser. *One in Christ* 29, no. 3: 269-75. Reprinted as "Ecumenical Amnesia," in *International Bulletin of Missionary Research* 18, no. 1 (January 1994): 2-5, where it appeared together with a response from Raiser (1994) and a rejoinder by Newbigin (94rtkr).

93rpma   "Religious Pluralism: A Missiological Approach." In *Theology of Religions: Christianity and Other Religions,* Studia Missionalia 42: 227-44. Rome: Pontifical Gregorian University. Contribution by Newbigin to a symposium at the Gregorian University in February 1993.

93ua   *Unfinished Agenda: An Updated Autobiography.* Edinburgh: Saint Andrew Press; London: SPCK; and Geneva: WCC Publications. See 85ua.

94awis   *A Word in Season: Perspectives on Christian World Missions.* Edited by Eleanor Jackson. Edinburgh: Saint Andrew Press; Grand Rapids: Eerdmans. Collection of works, most of them previously unpublished or published only in languages other than English, including: 1. "A Riverside Sermon" (extract from otherwise unpublished 60fwlb); 2. "The Pattern of the Christian World Mission" (first in a series of three lectures given in New York in late 1960); 3. "Missions and the Work of the Holy Spirit" (last in a series of three lectures given in New York in late 1960); 4. "Mission in a Modern City" (talk given in Scotland in the summer of

1974); 5. "The Pastor's Opportunities: Evangelism in the City" (87po); 6. "Does Society Still Need the Parish Church?" (talk given on 5 November 1985 at the Centre for Explorations in Social Concern); 7. "The Cultural Captivity of Western Christianity as a Challenge to a Missionary Church" (lecture given on 3 October 1994 in Stuttgart to members of the Evangelische Missionswerke organization); 8. "By What Authority?" (a portion of 94tam, later modified and expanded as 96tam); 9. "Our Missionary Responsibility in the Crisis of Western Culture" (presented at a conference held in Arnoldshain, FRG, May 1988); 10. "The Enduring Validity of Cross-Cultural Mission" (88evcc); 11. "Mission in the World Today" (address given on 12 November 1987 to the New College Missionary Society, Edinburgh); 12. "Reflections on the History of Missions" (paper prepared in anticipation of San Antonio 1989); 13. "Evangelism in the Context of Secularization" (English version of 90edcs); 14. "Mission in a Pluralist Society" (English translation of 91mipg); 15. "Mission Agenda" (paper delivered in Dublin in November 1992, celebrating the centenary of the Dublin University Mission); 16. "The Ecumenical Future and the WCC: A Missionary's Dream" (91md); and 17. "Learning to Live in the Spirit in Our European Home" (given at the Congress of the Arbeitsgemeinschaft Missionarischer Arbeit, EKD, Hannover 1992).

94cc   "Confessing Christ in a Multi-Religion Society." *Scottish Bulletin of Evangelical Theology* 12 (autumn): 125-36.

94ef   "An Echo from Finland." *Gospel and Culture* (U.K.), no. 20 (spring): 6.

94lrl   "Light of the Risen Lord." *Leading Light* 1, no. 3 (March): 10.

94pmps   "Pastoral Ministry in a Pluralist Society." In *Witnessing Church*. Madras: CLS. Contribution to a Festschrift in honor of Bishop Masilamani Azariah of Madras.

94rsv   Review of *Sharing a Vision*, by Archbishop George Carey. *Theology* 97 (March-April): 132-33.

94rtkr   "Reply to Konrad Raiser." *International Bulletin of Missionary Research* 18, no. 2 (April): 51-52. See 93reit and Raiser 1994.

94tam   "Truth and Authority in Modernity." In *Faith and Modernity*, edited by Philip Sampson, Vinay Samuel, and Chris Sugden, pp. 60-88. Oxford: Regnum Books. Presentation made to a conference of the Lausanne Committee on World Evangelisation held in Uppsala, Sweden, in 1993. A portion of the essay was republished as "By What Authority?" (chap. 8) in *A Word in Season* (see 94awis). A modified and expanded version of the essay was published as *Truth and Authority in Modernity* (see 96tam).

94wavh   "W. A. Visser 't Hooft 1900-1985: 'No Other Name.'" In *Mission Legacies: Biographical Studies of Leaders of the Modern Missionary Movement*, edited by Gerald H. Anderson et al., pp. 117-22. Maryknoll, N.Y.: Orbis.

95atfs   "As the Father Sent Me." *Missionary Herald* (Baptist Missionary Society, London) (July): 127-29.

95ew   "Evangelium und Wahrheit." *Evangelium und Wissenschaft* 29 (July): 4-17. Address given at a conference organized by Albrecht Hause in July 1993.

95fer   Foreword to *Everyman Revived: The Common Sense of Michael Polanyi.* Rev. ed., by Drusilla Scott, pp. iv-v. Grand Rapids: Eerdmans.

95fra   Foreword to *Roland Allen,* by Hubert J. B. Allen, pp. xiii-xv. Cincinnati: Forward Movement Publications.

95locs   "Leading Off: A Christian Society?" *Leading Light* 2, no. 1 (winter): 4, 18.

95os   *The Open Secret: An Introduction to the Theology of Mission.* Rev. ed. London: SPCK; Grand Rapids: Eerdmans. See 78os.

95pc   *Proper Confidence: Faith, Doubt, and Certainty in Christian Discipleship.* Grand Rapids: Eerdmans.

96lpe   "Lay Presidency at the Eucharist." *Mid-Stream* 35 (April): 177-82. Reprinted in *Theology* 99 (September/October 1996): 366-70.

96mic   "Modernity in Context." In *Modern, Postmodern, and Christian,* co-authored with John Reid and David Pullinger, Lausanne Occasional Paper no. 27, LCWE, pp. 1-12. Carberry, Scotland: Handsel.

96tam   *Truth and Authority in Modernity.* Christian Mission and Modern Culture Series, edited by Alan Neely, H. Wayne Pipkin, and Wilbert R. Shenk. Valley Forge, Pa.: Trinity Press International; Herefordshire, U.K.: Gracewing. A modified and expanded version of "Truth and Authority in Modernity" (see 94tam and chap. 8 of 94awis).

97blns   "Bishop Lesslie Newbigin: Senior Statesman of the World Christian Movement." *Vocatio* (Beeson Divinity School of Samford University) 10, no. 1 (fall): 2-4. Interview conducted by William R. O'Brien and Timothy George.

97com   "Culture of Modernity." In *Dictionary of Mission: Theology, History, Perspectives,* edited by Karl Müller, Theo Sundermeier, Stephen Bevans, S.V.D., Richard Bliese, pp. 98-101. Maryknoll, N.Y.: Orbis.

97dgc   "The Dialogue of Gospel and Culture: Reflections on the Conference of World Mission and Evangelism, Salvador, Brazil." *International Bulletin of Missionary Research* 21, no. 2 (April): 50-52.

97gitg   *The Gospel in Today's Global City.* Selly Oak Colleges Occasional Paper no. 16. Birmingham, U.K.: Selly Oak Colleges. Address given on 11 May 1996 in the Chapel of Saint Andrew's Hall for the launch of the Selly Oak Colleges' School of Mission and World Christianity.

97im   "An Indian Milestone." *Tablet* 251, no. 8200 (4 October): 1273.

97tapt   "The Trinity as Public Truth." In *The Trinity in a Pluralistic Age: Theological Essays on Culture and Religion,* edited by Kevin Vanhoozer, pp. 1-8. Grand Rapids and Cambridge, U.K.: Eerdmans. Presented at the Fifth Edinburgh Dogmatics Conference on "The Trinity in a Pluralistic Age" held at Edinburgh, 31 August to 3 September 1993.

98agt   "Announcing God's Tangible and Universal Kingdom." *Auburn Report*

(Forum on Faith & Society, Australia) 10, no. 5 (October): 8-10. The second in a two-part series. See 98ewm.

98bbln   *The Best of Bishop Lesslie Newbigin from the International Bulletin of Missionary Research.* New Haven, Conn.: Overseas Ministries Study Center. Including reprints of 82ccee, 85cwbc (*IBMR* 1987), 88evcc, 89rpuj, 93reit (*IBMR* 1994), and 97dgc.

98bim   "Bishops in Mission." In *Religion in Geschichte und Gegenwart,* edited by Hans Dieter Betz, Don S. Browning, Bernd Janowski, Eberhard Juengel, p. 1623. Tübingen: J. C. B. Mohr (Paul Siebeck).

98cmsc   "Can a Modern Society Be Christian?" In *Christian Witness in Society: A Tribute to M. M. Thomas,* edited by K. C. Abraham. Bangalore: Board of Theological Education, Senate of Serampore College. The Second Annual Gospel and Culture Lecture, presented at King's College London Chapel, King's College, London, on 1 December 1995 and distributed in an undated form by Gospel and Culture (U.K.). This essay was one of two by Newbigin used as the basis for a colloquium of scholars of the neo-Calvinist, Kuyperian tradition in Leeds in 1996. The other was a transcription of an address given at Duke University Divinity School (available in audio recording, 94gps). See also Newbigin's unpublished response to the colloquium (96gapt).

98dwhm   "Does What Happened Matter?" *Australian Christian* (25 March). Reprinted in the *European Evangelist* 43, no. 2 (summer 1998): 4. (Both of these journals are affiliated with the Christian Churches/Churches of Christ.)

98ewm   "Evangelism and the Whole Mission of the Church." *Auburn Report* (Forum on Faith & Society, Australia) 10, no. 4 (August): 7-9. Lecture given by Newbigin in the Practical Theology Department at Aberdeen University in November 1981, recorded in note form by one of the students present and later reconstructed in this edited version of those notes. The first in a two-part series. See 98agt.

98fp   *Faith and Power: Christianity and Islam in "Secular" Britain.* Coauthored with Jenny Taylor and Lamin Sanneh. London: SPCK. Newbigin coauthored the preface and "The Secular Myth" and authored "A Light to the Nations: Theology in Politics."

98ftf   "Face to Face with Ultimate Reality." *Third Way* (March): 17. Conversation with Russell Rook on 14 November 1997.

98spil   *Saint Paul in Limerick.* Carlisle: Solway.

98v   "Visser 't Hooft, Willem A(dolf)." In *Biographical Dictionary of Christian Missions,* edited by Gerald H. Anderson, pp. 706-7. New York, London, et al.: Simon and Schuster Macmillan.

98vjz   "Vijfentwintig Jaar Zending." In *Pinkstervuur in de 'Secular City,'* Report of De Nederlands Zendingsraad 1996-1997, pp. 74-78. Amsterdam: Nederlandse Zendingsraad. Newbigin's part in a conversation on the occasion of Jan van Butselaar's twenty-fifth anniversary of service as general secretary of the Nederlandse Zendingsraad, recorded on 13 September 1996 at the NCRV studio in Hilversum, the Netherlands, and translated for publication by Jan van Butselaar.

99wtb   *A Walk through the Bible*, with a foreword by Sandy Millar. London: SPCK. Presentations given at Focus 1997 (24-25 July) at Holy Trinity Brompton Church in London. Available on audio recording (97bo).

B. Selected Unpublished Manuscripts

Materials listed here are limited to those deemed especially significant for Newbigin research. Unless otherwise noted, items in this section are accessible in the archival collection "Lesslie Newbigin Papers" held in care of the Orchard Learning Resources Centre, Information Services, the University of Birmingham, Hamilton Drive, Weoley Park Road, Selly Oak, Birmingham B29 6QW, U.K. Care of the archival materials is under the general direction of Dr. Clive Field, librarian and director of information services at the University of Birmingham. Initial contact for access by prospective researchers should be made with Mrs. M. Nielsen, deputy director and services manager, telephone 0121-472-7245, fax 0121-415-2273, email <m.nielsen@westhill.ac.uk>.

In addition, there are archival collections of Newbigin's papers and correspondence in Geneva and Madras. In Geneva, the collection is at World Council of Churches, Ecumenical Centre Library, 150 route de Ferney, P.O. Box 2100, 1211 Geneva 2, Switzerland, telephone (41) 22-791-6279, fax (41) 22-710-2425. In Madras, the collection is in the care of The Archivist, The Bishop Newbigin Institute for Church and Mission Studies, Whites Road, Royapettah, Madras 600014, South India.

36r "Revelation." Theology paper submitted at Westminster College, Cambridge University, in partial fulfillment of a theology degree.

41kgip "The Kingdom of God and the Idea of Progress." Handwritten manuscript of four lectures given at United Theological College, Bangalore, India. [George R. Hunsberger]

51ott "Our Task Today: A Charge to Be Given to the Fourth Meeting of the Diocesan Council, Tirumangalam, 18-20 December, 1951."

57iwia "I When I Am Lifted Up. . . ." Sermon given at the Uniting Synod of the Congregational and Evangelical and Reformed Churches, Cleveland.

58oc/n "The Organization of the Church, Mission to the World." Paper presented to the meeting of the Joint Committee of the IMC and WCC, Nyborg, 14-17 August, leading to the publication *One Body, One Gospel, One World* (58obog). Fourteen pages. [WCC Archives.]

58oc/o "The Organization of the Church: Mission to the World." Paper presented to the IMC Staff Meeting, Oxford, 16-18 September, leading to the publication *One Body, One Gospel, One World* (58obog). Seventeen pages. [WCC Archives.]

58scmt "Summons to Christian Mission Today." Address given at the council dinner, North American Advisory Committee of the IMC, 14 November. Nine pages. [WCC Archives.]

60agsp "Address Given at the Service of Preparation for Holy Communion at the S.U.M. Quadrennial Conference, Athens." [WCC Archives.]

60cbww "The Cup of Blessing Which We Bless." Sermon preached on the text 1 Corinthians 10:16-17 at Grace Cathedral, San Francisco, 9 December, at the service of Holy Communion according to the Order of the Church of South India. Four pages.

60fbos "For by One Spirit." Address based on 1 Corinthians 12:13 given at the Presbyterian General Assembly, May, Cleveland. [WCC Archives.]

60fwlb "Forgetting What Lies Behind. . . ." Sermon preached at the Riverside Church, New York City, at the fiftieth anniversary observance of the Edinburgh 1910 World Missionary Conference, 25 May. [Titled "Faith in Action" in WCC Archives.]

60mcan "Mission of the Church to All the Nations." Address given at the NCC[CUSA] General Assembly, San Francisco, December 5. [WCC Archives.]

60npes "Notes on the 'Project of an Ecumenical Statement on the Nature and Basis of Religious Liberty.'" [WCC Archives.]

61ftd "First Tentative Draft of a Paper to Follow the IMC Paper 'One Body, One Gospel, One World.'" [WCC Archives.]

61pmmc "The Pattern of Ministry in a Missionary Church." Eleven pages. [WCC Archives.]

62mep "Missions in an Ecumenical Perspective." [WCC Archives.]

62mtg "The Mission of the Triune God." [WCC Archives.]

62uof "Unfaith and Other Faiths." Address delivered to the Twelfth Annual Assembly of the Division of Foreign Missions, NCCCUSA. Eight pages. [WCC Archives.]

63jamc "Jesus the Servant and Man's Community." Address given at a Congress of the Student Christian Movement.

63rsca "Rapid Social Change and Evangelism." Manuscript. Approximate date.

63wc "World Christianity: Result of the Missionary Expansion." Address given at Biblical Seminary, New York City. Approximate date.

64snc "Le Scandale des Non-Chrétiens." Four pages. [WCC Ecumenical Centre Library.]

70smd "Stewardship, Mission and Development." Address given at the Annual Stewardship Conference of the British Council of Churches, Stanwick, June.

73ck "The Church and the Kingdom." Manuscript written in response to a letter by Paul Löffler (dated "30 January 1973") encouraging further debate between Lesslie Newbigin and M. M. Thomas. The paper bears the date "July 1972," but it must certainly have been written in July 1973, responding as it does to Löffler's letter. A January 1972 date is impossible to conjecture for Löffler's letter since it refers to the March 1972 issue of *Religion and Society.*

76bsr8 "Bible Study on Romans 8." Bible study given at the Conference on "Church in the Inner City" held in Birmingham, U.K., September.

78eqfu "Episcopacy and the Quest for Unity." Notes of a contribution to a discussion at the Annual Conference of CCLEPE and Ecumenical Officers at Swanwick, September.

79pals "Presiding at the Lord's Supper." Manuscript written as a contribution to the discussion within the United Reformed Church regarding "the presidency at the Lord's Supper of members other than those ordained."

82m "Ministry." Address given at a conference in Croydon. Approximate date.

82urcm "URC Mission and Other Faiths Committee." A two-page essay critiquing "progressively liberal capitalism."

83ckc "Christ, Kingdom, and Church: A Reflection on the Papers of George Yule and Andrew Kirk." Approximate date.

83hswu "How Should We Understand Sacraments and Ministry?" Manuscript written for a consultation jointly mandated by the Anglican Consultative Council and the World Alliance of Reformed Churches, London, January.

85bpso "Background Paper for the Selly Oak Colleges' Staff." Two-page letter written for background information to those members of staff of the Selly Oak Colleges with regard to discussing a possible program outlined in Newbigin's book *The Other Side of 1984.* Recipients of the letter include: David Tennant, Grance Trenchard, Brian Wicker, Marius Felderhoff, Robert Wetzel, Marcella Hoesl, Maurice Sinclair, Dan Beeby, Martin Conway, and John Sargent.

85cfsw "Christian Faith in a Secularized World." Eight-page manuscript written ca. 1985 (as best determined from statements within the text).

85gpow "'Going Public' Operates with. . . ." Notes following an exchange of correspondence with Rev. Peter Wright about *Going Public: A Report on Ministry of Full-Time Chaplains in Polytechnics* (London: National Standing Committee of Polytechnic Chaplains). Also see 85rgp.

85rboc "The Role of the Bible in Our Church." Remarks given at a meeting of the Forward Policy Group of the United Reformed Church, 17-18 April.

85rgp "Re 'Going Public.'" Letter to Rev. Peter Wright regarding *Going Public: A Report on Ministry of Full-Time Chaplains in Polytechnics* (London: National Standing Committee of Polytechnic Chaplains). Also see 85gpow.

85rnwc Review of *A New World Coming,* by Andrew Kirk. Unpublished draft.

86eafm "England as a Foreign Mission Field." Reproduced text of an address given at the Assembly of the Birmingham Council of Christian Churches, March 10.

86olp "One of the Loveliest of the Psalms. . . ." Address given on the BBC.

86wiea "What Is the Ecumenical Agenda?" Two-page response to a letter from

Thaddeus Horgan, managing editor of *Ecumenical Trends,* asking Newbigin to write on this topic. Horgan had asked thirty persons each to write a four hundred word essay on this same theme for possible publication.

88hfff   "Human Flourishing in Faith, Fact and Fantasy." Paper presented to the Churches' Council on Health and Healing in Swanwick, U.K., in summer.

89dpa   "Discussion Paper on Authority." A working paper for the Gospel and Our Culture's discussion group on 4 September, meeting at Saint Andrew's Hall, Selly Oak, Birmingham, U.K. The paper discusses what Newbigin developed more fully in *The Gospel in a Pluralist Society* (89gps). It was later published in edited and sometimes considerably expanded form in several places. See 94awis (chap. 8 entitled "By What Authority?"), 94tam, and especially 96tam.

89os90   "The Other Side of 1990." A presentation at Clare College, Cambridge University. No date given, but likely 1989. Deuteronomy 26:1-11 and Hebrews 11:29–12:2 were the given texts.

89pcre   "The Place of Christianity in Religious Education." Paper written and presented in March 1989 in relation to the passage into law of the Education Reform Act (1988).

89uapv   "Unfinished Agenda: A Personal View of the Past, Present, and Future of Christian Mission." Nineteen-page working script of a BBC program in 1989 with contributions from John Hick, Kosuke Koyama, Kwame Bediako, Raymond Fung, Roger Hooker, and Hassan D'Qani Tafti. Available in audio recording (89uaav and 89uakp).

90fr   "First Reflections on the High Leigh Conference." Two-page critique of the first Gospel and Our Culture Conference at High Leigh Conference Centre, Hoddesdon, Hertfordshire, 15-17 October 1990. The conference on the theme "Mission to Our Culture in the Light of Scripture and the Christian Tradition" was the first of two regional conferences (three were originally planned) sponsored jointly by the Gospel and Our Culture and the British and Foreign Bible Society leading up to "The Gospel as Public Truth" National Consultation at Swanwick, U.K., in July 1992.

90rbh   "Response to L. A. (Bert) Hoedemaker." Manuscript written in response to an essay by Hoedemaker entitled "Enlightenment, Eclipse and the Problem of Western Christianity: Towards a Discussion with Lesslie Newbigin" (1990) in preparation for a conference in Oegstgeest, Holland, the Netherlands, at the Mission Training House, 23 November 1990. The essay and response were two of four papers used as the basis for discussion at the conference.

90rggd   "Response to G. G. de Kruijf." Manuscript written in response to an essay by de Kruijf entitled "The Christian Mission in the West" (1990) in preparation for a conference in Oegstgeest, Holland, the Netherlands, at the

Mission Training House, 23 November 1990. The essay and response were two of four papers used as the basis for discussion at the conference.

90witc   "What Is the Culture?" Address at the first regional conference jointly sponsored by the Gospel and Our Culture and the British and Foreign Bible Society, on the theme "Mission to Our Culture in the Light of Scripture and the Christian Tradition," held at High Leigh Conference Centre, Hoddesdon, Hertfordshire, 15-17 October 1990. Included in the conference booklet along with transcripts of other addresses by Donald English, Hugh Montefiore, Tom Houston, and Tom Smail.

91bafs   "Blasphemy and the Free Society." Six-page essay ca. 1991 focusing on the controversy surrounding the publication of Salman Rushdie's *The Satanic Verses*.

91bgn   "The Bible: Good News for Secularised People." Keynote address during the Europe/Middle East Regional Conference in Eisenach, Germany, in April 1991.

91m   "Missions." Five-page manuscript written ca. 1991 relating missions to homiletic theory and practice.

91patc   "Pluralism and the Church." Address presented at the second of two regional conferences jointly sponsored by the Gospel and Our Culture and the British and Foreign Bible Society, on the theme "Freedom and Truth in a Pluralist Society," held 10-12 April 1991 at the Swanwick Conference Centre. The other main speakers were David Ford, Paul Hiebert, and Andrew Walker.

91tr   "Theological Reflections on the Judgment of the U.S. Supreme Court in the Case of Edwards, Governor of Louisiana et al. versus Aguillard et al." Eight-page manuscript, ca. 1991.

93cmad   "The Christian Message." Three-page paper given by Newbigin at the annual Christmas dinner of the Indian YMCA in London in December 1993.

93gmwc   "The Gospel and Modern Western Culture." Talk given to the Swedish Missions Council.

94rcaw   "Reflections on *Creation Regained* by Albert Wolters." Two-page manuscript written as a response to Wolters's book.

94wkob   "What Kind of Britain?" Eleven-page manuscript, circulated among friends, of an address delivered in London in August 1994. Later developed into a book coauthored with Jenny Taylor and Lamin Sanneh (98fp).

95nblh   "New Birth into a Living Hope." Keynote address on the text 1 Peter 1:3 given on 28 August 1995 at the European Area Council of the World Alliance of Reformed Churches, meeting at Pollock Halls, Edinburgh, Scotland, from 28 August to 3 September 1995 on the theme "Hope and Renewal in Times of Change." The address was summarized on page 11 in *News and Views* (winter 1995) under the title "Edinburgh."

95rotb   "Reflections on the LMS/CWM Bicentennial: July 1995." Nine-page response to Konrad Raiser's keynote address on 12 July 1995 at the City Temple in London for the Bicentenary Celebrations of the London Missionary Society/Council for World Mission.

96gapt   "On the Gospel as Public Truth: Response to the Colloquium." Eleven-page response to a colloquium in Leeds in August 1996. Twenty-five scholars from the neo-Calvinist, Kuyperian tradition contributed papers for discussion, followed by Newbigin's written response. The event was organized by Mike Goheen. See also two papers by Newbigin which were used in preparation for the conference: a transcription of the audio recording 94gps, and the later published 98cmsc.

97ol   "Open Letter to All Ministers and Church Secretaries of the United Reformed Church for Action and to District Council Secretaries, Synod Clerks and the General Secretary for Information." Drafted by Newbigin, along with others, bearing their names at the bottom of the letter but bearing only his signature. A letter of protest against "Resolution 19" of the 1997 General Assembly of the United Reformed Church which, for the first time, explicitly authorized the ordination of persons in a homosexual relationship to the Ministry of Word and Sacraments. The other names appearing alongside Newbigin's are: Reverends Philip Morgan, Dan Beeby, Rose Barrett, Roger Cornish, Robert Courtney, Charles Croll, Alan Dunstone, Simon Ellis, John Hall, David and Mia Hilborn, Andrew Mills, Roger Scopes, Chris Vivian, Sally Willett, and Roger Whitehead.

C. Selected Audio and Video Materials

This section identifies audio and video recordings that are known to be generally accessible, either from the group or institution that made the recording or from some library or repository that makes it available. In most cases the source for procuring them is indicated in the reference. Repositories mentioned more than once are more fully identified here so that all the details need not be repeated for each reference.

Beardslee Library. Western Theological Seminary, Holland, Mich., U.S.A.
Christian Institute Tape Catalog, Newcastle-upon-Tyne, U.K.
Holy Trinity Brompton Teaching Tape Catalogue 97-98. Holy Trinity Brompton Church, Brompton Road, London, U.K.
The Reigner Recording Library. Union Theological Seminary, Richmond, Va., U.S.A.

54dv   *The Day of Victory.* Audio recording of a CBS *Church of the Air* radio program, on the text 2 Timothy 1:12. The Reigner Recording Library.

54flh   *Faith, Love, and Hope in the Life of the Church.* Audio recording of a sermon given at Seabury-Western Theological Seminary in Evanston, Ill., on 29 August 1954. The Reigner Recording Library.

54lhlu   *The Lord Is High and Lifted Up.* Audio recording of a sermon given at First Methodist Church in Evanston, Ill., on 29 August 1954, on the texts Isaiah 6 and Mark 13:3-13. The Reigner Recording Library.

54msa   *The Message of the Second Assembly.* Audio recording of Newbigin's address given at the Second Assembly of the World Council of Churches in Evanston, Ill., on 30 August 1954. The Reigner Recording Library.

57wcsi   *Work of the Church in South India.* Audio recording of an address given at Franklin Street Presbyterian Church in Baltimore on 14 July 1957. The Reigner Recording Library.

58sm5   *Sermon on Mark 5:27.* Audio recording of a sermon given as a radio broadcast by the BBC from the Flowerhill Parish Church in Airdrie, Scotland, in December 1958. The Reigner Recording Library.

60cle   *A Christian Life of Expectation.* Audio recording of a sermon given at Palo Alto, Calif., on 4 December 1960, on the text Matthew 24:9-14. The Reigner Recording Library.

60mpv   [*Missions: Their Purpose and Value.*] (Title devised by cataloguer.) Audio recording of an address at a popular meeting of the 1960 General Assembly of the United Presbyterian Church in the U.S.A., held 24 May 1960, 8:00 P.M., at the Public Music Hall, Cleveland. Presbyterian Historical Society, Presbyterian Church (USA), Philadelphia.

61mcwc   *The Mission and Calling of the World Council [of Churches].* Audio re-
          cording of an address by Newbigin ("The Missionary Dimension of the
          Ecumenical Movement") and an address by W. A. Visser 't Hooft ("The
          Calling of the World Council of Churches"), both given at the Third As-
          sembly of the World Council of Churches in New Delhi, India, on 19 No-
          vember 1961. The Reigner Recording Library. (Published as 62mdem.)

61mu   *Mission and Unity.* New York: Broadcasting & Film Commission, Na-
          tional Council of the Churches of Christ in the U.S.A. Audio recording
          of a radio program featuring Newbigin and W. A. Visser 't Hooft, with
          James W. Kennedy hosting, recorded in New York on 10 December 1961
          as a part of the Pilgrimage Series (No. 11). The Reigner Recording
          Library.

64se   *Study of Ephesians.* Atlanta: Sermons & Pictures Cassettes. Audio record-
          ing (on a set of five cassettes) of a series of Bible studies given at
          Montreat, N.C., that focuses on various themes: cosmic dimensions of
          the mission of the church, the unity and solidarity we can find in Christ,
          the Bible as the basis for the catholicity of the church, and both the unity
          and variety within the body of Christ. The Reigner Recording Library.

66fc   *The Finality of Christ.* New Haven, Conn.: Paul Vieth Christian Educa-
          tion Service, Yale Divinity School. Audio recording of the third of four
          Lyman Beecher Lectures at Yale University Divinity School given in April
          1966. The Reigner Recording Library. (See 69fc.)

84pcmp   *Post-Enlightenment Culture as a Missiological Problem: Can the West Be
          Converted?* Princeton: Princeton Theological Seminary. Audio recording
          (on six audio cassettes) of the Warfield Lectures given 19-22 March 1984.
          The titles of the lectures were: (1) "The Theory of Cross-Cultural Mis-
          sion and the Ideology of Pluralism"; (2) "Profile of a Culture: The In-
          ward and Outward Forms of Modernity"; (3) "Foolishness to the Greek:
          How Shall the Word be Heard?"; (4) "How Can We Know? The Scientific
          Frontier"; (5) "What Is to Be Done? The Political Frontier"; and
          (6) "Who Is Sufficient? The Call to the Church." Princeton Theological
          Seminary. (Published as 86fg.)

86gmc   *Global Mission of the Church.* Audio recording (on five cassettes) of a se-
          ries of five addresses at the Global Mission Conference at Montreat,
          N.C., 21-25 July 1986. The titles of the addresses were: (1) "In the Power
          of the Spirit"; (2) "Under the Sign of the Cross"; (3) "Discipling the Na-
          tions"; (4) "The Modern World as a Foreign Mission Field"; and
          (5) "From Idols to the Living God." The Reigner Recording Library.

89cw   *Concluding Worship.* Audio recording of a sermon given by Newbigin in
          Philadelphia at the "Continue the Journey Symposium" sponsored by
          the Bicentennial Committee, Presbyterian Church (U.S.A.) on 4 June
          1989, on the text John 13:36–14:6. The Reigner Recording Library.

89uaav   *Unfinished Agenda 1: Angry Voices.* Audio recording of an autobiographi-

289

cal presentation (given in Edinburgh) on a BBC Wales Radio 4 program on 12 March 1989. (See also the unpublished working script 89uapv.)

89uakf   *Unfinished Agenda 2: Keeping Faith.* Audio recording of an autobiographical presentation (given in Edinburgh) on a BBC Wales Radio 4 program on 19 March 1989. (See also the unpublished working script 89uapv.)

90ch/r   *Come Holy Spirit — Renew the Whole Creation.* Audio recording of a lecture given on 12 July 1990 to the Ecumenical Summer School at Saint Andrew's Hall, Selly Oak Colleges, on a theme chosen to coincide with the theme of the Seventh Assembly of the World Council of Churches. (Published as 90chs.)

90lfmc   *Leadership Formation for Missionary Congregations.* Audio recording of addresses to a joint meeting of the Board for Theological Education and the General Program Council of the Reformed Church in America and the Western Theological Seminary Faculty on 1 November 1990 in Holland, Mich., on the subthemes "The Missionary Congregation as Hermeneutic of the Gospel" and "Preparing Pastoral Leadership for Missionary Congregations." Beardslee Library.

90me/a   *Missionary Encounter of the Gospel with Our Western Culture.* Audio recording (on four audiocassettes) of the Osterhaven Lectures given at Western Theological Seminary in Holland, Mich., on 30-31 October 1990. The titles for the three lectures were: (1) "Believing and Knowing the Truth"; (2) "Affirming the Truth in the Church"; and (3) "Speaking the Truth to Caesar." A fourth cassette contains "Discussion and Questions." Beardslee Library. (Published as 91tt.)

90me/v   *Missionary Encounter of the Gospel with Our Western Culture.* Video recording (on three videocassettes) of the Osterhaven Lectures given at Western Theological Seminary in Holland, Mich., on 30-31 October 1990. The titles for the three lectures were: (1) "Believing and Knowing the Truth"; (2) "Affirming the Truth in the Church"; and (3) "Speaking the Truth to Caesar." Beardslee Library. (Published as 91tt.)

90wic   *What Is the Culture?* London: Catholic Missionary Education Centre. Audio recording of a lecture, with questions, answers, and comments, given at the High Leigh Consultation on "The Gospel and Our Culture" in October 1990.

91tt/a   *Think Tank.* Michigan City, Ind.: SWA. Audio recording of addresses given at an event sponsored by the Christian College Coalition on 7-9 June 1991, based on themes from the book *The Gospel in a Pluralist Society* (89gps). King College, Bristol, Tenn.

92gp/a   *The Gospel as Public Truth: Swanwick Opening Statement.* Audio recording of the opening address at the National Consultation of the Gospel and Our Culture entitled "The Gospel as Public Truth," held on 11-17

July 1992 at the Hayes, Swanwick, U.K. Reelife Recordings (Lancaster, Lancastershire, U.K.) No. GPT01. (Published as 92gpts.)

92ings   *It's No Good Shouting.* Thirty-minute video production forming the basis for a course for churches, groups, and individuals produced for the Gospel and Our Culture program. The video features Lamin Sanneh, George Carey, Frank Field, Jane Collier, Jeremy Begbie, Lawrence Osborn, Andrew Mawson, and others in addition to Newbigin, and contains highlights of "The Gospel as Public Truth" Consultation held in Swanwick, 11-17 July 1992.

94cfaw   *Christian Faith among World Religions.* Audio recording of a Bible School lesson given on 24 November 1994 at Holy Trinity Brompton Church. *Holy Trinity Brompton* Tape 76.

94cfws   *Christian Faith in the World of Science.* Audio recording of a Bible School lesson given on 10 November 1994 at Holy Trinity Brompton Church. *Holy Trinity Brompton* Tape 77.

94ght   *God the Holy Trinity.* Audio recording of a Bible School lesson given on 29 September 1994 at Holy Trinity Brompton Church. *Holy Trinity Brompton* Tape 78.

94gpsa   *The Gospel in the Public Square.* Audio recording of a Bible School lesson given on 8 December 1994 at Holy Trinity Brompton Church. *Holy Trinity Brompton* Tape 80.

94gpsb   *The Gospel in the Public Square* (Lectures I, II, and III). Audio recording (on three cassettes) of the Hickman Lectures given at the Convocation and Pastors School of the Duke University Divinity School on 24-26 October 1994. The third lecture was transcribed by George Vandervelde under the title "What Kind of Society?" for use as one of two papers by Newbigin to be discussed at the 1996 Leeds Consultation of scholars from the neo-Calvinist tradition (see 98cmsc and 96gapt). Duke University Divinity School Library, Duke University, Durham, N.C.

94gpt   *The Gospel as Public Truth.* Audio recording of an address given on 29 July 1994 at Holy Trinity Brompton Church. *Holy Trinity Brompton* Tape 224.

94jis   *Jesus the Incarnate Son.* Audio recording of a Bible School lesson given on 13 October 1994 at Holy Trinity Brompton Church. *Holy Trinity Brompton* Tape 79.

94lths   *Life Together in the Holy Spirit.* Audio recording of a Bible School lesson given on 27 October 1994 at Holy Trinity Brompton Church. *Holy Trinity Brompton* Tape 87.

94ret   *Renewal in the End Times.* Audio recording of a Bible School lesson given on 28 July 1994 at Holy Trinity Brompton Church. *Holy Trinity Brompton* Tape 240.

95astr   *Authority: Scripture, Tradition, Reason, Experience.* Audio recording of a

Bible School lesson given on 11 May 1995 at Holy Trinity Brompton Church. *Holy Trinity Brompton* Tape 94.

95coha   *The Church: One, Holy, Apostolic.* Audio recording of a Bible School lesson given on 1 June 1995 at Holy Trinity Brompton Church. *Holy Trinity Brompton* Tape 98.

95ctvi   *Creation: Things Visible and Invisible.* Audio recording of a Bible School lesson given on 18 May 1995 at Holy Trinity Brompton Church. *Holy Trinity Brompton* Tape 95.

95cuu   *Christ, Unique and Universal: Private Faith or Public Truth?* Audio recording of an address given as part of the "Evening Meeting" series. (No date given; estimated 1995.) *Christian Institute Tape Catalog*, tape EV3.

95fsra   *Fall, Sin, Redemption, Atonement, Justification.* Audio recording of a Bible School lesson given on 25 May 1995 at Holy Trinity Brompton Church. *Holy Trinity Brompton* Tape 96.

95gc   *Gospel and Culture.* Audio recording of an address given to a conference organized by the Danish Missions Council and the Danish Churches Ecumenical Council in Denmark on 3 November 1995.

95hdwk   *How Do We Know?* Audio recording of a Bible School lesson given on 5 May 1995 at Holy Trinity Brompton Church. *Holy Trinity Brompton* Tape 97.

95jfd   *Jesus' Farewell Discourse.* Audio recordings (on seven cassettes) of a series of Bible School lessons given at the autumn 1995 Bible School, October through December, at Holy Trinity Brompton Church on John 13–17. The series includes *Holy Trinity Brompton* Tapes 81 ("Introduction to John's Gospel," John 13:1-35 given on 2 October), 82 (John 13:36–14:31 on 16 October), 84 [*sic*] (John 15:1-17 on 30 October), 83 [*sic*] (John 15:18-21 on 13 November), 85 (John 16:16–17:19 on 28 November), 86 (John 17:13-26 on 11 December), and 87 ("Life Together in the Holy Spirit" given a year before, see 94lths).

95ltkg   *The Last Things: The Kingdom of God.* Audio recording of a Bible School lesson given on 8 June 1995 at Holy Trinity Brompton Church. *Holy Trinity Brompton* Tape 99.

95lwme   *LCA World Mission Event.* Audio recordings (on a set of four cassettes) of the addresses given at the 1975 Lutheran Church in America World Mission Event by Newbigin and David L. Vikner. Newbigin's addresses were entitled "World Mission in the Church," "The Gospel and the Religions," and "Mission as Liberation." The recordings also include Newbigin's "Response" following "An Evening with the Missionaries."

95n   *Nihilism.* Audio recording of an address that was part of the "Autumn Lectures: Modern Isms" series. *Christian Institute Tape Catalog*, tape MI3.

95r   *Romans.* Audio recording (on six cassettes) of a series of Bible study lessons given 17 January through 30 March 1995 at Holy Trinity Brompton Church. *Holy Trinity Brompton* Tapes 106-11.

95wswb   *Where Shall Wisdom Be Found?* Audio recording of a Bible School lesson given on 6 August 1995 at Holy Trinity Brompton Church. *Holy Trinity Brompton* Tape 425.

96ip   *Individual Prayer.* Audio recording of an address given sometime before Easter 1996 at Holy Trinity Brompton Church. *Holy Trinity Brompton* Tape 411.

96ms   *Mission Sunday.* Audio recording of an address given on 12 May 1996 at Holy Trinity Brompton Church on the texts Acts 1:1-11 and John 15. *Holy Trinity Brompton* Tape 1218.

96sl   *The Sovereign Lord.* Audio recording of an address given on 8 December 1996 at Holy Trinity Brompton Church. *Holy Trinity Brompton* Tape 423.

96swc   *Seven Words of the Cross.* Audio recording of a presentation given on Good Friday 1996 at Holy Trinity Brompton Church. *Holy Trinity Brompton* Tape 421.

97bo   *Bible Overview.* Audio recording (on two cassettes) of presentations given at Focus 1997 on 24-25 July at Holy Trinity Brompton Church. *Holy Trinity Brompton* Tapes 1080-81. Published as 99wtb.

97bow   *Building on the Word: III. Moses and IV. Jeremiah.* Audio recording (on two cassettes) of presentations given with Sandy Millar and Simon Downham at Focus 1997 on 23-24 July at Holy Trinity Brompton Church. *Holy Trinity Brompton* Tapes 1067-1068.

97tgps   *The Gospel in a Pluralist Society.* Audio recording (on two cassettes) of a "Missionary Sermon" and an "Afternoon Lecture" on the theme, both presented on 24 June 1997 at the Beeson Divinity Chapel of Samford University in Birmingham, Ala. Beeson Divinity School Media Center tapes CA-1480 and CA-1481.

97lnth   *Lesslie Newbigin (1909-1998): Two of His Last Messages.* Video recording (on one cassette) of a "Missionary Sermon" and an "Afternoon Lecture," both presented on 24 June 1997 at the Beeson Divinity Chapel at Samford University in Birmingham, Ala. Beeson Divinity School Media Center. See 97gps.

97mcsb   *Mission and Culture: Shaped by a Book.* Audio recording (on two cassettes) of messages (Parts One and Two) given on 6 October 1997 at Hothorpe Hall, Leicestershire, England, for the Fellowship of Churches of Christ of Great Britain and Ireland LINK Conference, the theme of which was "On the Move? AD 2000+."

97sigj   *South Indian Golden Jubilee.* A six-minute prerecorded message for the service of Holy Communion, played in Newbigin's absence as his participation in the 26-28 September 1997 celebration by the Church of South India of its golden jubilee. The celebration was held in Madras on the theme "Unite, Liberate, Celebrate." (Newbigin was the only one of the original Church of South India bishops still alive.) See Webster 1998.

D. Published Reviews of Newbigin's Books

48rc   *The Reunion of the Church: A Defence of the South India Scheme*

Douglas, H. P. *Theology Today* 6 (January 1950): 576-58.
Mathews, James K. *Religion in Life* 18, no. 4 (autumn 1949): 619-20.
Nichols, James Hastings. *Journal of Religion* 30 (1950): 294-96.
Wedel, Theodore O. *International Review of Missions* 38 (1949): 100-102.
Yochum, R. *Lutheran Quarterly* 2 (February 1950): 102-3.

51sid   *South India Diary* (Swedish edition: *Sydindisk Dagbok*)

Estborn, Sigfrid. *Svensk Missionstidskrift* 52 (1964): 55-57.

51sid   *South India Diary* (American edition: *That All May Be One*)

Barclay, W. *Expository Times* 62 (1951): 383-84.
Nelson, J. Robert. *International Review of Missions* 41 (1952): 418.

53hg   *The Household of God*

Bishop of Derby. *Scottish Journal of Theology* 7 (March 1954): 99-104.
Fagerberg, H. "Institution and Spirit: New Works on the Church." *Ecumenical Review* 7 (1954-55): 196-200.
Fernell, William O. *International Review of Missions* 43 (1954): 336-38.
Huxtable, J. *Congregational Quarterly* 32 (April 1954): 176.
Leiper, Henry S. *Religion in Life* 23, no. 2 (September 1954): 316-17.
Peter, J. F. *Reformed Theological Review* 13 (June 1954): 59.
Price, T. D. *Review and Expositor* 52 (January 1955): 101-3.

53hg   *The Household of God* (French edition: *L'Eglise, Peuples des Croyants, Corps du Christ, Temple de l'Esprit*)

Thils, Gustave. *Ephemerides Theologicae Lovanienses* 39 (1963): 159-60.
Unsigned. *Irénikon* 33 (1960): 115.

56ss   *Sin and Salvation*

Boozer, J. *Journal of Bible and Religion* 25 (October 1957): 388.
Braun, N. H. *Japan Christian Quarterly* 24 (April 1958): 182-83.
Morgan, R. L. *Interpretation* 12 (July 1958): 362.

58obog   *One Body, One Gospel, One World*

Aske, Sigurd. *Lutheran World* 6 (1959-60): 201-3.
Hoggard, J. Clinton. *Chaplain* 16, no. 2 (April 1959): 53-54.

58obog   *One Body, One Gospel, One World* (French edition: *La Mission Mondiale de l'Eglise*)

Unsigned. *Verbum Caro* 15 (1961): 413-14.

60pp/ 60whal	*A Decisive Hour for the Christian Mission,* by Norman Goodall, J. E. Lesslie Newbigin, W. A. Visser 't Hooft, and D. T. Niles Kitagawa, D. "Toward Rethinking Missions." *Ecumenical Review* 13 (1960-61): 107-11.
60rc	*The Reunion of the Church: A Defence of the South India Scheme,* second revised edition Communauté, de Taizé. *Ecumenical Review* 13 (January 1961): 268-70. Houghton, Frank. *Churchman* 74 (April-June 1960): 129-30. Sasse, Hermann. *Reformed Theological Review* 21 (February 1962): 24-27. Sully, T. Donald. "Uniting the Ministries." *Church Quarterly Review* 162, no. 343 (April-June 1961): 210-23.
61ftow	*A Faith for This One World?* Devanandan, Paul D. *National Christian Council Review* 82 (1962): 127-28. Kirkpatrick, Dow. *Religion in Life* 31, no. 4 (autumn 1962): 651.
61ftow	*A Faith for This One World?* (French edition: *L'Universalisme de la Foi Chrétienne*) Mehl, R. *Revue d'Histoire et de Philosophie Religieuses* 45, nos. 3-4 (1965): 403-4. D.T.S. *Irénikon* 37, no. 1 (1964): 148-49. Thils, Gustave. *Ephemerides Theologicae Lovanienses* 40 (1964): 507-8.
61icd	*Is Christ Divided? A Plea for Christian Unity in a Revolutionary Age* Arndt, Elmer J. F. *Theology and Life* 5 (February 1962): 82-84. Piet, John H. *Reformed Review* 15 (March 1962): 60-61.
63rtdt	*The Relevance of Trinitarian Doctrine for Today's Mission* West, Charles C. *International Review of Missions* 53 (April 1964): 245-46.
63rtdt	*The Relevance of Trinitarian Doctrine for Today's Mission* (American edition: *Trinitarian Faith and Today's Mission*) Barksdale, J. *Japan Christian Quarterly* 31 (April 1965): 129-30. Nelson, J. Robert. *Religion in Life* 33, no. 4 (autumn 1964): 642-43.
66hrsm	*Honest Religion for Secular Man* Hay, C. *Australian Biblical Review* 14 (December 1966): 78-79. Mitton, Charles Leslie. *Expository Times* 77 (August 1966): 321-22.

Nugent, Alan H. *Religion and Society* (Bangalore) 13 (September 1966): 63-65.

Wilkinson, A. *London Quarterly and Holborn Review* 191 (October 1966): 330-31.

66hrsm   *Honest Religion for Secular Man* (French edition: *Une Religion pour um Monde Séculier*)

Queralt, Antonio. *Gregorianum* 49 (1968): 592-93.

69fc   *The Finality of Christ*

Berkhof, Hendrikus. *International Review of Mission* 59 (January 1970): 94-95.

72jij   *Journey into Joy*

John, Mathew P. *National Christian Council Review* 92 (November 1972): 371.

77gs   *The Good Shepherd* (1985 edition)

Horton, William D. *Expository Times* 97, no. 8 (May 1986): 253-54.

Idle, Christopher. *Churchman* 100, no. 1 (1986): 78-79.

78cic   *Christianity in the Classroom,* by Newbigin et al.

Holm, J. *Theology* 81 (November 1978): 474-75.

78os   *The Open Secret: Sketches for a Missionary Theology*

Bartholomew, Craig. Internet address: www.uovs.ac.za/arts/phil/nuances/n-e3a.txt.

Bengson, G. A. *Trinity Seminary Review* 1, no. 2 (fall 1979): 37-39.

Branson, M. R. *Christianity Today* 24 (25 January 1980): 32.

Dahlberg, Raymond L. *Covenant Companion* (15 January 1982).

Drummond, Donald Craig. *Japan Christian Quarterly* 46, no. 3 (summer 1980): 186-88.

Goldsmith, M. *Churchman* 93, no. 4 (1979): 355-56.

Hannum, E. Louise. "Missionary Theology." *Living Church* (22 July 1979): 11-12.

Hoedemaker, B. *International Review of Mission* 68 (October 1979): 455-57.

Howard, David M. *Evangelical Missions Quarterly* 15, no. 4 (October 1979): 248-50.

Manning, Herbert E. *Presbyterian Outlook* 161, no. 42 (19 November 1979): 15.

Meyers, Kurt. *Trinity Seminary Review* (fall 1979).

Peterson, R. L. *Princeton Seminary Bulletin* 2, no. 2 (1979): 191-93.

Piet, J. H. *Reformed Review* 33 (winter 1980): 112.

Robertson, J. S. *Theology* 83 (May 1980): 220-21.

Robinson, D. W. B. *Reformed Theological Review* 38 (September-December 1979): 84-85.

Scherer, J. A. *Occasional Bulletin of Missionary Research* 4 (April 1980): 89.

Smith, N. J. *Missionalia* 7, no. 2 (August 1979): 92-93.

Tangelder, Johan D. "An Evaluation of Missiology Today." *Calvinist Contact* (1 June 1979): 16.

Wendland, E. H. *Wisconsin Lutheran Quarterly* 76, no. 2 (April 1979): 170-71.

80ykc   *Your Kingdom Come* (American edition: *Sign of the Kingdom*)

Aaseng, R. E. *Book Newsletter of Augsburg Publishing House,* no. 494 (November-December 1981).

Bauer, Arthur O. *World Encounter* (summer 1981).

Bosch, David J. *Missionalia* 10, no. 1 (April 1982): 35.

DeWaard, H. *Vox Reformata* 38 (May 1982): 53.

Hunt, George Laird. *Presbyterian Outlook* 163, no. 29 (10 August 1981): 2.

Macpherson, F. *Scottish Journal of Theology* 35, no. 5 (1982): 462-63.

Martin, Joseph M. *Journal of the American Scientific Affiliation* 35, no. 3 (September 1983): 186.

Meyer, Dale A. *Concordia Journal* (May 1982): 117.

Piet, John H. *Reformed Review* 35, no. 2 (winter 1982): 119-20.

Rowold, Henry. *Currents in Theology and Mission* 9 (October 1982): 316.

Shenk, Wilbert R. *Provident Book Finder* (January/February 1982).

Wendland, E. H. *Wisconsin Lutheran Quarterly* 79, no. 3 (summer 1982): 239.

Unsigned. *CAPS Bulletin* 7, no. 3 (1981).

82lhc   *The Light Has Come*

Atkinson, J. *Scottish Journal of Theology* 37, no. 1 (1984): 115-17.

Chilton, B. D. *Churchman* 97, no. 2 (1983): 160-61.

Dixon, Michael E. *Sharing the Practice* 6, no. 3 (May/June 1983): 17.

Klein, W. W. *Journal of the Evangelical Theological Society* 26 (December 1983): 501.

R.P.M. *Presbyterian Layman* 30, no. 6 (November/December 1997).

McAlpine, T. H. *Theological Students Fellowship Bulletin* 6, no. 2 (November-December 1982): 17.

McDonnell, Rea, S.S.N.D. *Biblical Theology Bulletin* 13 (July 1983): 101-2.

Michaels, J. R. *Christian Scholar's Review* 13, no. 1 (1984): 65-66.

Nisly, Paul W. *Provident Book Finder* (September/October 1993).

Phelan, J. E. *Covenant Quarterly* 42 (February 1984): 37-38.

Piet, J. H. *Reformed Review* 36 (spring 1983): 158-59.

Reif, Gary L. *Sharing the Practice* 22, no. 2 (1999): 24.

Sire, James W. *Bible Newsletter* (February 1983): 6.

83os84   *The Other Side of 1984: Questions for the Churches*

Allen, C. *Ching Feng* 28, nos. 2-3 (1984): 164-65.

Blochliger, M. *Neue Zeitschrift für Missionswissenschaft* 41 (1985): 311-12.

Bosch, David, *Missionalia* 12, no. 3 (November 1984): 146.

Cragg, K. *International Bulletin of Missionary Research* 8 (October 1984): 180-81.

Gawith, A. R. "The Future of the Welfare State: A Time for Pragmatism." *Crucible* (July/September 1984): 112-22.

Hafner, Hermann. *Evangelium und Wissenschaft* 29 (July 1995): 53-55.

Harvey, R. *Missionary Herald* (Baptist Missionary Society, London) (1983).

Kosmahl, H. J. *Africa Theological Journal* 13, no. 3 (1984): 206-8.

Murray, Douglas M. *Scottish Journal of Theology* 39, no. 3 (1986): 402-4.

Oxland, J. S. *Christian Statesman* (spring 1984).

Puddefoot, J. C. *Convivium* 18 (March 1984): 16-19.

Recker, R. R. *Calvin Theological Journal* 20 (November 1985): 337-38.

Selly Oak Journal, no. 2 (January 1985). A series of six responses to *The Other Side of 1984:* "Origins and On-Goings" by Philip Morgan; "A Muslim Response" by Hasan Askari; "Mediaeval University or Post-Enlightenment Academy?" by Dan Beeby; "Some Epistemological Queries" by Marius Felderhoff; "A Third World Perspective" by Patrick Kalilombe; "The Social Nature of Belief" by Ann Myler; and "Witness to a Way of Life" by Norman Solomon. The issue includes an introductory article (85hiao) and rejoinder (85rtr) by Newbigin.

Shenk, Calvin E. *Missiology* 13 (April 1985): 226-28.

Siwu, Richard A. D. *Asia Journal of Theology* 1, no. 1 (April 1987): 251-52.

Slack, K. *Christian Century* 101, no. 1 (4-11 January 1984): 6-7.

Spanner, Douglas C. *Churchman* 104, no. 4 (1990): 371-72.

Stockwell, Eugene. *CWME Letter* 27 (September 1984).

Thomas, M. M. "Mission and Modern Culture." *Ecumenical Review* 36, no. 3 (July 1984): 316-22.

Toon, P. *Christian Century* 101, no. 13 (18 April 1984): 405-7.

Vander Bent, A. J. "Christianity and Culture: An Analytical Survey of Some Approaches." *Ecumenical Review* 39, no. 2 (1987): 222-27.

Verstraelen, Frans J. *Wereld en Zending* 14, no. 4 (1985): 370-71.

Walker, Bridget. *Movement: SCM Journal* 57.

Whitehouse, W. A. "The Other Side of 1984: Out of the Ghetto." *Reform* (January 1984).

85ua   *Unfinished Agenda*

Bailey, J. Martin. *New World Outlook* (July/August 1986).

Baker, Wesley C. "A Twentieth-Century Pilgrimage." *Presbyterian Survey* 77 (March 1987): 44-45.

Cairns, David. *Life and Work* (Church of Scotland) (1986).

Dekar, Paul R. *Theodolite* 7, no. 7 (1986): 46-47.

J.M.F. *Episcopalian* (December 1986).

Fonner, Michael G. *East Asia Journal of Theology* 4, no. 2 (October 1986): 203-4.

Gensichen, Hans Werner. *Zeitschrift für Mission* 22, no. 4 (1996): 257-60.

Genzen, Gary C. *Sharing the Practice* 9, no. 3 (summer 1986): 52-53.

Gros, Jeffrey, F.S.C. *Review for Religious* 46, no. 2 (March/April 1987): 313.

Handy, Robert T. *Journal of Ecumenical Studies* 25 (spring 1988): 306-8.

Heideman, Eugene. *Church Herald* 43, no. 3 (7 February 1986): 22.

Hinson, E. Glenn. *Review and Expositor* 83, no. 4 (fall 1986): 637-38.

Hunt, George Laird. *Presbyterian Outlook* 168, no. 6 (17 February 1986): 9-10.

Jones, Tracey K., Jr. *Missiology* 14, no. 4 (October 1986): 518-19.

Kruger, H. *Ökumenische Rundschau* 35, no. 1 (1986): 126-27.

Lewicki, Roman, S.J. *Vidyajyoti* 52, no. 1 (January 1988): 63.

Long, Charles H. "Friendly Critic." *Living Church* (15 June 1986).

Maris, David L. *Reformed Review* 40, no. 3 (spring 1987): 260.

Neely, Alan. *Faith and Mission* 4, no. 1 (fall 1986): 106.

"Presbuteros" [pseud.]. *Expository Times* 97 (October 1985): 32.

Quek, Peter. *Asia Journal of Theology* 3 (April 1989): 369-71.

Rathmair, Franz. *Mission Focus* (June 1986): 30.

Ryerson, Charles A. *Theology Today* 43, no. 3 (October 1986): 459-60 and *International Bulletin of Missionary Research* 11, no. 2 (April 1987): 90.

Saayman, Willem A. *Evangelical Review of Theology* 13 (January 1989): 95-96.

Saayman, Willem A. *Missionalia* 14, no. 2 (August 1986): 111.

Sachs, William L. *Church History* 57 (September 1988): 422.

Sugeno, Frank E. *Anglican Theological Review* 69, no. 2 (April 1987): 209-11.

Walker, Susan. *Canadian Churchman* (March 1986).

Wicki, J. *Neue Zeitschrift für Missionswissenschaft* 42 (1986): 297-98.

Willson, Robert. *Saint Mark's Review* 123-24 (September-December 1985): 71-72.

Unsigned. *MARC Newsletter* (May 1986).

86fg   *Foolishness to the Greeks: The Gospel and Western Culture*

Augsburger, Myron S. *Mission Focus* (June 1987): 27.

Bailey, E. *Journal of Beliefs* (February 1987).

Benge, Chris. *Shaker* 46 (1986).

Berkhof, Hendrikus. *Soteria* 3, no. 4 (1986): 33-35.

Blaser, Klauspeter. *Revue de Théologie et de Philosophie* 119, no. 3 (1987): 414-15.

Burningham, G. *Anglican Catholic* (autumn 1986).

Cairns, D. *Life and Work* (January 1987).

Charles, E. *Christian Socialist* (winter 1986): 6.

Chinnappan, M. V. *Vidyajyoti* 52, no. 1 (January 1988): 58-59.

Cotterell, Peter. *Themelios* 12, no. 3 (April 1987): 102-3.

Davies, J. *Christian: Living for a Change* (May/June 1987): 25.

Deist, Ferdinand. *Missionalia* 14, no. 3 (November 1986): 152.

DeWaard, H. *Vox Reformata* 47 (November 1986): 63-64.

Divarkar, Parmananda R. *International Bulletin of Missionary Research* 11, no. 2 (April 1987): 80.

Easton, Esther. *Concern* (October 1986).

Eitel, Keith. *Criswell Theological Review* 4, no. 1 (fall 1989): 218-19.

Fakes, Dennis R. *Sharing the Practice* 10, no. 3 (summer 1987): 46-47.

Fountain, Ossie. *Journal* (U.K.) (1987).

Hafner, Hermann. *Evangelium und Wissenschaft* 29 (July 1995): 53-55.

Hart, Trevor. *Evangelical Quarterly* 61 (October 1989): 374-75.

Heim, David. *Christian Century* 104, no. 28 (7 October 1987): 864-65.

Kritzinger, J. J. *Skrif en Kerk* 9, no. 2 (1988): 230-32.

Landwehr, Arthur J. *Circuit Rider* (April 1987).

Miller, Jim. *Africa Journal of Evangelical Theology* 9, no. 2 (1990): 42-45.

Murray-Rust, David. "Mission to Our Own Culture." *Friend* 144, no. 43 (October 1986): 1369-70.

Olney, Fred. *Christian Arena* (September 1987): 21.

Oosterwal, Gottfried. *Missiology* 15, no. 2 (April 1987): 98-99.

Pallmeyer, Paul. *Book Newsletter of Augsburg Publishing House*, no. 526 (March-April 1987): 6-7.

Piet, John H. *Reformed Review* 40, no. 2 (winter 1987): 164-65.

Platten, Stephen. *Theology* 90 (May 1987): 222-23.

Richardson, P. *Reader* (August 1987).

Rodd, C. S. *Expository Times* 98, no. 3 (December 1986): 65-66.

Schwarz, Brian, H. *Lutheran Theological Journal* 21 (December 1987): 153-55.

Schwarz, W. *Guardian* 27, no. 10 (1986).

Shannon, Harper. *Alabama Baptist* (1 September 1988).

Spanner, Douglas. *Churchman* 103, no. 2 (1989): 169-70.

Stafford, Tim. "Bringing the Gospel Back Home." *Christianity Today* 30, no. 13 (19 September 1986): 57-58.

Suurmond, J. J. *Bijdragen: Tijdschrift voor Philosophie en Theologie* 51 (1990): 210.

Thomson, Alexander. *Scottish Journal of Theology* 41, no. 4 (1988): 541-43.

Wadsworth, K. *Reform* (January 1987): 23.

Walker, D. F. *Asia Journal of Theology* 1 (October 1987): 563-64.

Watson, David Lowes. *Journal of the Academy for Evangelism in Theological Education* 2 (1986-87): 91.

Weld, Wayne. *Covenant Quarterly* 45, no. 3 (August 1987): 152.

Williams, Stephen. *Scottish Bulletin of Evangelical Theology* 7 (spring 1989): 54-55.

Unsigned. *Expository Times* 98 (December 1986): 65-66.

Unsigned. *Pacific Theological Review* 21, no. 2 (spring 1988).

Unsigned. *Theological Educator* 54 (fall 1996): 137.

Unsigned. *This World* 24 (winter 1989): 150-51.

86fg   **Foolishness to the Greeks: The Gospel and Western Culture** (German edition: *Den Griechen eine Torheit: Das Evangelium und Unsene Westliche Kultur*)

Weiss, Thomas. *Ökumenische Rundschau* 41 (January 1992): 125-26.

87mcw   **Mission in Christ's Way**

Bosch, David. *Missionalia* 16, no. 1 (April 1988): 50.

Janzon, Göran. *Svensk Missionstidskrift* 77, no. 2 (1989): 51.

Rees, Paul S. *International Bulletin of Missionary Research* 13 (April 1989): 82.

Svensson, Bertil. *Svensk Missionstidskrift* 78, no. 3 (1990): 71.

89gps   **The Gospel in a Pluralist Society**

Barber, Bruce. *Pacifica: Australian Theological Studies* 3 (October 1990): 356-58.

Bauer, Louis E. *Practice* (1990).

Berends, W. *Vox Reformata* 56 (1991): 81-82.

Boisclair, Regina A. *Journal of Ecumenical Studies* 29 (spring 1992): 282-83.

Bosch, David J. *Missionalia* 19, no. 1 (April 1991): 88-89.

Chiarini, Franco. *Protestantesimo* 52 (1997): 210-11.

Clapp, Rodney. "The Blessings of Postmodernism." *Christianity Today* 35 (14 January 1991): 36-38.

D'Costa, Gavin. *Expository Times* 102 (December 1990): 90.

D'Costa, Gavin. *King's Theological Review* 13 (autumn 1990): 54-55.

Doenecke, Justus. "Distinguished Missionary." *Living Church* (29 July 1990).

Ellingworth, Paul. *Evangelical Quarterly* 63 (October 1991): 368-69.

Fackre, Gabriel. *Journal of the Academy for Evangelism in Theological Education* 7 (1991-92): 100-102.

Ford, David. *The Gospel and Our Culture* (U.K.), no. 5 (spring 1990): 4.

Forster, Peter. *Themelios* 17 (October-November 1991): 34-35.

Fountain, Ossie. *CBRF Journal* 124 (March 1991): 38-39.

Gill, Kevin. "A Critical Review of *The Gospel in a Pluralist Society* by Lesslie Newbigin." *Ratio* (spring 1993).

Gilmore, Alec. *Theological Book Review* 2, no. 2 (January 1990): 20.

Girardet, Giorgio. *Protestantesimo* 45, no. 3 (1990): 233-34.

Greenfield, Guy. *Southwestern Journal of Theology* 33, no. 3 (summer 1991): 51.

Hedlund, Roger E. *Evangelical Review of Theology* 15 (April 1991): 180-81.

Henry, Paul. *Mission and Ministry* 8 (winter 1991): 19-23.

Hertzler, Daniel. *Gospel Herald* (10 July 1990).

Hertzler, Daniel. *En Christo* 4 (January 1991): 20-21. (Spanish translation of review in *Gospel Herald*, 10 July 1990.)

Lewicki, Roman, S.J. *Vidyajyoti* 59, no. 5 (May 1995): 345-46.

Lewis, Christopher. *Theology* 93 (September-October 1990): 395-96.

Lindbeck, George. *International Bulletin of Missionary Research* 14 (October 1990): 182.

McKaughan, Larry. *Disciple* (September 1992): 28-29.

Miller, Jim. *Africa Journal of Evangelical Theology* 9, no. 2 (1990): 42-45.

Mullins, Mark R. *Japan Christian Quarterly* 56, no. 4 (fall 1990): 249-50.

Nussbaum, Stan. *Gospel and Our Culture* (U.K.), no. 4 (winter 1990): 4.

Percell, Emery A. *Quarterly Review* 10 (winter 1990): 97-103.

Phillips, Timothy. *Evangelical Missions Quarterly* 27 (April 1991): 207-9.

Poitras, Edward W. *Perkins Journal* 43 (July-October 1990): 45-46.

Rajashekar, J. Paul. *International Review of Mission* 80 (January 1991): 130-32.

Ray, John. *Go* (Interserve, London) (April-June 1990): 15.

Rempel, Erwin. *Mennonite* 105 (10 July 1990): 310.

Sanneh, Lamin. "Particularity, Pluralism and Commitment." *Christian Century* 107 (31 January 1990): 103-8.

Skjevesland, Olav. *Luthersk Kirketidende* (21 August 1998).

Sparks, O. Benjamin, III. *Journal for Preachers* 16, no. 3 (1993): 31-33.

Stroup, George W. *Homiletic* 16, no. 1 (1991): 30-31.

Van der Merwe, Petrus Johannes. *Hervormde Teologiese Studies* 51 (March 1995): 255-56.

Watson, David Lowes. *Journal of the Academy for Evangelism in Theological Education* 5 (1989-90): 93.

Weber, Philippe. *Revue Théologique de Louvain* 22, no. 3 (1991): 423.

Weld, Wayne C. *Covenant Quarterly* 49 (fall 1991): 47-48.

Weld, Wayne C. *Covenant Quarterly* (February 1998): 35-38.
White, James J. *Lutheran Partners* (March/April 1991): 51.
Wolanin, Adam. *Gregorianum* 78, no. 1 (1997): 173-74.
Won Yong, Ji. *Concordia Journal* 16 (July 1990): 283-84.
Unsigned. *Advance* (April 1991).
Unsigned. *Polis* (June 1990).

91tt   *Truth to Tell: The Gospel as Public Truth*

Allen, C. Leonard. *Restoration Quarterly* 34, no. 2 (1992): 127.
Bailey, Raymond. *Review and Expositor* 89 (fall 1992): 585.
Baldner, Steven. *Canadian Catholic Review* (February 1993): 26-28.
Braaten, Carl E. *Lutheran Forum* 27 (November 1993): 53-54.
Briggs, John H. Y. *Baptist Quarterly* 34 (July 1992): 302-3.
Cogswell, James A. *Presbyterian Outlook* 174, no. 5 (10 February 1992): 9-10.
De Gruchy, John W. *Journal of Theology for Southern Africa* 81 (December 1992): 88.
Goheen, Michael W. *Pro Rege* 21, no. 3 (March 1993): 23-24.
Henderson, John M., III. *Probe Vanguard* (November/December 1991).
Hiebert, Paul G. *Evangelical Missions Quarterly* 31 (October 1995): 504-5.
Hillman, Eugene. *Religious Studies Review* 19, no. 1 (January 1993): 52.
Hunsberger, George R. *Reformed Review* 45 (winter 1991): 173; "Book Note" in *Journal of the Academy for Evangelism in Theological Education* 6 (1990-91): 89.
Kettle, David. *Stimulus* 2 (May 1994): 44-45.
Klafehn, Richard K. *Augsburg Fortress Book Newsletter* (winter 1993).
Marshall, David. *Presbyterian Record* (April 1992): 32-33.
Page, Don. *Christian Week* (Canada) (3 March 1992).
Peel, David. *Reform* (May 1992).
Rodríguez, Pedro. *Scripta Theologica* 26 (May-August 1994): 847.
Root, James P. "Religion in Review." *Herald-Times* (9 November 1991).
Rynkiewich, Michael A. *Asbury Theological Journal* 51, no. 2 (fall 1996): 120-22.
Spanner, Douglas C. *Churchman* 106, no. 4 (1992): 362-64.
Stroup, George W. *Homiletic* 17, no. 1 (1992): 28-29.
Townsend, Michael J. *Expository Times* 103 (June 1992): 284.
Watson, David Lowes. *Journal of the Academy for Evangelism in Theological Education* 6 (1990-91): 89.
Williams, John. *Anvil: An Anglican Evangelical Journal for Theology and Mission* 9, no. 3 (1992): 282-83.
Williams, Stephen. *Themelios* 18 (October 1992): 32.
Unsigned. *Vidyajyoti* 57, no. 8 (August 1993): 505-6.

93ua   *Unfinished Agenda: An Updated Autobiography*

Keskitalo, Jukka. *Teologisk Tidskrift* 102 (1997).

Sanneh, Lamin O. *International Bulletin of Missionary Research* 20 (January 1996): 36.

94awis   *A Word in Season: Perspectives on Christian World Missions*

Cracknell, Kenneth. *Expository Times* 107 (December 1995): 90-91.

Dahlberg, Raymond L. *Missiology* 24 (July 1996): 430-31.

DeWaard, H. *Vox Reformata* 61 (1996): 152-53.

Gros, Jeffrey. *Journal of Ecumenical Studies* 34 (spring 1997): 242-43.

Keskitalo, Jukka. *Teologisk Tidskrift* 102 (1997).

Kinnamon, Michael. *Lexington Theological Quarterly* 30 (summer 1995): 124-25.

Leupp, Roderick T. *Christian Librarian* (September 1996): 109-10.

Olson, Roger E. *Books and Culture* 2 (January-February 1996): 27.

Ramachandra, Vinoth. *Themelios* 22 (April 1997): 68-69.

Scherer, James A. *Lutheran Quarterly* 9 (autumn 1995): 340-41.

Stockwell, Eugene L. *International Bulletin of Missionary Research* 19 (July 1995): 128-29.

95os   *The Open Secret: An Introduction to the Theology of Mission,* revised edition

Alemany, José J. *Estudios Eclesiasticos* (Spain) 73 (1998).

Cressey, Martin. *Ecumenical Review* 49, no. 3 (July 1997): 387-88.

Editor. *Reformation and Revival* (fall 1998): 182-85.

Hexham, Irving. *Canadian Evangelical Report* 13 (fall 1996).

Holland, Grace. *Ashland Theological Journal* 30 (1998).

Keskitalo, Jukka. *Teologisk Tidskrift* 102 (1997).

Kritzinger, J. J. *Missionalia* 26, no. 2 (August 1998): 291.

Meyerink, Paul R. *Reformed Review* 49, no. 3 (spring 1996): 223-24.

95pc   *Proper Confidence: Faith, Doubt, and Certainty in Christian Discipleship*

Alemany, José J. *Estudios Eclesiasticos* (Spain) 73 (1998).

Bush, Peter. *Presbyterian Record* (May 1998): 44-45.

Cogswell, James A. *Presbyterian Outlook* 177, no. 34 (2 October 1995): 8.

Drew, Gavin. *Stimulus* 4 (February 1996): 10-11.

D.W.H. *Bookstore Journal* (June 1995).

Heim, S. Mark. *Religious Studies Review* 21, no. 4 (October 1995): 315-16.

Keskitalo, Jukka. *Teologisk Tidskrift* 102 (1997).

Lesser, R. H. *Vidyajyoti* 61, no. 8 (August 1997): 569-71.

Long, Robert. *St. Mark's Review* 163 (spring 1995): 43-44.

Olson, Roger E. *Books and Culture* 2 (January-February 1996): 27.

Osborn, Lawrence. *Theology* 99 (March-April 1996): 142-43.

Trost, Frederick R. *Princeton Seminary Bulletin* 17, no. 3 (1996): 388-90.

J.D.W. *Regent's Reviews* (U.K.) (spring 1996).

West, Charles C. *International Bulletin of Missionary Research* 19 (October 1995): 180-81.

Wright, James. *Logia* 5, no. 4 (1996): 50

Unsigned. *Editors Newsletter* (July/August/September 1995).

96tam   **Truth and Authority in Modernity**

Keskitalo, Jukka. *Teologisk Tidskrift* 102 (1997).

E. Selected Engagements with Newbigin's Thought

Aleaz, K. P. 2001. "The Globalization of Poverty and the Exploitation of the Gospel." In *A Scandalous Prophet: The Way of Mission after Newbigin,* edited by Thomas F. Foust, George R. Hunsberger, J. Andrew Kirk, and Werner Ustorf, pp. 165-73. Grand Rapids: Eerdmans.

Anastasios (Yannoulatos). 2000. "Problems and Prospects of Inter-religious Dialogue: An Eastern Orthodox Perspective." *Ecumenical Review* 52, no. 3 (July): 351-57. Written in tribute to Lesslie Newbigin.

Anderson, Gerald H. 1982. "Cross-currents in Mission." *International Bulletin of Missionary Research* 6, no. 4 (October): 145. Editorial comments on a dialogue in that issue of the journal between Newbigin (82ccee and 82lnr), Paul Schrotenboer (1982), and C. Peter Wagner (1982).

————. 1988. "Modernity and the Everlasting Gospel: Assessing the Newbigin Thesis." *International Bulletin of Missionary Research* 12, no. 4 (October): 1. Editorial comments on a dialogue in that issue of the journal involving Newbigin (88rds) in response to an article on his thought by David M. Stowe (1988), with comment on both by Charles C. West (1988).

————. 1989. "The Truth of Christian Uniqueness." *International Bulletin of Missionary Research* 13, no. 2 (April): 49. Editorial comments on essays within that issue of the journal by Newbigin (89rpuj) and Johannes Verkuyl (1989).

————. 1994. "Mission to Western Culture." *International Bulletin of Missionary Research* 18, no. 1 (January): 1. Editorial comments on essays within that issue of the journal by Newbigin (a republication of 93reit), H. Dan Beeby (1994), and Wilbert R. Shenk (1994). See also Konrad Raiser's response to Newbigin's article in the succeeding issue (Raiser 1994) and Newbigin's reply to it (94rtkr).

————. 1998. "Lesslie Newbigin, 1909-1998." *International Bulletin of Missionary Research* 22, no. 2 (April): 49.

Aydin, Mahmut. 2001. "Globalization and the Gospel: A Muslim View." In *A Scandalous Prophet: The Way of Mission after Newbigin,* edited by Thomas F. Foust, George R. Hunsberger, J. Andrew Kirk, and Werner Ustorf, pp. 174-81. Grand Rapids: Eerdmans.

Barns, Ian. 1994. "Christianity in a Pluralist Society: A Dialogue with Lesslie Newbigin." *St. Mark's Review (Canberra)* 158 (winter): 27-37.

Bassham, Rodger. 1996. Review of *Many Voices in Christian Mission: Essays in Honour of J. E. Lesslie Newbigin, World Christian Leader,* edited by Francis T. Dayanandan and Israel Selvanayagam. *Missiology* 24 (July): 403-4.

Beeby, H. Dan. 1994. "A White Man's Burden, 1994." *International Bulletin of Missionary Research* 18, no. 1 (January): 6-8. See Gerald H. Anderson (1988).

————. 1998a. "James Edward Lesslie Newbigin (1909-1998): Missionary Thinker." *Mission Studies* 15, no. 1: 10-13.

————. 1998b. "Lesslie Newbigin Remembered." *International Bulletin of Missionary*

Research 22, no. 2 (April): 52. Also published as "Lesslie Newbigin," *Gospel and Our Culture* (North America) Special Edition (1998): 2-3. An address given at Newbigin's funeral service at the Dulwich Grove United Reformed Church in London on Saturday, 7 February 1998.

———. 1998c. "The Right Reverend Lesslie Newbigin." *Independent* (England) 4 (February). Obituary.

———. 1998d. "Walking with Lesslie — A Personal Perspective." *Bible in TransMission* Special Issue: 9-10.

———. 1999. "Understanding a Giant's Theology." Review of *Bearing the Witness of the Spirit,* by George R. Hunsberger (1998b). *Evangelical Missions Quarterly* 35, no. 2 (April): 226, 228. Also published in the Gospel and Our Culture (U.K.) 25 (summer 1999): 8.

———. 2000. "No Loose Canon." *International Review of Mission* 89, no. 355 (October).

Berkhof, Hendrikus. 1985. Foreword to *Verder dan "1984": Missionaire Confrontatie met de Moderne Cultur,* by Lesslie Newbigin (83os84). Kampen: Kok.

Bevans, Stephen, S.V.D. 1999. "Living between Gospel and Context: Models for a Missional Church in North America." In *Confident Witness — Changing World: Rediscovering the Gospel in North America,* pp. 141-54. Grand Rapids: Eerdmans.

Blake, Eugene Carson. 1969. "Tribute to Bishop Lesslie Newbigin." In *Bishop Newbigin's Sixtieth Birthday Celebration Brochure.* Madras.

Bosch, David J. 1991. *Transforming Mission: Paradigm Shifts in Theology of Mission.* American Society of Missiology Series, no. 16. Maryknoll, N.Y.: Orbis.

———. 1995. *Believing in the Future: Toward a Missiology of Western Culture.* Valley Forge, Pa.: Trinity Press International.

Boyd, Robin H. S. 1990. "A Barthian Theology of Interfaith Dialogue?" *Pacifica: Australian Theological Studies* 3: 288-303.

Brattinga, Teije. 1990. "Behoefte aan een Bescheiden Zending." In Brinkman and Noordegraaf 1990, pp. 69-77.

Brink, Gijsbert van den. 1992. "Lesslie Newbigin als postmodern apologeet." *Nederlands Theologisch Tijdschrift* 46 (October): 302-19 (English abstract, p. 334).

Brinkman, Martien E. 1990. "Voorbij Newbigin?" In Brinkman and Noordegraaf 1990, pp. 111-17.

Brinkman, Martien E., and Herman Noordegraaf, eds. 1990. *Het Evangelie in het Westen: Nederlandse Reacties op Lesslie Newbigin.* Kampen: Kok.

Brown, George, Jr., George R. Hunsberger, Christopher B. Kaiser, and Craig Van Gelder. 1991. "Selected Annotated Bibliography of Missiology: The Gospel and Our Culture." *Missiology* 19, no. 4: 495-98.

Brownson, James V. 1991. "The Gospel as 'Event'?" *Gospel and Our Culture* (North America) 3, no. 2 (July): 1-3. A response to 91gpt.

———. 1998. *Speaking the Truth in Love: New Testament Resources for a Missional*

Hermeneutic. Christian Mission and Modern Culture Series. Harrisburg, Pa.: Trinity Press International.

Brueggemann, Walter. 1999. Foreword in *Journal for Preachers* 22, no. 3 (Easter): 1-2.

Bruggeman, Antonio, S.J. 1965. *The Ecclesiology of Lesslie Newbigin.* Excerpta ex Dissertatione ad Lauream in Facultate Theologica Pontificiae Universitatis Gregorianae. Ranchi, India: Pontifica Universitas Gregoriana.

Burce, Jerome Edward. 1996. "Why and Whither Zion? Discovering Churchly Purpose at a Lutheran Congregation in New England." D.Min. diss., Hartford Seminary, Hartford, Conn.

Castro, Emilio. 2000. *International Review of Mission* 89, no. 355 (October).

Cavert, Samuel McCrea. 1961. *On the Road to Christian Unity: An Appraisal of the Ecumenical Movement.* New York: Harper and Bros. Particular attention is given to chap. 4 of 53hg.

Chapman, Thomas Gregory. 1992. "A Phenomenological Method of Post-Dialogue within a World of Religious Pluralism." Ph.D. diss., Southern Baptist Theological Seminary, Louisville, Ky.

Church of England Newspaper, The. 1992. *The Gospel as Public Truth: Applying the Gospel in the Modern World.* London: CENBooks. A booklet containing a series of articles based on the Gospel and Our Culture 1992 Swanwick Consultation and published in the *Church of England Newspaper.* Newbigin wrote the introduction (92igpt). Other articles include: "Science versus Religion as the Holder of Public Truth" by Drusilla Scott; "The Global West and the Missing Categories" by H. Dan Beeby; "The Church and the Challenge of the New Age" by Lawrence Osborn; "The Idol in Every Living Room" by Iwan Russell-Jones; "The Gospel and the Arts" by Richard Russell; "The Gospel and the Market Place" by Jane Collier; and "The Gospel and the World of Politics" by E. J. Korthals Altes.

Clarke, Sundar. 1994. "A Man of Unique Combinations." In *Many Voices in Christian Mission: Essays in Honour of J. E. Lesslie Newbigin, World Christian Leader,* edited by T. Dayanandan Francis and Israel Selvanayagam, pp. 1-2. Madras: CLS.

Conway, Martin. 1994. "God-Open, World-Wide, and Jesus-True: Lesslie Newbigin's Faith Pilgrimage." *Mission Studies* 11, no. 2: 191-202. Also published in *Mid-Stream,* 34, no. 1 (1995): 21-33 and in a slightly shorter version as "Profile: Lesslie Newbigin's Faith Pilgrimage" in the *Epworth Review* 21 (1994): 27-36.

―――. 1998a. "Appreciation: Lesslie Newbigin." *Guardian* (England), 14 (February). A supplement to the obituary previously printed by the *Guardian* under the names of Conway and Christopher Driver without Conway's knowledge. See Conway and Driver 1998.

―――. 1998b. "Lesslie Newbigin." *Tablet* (England), 7 February. Obituary.

―――. 2000. "The Open Secret for the Open Society: Unity, Mission and Social Responsibility as Inescapably Inter-related Challenges." *Ecumenical Review* 52, no. 3 (July): 367-78. Written in tribute to Lesslie Newbigin.

Conway, Martin, and Christopher Driver. 1998. "Preaching the Gospel of Unity."

Guardian (England), 6 February. Obituary. This obituary was published from notes left at his death by the late Christopher Driver. The *Guardian* subsequently apologized to Martin Conway for the many mistakes and for not having contacted him before publication, and printed a retraction entitled "Corrections and Clarifications," *Guardian* (England), 7 February 1998. Later a supplemental obituary by Conway was published (Conway 1998a).

Coventry, John, S.J. 1991. "Word of God?" *Gospel and Our Culture* (U.K.) 10 (summer): 1-2. A response to 91gpt. See also Newbigin's response (91r).

Cruchley-Jones, Peter. 2001. "Entering Exile: Can There Be a Missiology for 'Not My People'?" In *A Scandalous Prophet: The Way of Mission after Newbigin*, edited by Thomas F. Foust, George R. Hunsberger, J. Andrew Kirk, and Werner Ustorf, pp. 23-36. Grand Rapids: Eerdmans.

Davidson, Gary Charles. 1996. "Where Alone Peace and Justice Embrace: A Confessional Understanding of Pluralist Society in the Thought of J. E. Lesslie Newbigin." M.Div. thesis, Emmanuel School of Religion, Johnson City, Tenn.

D'Costa, Gavin. 1986. *Theology and Religious Pluralism: The Challenge of Other Religions.* Oxford and New York: Basil Blackwell.

de Knijff, H. W. 1990. "Newbigins Reactie op de Verlichting." In Brinkman and Noordegraaf 1990, pp. 61-68.

de Kruijf, G. G. 1990. "The Christian Mission in the West." Unpublished paper in preparation for a conference at the Mission Training House in Oegstgeest in the Netherlands, 23 November 1990, to which Newbigin wrote a response (90rggd). See also L. A. (Bert) Hoedemaker 1990.

Devadhar, Sudarshana. 1987. "Stanley J. Samartha's Contribution to the Interfaith Dialogue." Ph.D. diss., Drew University, N.J.

Devanesen, Chandran D. S. 1969. "Lesslie Our Bishop." In *Bishop Newbigin's Sixtieth Birthday Celebration Brochure.* Madras.

Dewey, Margaret. 1984. "Theology as Mission: Fr. Kelly's Vision in 1984." *Society of the Sacred Mission* (England) (November): 3-4.

———. 1987. "The Gospel and Western Culture." In *Thinking Mission*, no. 53. London: United Society for the Propagation of the Gospel, January 1987. The *Thinking Mission* series selects from two journals, the *International Review of Mission* and the *Ecumenical Review*, to provide summaries of current missionary thinking.

De Wit, John. 1990. *Another Way of Looking: Helping You Challenge the Assumptions of Today's Culture.* Swindon, U.K.: Bible Society Publication. An attempt to embrace the principles of the Gospel and Our Culture Movement and utilize them to create a series of studies for members of Christian congregations. See 90f.

Dharmaraj, A. C. 1969. "My Personal Reminiscences of Bishop Lesslie Newbigin." In *Bishop Newbigin's Sixtieth Birthday Celebration Brochure.* Madras.

Doraisamy, Solomon. 1994. "A Missionary by Call, Commission and Commitment." In *Many Voices in Christian Mission: Essays in Honour of J. E. Lesslie Newbigin,*

World Christian Leader, edited by T. Dayanandan Francis and Israel Selvanayagam, pp. 5-9. Madras: CLS.

Duraisingh, Christopher. 1990. "Editorial." *International Review of Mission* 79 (January): 1-5.

Fackre, Gabriel. 1983. "The Scandals of Particularity and Universality." *Mid-Stream* 22, no. 1: 32-52.

Fleming, John. 1959. "Some Aspects of the Biblical and Theological Basis of the Christian Ministry." *South East Asia Journal of Theology* 1, no. 2: 22-34.

Flett, John, ed. 1998. *Collision Crossroads: The Intersection of Modern Western Culture with the Christian Gospel.* Auckland, New Zealand: DeepSight Trust. Including essays by John Flett, Harold Turner, Lawrence Osborn, George Hunsberger, Murray Rae, Ian Kemp, Bruce Hamill, and David Kettle.

Forrester, Duncan B. 2001. "Lesslie Newbigin as Public Theologian." In *A Scandalous Prophet: The Way of Mission after Newbigin,* edited by Thomas F. Foust, George R. Hunsberger, J. Andrew Kirk, and Werner Ustorf, pp. 3-12. Grand Rapids: Eerdmans.

Foust, Thomas F. 1998. "Lesslie Newbigin." *Bible in TransMission* Special Issue: 2. A chronology of Newbigin's life.

———. 2000. "The Missiological Approach to Modern Western Culture according to Lesslie Newbigin and Dean E. Walker." Ph.D. diss., University of Birmingham, U.K.

———. 2001. "Lesslie Newbigin's Epistemology: A Dual Discourse?" In *A Scandalous Prophet: The Way of Mission after Newbigin,* edited by Thomas F. Foust, George R. Hunsberger, J. Andrew Kirk, and Werner Ustorf, pp. 153-62. Grand Rapids: Eerdmans.

Foust, Thomas F., and George R. Hunsberger, comps. 2001. "Bishop J. E. Lesslie Newbigin: A Comprehensive Bibliography." In *A Scandalous Prophet: The Way of Mission after Newbigin,* edited by Thomas F. Foust, George R. Hunsberger, J. Andrew Kirk, and Werner Ustorf, pp. 249-325. Grand Rapids: Eerdmans.

Foust, Thomas F., George R. Hunsberger, J. Andrew Kirk, and Werner Ustorf, eds. 2001. *A Scandalous Prophet: The Way of Mission after Newbigin.* Grand Rapids: Eerdmans. Selected papers resulting from the conference "After Newbigin: A Colloquium in Honour of Lesslie Newbigin" sponsored by the School of Mission and World Christianity, the Selly Oak Colleges, and the British and Foreign Bible Society, on 2-3 November 1998.

Francis, T. Dayanandan, and Israel Selvanayagam, eds. 1994. *Many Voices in Christian Mission: Essays in Honour of J. E. Lesslie Newbigin, World Christian Leader, Presented on the Occasion of His Eighty-fifth Birthday.* Madras: CLS. The volume contains a foreword by the Most Rev. Dr. Vasant P. Dandin; tributes by Sundar Clarke, Paulos Mar Gregorios, Solomon Doraisamy, P. Victor Premasagar, John H. Piet, and S. Kulandran; articles by J. Russell Chandran, Emilio Castro, Walter J. Hollenweger, Yeow Choo-Lak, Gnana Robinson, M. Azariah, Charles A. Ryerson, Samuel Amirtham, Duncan B. Forrester, P. Victor

Premasagar, Israel Selvanayagam; and a selected bibliography compiled by Eleanor Jackson expanding on the bibliography of George R. Hunsberger (1987).

Franks, Martha. 1998. "Election, Pluralism, and the Missiology of Scripture in a Postmodern Age." *Missiology* 26, no. 3 (July): 329-43.

Gelwick, Richard. 2000-2001. "Christian Faith in a Pluralist Society." *Tradition and Discovery* (The Polanyi Society) 27, no. 2: 39-45.

Glasser, Arthur F. 1979. "Reconciliation between Ecumenical and Evangelical Theologies and Theologians of Mission." *Missionalia* 7, no. 3: 99-114.

Gnanadason, I. R. H. 1969. "Bishop Newbigin — An Appreciation." In *Bishop Newbigin's Sixtieth Birthday Celebration Brochure*. Madras.

Goheen, Michael W. 1999a. Review of *Bearing the Witness of the Spirit*, by George R. Hunsberger (1998b). *International Bulletin of Missionary Research* 23, no. 2 (April): 80.

———. 1999b. "Mission and the Public Life of Western Culture: The Kuyperian Tradition." *Gospel and Our Culture* (U.K.) 26 (autumn): 6-8.

———. 1999c. "Toward a Missiology of Western Culture." *European Journal of Theology* 8, no. 2: 155-68.

———. 2000. "As the Father Has Sent Me, I Am Sending You: Lesslie Newbigin's Missionary Ecclesiology." Ph.D. diss., University of Utrecht, the Netherlands.

———. 2001. "The Missional Calling of Believers in the World: Lesslie Newbigin's Contribution." In *A Scandalous Prophet: The Way of Mission after Newbigin*, edited by Thomas F. Foust, George R. Hunsberger, J. Andrew Kirk, and Werner Ustorf, pp. 37-54. Grand Rapids: Eerdmans.

Gorringe, Timothy. 1998. "The Right Reverend Lesslie Newbigin." *Church Times* (England), 6 February.

Graham, Elaine, and Heather Walton. 1991. "A Walk on the Wild Side: A Critique of the Gospel and Our Culture." *Modern Churchman* 33, no. 1: 1-7. See 92goc for Newbigin's response. A response to all three is offered by John Reader (1993).

Greene, Colin J. D. 1998. "Lesslie Newbigin — A Bible Society Perspective." *Bible in TransMission* Special Issue: 14-15.

———. 2001. "Trinitarian Tradition and the Cultural Collapse of Late Modernity." In *A Scandalous Prophet: The Way of Mission after Newbigin*, edited by Thomas F. Foust, George R. Hunsberger, J. Andrew Kirk, and Werner Ustorf, pp. 65-72. Grand Rapids: Eerdmans.

Griffioen, Sander. 1990. "Newbigins Cultuurfilosophie." In Brinkman and Noordegraaf 1990, pp. 49-60.

Guder, Darrell L. 1985. *Be My Witnesses: The Church's Mission, Message, and Messengers*. Grand Rapids: Eerdmans.

———. 1994. "Evangelism and the Debate over Church Growth." *Interpretation* 48, no. 2 (April): 145-55.

———. 1999-2000. Review of *Bearing the Witness of the Spirit*, by George R. Hunsberger (1998b). *Reformed Review* 53, no. 2 (winter): 147.

————. 2000. *The Continuing Conversion of the Church.* Gospel and Our Culture Series. Grand Rapids: Eerdmans.

————, ed. 1998. *Missional Church: A Vision for the Sending of the Church in North America.* Gospel and Our Culture Series. Grand Rapids: Eerdmans. Coauthored by Lois Barrett, Inagrace T. Dietterich, George R. Hunsberger, Alan J. Roxburgh, and Craig Van Gelder.

Haaramäki, Ossi. 1983. "Mission and Unity in the Missionary Ecclesiology of Max A. Warren." *International Review of Mission* 72 (April): 267-71. See Newbigin's rejoinder, 83rmu.

Hardy, Daniel. 2001. "A Response to the Consultation." In *A Scandalous Prophet: The Way of Mission after Newbigin,* edited by Thomas F. Foust, George R. Hunsberger, J. Andrew Kirk, and Werner Ustorf, pp. 227-33. Grand Rapids: Eerdmans.

Hathaway, Alden M. 1995. "A Christian Society?" *Trinity* (Episcopal Diocese of Pittsburgh) 16, no. 6 (March): 12. Republished in the *Gospel and Our Culture* (North America) 7, no. 3 (September 1995): 4-5.

Hauerwas, Stanley, and William H. Willimon. 1991. "Why *Resident Aliens* Struck a Chord." *Missiology* 19, no. 4 (October): 419-29.

Heim, S. Mark. 1988. "Mission and Dialogue: Fifty Years after Tambaram." *Christian Century* 105 (6 April): 340-43.

————. 1999. Review of *Bearing the Witness of the Spirit,* by George R. Hunsberger (1998b). *Theology Today* 56, no. 2: 266, 268.

Heinrich VII, Prinz Reuss. 1986. "Christian Politics." *Theology* 89: 41-42.

Hendrick, John R. "Pete." 1993. "Two Ways of Realizing the Vision of the PC(U.S.A.) for Its Congregations: Congregations with Missions and/or Missionary Congregations." *Insights* (Austin Presbyterian Theological Seminary) 108, no. 2 (fall): 59-68. Republished as "Congregations with Missions vs. Missionary Congregations," in Hunsberger and Van Gelder 1996, pp. 298-307.

Hertig, Paul, and Young Lee Hertig. 1999. "'The Christian Mission and Modern Culture' Trinity Press International Series." *Missiology* 27, no. 2 (April): 261-71.

Hick, John. 1995. *The Rainbow of Faiths.* London: SCM Press. See especially pp. 33-44 and 49-50.

Hoedemaker, L. A. (Bert). 1990a. "Enlightenment, Eclipse and the Problem of Western Christianity: Towards a Discussion with Lesslie Newbigin." Unpublished paper in preparation for a conference at the Mission Training House in Oegstgeest in the Netherlands, 23 November 1990, to which Newbigin wrote a response (90rbh). See also G. G. de Kruijf 1990.

————. 1990b. "Verlichting als Verduistering?" In Brinkman and Noordegraaf 1990, pp. 97-110.

————. 1998. *Secularization and Mission: A Theological Essay.* Christian Mission and Modern Culture Series. Harrisburg, Pa.: Trinity Press International.

————. 2001. "Rival Conceptions of Global Christianity: Mission and Modernity, Then and Now." In *A Scandalous Prophet: The Way of Mission after Newbigin,* edited by Thomas F. Foust, George R. Hunsberger, J. Andrew Kirk, and Werner Ustorf, pp. 13-22. Grand Rapids: Eerdmans.

Hollis, Michael. 1974. "Lesslie Newbigin: Versöhnung in der Bewahrung." In *Ökumenische Gestalten: Brückenbauer der einen Kirche,* edited by Günter Gloede, pp. 340-48. Berlin: Evangelische Verlagsanstalt.

Hunsberger, George R. 1987. "The Missionary Significance of the Biblical Doctrine of Election as a Foundation for a Theology of Cultural Plurality in the Missiology of J. E. Lesslie Newbigin." Ph.D. diss., Princeton Theological Seminary, Princeton, N.J. Published with minor revisions as *Bearing the Witness of the Spirit: Lesslie Newbigin's Theology of Cultural Plurality* (Hunsberger 1998b).

————. 1989. Review of *Theology and Religious Pluralism: The Challenge of Other Religions,* by Gavin D'Costa. *International Bulletin of Missionary Research* 13, no. 2 (April): 82-83.

————. 1991a. "The Changing Face of Ministry: Christian Leadership for the Twenty-First Century." *Reformed Review* 44, no. 3: 224-45.

————. 1991b. "The Newbigin Gauntlet: Developing a Domestic Missiology for North America." *Missiology* 19, no. 4 (October): 391-408. Republished in Hunsberger and Van Gelder 1996, pp. 3-25.

————. 1993. "Acquiring the Posture of a Missionary Church. *Insights* (Austin Presbyterian Theological Seminary) 108, no. 2 (fall): 19-26. Reprinted in Hunsberger and Van Gelder 1996, pp. 289-97. Reprinted in abridged form in Flett 1998, pp. 39-45.

————. 1994. "Is There Biblical Warrant for Evangelism?" *Interpretation* 48, no. 2 (April): 131-44.

————. 1995. "Cutting the Christendom Knot." In *Christian Ethics in Ecumenical Context,* edited by Shin Chiba, George R. Hunsberger, and Lester Edwin J. Ruiz, pp. 53-71. Grand Rapids: Eerdmans.

————. 1998a. "Apostle of Faith and Witness." *Gospel and Our Culture* (North America) Special Edition: 1-2.

————. 1998b. *Bearing the Witness of the Spirit: Lesslie Newbigin's Theology of Cultural Plurality.* Gospel and Our Culture Series, ed. Craig Van Gelder. Grand Rapids: Eerdmans. See Hunsberger 1987.

————. 1998c. "Conversion and Community: Revisiting the Lesslie Newbigin–M. M. Thomas Debate." *International Bulletin of Missionary Research* 22, no. 3 (July): 112-17.

————. 1998d. "Cultivating Ways of Christ for People in the Postmodern Transition: Resources in the Vision of Lesslie Newbigin." *Journal for Preachers* 22, no. 1 (Advent): 12-18. Republished as "Renewing Faith during the Postmodern Transition," *Bible in TransMission* Special Issue: 10-13, and as "Cultivating Ways of Christ in the Postmodern Transition: Resources for Pastoral Leaders" in four installments in the *Gospel and Our Culture* (North America) 11 (1999), nos. 1:3, 2:3, 3:3, and 4:3.

————. 1999a. "Biography as Missiology: The Case of Lesslie Newbigin." *Missiology* 27, no. 4 (October): 523-31.

————. 1999b. "Lesslie Newbigin and His Impact on the Western Church." *ReNews* (Presbyterians for Renewal) 10, no. 4 (December): 14.

————. 2001a. "The Church in the Postmodern Transition." In *A Scandalous Prophet: The Way of Mission after Newbigin*, edited by Thomas F. Foust, George R. Hunsberger, J. Andrew Kirk, and Werner Ustorf, pp. 95-106. Grand Rapids: Eerdmans.

————. 2001b. "Faith and Pluralism: A Response to Richard Gelwick." *Tradition and Discovery* (The Polanyi Society) 27, no. 3: 19-29.

Hunsberger, George R., Alan Reynolds, and Howard J. Van Til. 1992. "'The Gospel as Public Truth': North American Reflections on a British Consultation July 11-17, 1992." *Gospel and Our Culture* (North America) 4, no. 3 (December): 1-3. Including "The Swanwick Consultation: Some Personal Reflections" (Van Til), "The View from Western Canada" (Reynolds), and "British and American Comparisons" (Hunsberger).

Hunsberger, George R., and Craig Van Gelder, eds. 1996. *The Church between Gospel and Culture: The Emerging Mission in North America*. Gospel and Our Culture Series. Grand Rapids: Eerdmans.

Jackson, Eleanor. 1998. "J. E. Lesslie Newbigin." *Occasional Newsletter of the British and Irish Association for Mission Studies*, n.s., no. 10 (March): 1-2.

————. 2001. *Walking in the Light: A Biographical Study of Lesslie Newbigin*. Carlisle: Paternoster.

Jackson, Graeme. 1991. "A Letter and a Response." *Gospel and Our Culture* (U.K.), no. 8 (winter): 4. A response to an article by Newbigin (90tp), with a rejoinder to Newbigin's reply (91rbn).

Jantz, Harold. "Galileo Reversed: Abbotsford's Trial by Media over Creationism." *Christian Week* (Canada).

Janzon, Göran. 1988. "Kristen tro och religionerna: en kommenterande litteratur-översikt." *Svensk Missionstidskrift* 76, no. 1: 50-58.

Jeffery, Robert M. C. 2001. "Globalization, Gospel, and Cultural Relativism." In *A Scandalous Prophet: The Way of Mission after Newbigin*, edited by Thomas F. Foust, George R. Hunsberger, J. Andrew Kirk, and Werner Ustorf, pp. 195-200. Grand Rapids: Eerdmans.

Jenkins, Simon. 1995. "Leading Light Interview: Gospel and Culture." *Leading Light* 2, no. 1 (winter): 8-9.

Kenneson, Philip. 2001. "Trinitarian Missiology: Mission as Face-to-Face Encounter." In *A Scandalous Prophet: The Way of Mission after Newbigin*, edited by Thomas F. Foust, George R. Hunsberger, J. Andrew Kirk, and Werner Ustorf, pp. 76-83. Grand Rapids: Eerdmans.

Keskitalo, Jukka. 1988. "Kolmiyhteisen Jumalan Missio: Lesslie Newbigin Lähetyskäsityksen Teologinen Perusta." M.Th. thesis, University of Helsinki. An abstract in English is available from the author, entitled "The Mission of the Triune God: The Theological Basis of Lesslie Newbigin's Missiology."

———. 1992. "Church and Mission: Lesslie Newbigin's Missionary Ecclesiology" (in Finnish). Lisenciate (postgraduate) thesis, University of Helsinki.

———. 1999. "Kristillinen usko ja moderni kulttuuri: Lesslie Newbigin käsitys kirkon missiosta modernissa länsimaisessa kulttuurissa" (Finnish). Helsinki: Suomalainen Teologinen Kirjallisuusseura. Th.D. thesis, University of Helsinki. A ten-page summary in English, entitled "The Christian Faith and Modern Culture: Lesslie Newbigin's View of the Church's Mission in Modern Western Culture," is included on pp. 365-76.

Kettle, David. 1993. "On Handling Cultural Assumptions. . . ." *Gospel and Culture Newsletter* (U.K.), no. 16 (spring): 8. Also published in *New Slant* (New Zealand) 3 (August 1993): 3-4.

———. 2001. "Gospel, Authority, and Globalization." In *A Scandalous Prophet: The Way of Mission after Newbigin*, edited by Thomas F. Foust, George R. Hunsberger, J. Andrew Kirk, and Werner Ustorf, pp. 201-14. Grand Rapids: Eerdmans.

Kirk, J. Andrew. 2001. "Mission in the West: On the Calling of the Church in a Postmodern Age." In *A Scandalous Prophet: The Way of Mission after Newbigin*, edited by Thomas F. Foust, George R. Hunsberger, J. Andrew Kirk, and Werner Ustorf, pp. 115-27. Grand Rapids: Eerdmans.

Klopfeusfein, Maria. 1961. "Lesslie Newbigin: Mission und Einheit der Kirche." Postgraduate thesis, University of Berne.

Knitter, Paul F. 1985. *No Other Name? A Critical Survey of Christian Attitudes toward the World Religions*. London: SCM Press.

Kulandran, S. 1994. "Reminiscences and Reflections." In *Many Voices in Christian Mission: Essays in Honour of J. E. Lesslie Newbigin, World Christian Leader*, edited by T. Dayanandan Francis and Israel Selvanayagam, pp. 26-28. Madras: CLS.

Langerak, Ana. 1998. "Bishop Lesslie Newbigin: In Grateful Memory." *International Review of Mission* 87 (January): 6-7.

Lehmann-Habeck, Martin. 1984. "What We Have Seen and Heard: Confession and Resistance Today." *International Review of Mission* 73 (October): 397-404.

Lewis, Philip. 1999. "Newbigin's Theological Assumptions." Review of *Bearing the Witness of the Spirit*, by George R. Hunsberger (1998b). *Expository Times* 110 (June): 304.

Little, Dale W. 2000. "The Significance of Theology of the Holy Spirit for Theology of Religion and for Theology of Mission with Special Reference to the Writings of Lesslie Newbigin and Clark Pinnock." Ph.D. diss., Trinity Evangelical Divinity School, Deerfield, Ill.

Löffler, Paul. 1989. "Die Mission kehrt zuruck: Lesslie Newbigin's Beitrag zu einem Missionverstandnis für unseren Kontext." *Ökumenische Rundschau* 38: 147-57.

Long, Thomas E. 1990. "Eschatological Dimensions of Church and Kingdom in

Lesslie Newbigin, John Zizioulas, Jürgen Moltmann, and Hans Küng." Master of Theology thesis, Divinity School, Duke University.

Longley, Clifford. 1989. "Inquest on the Enlightenment." *Times*, Saturday, 25 March.

Lundy, Mary Ann. 1998. "Press Release: Bishop Lesslie Newbigin." Geneva: World Council of Churches Office of Communication, 2 February. Signed by Ms. Mary Ann Lundy, WCC Acting General Secretary, in the absence of General Secretary Rev. Dr. Konrad Raiser, away on a visit to Russia.

McKay, Margaret. 1998. "The Right Reverend Lesslie Newbigin." *Church Times* (England), 27 February.

Montefiore, Hugh, ed. 1992. *The Gospel and Contemporary Culture*. Introduction by Hugh Montefiore. London and New York: Mowbray.

Muck, Terry C. 1993. "The Gospel and Our Culture Network: A Comparative Analysis." *Insights* (Austin Presbyterian Theological Seminary) 108, no. 2 (fall): 7-18.

Neal, John C. 1993. "Contemporary Mission for Multicultural Congregations in a Pluralistic Parish." D.Min. diss., Columbia Theological Seminary.

Nixon, Robin. 1977. "Ecumenism, Models of the Church and Styles of Authority." *Churchman* 91 (July): 229-41. A review of Newbigin's book *Household of God* (53hg) and of *Models of the Church* by Avery Dulles.

Noordegraaf, Herman, and Jan J. Van Capelleveen. 1990. "Een Problematische Opdracht." In Brinkman and Noordegraaf 1990, pp. 7-20.

Northcott, Cecil. 1961. "Newbigin and New Delhi." *Christian Century* 78 (5 July): 822-23.

Ofstad, Kristin. 1991. "In Response to Anne Riggs." *Gospel and Our Culture* (U.K.), no. 11 (autumn): 4. See Riggs 1991.

———. 1992. "In Response to Rev. Bernard Thorogood's Letter in Newsletter 12." *Gospel and Our Culture* (U.K.), no. 13 (summer): 2-3. See Thorogood 1992.

———. 1993. "The Gospel and Our Culture Network in North America — Chicago Consultation." *Gospel and Our Culture* (U.K.), no. 16 (spring): 6-7.

Osborn, Lawrence. 1992. Review of *Missiology* 19, no. 4 (October 1991). *Gospel and Our Culture* (U.K.), no. 12 (spring): 3-4.

Oscarsson, Gunne. 1990. "Evangeliet och var Kultur: dialog for omvandelse." *Svensk Missionstidskrift* 78, no. 4: 6-10.

Osthathios, Geevarghese Mar. 1983. "More Cross-Currents in Mission." *International Bulletin of Missionary Research* 7, no. 4 (October): 175-76.

Ottati, Douglas F. 1993. "Whose Gospel? Which Culture?" *Insights* (Austin Presbyterian Theological Seminary) 108, no. 2 (fall): 41-57.

Paulos Mar Gregorios. 1994. "Tribute to a Great Soul." In *Many Voices in Christian Mission: Essays in Honour of J. E. Lesslie Newbigin, World Christian Leader*, edited by T. Dayanandan Francis and Israel Selvanayagam, pp. 3-4. Madras: CLS.

Piet, John H. 1994. "What I Owe to Lesslie Newbigin." In *Many Voices in Christian Mission: Essays in Honour of J. E. Lesslie Newbigin, World Christian Leader*, edited by T. Dayanandan Francis and Israel Selvanayagam, pp. 11-25. Madras: CLS.

Pope-Levinson, Priscilla. 1998. "Evangelism in the World Council of Churches Part Three: The First Decade." *International Review of Mission* 87 (January): 95-111. Pope-Levinson gives particular attention to Newbigin's article "Mission to Six Continents" (70msc).

Premasagar, P. Victor. 1994. "Newbigin — God's Gift to the Church in India." In *Many Voices in Christian Mission: Essays in Honour of J. E. Lesslie Newbigin, World Christian Leader,* edited by T. Dayanandan Francis and Israel Selvanayagam, p. 10. Madras: CLS.

Price, Lynne. 2001. "Churches and Postmodernity: Opportunity for an Attitude Shift." In *A Scandalous Prophet: The Way of Mission after Newbigin,* edited by Thomas F. Foust, George R. Hunsberger, J. Andrew Kirk, and Werner Ustorf, pp. 107-14. Grand Rapids: Eerdmans.

Raiser, Konrad. 1994. "Is Ecumenical Apologetics Sufficient? A Response to Newbigin's 'Ecumenical Amnesia.'" *International Bulletin of Missionary Research* 18, no. 2 (April): 50-51. See 93reit and 94rtkr and Gerald H. Anderson 1994.

Ramachandra, Vinoth. 1996. *The Recovery of Mission: Beyond the Pluralist Paradigm.* Grand Rapids: Eerdmans. Especially noteworthy is Chapter 5, "Engaging Modernity," pp. 143-76.

Reader, John. 1993. "Theology, Culture and Post-Modernity: In Response to Graham, Walton and Newbigin." *Modern Churchman* 34, no. 5: 58-63. A response to E. Graham and H. Walton (1991) and Newbigin (92goc).

Reardon, Martin. 1998. "Lesslie Newbigin: 1909-1998." *Pilgrim Post* (England) (March/April): 9. Obituary.

Reilly, John, S.J. 1978. "Evangelism and Ecumenism in the Writings of Lesslie Newbigin and Their Basis in His Christology." Ph.D. diss., Pontificiae Universitatis Gregorianae, Rome.

————. 1979. *Evangelism and Ecumenism in the Writings of Lesslie Newbigin and Their Basis in His Christology.* Excerpta ex dissertatione ad Doctoratum in Facultate Theologiae Pontificiae Universitatis Gregorianae. Rome: Pontificiae Universitas Gregorianae.

Richmond, Helen. 1995. "Daring to Believe: Exploring the Missiology of Lesslie Newbigin." M.A. thesis, Sydney College of Divinity.

Riggs, Anne. 1991. "Gospel and Our Culture: An Alternative View?" *Gospel and Our Culture* (U.K.), no. 11 (autumn): 3.

Roach, Corwin C. 1949. "Recent Books on Unity." *Anglican Theological Review* 31: 34-38. The books reviewed include: *Lambeth and Unity* by L. Haselmayer; *Church and Churches* by C. Smith; and *Reunion of the Church* by Newbigin (48rc).

Roberts, Michael A. 1996. "Developing a Teaching Guide for Presbyterian Newcomers." D.Min. diss., Austin Presbyterian Theological Seminary, Austin, Tex.

Robinson, Martin. 1996. *To Win the West.* Crowborough, East Sussex: Monarch Publications. Especially noteworthy are Robinson's comments regarding Newbigin's book *The Household of God* on pp. 149-52.

————. 1998a. "A Passion for Mission." *Bible in TransMission* Special Issue: 2.

————. 1998b. "The Rt. Revd. Lesslie Newbigin." *Bible in TransMission* (spring): 3.

Rowold, Henry. 1999. Review of *Bearing the Witness of the Spirit*, by George R. Hunsberger. *Missio Apostolica.*

Russell-Jones, Iwan. 1998. "Lesslie Newbigin: The Greater Blessing." *Ship of Fools* (http://cargo.ship-of-fools.com/Features98/Newbigin/NewbiginIwan.html).

Sanneh, Lamin O. 1993. *Encountering the West: Christianity and the Global Cultural Process.* Maryknoll, N.Y.: Orbis. See especially pp. 63-83.

Schmidt-Leukel, Perry. 2001. "Mission and Trinitarian Theology." In *A Scandalous Prophet: The Way of Mission after Newbigin,* edited by Thomas F. Foust, George R. Hunsberger, J. Andrew Kirk, and Werner Ustorf, pp. 57-64. Grand Rapids: Eerdmans.

Schrotenboer, Paul G. 1982. "Responses to the Article by Lesslie Newbigin." *International Bulletin of Missionary Research* 6, no. 4 (October): 152-53. A response to Newbigin's article (82ccee), to which Newbigin replied with a rejoinder. See also Gerald H. Anderson (1982) and C. Peter Wagner (1982).

Schwarz, Brian. 1985. "Take Up Your Bed and Walk." *Point: Forum for Melanesian Affairs,* no. 7: 245-61.

Shaw, Mark. 1997. *Ten Great Ideas from Church History.* Downers Grove, Ill.: InterVarsity. Shaw criticizes Newbigin's analysis of denominationalism and unity (see especially pp. 64-65).

Shenk, Wilbert R. 1990. "Report on a European Assignment." *Gospel and Our Culture* (North America) 2, no. 2 (October): 1-2.

————. 1991a. "Canvassing the Future." *Gospel and Our Culture* (North America) 3, no. 2 (July): 4-5.

————. 1991b. "Report on a European Assignment (Part 2)." *Gospel and Our Culture* (North America) 3, no. 1 (March): 2-4.

————. 1993. "The Culture of Modernity as a Missionary Challenge." In *The Good News of the Kingdom,* edited by Charles Van Engen et al., pp. 192-99. Maryknoll, N.Y.: Orbis. Republished in Hunsberger and Van Gelder 1996, pp. 69-78.

————. 1994. "Encounters with 'Culture' Christianity." *International Bulletin of Missionary Research* 18, no. 1 (January): 8-13.

————. 1998a. "Lesslie Newbigin's Contribution to the Theology of Mission." *Bible in TransMission* Special Issue: 3-6. Republished in slightly expanded form in *International Bulletin of Missionary Research* 24, no. 1 (January 2000).

————. 1998b. "A Tribute to Bishop Newbigin." *Gospel and Our Culture* (North America) Special Edition: 4.

Sicard, Harald von. 1962. "Missionens självbesinning" [notes from Graaf S. C. van Randwijck, N. A. Nissiotis, J. E. Lesslie Newbigin on mission work and ecumenism]. *Svensk Missionstidskrift* 50, no. 4: 205-8.

Slack, Kenneth. 1998. "The Right Reverend Lesslie Newbigin." *Times Newspaper* (London), Saturday, 31 January, p. 25. Obituary, edited from a short piece written several years earlier by Slack, who in the meantime had died.

Spindler, Marc R. 1987. "Witness under Cross-Examination." *Mission Studies* 4, no. 2: 67-73. A rejoinder to D. Bosch, L. Newbigin, G. M. Soares-Prabhu, H. D. Beeby, and J. Parratt.

Stafford, Tim. 1996. "God's Missionary." *Christianity Today* 40 (9 December): 24-33.

Stockwell, Eugene L. 1987. "Editorial: 1912-1987." *International Review of Mission* 76 (April): 1-7.

Stowe, David M. 1988. "Modernization and Resistance: Theological Implications for Mission." *International Bulletin of Missionary Research* 12, no. 4: 146-51. A response to Newbigin's proposals for a missionary encounter with Western culture to which Newbigin replied in 88rds. See also Charles C. West's comments on their dialogue (1988).

Stromberg, Jean. 1988. "Christian Witness in a Pluralist World: Report on a Mission/Dialogue Consultation." *International Review of Missions* 77: 412-36. A report of the discussion that took place at the fiftieth anniversary of the 1938 Tambaram missionary conference, convened by the World Council of Churches and gathered in Mahabalipuram, India. The discussion centered around the issues raised for Christian witness in the midst of a pluralist society. The group had heard papers or presentations by Newbigin, Stanley Samartha, Diana Eck, Carl Hallencreutz, M. M. Thomas, Bishop Anastasios, Wilfred Cantwell Smith, and Christopher Duraisingh.

Sundkler, Bengt. 1954. *Church of South India: The Movement Towards Union, 1900-1947.* London: Lutterworth. See especially pp. 301-48.

Taber, Charles R. 2001. "The Gospel as Authentic Meta-Narrative." In *A Scandalous Prophet: The Way of Mission after Newbigin,* edited by Thomas F. Foust, George R. Hunsberger, J. Andrew Kirk, and Werner Ustorf, pp. 182-94. Grand Rapids: Eerdmans.

Taylor, Jenny. 1992a. "Carey Says: Decade Doomed without Contextualisation." News release published and circulated by the Gospel and Our Culture program giving a summary of the Gospel and Our Culture's National Consultation that took place at the Hayes, Swanwick, 11-17 July 1992.

———. 1992b. "Modern Society at Dead End." News release published and circulated by the Gospel and Our Culture program heralding the launch of the book *The Gospel and Contemporary Culture,* which was to provide material for consideration of the upcoming Gospel as Public Truth Consultation at the Hayes, Swanwick, 11-17 July 1992.

———. 2001. "Lesslie Newbigin's Understanding of Islam." In *A Scandalous Prophet: The Way of Mission after Newbigin,* edited by Thomas F. Foust, George R. Hunsberger, J. Andrew Kirk, and Werner Ustorf, pp. 215-24. Grand Rapids: Eerdmans.

Taylor, Michael H. 2001. "Afterword." In *A Scandalous Prophet: The Way of Mission after Newbigin,* edited by Thomas F. Foust, George R. Hunsberger, J. Andrew Kirk, and Werner Ustorf, pp. 238-42. Grand Rapids: Eerdmans.

Taylor, Richard W. 1972. "On Acknowledging the Lordship of Jesus Christ without Shifting Tents." *Religion and Society* 19, no. 1: 59-68.

Thomas, Joe Matthew. 1996. "The Centrality of Christ and Inter-religious Dialogue in the Theology of Lesslie Newbigin." Ph.D. diss., Faculty of Theology, University of St. Matthew's College, Toronto.

Thomas, M. M. 1969. "What Bishop Newbigin Has Meant to Me." In *Bishop Newbigin's Sixtieth Birthday Celebration Brochure*. Madras.

————. 1971. *Salvation and Humanisation: Some Crucial Issues of the Theology of Mission in Contemporary India*. Madras: CLS.

————. 1977. *Some Theological Dialogues*. Madras: CLS. Based on correspondence with Philippe Maury, Hendrik Kraemer, M. A. C. Warren, H. H. Wolf, Arend van Leeuwen, Hendrik Berkhof, Lesslie Newbigin, and Donald A. McGavran.

————. 1987. *Risking Christ for Christ's Sake: Towards an Ecumenical Theology of Pluralism*. Geneva: World Council of Churches.

————. 1990. *My Ecumenical Journey, 1947-1975*. Trivandrum: Ecumenical Publishing Centre. An autobiography in which Newbigin is often mentioned.

Thomas, M. M., Lesslie Newbigin, and Alfred Krass. 1972. "Baptism, the Church, and Koinonia: Three Letters and a Comment." *Religion and Society* 19, no. 1: 69-90.

Thomas, Winburn T. 1960. "Commemorating the World Missionary Congress [Edinburgh 1910]." *Christian Century* 77 (15 June): 733-34.

Thorogood, Bernard G. 1990. "Apostolic Faith: An Appreciation of Lesslie Newbigin, Born 8 December 1909." *International Review of Mission* 79 (January): 66-85.

————. 1991. "Newbigin, (James Edward) Lesslie." In *Dictionary of the Ecumenical Movement,* edited by Nicholas Lossky, José Míguez Bonino, John Pobee, Thomas F. Stransky, C.S.P., Geoffrey Wainwright, and Pauline Webb, pp. 725-26. Geneva: WCC Publications; Grand Rapids: Eerdmans.

————. 1992. "Letter." *Gospel and Our Culture* (U.K.), no. 12 (spring): 3. A response to Kristin Ofstad 1991.

Trompf, Garry. 1977. "Secularisation for Melanesia?" *Point: Forum for Melanesian Affairs* 6, no. 1: 208-25.

Turner, Harold. 1998. "Lesslie Newbigin — A New Zealand Perspective." *Bible in TransMission* Special Issue: 7-8.

University of British Columbia Graduate and Faculty Christian Forum. 1993. "Newbigin: Modernism and the Roots of Disbelief." *Gospel and Our Culture* (North America) 5, no. 1 (March): 2-4. Notes from a symposium held at Regent College, Saturday, 25 April 1992, Vancouver, Canada.

Ustorf, Werner. 1992. *Christianized Africa — De-Christianized Europe? Missionary Inquiries into the Polycentric Epoch of Christian History*. Seoul: Tyrannus. Includes an examination of Newbigin's theology, especially part II, section 8 (pp. 149-63), entitled "A Partisan's View: Lesslie Newbigin's Critique of Modernity," with particular reference to *The Other Side of 1984: Questions for the Churches* (83os84) and *Truth to Tell: The Gospel as Public Truth* (91tt).

————. 2001. "The Emerging Christ of Post-Christian Europe." In *A Scandalous*

Prophet: The Way of Mission after Newbigin, edited by Thomas F. Foust, George R. Hunsberger, J. Andrew Kirk, and Werner Ustorf, pp. 128-44. Grand Rapids: Eerdmans.

van Butselaar, G. Jan. 2000. "Mission and Unity: An Uneasy Affair?" *Ecumenical Review* 52, no. 3 (July): 358-66. Written in tribute to Lesslie Newbigin.

————. 2001. "Two Wonderful, Bewildering Days." In *A Scandalous Prophet: The Way of Mission after Newbigin,* edited by Thomas F. Foust, George R. Hunsberger, J. Andrew Kirk, and Werner Ustorf, pp. 234-37. Grand Rapids: Eerdmans.

Van Engen, Charles. 1997. "Mission Theology in the Light of Postmodern Critique." *International Review of Mission* 86 (October): 437-61. Special attention given to Newbigin's concept of the congregation as the hermeneutic of the gospel.

Van Gelder, Craig, ed. 1999. *Confident Witness — Changing World: Rediscovering the Gospel in North America.* Gospel and Our Culture Series. Grand Rapids: Eerdmans.

Van Leeuwen, Arend Theodoor. 1964. *Christianity in World History: The Meeting of the Faiths of East and West.* New York: Scribner.

Van Leeuwen, Mary Stewart. 1995. "Principalities, Powers, and Gender Relations: Some Reflections for Patient Revolutionaries." *CRUX* 31, no. 3 (September): 9-16.

Van Lin, Jan. 1990. "Zending, Dialoog en Eenheid van de Kerken." In Brinkman and Noordegraaf 1990, pp. 79-95.

Vaughan, Patrick H. 1987. "Non-Stipendiary Ministry in the Church of England: A History of the Development of an Idea." Ph.D. thesis, University of Nottingham.

Veldhorst, Berend J. 1990a. "A Christian Voice in a World without God." Ph.D. thesis, State University of Utrecht, the Netherlands, ca. 1990.

————. 1990b. "Luisteren naar Newbigin." In Brinkman and Noordegraaf 1990, pp. 37-48.

Verkuyl, Johannes. 1978. *Contemporary Missiology.* Grand Rapids: Eerdmans. See especially pp. 56-57.

Villian, Maurice. 1963. *Unity: A History and Some Reflections.* London: Harvill. Translated by J. R. Foster from the third revised and augmented edition of *Introduction à L'Oecuménisme* (Tournai: Casterman).

Visser 't Hooft, Willem Adolf. 1966. "Lesslie Newbigin." *International Review of Mission* 55 (January): 96-97. Written upon Newbigin's retirement as editor of the *International Review of Mission.*

Wagner, C. Peter. 1982. "Responses to the Article by Lesslie Newbigin." *International Bulletin of Missionary Research* 6, no. 4 (October): 152-53. A response to Newbigin's article (82ccee), to which Newbigin replied with a rejoinder. See also Gerald H. Anderson (1982) and Paul G. Schrotenboer (1982).

Wainwright, Geoffrey. 2000. *Lesslie Newbigin: A Theological Life.* New York: Oxford University Press. An intellectual and spiritual biography.

Walker, Andrew. 1995. "A Year of Action." *Gospel and Culture* (U.K.) (December): 1-2.

———. 1998. "Lesslie Newbigin: Remembering Lesslie." *Ship of Fools* (http://cargo.ship-of-fools.com/Features98/Newbigin/NewbiginWalker.html).

Walls, Andrew F. 2001. "Enlightenment, Postmodernity, and Mission." In *A Scandalous Prophet: The Way of Mission after Newbigin,* edited by Thomas F. Foust, George R. Hunsberger, J. Andrew Kirk, and Werner Ustorf, pp. 145-52. Grand Rapids: Eerdmans.

Ward, Heather. 2001. "The Use and Misuse of 'Metaphor' in Christian Theology." In *A Scandalous Prophet: The Way of Mission after Newbigin,* edited by Thomas F. Foust, George R. Hunsberger, J. Andrew Kirk, and Werner Ustorf, pp. 73-75. Grand Rapids: Eerdmans.

Watson, David Lowes. 1991. "Christ All in All: The Recovery of the Gospel for North American Evangelism." *Missiology* 19, no. 4 (October): 443-59. Republished in Hunsberger and Van Gelder 1996, pp. 177-197.

Webster, John C. B. 1998. "The Church of South India Golden Jubilee." *International Bulletin of Missionary Research* 22, no. 2 (April): 50.

Wehrli, Eugene S. 1955. *Rediscovering the Church: A Study Guide for Lesslie Newbigin's Book "The Household of God."* St. Louis: United Student Fellowship, in cooperation with the United Student Christian Council.

West, Charles C. 1988. "Mission to the West: A Dialogue with Stowe and Newbigin." *International Bulletin of Missionary Research* 12, no. 4 (October): 153-56. See David M. Stowe (1988) and Newbigin's reply (88rds).

———. 1991. "Gospel for American Culture: Variations on a Theme by Newbigin." *Missiology* 19, no. 4 (October): 431-41. Republished in Hunsberger and Van Gelder 1996, pp. 214-27.

———. 1998a. "God, the Gospel and Human Truth." In *Mission Today: Challenges and Concerns,* edited by Abraham P. Athyal and Dorothy Yoder Nyce, pp. 133-48. Chennai, India: Gurukul Lutheran Theological College and Research Institute. Excerpts republished in the *Gospel and Our Culture* (North America) 10, no. 4 (December): 5, 8.

———. 1998b. "Newbigin, J(ames) E(dward) Lesslie." In *Biographical Dictionary of Christian Missions,* edited by Gerald H. Anderson, p. 491. New York, London, et al.: Simon and Schuster Macmillan.

———. 1999a. *Power, Truth, and Community in Modern Culture.* Christian Mission and Modern Culture Series. Harrisburg, Pa.: Trinity Press International.

———. 1999b. Review of *Bearing the Witness of the Spirit,* by George R. Hunsberger (1998b). *Missiology* 27, no. 3 (July): 405-6.

Westerlund, George. 1998. Review of *Bearing the Witness of the Spirit,* by George R. Hunsberger. *Library Journal* (August): 100.

Weston, Paul. 1999. "Gospel, Mission and Culture: The Contribution of Lesslie Newbigin." In *Witness to the World,* edited by David Peterson, pp. 32-62. Carlisle: Paternoster.

Wiles, Maurice. 1979. "Comment on Lesslie Newbigin's Essay." In *Incarnation and*

Myth: The Debate Continues, edited by Michael Goulder, pp. 211-13. Grand Rapids: Eerdmans.

Williams, John. 1993. "The Gospel as Public Truth: A Critical Appreciation of the Theological Programme of Lesslie Newbigin." *Anvil* 10, no. 1: 11-24. Also see *Evangelical Review of Theology* 18 (October 1994): 299-376.

Williams, Stephen. 1986. "Theologians in Pursuit of the Enlightenment." *Theology* 89, no. 7 (September): 368-74.

————. 1995. *Revelation and Reconciliation: A Window on Modernity.* Cambridge: Cambridge University Press.

Willimon, William H. 1999. "Preaching as Missionary Encounter with North American Paganism (in Homage to Lesslie Newbigin, 1909-1998)." *Journal for Preachers* 22, no. 3 (Easter): 3-10.

Wingate, Andrew. 1983. "An Experiment in Local Non-Stipendiary Ordained Ministry: A Case Study from Tamil Nadu." *Religion and Society* 30: 45-60.

————. 1984. "NSM in India." *Theology* 87 (July): 259-65.

Wood, Ralph C. 1999. Review of *Bearing the Witness of the Spirit,* by George R. Hunsberger. *Modern Theology* 15, no. 4 (October): 509-11.

Yannoulatos, Anastasios, et al. 1990. "In Tribute to Bishop Lesslie Newbigin." *International Review of Mission* 79 (January): 86-101. Tributes on the occasion of Newbigin's eightieth birthday.

Yates, Timothy. 1998. "Editorial." *Occasional Newsletter of the British and Irish Association for Mission Studies,* n.s., 10 (March): 1.

Young, Frances. 2001. "The Uncontainable God: Pre-Christendom Doctrine of Trinity." In *A Scandalous Prophet: The Way of Mission after Newbigin,* edited by Thomas F. Foust, George R. Hunsberger, J. Andrew Kirk, and Werner Ustorf, pp. 84-91. Grand Rapids: Eerdmans.

Zub, David. 1996. "Commitment with Confidence (Not Certainty): Observations on Lesslie Newbigin." *Touchstone* 14 (May): 50-56.

[Unknown]. ca. 1961. "The Church as 'Simul Justus et Peccator'? — The Challenge of L. Newbigin." Seminar No. 6, n.d, ca. 1961. This document can be found in the Archives Collection at the Central Library of the Selly Oak Colleges.

[Unknown]. n.d. *"The Other Side of 1984": A Study Guide.* York, England: Diocese of York, Church of England. This is a ten-page booklet divided into five studies. It was written to be used as a study guide to Newbigin's book *The Other Side of 1984* for use in the churches in York.

[Unknown]. 1987. "Newbigin, Rt. Rev. Lesslie." *The International Who's Who 1987-88.* 51st ed. London: Europa Publications.

F. Ongoing Expressions of the Gospel and Our Culture Movement

The Gospel and Our Culture movement began in the United Kingdom in the early 1980s under the influence of Bishop Newbigin's challenge to the churches of the West to engage what he called the most important missionary challenge of the latter part of the twentieth century — the missionary encounter of the gospel with Western culture. His book *The Other Side of 1984* sparked the movement in Britain, which first took form as the Gospel and Our Culture Programme of the British Council of Churches. That program later merged with the C. S. Lewis Society to form Gospel and Culture, and after a brief cessation re-formed itself as the Gospel and Our Culture, a registered company owned by the British and Foreign Bible Society, Stonehill Green, Westlea, Swindon, SN5 7DG, U.K. It has now gone again to an independent basis. The network coordinator is Rev. David Kettle, who may be contacted at <DJK@kettle.force9.co.uk>. The U.K. network maintains a website at <http://www.gospel-culture.org.uk>.

In North America, the Gospel and Our Culture Network formed in the late 1980s under the influence of Newbigin and others as an effort to engage the same challenge within the specific context of the U.S.A. and Canada. Coordinated by Rev. George R. Hunsberger, the network maintains a cycle of research, consultation, and publication to encourage the encounter of the gospel with North American culture and to stimulate the transformation of the life and witness of the churches. The office of the North American network is located at Western Theological Seminary, 101 E. 13th Street, Holland, Michigan 49423, U.S.A., telephone 1-616-392-8555. The coordinator can be reached at <georgeh@westernsem.org> and the administrative assistant, Judy Bos, can be reached at <judy@westernsem.org>. The GOCN website is located at <http://www.gocn.org>.

In the last few years the Canadians of the GOCN in North America have begun to form their own expression of the network with particular focus on the Canadian situation. Rev. Alan J. Roxburgh coordinates a team guiding that effort. He can be contacted at <alanroxburgh@home.com>.

A parallel movement has emerged in New Zealand. The Deepsight Trust, formerly known as the Gospel and Cultures Trust, was founded and led initially by Harold Turner. A web presence is maintained by the group's secretary, John Flett. Flett also publishes *In Slant,* the regular newsletter of Deepsight Trust. He can be contacted at <http://www.deepsight.org> as well as at <jflett@deepsight.org>.

A consortium of the British, North American, and New Zealand organizations has announced the formation of a website for Newbigin studies at <www.newbigin.net>. With the assistance of a grant from the Council for World Mission, this bibliography will be made available online in a fully searchable form and will be continually expanded and updated.

A South African expression of the movement has begun with an e-mail newsletter and discussion group, produced and moderated by Jan Nieder-Heitmann, connecting together people who in various ways have been working at these issues in that context. Nieder-Heitmann can be contacted at <jniederh@mweb.co.za>.

In addition, an international project led by Wilbert R. Shenk has produced a body of research and reflection in pursuit of a missiology of Western culture. Shenk, a professor at Fuller Theological Seminary's School of World Mission, has coedited with H. Wayne Pipkin and Alan Neely a series of monographs entitled Christian Mission and Modern Culture (Trinity Press International, Harrisburg, Pa., U.S.A.).